The
African American
Encyclopedia

Second Edition

The
African American
Encyclopedia

Second Edition

Volume 8
Ran-Sud

Editor, First Edition
Michael W. Williams

Consulting Editor, Supplement to First Edition
Kibibi Voloria Mack

Advisory Board, Second Edition

Barbara Bair
Duke University

Carl L. Bankston III
Tulane University

David Bradley
City University of New York

Shelley Fisher Fishkin
University of Texas, Austin

Wendy Sacket
Coast College

Managing Editor, Second Edition
R. Kent Rasmussen

Marshall Cavendish
New York • London • Toronto • Sydney

Project Editor: McCrea Adams
Production Editor: Cindy Beres
Assistant Editor: Andrea Miller
Research Supervisor: Jeffry Jensen
Photograph Editor: Philip Bader
Page Layout: William Zimmerman

Marshall Cavendish Corporation
99 White Plains Road
Tarrytown, New York 10591-9001

© 2001 Marshall Cavendish Corporation
Printed in the United States of America
09   08   07   06   05   04   03   02   01   5   4   3   2   1

Library of Congress Cataloging-in-Publication Data

The African American encyclopedia.—2nd ed. / managing editor, R. Kent Rasmussen.
    p. cm.
Includes bibliographical references and index.
1. Afro-Americans—Encyclopedias. I. Rasmussen, R. Kent.
E185 .A253   2001
973′.0496073′003—dc21
ISBN 0-7614-7208-8 (set)   00-031526
ISBN 0-7614-7216-9 (volume 8)   CIP

∞ This paper meets the requirements of ANSI/NISO Z39.48-1992 (R1997)
Permanence of Paper for Publications and Documents in Libraries and Archives

Contents

Contents

The
African American
Encyclopedia

Second Edition

Ranger, Joseph (b. c. 1760): Patriot. Ranger was a free black man who served in the American Navy during the AMERICAN REVOLUTION. After the sinking of the *Jefferson* by the British, Ranger enlisted on the *Patriot*. Following the defeat of the *Patriot*, Ranger and the rest of the crew were taken prisoner. Ranger was released when the British surrendered, and continued to serve aboard Virginia ships until 1787.

Ransier, Alonzo Jacob (1834, Charleston, South Carolina—August 17, 1882, Charleston, South Carolina): RECONSTRUCTION-era politician. Ransier served in the SOUTH CAROLINA state house of representatives from 1868 until 1870, then became lieutenant governor in 1870. He entered the House of Representatives in 1873, serving on the Committee on Manufactures. After leaving Congress, he was appointed as U.S. internal revenue collector (1875

Reconstruction-era statesman Alonzo Jacob Ransier. *(Associated Publishers, Inc.)*

and 1876) for the Second District of South Carolina.

See also: Congress members; Politics and government.

Rap: Also known as HIP-HOP, rap emerged as a primary cultural form in urban ghettos during the late 1970's. Characterized by inventive lyrics and densely textured music, rap had grown by the 1990's into a major force in American popular culture with a large multicultural audience.

Cultural Background

Grounded in the oral traditions of West African culture, "rapping" in its general sense refers to the creative everyday use of language in the African American community. In African American music, rapping encompasses the sermons of the gospel church, the talking blues of Blind Willie MCTELL, the hyperbolic rock-and-roll lyrics of Chuck BERRY, and the jazz poetry of Gil Scott-Heron and the LAST POETS. The two most important African American predecessors of rap music were James BROWN and George Clinton (founder of PARLIAMENT/FUNKADELIC), who sometimes spoke or shouted their lyrics over rhythmically intense funk music. The most immediate sources of rap, however, were the Jamaican disc jockeys of the 1960's and 1970's. Playing a variety of soul and REGGAE hits, the disc jockeys frequently talked over the "dub," or instrumental, sides of the records. Both this style of rapping and the use of sound systems with impressive arrays of speakers and turntables anticipated the form of early rap.

Early Development

Rap as a distinct form originated in NEW YORK CITY during the mid-1970's. Reacting against the elitism of New York's interracial disco clubs, disc jockeys such as Kool DJ Herc, Afrika Bambaataa, and Grandmaster Flash were hosting dances on street corners or in makeshift clubs in the South Bronx as early as 1973. By 1976 these dances had become an important part of street culture in Brooklyn, Queens, and Harlem, where they developed alongside graffiti art and break dancing. By the end of the decade, African American performers had divided the functions of the Jamaican disc jockeys between the "DJ" (who operated the turntables) and the "MC" (or rapper).

Rap's emergence in the recording industry was centered on Sylvia Robinson's Sugarhill Records. Essentially a novelty record, the Sugarhill Gang's "Rapper's Delight" (1979) established a market for more authentic records such as Harlem rapper Kurtis Blow's "The Breaks" (1980); "The Adventures of Grandmaster Flash on the Wheels of Steel" (1981), which incorporated samples of hits by Chic, Blondie, and Queen; "The New Rap Language" (1980) by Spoonie Gee and the Treacherous Three; "Looking for the Perfect Beat" (1982) by Bambaataa's Soul Sonic Force; and "The Message" (1982) by GRANDMASTER FLASH AND THE FURIOUS FIVE. The first explicitly political rap record, "The Message" drew attention to conditions in America's ghettos and was widely viewed as an expression of black America's anger over the policies of the Ronald REAGAN ADMINISTRATION.

Commercial Success

Throughout the mid-1980's, rap music provided a gauge of the frustration and violence in poor black neighborhoods. The first of many rappers from stable, middle-class backgrounds, RUN-D.M.C. articulated the growing frustration in "It's Like That" (1983). Philadelphia rapper Schooly D's "P.S.K.—What Does It Mean?" (1985) and Boogie Down Productions' "Criminal Minded" (1987) highlighted the violent potential of this situation, anticipating the GANGSTA style of West Coast rap. Run-D.M.C.'s sparse but insistent rhythm

tracks, frequently overlaid with rock guitar lines, established the dominant style of the rap that first attracted widespread attention outside the black community. White producer Rick Rubin and his black partner Russell Simmons of the Def Jam production company pioneered rap's popularity in a series of records by Run-D.M.C., L.L. COOL J., and white rappers the Beastie Boys. Producers, including Marley Marl, DJ Red Alert, Mr. Magic, Hurby Luv Bug, and the Bomb Squad (Hank and Keith Shocklee and Eric Sadler), continued to play a major role in the development of rap.

The development of rap during the 1980's can be charted through a series of records that created new styles. Eric B. and Rakim's "Follow the Leader" (1988), for example, replaced the relatively spare Run-D.M.C. style with dense textures that made heavy use of "sampling"—the digital recording and reuse of bits of music, speech, or sound from earlier recordings. One of the most significant records in this new style was E.P.M.D.'s "Strictly Business" (1988), which reasserted the connection between rap and reggae by including lengthy samples from Bob Marley's "I Shot the Sheriff." While Eric B. and Rakim, Big Daddy Kane, and E.P.M.D. continued to direct their raps primarily to an African American audience, the late 1980's saw the increasing popularity of rap with a mainstream audience, much of which was introduced to the form through videos. Among the rappers whose stardom was based significantly on videos were Jazzy Jeff and the Fresh Prince, M.C. HAMMER, Tone Loc, and white rapper Vanilla Ice.

In 1988 a rap category was added to the Grammy Awards. The award was not presented on the Grammy telecast, however, leading its first recipients, D.J. Jazzy Jeff and the Fresh Prince, to boycott the ceremony. The next year the presentation was made on the air, and the broadcast of the awards show included

(continued on page 2105)

Notable Rap Groups

Bone Thugs-N-Harmony (Layzie and Krazie Bone, Wish Bone, Flesh-and-Bone, and Bizzie Bone). In 1993 the group released an undistinguished debut album; however, their 1996 single "Tha Crossroads" reached number one on the charts two weeks after its release—the fastest rise since the Beatles' 1964 "Can't Buy Me Love." The recording won a Grammy Award.

De La Soul (Posdnuos [Kelvin Mercer], P. A. Pasemaster Mase/Baby Huey Maseo [Vincent L. Mason], and Trugoy the Dove [David Jolicoeur]). De La Soul's first album, *3 Feet High and Rising* (1989), featured sampling of the 1968 Turtles hit "You Showed Me" that prompted a lawsuit challenging the uncompensated appropriation of copyrighted material. De La Soul's second album, *De La Soul Is Dead* (1991) incorporated a storybook theme with dark overtones. In 1993 the group released the album *Buhloone Mind State*.

Digital Underground. Digital Underground came out of the OAKLAND, CALIFORNIA, rap scene and was known for elaborately staged concerts, flashy costumes, and comedy sketches. *Sex Packets* (1990) contained the popular single, "The Humpty Dance." Later, the group released a short album, entitled *This Is an E.P. Release* (1991), that contained remixes of some of the songs featured on the *Sex Packets* album.

E.P.M.D. (Erick Sermon and Parrish Smith). The duo's stage name is an abbreviation for "Erick and Parrish Making Dollars." Their albums include *Strictly Business* (which incorporates reggae samples from Bob Marley's "I Shot the Sheriff"), *Unfinished Business* (1989), and *Business as Usual* (1990).

Fat Boys (Mark Morales, Darren Robinson, and Damon Wimbley). The trio produced albums such as *The Fat Boys, Big and Beautiful,* and *The Fat Boys Are Back* (1985). It was featured in the rap film *Krush Groove* (1985) and in the comedy *Disorderlies* (1986). The sound track of the film contained their version of the Beatles' hit "Baby, You're a Rich Man." *Crushin'* (1987) featured a remake of "Wipeout," a collaboration with the Beach Boys.

Grandmaster Flash and the Furious Five. *See main text entry.*

Naughty by Nature. The group's members—Vinnie, Treatch, and DJ K.G.—became known for their streetwise rap style. In collaboration with Benny Medina and Queen Latifah, they produced the self-titled *Naughty by Nature* album in 1991. The album's hit single "O.P.P." combined a sample from the Jackson 5's classic "ABC" with a hard-core rap sound, resulting in the first gold rap single of the 1990's. In 1995 *Poverty's Paradise* won a Grammy Award.

N.W.A. *See main text entry.*

Public Enemy. *See main text entry.*

Salt-N-Pepa (Cheryl "Salt" James, Sandy "Pepa" Denton, and Dee Dee "DJ Spinderella" Roper). The group's first album, *Hot, Cool, and Vicious,* went platinum on the same day in 1988 that the single "Push It" went gold. The success of "Push It" made Salt-N-Pepa the first female rap group to have a gold record. The group's second album, *A Salt with a Deadly Pepa,* was released in 1988 and also sold more than one million copies. The group had also had a song on the sound track of the gang film *Colors* (1988). *Black's Magic* was released in 1990, and the group won a Grammy Award in 1994 for "None of Your Business."

Run-D.M.C. *See main text entry.*

2 Live Crew. *See main text entry.*

Whodini (Jalil Hutchins, Ecstasy, and DJ Grandmaster Dee). Whodini was one of the early rap crews and gained popularity based on its funky, danceable rhythms and spooky, horror-film sound. Its best known hit was the single "The Freaks Come Out at Night," released from its second album, *Escape* (1985), and featured on the sound track of *The Jewel of the Nile* (1985).

Wu-Tang Clan (RZA, Ghost Face Killa, Raekwon, Ol' Dirty Bastard, and Genius). The group derived its philosophical principles from the ancient Shao-Lin monks. The rap crew's nine members also became well-known solo performers. The group's debut album, *Enter the Wu-Tang (36 Chambers)* (1993), was enthusiastically received. Within three years, five Wu-Tang Clan-related albums had been released.

Notable Rap Musicians

Bambaataa, Afrika (b. Apr. 10, 1960, New York, N.Y.). Bambaataa founded Zulu Nation, a cultural organization promoting hip-hop style. Bambaataa and the Soul Sonic Force, with producer and keyboardist Arthur Baker, recorded the rap singles "Looking for the Perfect Beat" and "Planet Rock" in 1983. The group appeared in the film *Beat Street* (1984), which chronicled the development of rap and break dancing.

Blow, Kurtis (Kurt Walker; b. 1956 or 1957). Known as the "Platinum Prince," Blow is considered one of the pioneers of rap music. Originally a break dancer, Blow started his career as a disc jockey in 1972, playing music at house parties, but he soon began composing rap lyrics and rhymes. His first hit was "Christmas Rappin'," a 1979 single that sold half a million copies and became the first rap hit. Blow's next release, a twelve-inch single entitled "The Breaks," went on to sell more than five hundred thousand copies in 1980. Blow released an album in 1984 called *Ego Trip*.

Coolio. *See main text entry.*

Dr. Dre. *See main text entry.*

Eazy-E (Eric Wright; Sept. 7, 1963, Compton, Calif.— Mar. 26, 1995, Los Angeles, Calif.). As a founding member of the rap music group N.W.A. (Niggaz with Attitude), Eazy-E was a pioneer of West Coast GANGSTA RAP. After the group broke up in the wake of contract disputes, he became president of the independent rap label Ruthless Records. In 1996 his record label posthumously released Eazy-E's final album, *Str8 Off the Streetz of . . . Compton*.

Father MC. Father MC was one of the first rap stars to popularize the Love Rap image, combining a rhythm-and-blues sound with rap lyrics. He recorded several albums, and his rap singles became a staple of many black radio stations.

Fresh, Doug E. (Doug E. Davis; b. Sept. 17, 1966, New York, N.Y.). Fresh became known as the "Human Beat Box" in tribute to his ability to use his hands and body to imitate all the electronic and mechanical noises usually made by rap deejays on a record turntable. His first big hit, "The Show," fea-

tured rapper Ricky "Slick Rick" Walters. His album *Doin' What I Gotta Do*, recorded with the New Get Fresh Crew, was released in 1992 on HAMMER's Bust It record label.

Hammer. *See main text entry.*

Heavy D. (Dwight Myers; b. 1967, Mount Vernon, N.Y.). Lead singer for the rap group Heavy D. and the Boyz. The group is best known for a mixture of upbeat dance rap tunes and mellow rap ballads. Heavy D. formed his group in 1986 and with it has recorded *Living Large* (1987), *Big Tyme* (1989), and *Peaceful Journey* (1991).

Ice Cube. *See main text entry.*

Museum of Modern Art, Film Stills Archive

Ice-T (Tracey Marrow; b. Newark, N.J.). A rap singer, producer, and actor, Ice-T released his first album, *Rhyme Pays*, in 1987; it was followed by *Power* and *The Iceberg*. Ice-T collaborated with Quincy JONES on Jones's 1990 album *Back on the Block* and received a Grammy Award for his work. Ice-T also appeared in films, beginning in the late 1980's, including *Colors* (1988), *New Jack City* (1991), and *Ricochet* (1991). His fourth album, *OG Original Gangster*, was released in 1991, sold more than a half million copies before the end of the year, and reached number fifteen on *Billboard* magazine's album chart.

Kane, Big Daddy (Antonio Hardy; b. 1968, Brooklyn, N.Y.). Although best known as a rap music artist, Kane is also a songwriter and record producer. His albums, a blend of lively rap vocals and smooth rap ballads, include *Long Live the Kane* (1987), *It's a Big Daddy Thing* (1990), *Taste of Chocolate* (1990), and *Prince of Darkness* (1991).

Kool Moe Dee (b. 1962?). Kool Moe Dee's 1985 debut album, *I'm Kool Moe Dee*, contained the single "Go See the Doctor," one of the first rap songs to address the topic of sexually transmitted diseases. His second album contained the title track "How Ya Like Me Now" (1987), a taunting rap addressed to his rival, L.L. Cool J. He released *Knowledge Is King* in 1989. Kool Moe Dee also collaborated with Quincy Jones on his single "Back on the Block" from the sound track to *Listen Up! The Lives of Quincy Jones* (1990).

KRS-One (Kris Parker; b. 1964, New York, N.Y.). Parker adopted the stage name KRS-One (Knowledge Reigns Supreme Over Nearly Everyone) and began writing songs with Scott Sterling. Singles included "Listen to Our Minds" and the hit "Crack Attack." Their debut album, *Criminal Minded*, was released in 1986. Parker and Sterling cowrote the song "Stop the Violence." Before the single was released on their second album, *By Any Means Necessary* (1988), Sterling was killed in a drive-by shooting in August of 1987. Sterling's death prompted Parker to organize the Stop the Violence movement.

L.L. Cool J. *See main text entry.*

M.C. Lyte. *See main text entry.*

Queen Latifah. *See main text entry.*

Rock, Chubb (Richard Simpson; b. 1968, Jamaica). Rock is known for his up-tempo rap tunes. The performer, who was raised in Brooklyn, cowrote and coperformed the popular song "Just Ask Me To," which was on the sound track for the film *Boyz 'N the*

Hood (1991). His albums include *And the Winner Is . . .* (1989) and *The One* (1991).

Shakur, Tupac. *See main text entry.*

Sister Souljah. *See main text entry.*

AP/Wide World Photos

Slick Rick (b. England). Slick Rick, or Ricky Walters, was one of the early rap acts to be managed by Russell Simmons, who signed him to his Def Jam rap label. Walters was charged with attempted murder for a shooting that occurred in 1990. While awaiting trial (at which he was convicted), Walters recorded several singles and accompanying videos. He released the album *The Ruler's Back* in 1991.

Snoop Dogg. *See main text entry.*

Young M.C. (Marvin Young; b. 1968, London, England). Young M.C. had a million-selling single with "Bust a Move." His albums include *Stone Cold Rhymin'* (1989) and *Brainstorm* (1991). In 1990 he won both an American Music Award and a Grammy Award.

---

a rap number by the previous year's winners.

In 1990 M.C. Hammer's *Please Hammer Don't Hurt 'Em* was the year's best-selling album, and by the early 1990's, rap had become a central element of American pop culture. Some observers noted that a rap artist apparently needed also to be appearing in a television situation comedy in order to win a Grammy Award, as evidenced by the number of winning rappers with acting credits, such as Will SMITH and QUEEN LATIFAH. Nevertheless, as political pressure on record companies eased and mainstream audiences grew accustomed to rap, even hard-core rappers achieved critical recognition.

Controversies

As rap's popularity increased, a series of controversies developed concerning both style and content. Widespread sampling led to a series of copyright suits, and by the early 1990's, most rap producers were either paying royalties to their sources or creating their own versions of material they previously might have sampled. As rap expanded beyond its original East Coast and New York City base, both electronic and print media focused attention on its political and social impact. Many LOS ANGELES-based rappers, including Ice-T and N.W.A., acknowledged gang affiliations, generating questions concerning the relationship between rap and violence in inner cities. N.W.A., which included Dr. Dre, Eazy-E, and Ice Cube, released the influential album *Straight Outta Compton*, containing "F tha Police," in 1988.

By the 1990's, Los Angeles and New York City were both major rap centers, and a fierce rivalry had grown between East Coast and West Coast rappers—and in particular between New York-based Bad Boy Entertainment, headed by Sean "Puffy" Combs (Puff Daddy), and Los Angeles-based Death Row Records, headed by Suge Knight (and Dr. Dre until 1996). Both camps produced gritty gangsta rap, and artists involved with both had numerous scrapes with the police. A number of rap stars were involved in drug arrests or assault and murder indictments.

Tupac Shakur, recording under the name 2Pac, and Snoop Dogg (Snoop Doggy Dogg) were major West Coast stars, and the Notorious B.I.G. (or Biggie Smalls) was a New York-based star. Shakur's first album, *2Pacalypse Now*, came out in 1991, Snoop Dogg's *Doggystyle* appeared in 1993 (he had already made a name for himself rapping on Dr. Dre's 1992 *The Chronic*), and the Notorious B.I.G.'s *Ready to Die* was released in 1994. Shakur spent parts of 1995 and 1996 in prison for sexual assault; upon his release he recorded *All Eyez on Me* (1996), which sold roughly five million copies.

Tupac Shakur was murdered in September of 1996. Six months later, in March of 1997, the Notorious B.I.G. was murdered. Members of the New York rap community were rumored to be responsible for the first murder, and the second murder was widely rumored to be a West Coast response to the first.

Many in the rap world realized that gangsta rivalries had gotten out of control and called for a truce all around. Bone Thugs-N-Harmony's Grammy Award-winning single "Tha Crossroads" (1996) recalled the deaths of friends who had been victims of gang vio-

Puff Daddy performing at the American Music Awards in early 1998. *(AP/Wide World Photos)*

Ice-T was one of several successful rappers who have admitted to having had gang affiliations. *(Sire Records Co.)*

lence. While mainstream media identified rap as a source of violence, many rappers contributed their energy to benefit programs such as the "Stop the Violence" movement and "Human Education Against Lies" programs developed by KRS-One of Boogie Down Productions and the "We're All in the Same Gang" project of the West Coast Rap All-Stars. Allegations were made concerning the acceptance of violence against women in the raps of gangsta rappers such as N.W.A., the sexually explicit lyrics of Miami's 2 LIVE CREW, and the alleged anti-Semitism of PUBLIC ENEMY. At their most extreme, these controversies resulted in boycotts of specific rap groups and the arrest of record-store employees for selling allegedly obscene material.

Snoop Dogg had his own legal problems; arrested for murder in 1993, he was eventually acquitted early in 1996. Although the popularity of gangsta rap was fading, both Snoop Dogg's and Puff Daddy's careers continued beyond the controversies. Puff Daddy's *No*

Way Out (1997) won the 1997 Grammy Award for best rap album, and Snoop Dogg released *The Doggfather* (1996) and *Da Game Is to Be Sold, Not to Be Told* (1998). Dr. Dre continued as well, releasing *Dr. Dre 2001* in 1999 on his own Aftermath label.

Diversity of Rap

One unfortunate aspect of rap's public image was the degree to which the controversies obscured the diversity of expression in the form. The politics of rap covers most of the political spectrum, from the militancy of Public Enemy's *It Takes a Nation of Millions to Hold Us Back* (1988) and 2 Black 2 Strong's "Burn Baby Burn" (1990) to the encompassing humanism of Boogie Down Productions' *Edutainment* (1990) and the black feminism of Queen Latifah's *All Hail the Queen* (1989).

Paralleling the popularity of gangsta rap was always the continuing popularity of less confrontational forms of rap and the growth of alternative rap styles typified by the work of such artists as Arrested Development, the Fugees, Digable Planets, and many others. *The Score* (1996) by the Fugees won the 1996 Grammy Award for best rap album, and the group's Lauryn Hill went on to major solo success with *The Miseducation of Lauryn Hill* (1998), which won a Grammy Award for album of the year. Genial rapper and film star Will Smith remained successful. In 1997 he put out his first solo record, *Big Willie Style*, which contained the title song from the film *Men in Black*; the song earned Smith his third Grammy Award. His *Willenium* was released in 1999.

COOLIO became one of the biggest rap stars of the mid-1990's. His debut album, *It Takes a Thief* (1994) became an instant success, and it eventually sold more than one million copies. The follow-up, *Gangsta's Paradise* (1995), won him the 1995 Grammy Award for best rap solo performance for the title song. *My Soul* (1997), Coolio's third album, was also a hit; it contained the single "C U When U Get There."

In late 1995 the governor of Massachusetts gave the rap group Salt-N-Pepa a citation honoring them for displaying positive images of young women with their music. Members of the group, left to right: Sandy Denton, Dee Dee Roper, and Cheryl James. *(AP/Wide World Photos)*

Two of the dominant tendencies of rap during the late 1980's and early 1990's were a growing emphasis on AFROCENTRICITY and the increased presence of African American women rappers. Raps such as Stetsasonic's "A.F.R.I.C.A." (1987), which samples a Jesse JACKSON speech, and the antiapartheid collaboration *Sun City* (1985) demonstrated a longstanding interest in the "motherland." It was only with the emergence of X Clan, Isis, and the Jungle Brothers in the late 1980's, however, that this interest took the form of a serious encounter with West African philosophical traditions.

Although women had been involved in rap since the beginning, most early women rappers followed patterns established by their male counterparts. The verbal duels between M.C. LYTE and Antoinette, for example, followed the pattern established by L.L. Cool J. and Kool Moe Dee, while hard-core groups such as B.W.P. (Bitches with Problems) responded in kind to the sexual explicitness of N.W.A. With the emergence of Salt-N-Pepa, Monie Love, Yo-Yo, and Queen Latifah, black women began to create raps reflecting women-centered visions such as those of writers Toni MORRISON and Alice WALKER.

In the early 1990's a new generation of black rappers (including A Tribe Called Quest, Digital Underground, Naughty by Nature, De La Soul, P.M. Dawn, and Poor Righteous Teachers) assumed important roles in a scene that included Chicano (Kid Frost), Samoan (the Boo-Yaa T.R.I.B.E.), Latino (Mellow Man Ace), English (Monie Love), and European American (3rd Bass) rappers. In addition, rock acts such as Faith No More and R.E.M. collaborated with rap acts and experimented with rap themselves.

Rap became a staple of music television and provided the sound track for a number of films, including *Wild Style* (1982) and *Boyz 'n the Hood* (1991). The lines dividing rap from other forms of black music appeared increasingly blurred in the 1990's. In addition to the use of rap in popular or RHYTHM-AND-BLUES songs by African American entertainers such as Bobby Brown and Neneh Cherry, several significant hybrid forms developed. Of particular significance were hip-house, a combination of rap with Chicago HOUSE MUSIC, and the dance hall reggae of Jamaican performers such as Shabba Ranks, which reasserted the connection between rap and the musical traditions of the African diaspora.

—*Craig Werner*
—*Updated by McCrea Adams and Janet Long*
See also: Recording labels.

Suggested Readings:

Alexander, Frank, and Heidi S. Cuda. *Got Your Back: The Life of a Bodyguard in the Hardcore World of Gangsta Rap*. New York: St. Martin's Press, 1998.

Costello, Mark, and David F. Wallace. *Signifying Rappers: Rap and Race in the Urban Present*. New York: Ecco Press, 1990.

Fernando, S. H. *The New Beats: Exploring the Music, Culture, and Attitudes of Hip-Hop*. New York: Anchor Books/Doubleday, 1994.

George, Nelson. *Buppies, B-boys, Baps, and Bohos: Notes on Post-soul Black Culture*. New York: HarperPerennial, 1994.

_____. *Hip Hop America*. New York: Viking Press, 1998.

Kitwana, Bakari. *The Rap on Gangsta Rap: Who Run It? Gangsta Rap and Visions of Black Violence*. Chicago: Third World Press, 1994.

Ro, Ronin. *Gangsta: Merchandizing the Rhymes of Violence*. New York: St. Martin's Press, 1996.

Rose, Tricia. *Black Noise: Rap Music and Black Culture in Contemporary America*. Hanover, N.H.: Wesleyan University Press: Published by University Press of New England, 1994.

Spencer, Jon M., ed. *The Emergency of Black and the Emergence of Rap*. Durham, N.C.: Duke University Press, 1991.

Stancell, Steven. *Rap Whoz Who: The World of Rap Music*. New York: Schirmer Books, 1996.

Stanley, Lawrence A., ed. *Rap: The Lyrics*. New York: Penguin Books, 1992.

Toop, David. *Rap Attack Two: African Rap to Global Hip Hop*. New York: Serpent's Tail, 1992.

Winfield, Betty H., and Sandra Davidson, eds. *Bleep! Censoring Rock and Rap Music*. Westport, Conn.: Greenwood Press, 1999.

Rapier, James Thomas (November 13, 1837, Florence, Alabama—May 31, 1883, Montgomery, Alabama): RECONSTRUCTION-era politician; U.S. representative from ALABAMA during RECONSTRUCTION. Rapier was the youngest son of John H. Rapier, a barber who had been granted his freedom in 1829, and his wife Susan, a free black woman. James attended a black school in Nashville, TENNESSEE, and worked as a roustabout on the Mississippi River before moving to Canada. In 1856 he entered school in the black community of Buxton, Ontario, and subsequently attended normal school in Toronto. He received his teaching certificate in 1863 and returned to Buxton to teach. Late in 1864, Rapier moved to Nashville, where he worked as a reporter for a northern newspaper and raised cotton on rented land.

After delivering the keynote address at the Tennessee Negro Suffrage Convention in 1865, Rapier decided to return to Alabama, where he became a wealthy cotton planter and established his own newspaper. He entered state politics, becoming chairman of the Alabama REPUBLICAN PARTY's first platform com-

Reconstruction-era statesman James T. Rapier. *(Associated Publishers, Inc.)*

mittee and serving as a delegate to the state constitutional convention in 1867. Falsely charged in a conspiracy to burn a women's academy, Rapier fled for his life to Montgomery. Within a year, he was cleared of the charges and resumed his political activities.

Rapier traveled to WASHINGTON, D.C., in 1869 to attend the first convention of the National Negro Labor Union, an organization dedicated to protecting black people's right to work, acquire land, and gain an education. In 1870 Rapier ran for election as Alabama secretary of state, but he was defeated. In 1872 he was nominated as the Republican candidate for the state's Second Congressional District, and he won the election in November, becoming the second black representative from Alabama.

Rapier became a member of the House Committee on Education and Labor. He successfully campaigned for passage of legislation to make Montgomery a federal port and lobbied for support of a new Civil Rights Act. Rapier lost his race for reelection in 1874 and unsuccessfully contested the election results. Undeterred, Rapier sought the Republican nomination for the Fourth Congressional District seat in 1876 and won. His opponent for the nomination was the seat's black incumbent, Jeremiah Haralson, who decided to run as an independent candidate for the seat. The resulting division of voters in this black-majority district guaranteed the success of the Democratic candidate. After his loss, Rapier accepted an appointment as an internal revenue collector in Alabama. He became a financial supporter of the Exoduster movement, using his income from cotton farming to sponsor black migrants willing to settle lands in Kansas. Declining health forced Rapier to resign his federal collector's post. He died of TUBERCULOSIS.

See also: Congress members; Politics and government.

Raspberry, William (b. October 12, 1935, Okolona, Mississippi): Journalist and nationally syndicated COLUMNIST. As the child of two schoolteachers, James Lee and Willie Mae Tucker Raspberry, William James Raspberry learned to value reading and education. While attending Indiana Central College, from which he graduated with a bachelor's degree in 1960, Raspberry went to work in 1956 as a reporter for the *Indianapolis Recorder*, a black weekly newspaper. He served as a photographer, proofreader, and editorial writer and eventually rose to associate managing editor before he was drafted into the U.S. Army in 1960.

After his discharge from the army in 1962, Raspberry moved to WASHINGTON, D.C., where he took a job as a teletype operator at

Columnist William Raspberry on learning he was to receive a Pulitzer Prize for commentary in early 1994. *(AP/Wide World Photos)*

The Washington Post. He was soon promoted to writing obituaries before serving as a general assignment reporter on the paper's city desk. Raspberry served as assistant city editor for a year before being asked in 1966 to take over "Potomac Watch," a column that focused on local issues. On November 12, 1966, he was married to Sondra Patricia Dodson; the couple eventually reared three children.

Raspberry gradually transformed the "Potomac Watch" column to suit his own personality and his interest in education, criminal justice, and minority problems. His column, appearing three times a week, began exploring more issues of national interest and was picked up for distribution by *The Washington Post* syndicate. Raspberry also contributed articles on race relations and public education to popular magazines, taught journalism at HOWARD UNIVERSITY from 1971 to 1973, and served as commentator and discussion panelist on Washington television stations between 1973 and 1975.

Raspberry was named journalist of the year in 1965 by the Capital Press Club for his coverage of the WATTS RIOTS in Los Angeles. From 1979 to 1986, he served as a member of the Pulitzer Prize board; in 1982 he was first nominated for a Pulitzer Prize for Commentary and won the award in 1994. He also received the Liberty Bell award from the Federal Bar Association, as well as honorary degrees from Georgetown University, the University of Maryland, Indiana University, and Virginia State University.

Raspberry selected sixty-one of his columns, most of them written between 1988 and 1991, and published them in the collection *Looking Backward at Us* (1991). The book's four sections—On Education, On Criminal Justice, On Family, and On Racial Matters—reflect his predominant themes. Raspberry's writing resists easy classification as liberal or conservative. Although racial issues tend to appear in each section of the book, Raspberry is equally likely to stress what African Americans should do to help themselves as he is to call for government help in overcoming the damaging effects of racism on minorities. He criticizes conservative black economists who expect market forces alone, without government intervention, to overcome the effects of racial discrimination in hiring. For Raspberry, deterioration of FAMILIES, violence, TEENAGE PREGNANCY, and SUBSTANCE ABUSE constitute the major forces threatening black America. His writing presents eloquent arguments that these are problems, unlike racism, that the African American community can and should attack through their own efforts.

Rastafarianism: Syncretic RELIGION with roots in JAMAICA and AFRICA. The word "Rastafari" comes from the title and name of Ras (prince) Tafari Makonnen, an Ethiopian nobleman who in 1930 was crowned Emperor Haile Selassie I, King of Kings, Lord of Lords, Conquering Lion of the Tribe of Judah. Through much of of the mid-twentieth century, Haile Selassie was a unique icon of black African pride on a continent dominated by European colonialism.

Inspired by references to the Lion of the Tribe of Judah in the Bible (especially Revelation 5:2-5), Rastafarians believe that Haile Selassie is the Living God, the Returned Messiah, who will overturn centuries of European colonial domination and eventually lead the scattered peoples of African origin back to Africa. Rastafarians have different views on the overthrow of Haile Selassie in 1974 and his death in 1975. Some believe that the emperor never really died and will return to power. Others maintain that as a monarch he was human, and did die, but that as a manifestation of Jah, or God, Haile Selassie's spirit continues to be divine. While he was alive, Haile Selassie himself never acknowledged Rastafarians.

Ethiopian emperor Haile Selassie, seen holding court in 1935, never claimed the divinity attributed to him by Rastafarians. *(AP/Wide World Photos)*

Beliefs and Practices

Rastafarians see people of AFRICAN HERITAGE as black Hebrews, in exile and in bondage. Since Ethiopia, in the ancient world, referred not only to the modern nation of Ethiopia but also to all of black Africa, and since Ethiopians have maintained that they are descended from the Hebrew tribe of Israel, Rastafarians see Africans as the true Israelites. Drawing on biblical images, they refer to the lands in which Africans were settled through SLAVERY as "Babylon." Babylon, or Western civilization, is decadent and corrupt in their view. The society based on European traditions has strayed from divine inspiration, and the white, Western oppressors are people who follow their own intellects, rather than the teachings of holiness.

Western civilization, the Rastafari believe, has corrupted black people, as well as white people. It has led black people to despise their own identities as Africans. The Africans have also sinned, however. It was precisely because blacks had strayed from holy ways of living that the Europeans were able to enslave the peoples of Africa and tear them away from the African heritage.

Maintenance of the divine principles of life is the basic goal of Rasta. These principles are maintained through worshiping Jah in ritual and chanting and in correct daily behavior and thought. An important part of correct daily behavior is the consumption of proper foods, known as "ital" foods. Strict Rastafarians are vegetarians, since eating flesh or animal products makes a cemetery of the stomach. Rastafarians often use grated coconut in their foods as a replacement for the flavoring of meat. Alcohol is also forbidden as inconsistent with healthful living. Fresh fruits and vegetables constitute a major part of the ital diet.

The practice of smoking marijuana, or ganja, is seen by some non-Rastafarians as one of the more questionable aspects of the religion. Rastafarians, however, see smoking "the wisdom weed" as a religious ritual. They believe that it can be used to induce a peaceful and contemplative state of mind. Generally, a set ritual is used in smoking. The ganja is produced wrapped in a newspaper or a paper bag. It is cut up with a knife and then rolled into a cigarette, known as a "spliff," or put into a chillum pipe. The group of smokers will repeat a prayer together. Each smoker will inhale deeply several times and then pass the spliff or pipe on to the next smoker.

Among the most visible distinguishing characteristics of Rastafarians are the long ringlets, or dreadlocks, worn by many adherents. Part of the appeal of dreadlocks for people asserting the value of African origin is that only black people have hair that will naturally form ringlets as it grows. Rastafarians will also sometimes assert that the dreadlocks act as wires that transmit Jah's energy to the worshiper. For most Rastafarians, the hair should not be combed, but simply washed in pure water, although some groups do practice combing.

Importance of Marcus Garvey

Although Rastafarianism is often thought of as a Jamaican faith that has only relatively recently begun to spread in the United States, there are profound historical links between African Americans and the origins of Rastafarianism on the island. When the English invaded Jamaica in 1655 and the Spanish colonists fled, many of the slaves of the Spanish fled to the mountains. Known as "MAROONS," these descendants of Africans fought guerrilla wars against the British and maintained a tradition of independence and opposition to European domination.

Marcus GARVEY's ancestors were Jamaican Maroons. In the early twentieth century, the young Garvey traveled around Latin America and the Caribbean and eventually made his way to London, where he worked as a printer, studied African civilizations, and read Booker T. WASHINGTON's *Up from Slavery*, a work that had a profound influence on Garvey. He returned to Jamaica in 1914 and founded an organization with the goal of establishing black educational institutions on the model of Washington's TUSKEGEE INSTITUTE.

In 1916 Garvey went to the United States, hoping to receive guidance from Washington. Washington died before they could meet, but Garvey settled in NEW YORK CITY, in Harlem, where he established the UNIVERSAL NEGRO IMPROVEMENT ASSOCIATION (UNIA). Garvey became convinced that people of African heritage would never achieve true equality and freedom in the lands where they had been enslaved, and he began to proclaim that all the people of Africa and the black people of the United States were one nation, and that the return of the black race to Africa would restore that continent to glory.

The UNIA became one of the largest pan-African organizations in history, and Garvey became known as the foremost exponent of the "back-to-Africa" movement. Since Garvey claimed that the deliverance of the black race would come when a black king was crowned in Africa, he became, in the eyes of Rastafarians, a prophet of the coming of Ras Tafari. The U.S. government imprisoned Garvey on mail-fraud charges in 1924. After President Calvin Coolidge pardoned him in 1927, Garvey was deported back to Jamaica and spent the rest of his life traveling around the world trying to put his organization together again.

Garvey never managed to regain the influence he had held before his imprisonment. He did, however, help to shape pan-African ideology in his native Jamaica and in the United States. The red, black, green, and gold colors he popularized as the colors of PAN-AFRICANISM continue to have symbolic meaning both for Rastafarians and for North American black liberation movements. However, Garvey himself never had anything directly to do with Rastafarianism.

The Development of Rastafarianism in Jamaica

The coronation of Haile Selassie in St. George's Cathedral in Addis Ababa was taken by many followers of Garvey as the beginning of the fulfillment of the pan-African dream. In Jamaica, four ministers, who had apparently been Garveyites, were particularly inspired by this event. Leonard Howell, Joseph Hibbert, Archibald Dunkley, and Robert Hinds each claimed to have received the revelation that Haile Selassie was the Messiah of black people.

The Rastafarian faith grew gradually from the 1930's through the 1950's. In 1949 a group of militant Rastafarian political activists formed a movement known as Young Black Faith. According to sociologist Barry Chavannes, the members of Young Black Faith institutionalized the use of ganja as a Rastafarian ritual and adopted the practice of wearing long, uncombed hair as an expression of their rejection of society.

In the 1950's and 1960's, Rastafarians became a part of Jamaican life, never accepted by the police or officialdom, but increasingly visible. At the same time, as a result of political violence and unemployment in Jamaica, Jamaican migrants began to move in large numbers to Canada and the United States, bringing the Rastafarian religion back to the region where Garvey had done much of his work.

Migration, Reggae, and North American Rastafarianism

Rastafarianism has grown from a Jamaican faith to an international religion as a result of the migration of Jamaicans to other places and as a result of the global popularity of REGGAE music. From the 1950's to the 1960's, Canada was a primary destination for migrants from Jamaica, who settled chiefly in Toronto and Montreal, creating distinct Rastafarian communities in these cities. Since the 1970's, the overwhelming majority of the roughly twenty thousand people who emigrate from Jamaica every year have settled in the United States. Most Jamaican immigrants to the United States have settled in the large cities of the eastern seaboard, Houston, Texas, and the major cities of California.

While Rastafarianism may have been planted on North American soil by immigrants, however, it owes its spread to the popularity of reggae music, particularly through the agency of Bob Marley. Rastafarians place a strong value on artistic expression in all forms. They are known for their woodcarving, painting, poetry, and music. It is not surprising that

Wearing his hair in long dreadlocks, reggae singer Bob Marley was a roving apostle for Rastafarianism through the last years of his life. (*AP/Wide World Photos*)

they became major performers of Jamaican styles of music.

Bob Marley was a dynamic writer and musician, who expressed the concerns of the Jamaican people and the liberationist ideals of the Rastafarian faith. By the 1970's, his songs were known to people all over the island. Marley's albums *Catch a Fire* and *Natty Dread* brought him worldwide fame. In 1976, after he was the victim of a shooting, Marley left Jamaica for nearly incessant tours of the world, bringing both his music and his religion to parts of the globe far from his native island. Other Rastafarian Jamaican musicians followed Marley's rise to fame. By the time Bob Marley died of cancer in 1981, reggae music had become an institution, and Marley himself had become a cultural icon.

Through reggae music, not only the fashions but also many of the attitudes and even beliefs of Rastafarianism became part of the

North American artistic scene. American musical groups such as See-I and Babylon Warriors, in Washington, D.C.; Roots Reggae, in Southern California; and Jah Ma Roots and Healin' of the Nations, in Boston; have professed the Rastafarian faith.

Rastafarianism in North America in 2000
Although Rastafarianism is widely known in North America, it still has relatively few American adherents, compared with other systems of religious belief. A solid statistical study of religion in the United States conducted in 1991 by the ICR Survey Research Group on behalf of the Graduate School of the City University of New York concluded that there are fewer than 50 thousand Rastafarians in the American population of more than 250 million. (By contrast, there are about 1.4 million Muslims in the country.)

These numbers do not, however, reveal how many North Americans have been influenced by Rastafarian ideals. The pan-African ideals and many forms of belief and expression have been shared by African American groups, such as the ill-fated MOVE ORGANIZATION. Many who have not professed the Rastafarian faith have been profoundly moved by reggae music. Alice WALKER, the author of *The Color Purple*, wrote an article in the magazine *Mother Jones* in which she described the influence of Bob Marley's music on her and told how she had made a pilgrimage to Marley's mausoleum.

Somewhat ironically, through reggae the pan-African faith of Rastafarianism began to cross racial boundaries. The music reached widespread popularity in the late 1970's, a time not too far removed from the height of the American "hippie" movement, and long hair, mysticism, and music with a strong beat touched chords that had become familiar in American culture. White young people began to cultivate dreadlocks, although theirs were rarely as natural as those of the original black believers. Gary Himmelfarb, a young Jewish American with a love of Jamaican music and culture who sported dreadlocks himself, took the name "Dr. Dread" and started one of the first and most influential reggae radio programs.

The spread of Rasta images has created the phenomenon known as "fashion dread." People who have no belief in pan-Africanism and do not maintain an ital diet may be found wearing dreadlocks and woolen tams in African liberation colors, smoking ganja in chillum pipes, and dancing to a reggae beat.

The popularization of Rastafarianism through music also has had its negative effects. In Jamaica, the followers of the faith were long known for advocating nonviolence. As dreadlocks and other trappings of the religion became part of Jamaica's youth culture, though, criminals and arms smugglers became attracted to these forms of expression. Some of these pseudo-Rastas made their way to the United States and Canada. This did not help alleviate the suspicion of the dreadlocked Africans in many segments of American society.

While Rastafarianism has found acceptance in American minority communities and among American youth, it has also been viewed with uneasiness. In 1979 and in 1980, CBS aired two documentaries on Rastafarians. In these, members of the Jamaican religion were largely portrayed as drug users, smugglers, and agents of the Soviets and Cubans. In 1983 nationally syndicated columnist Jack Anderson wrote of a secret New York City Police Department report that warned officers of "criminal elements of the Rastafarian religious sect" who had been trained by the Cubans in guerrilla warfare.

A number of Rastafarians have found themselves in American prisons. This is partially a result of American laws against marijuana use, partially a result of the fact that elements of Rastafari belief have been taken up by law breakers, and partially a result of the fact that some individuals already in prison have converted to Rastafarianism, just as other prisoners have converted to ISLAM or born-again Christianity.

The beliefs and practices of imprisoned American Rastafarians have put them at odds with the institutions that hold them. In 1986 the New York State Appeals Court ruled that New York prison officials could not force Rastafarian inmate Alfredo Lewis to cut off his four foot-long dreadlocks, a ruling upheld by the U.S. SUPREME COURT in 1990. In matters of diet, Rastafarian prisoners have been less successful. In 1987, responding to a suit filed by American Rastafarian prisoners Altha Nomad and Terry Lawson, a U.S. district court judge ruled that the Virginia state penitentiary did not violate their rights to religious freedom when it gave them foods with preservatives, artificial flavorings and additives, and other food items forbidden in the ital diet.

—*Carl L. Bankston III*

See also: Immigration and ethnic origins of African Canadians; Jamaica and Jamaican Americans.

Suggested Readings:

Barrett, Leonard E. *The Rastafarians*. Rev. ed. Boston: Beacon Press, 1997.

Chevannes, Barry. *Rastafari: Roots and Ideology.* Syracuse, N.Y.: Syracuse University Press, 1994.

_____, ed. *Rastafari and Other African-Caribbean Worldviews*. New Brunswick, N.J.: Rutgers University Press, 1998.

Clarke, Peter B. *Black Paradise: The Rastafarian Movement*. Rev. ed. San Bernardino, Calif.: Borgo Press, 1994.

Nicholas, Tracy, and Bill Sparrow. *Rastafari: A Way of Life*. Garden City, N.Y.: Anchor Books, 1979.

Turner, Terisa E., and Bryan J. Ferguson, eds. *Arise Ye Mighty People! Gender, Class, and Race in Popular Struggles*. Trenton, N.J.: Africa World Press, 1994.

Rattley, Jessie Meinfield (b. May 4, 1929, Birmingham, Alabama): Businesswoman and politician. Rattley received her bachelor of science degree from HAMPTON INSTITUTE in 1951. She founded Peninsula Business College in Newport News, Virginia, in 1952 and became its director. Rattley went on to teach at an all-black public high school in Newport News and established its business department to train minority students. In 1970 she became the first African American and the first woman to be elected to the Newport News city council, and she was reelected to the council in 1974, 1978, and 1982. As councilwoman, Rattley was active in city planning and redevelopment and served on the library board. She was the first African American to be elected to the Virginia Municipal League executive committee in 1974. She also served as president of the National Black Caucus of Local Elected Officials and as president of the National League of Cities in 1982. Rattley was elected vice-mayor of Newport News in 1976 and was elected to a four-year term as mayor in 1986.

See also: Politics and government.

Reagan administration: When Ronald Reagan was elected president over incumbent Democrat Jimmy Carter in 1980, he had already had a long career as a spokesperson for the conservative wing of the REPUBLICAN PARTY. A generally popular president, Reagan was easily reelected in 1984. During his two terms, his administration effected significant changes in the federal government. Reagan wanted to cut the size and spending of the government drastically. His administration reduced funding for agencies involved with defending and enforcing CIVIL RIGHTS. He also appointed like-minded conservatives to head government agencies and serve as judges.

Few African Americans voted for Reagan in 1980. Since his campaign called for a reduction

Notable African American Appointees in the Reagan Administration

Samuel R. Pierce, Jr.	Secretary of Housing and Urban Development
Lenora Alexander	Director of Women's Bureau (Labor Department)
Melvin Humphrey	Director of Office of Small Business Administration
Clarence Pendleton, Jr.	Chair of U.S. Commission on Civil Rights
Clarence Thomas	Assistant secretary of Education; chair of the Equal Employment Opportunity Commission
C. Everett Wallace	Deputy assistant secretary of Housing and Urban Development
Lance H. Wilson	Executive assistant to secretary of Housing and Urban Development

in the size and responsibility of the federal government, many blacks feared that Reagan's election would usher in an assault on civil rights legislation and affirmative action programs. Indeed, he argued that policies such as forced school busing to desegregate schools and the use of quotas in affirmative action programs undermined free enterprise and tainted the achievements of successful African Americans. Once he was in office, Reagan's New Federalism approach restored the power of states' rights, and his presidency enjoyed considerable support among conservative southerners.

Reagan was strongly criticized by several prominent African Americans for what they saw as his callous stance on racial issues. He did receive some support from affluent black CONSERVATIVES and young men, but the majority of blacks did not embrace his presidency. His approval rating never exceeded 30 percent among African Americans, and in the 1984 election they voted for the Democratic candidate, Walter Mondale, by a ten-to-one margin.

The president's lackluster commitment to racial equality may be seen through an examination of the records of two of his chief African American appointments. Reagan selected Samuel Pierce, Jr., to serve as the secretary of Housing and Urban Development (HUD). A prominent Wall Street lawyer, Pierce had served as an assistant to the undersecretary of labor during the Dwight Eisenhower administration in the 1950's and later as a general counsel to the Treasury Department under

President Richard Nixon. Under his leadership, HUD self-destructed. Instead of promoting low-income housing, Pierce allowed funds to be diverted toward the construction of luxury apartments, golf courses, and other projects supported by wealthy Reagan supporters. Although he was the only cabinet member to remain in office for all of Reagan's presidency, other members of the administration say that he possessed very little power or influence. Aides often referred to him as Silent

Official portrait of President Ronald Reagan. *(Library of Congress)*

Sam, and most political insiders viewed him as a token appointment.

Reagan also selected Clarence PENDLETON for the U.S. COMMISSION ON CIVIL RIGHTS. While the commission had previously acted as the government's conscience on racial matters, Pendleton helped restructure the organization to reflect the conservative ideological beliefs shared by many of Reagan's conservative friends. Pendleton attacked affirmative action and argued that African Americans should shift toward economic self-help instead of relying on government-sponsored development programs.

While Pendleton's positions received some backing from conservative upper-class blacks, his actions added to the general belief among African Americans that Reagan's administration hoped to roll back civil rights legislation. Both the NATIONAL URBAN LEAGUE and the SOUTHERN CHRISTIAN LEADERSHIP CONFERENCE (SCLC) accused the president of intensifying racial polarization, and most black organizations concluded that Reagan offered little to the majority of African Americans who desired proactive federal protection for school desegregation, equal employment, and affordable housing. Another conservative Reagan appointee was future U.S. SUPREME COURT justice Clarence THOMAS, appointed to head the EQUAL EMPLOYMENT OPPORTUNITY COMMISSION (EEOC).

Reagan's lack of popularity among blacks can also be attributed to his indifferent stance toward civil rights violations. During his presidency, the Justice Department failed to investigate complaints concerning voting rights and RACIAL DISCRIMINATION. The president also lobbied Congress not to extend the VOTING RIGHTS ACT OF 1965, legislation that had forced the South to accept African Americans' constitutional right to register to vote. His veto of the 1988 Civil Rights Restoration Act further strengthened African American disapproval.

—*Robert D. Ubriaco, Jr.*

See also: Carter administration; Bush administration; Eisenhower administration; Housing and Urban Development, Department of (HUD).

Reconstruction: The central issue of the post-CIVIL WAR United States was the role of African Americans in American society. The Reconstruction period, the time during which the former states of the CONFEDERACY underwent political change and achieved readmission to the United States, is generally regarded as lasting from 1865 to 1877, but some scholars disagree on its starting date.

Actually, President Abraham Lincoln began the process of restoring the seceded states to the Union before the Civil War had ended. The president's lenient terms, apparently prompted by his desire to hurt Confederate morale by getting back some of the seceded states, struck many in Congress as too generous. Lincoln was ready to welcome back a rebel state if 10 percent of its 1860 voters swore allegiance to the United States and wrote a new state constitution that ended SLAVERY. In his last public address—on April 11, 1865, two days after Confederate General Robert E. Lee's surrender—Lincoln also expressed his wish that the new southern state governments being set up under his Reconstruction program would grant at least some African Americans, including Union army veterans, the right to vote. Outraged at the president's suggestion, Confederate sympathizer John Wilkes Booth assassinated him.

Presidential Reconstruction Under Johnson
The new president, Andrew Johnson, at first seemed tougher on the former Confederacy than Lincoln had been. Johnson said that 50 percent of a state's 1860 voters would have to swear allegiance to the United States before a new state government would be established, adding that members of certain groups who

had been loyal to the Confederacy, including those worth more than twenty thousand dollars in taxable property, would have to apply to him if they wished a pardon. Johnson, however, readily granted clemency; by the end of his administration, he had excused all save a very few former Confederates.

Johnson offered African Americans nothing, but they took the initiative to improve their own lives. They built schools and churches, organized mutual-aid societies, and met in conventions all over the South to demand full rights of citizenship. Perhaps half of the African American population was on the road in 1865, some looking for family loved ones taken from them by the internal slave trade and others moving to cities in search of work.

Southern state legislatures organized under Johnson's Reconstruction program showed their hostility to African American as-

pirations by passing laws known as BLACK CODES. Though the black codes granted former slaves the right to legally recognized marriages, their main goal was to limit African American economic options. In MISSISSIPPI, for example, African Americans had to sign year-long contracts as a condition of employment and were forbidden to rent land in rural areas. In SOUTH CAROLINA, African Americans who held any job other than agricultural worker or servant had to pay a special tax.

Congress Reacts

The U.S. Congress responded to this virtual reenslavement of African Americans by denying seats to the newly elected U.S. senators and representatives from the South and by trying to mitigate the effects of the black codes. In early 1866, Congress passed and sent to Johnson two bills, one to guarantee African Ameri-

Meetings such as this Colored National Convention session in Nashville, Tennessee, were common during Reconstruction. *(Associated Publishers, Inc.)*

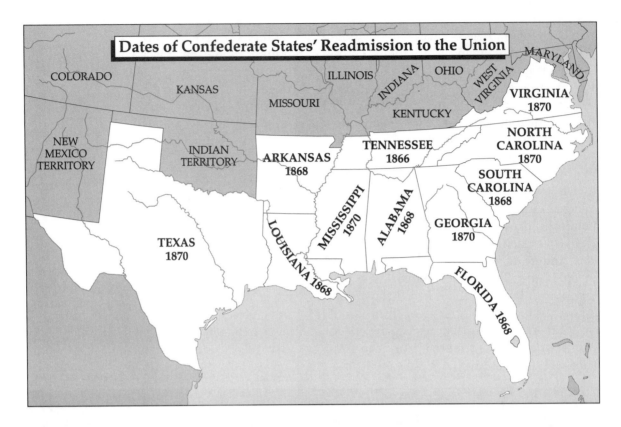

Dates of Confederate States' Readmission to the Union

COLORADO

KANSAS

ILLINOIS

INDIANA

OHIO

WEST VIRGINIA

MARYLAND

MISSOURI

KENTUCKY

VIRGINIA
1870

NEW MEXICO TERRITORY

INDIAN TERRITORY

ARKANSAS
1868

TENNESSEE
1866

NORTH CAROLINA
1870

SOUTH CAROLINA
1868

MISSISSIPPI
1870

ALABAMA
1868

GEORGIA
1870

TEXAS
1870

LOUISIANA 1868

FLORIDA 1868

cans citizenship and certain CIVIL RIGHTS, the other to extend the one-year life span of the Bureau of Refugees, Freedmen, and Abandoned Lands, better known as the FREEDMEN'S BUREAU. Johnson vetoed both bills, claiming, among other things, that they were not in the best interests of whites.

Congress stood up to Johnson. On April 9, members voted to override his veto of the Civil Rights Act of 1866, making it the first major piece of legislation in U.S. history to become law without the president's signature. Congress sustained Johnson's veto of the Freedmen's Bureau extension, only to override it a few months later when he turned down another bill to extend the life of the agency. The Freedmen's Bureau, despite Johnson's objections, continued negotiating labor contracts between planters and former slaves, distributing food rations, setting up hospitals and universities, and managing about four thousand primary schools.

Some of these elementary schools fell prey to the forces of hate, as was the case during MEMPHIS, TENNESSEE, and NEW ORLEANS race riots in 1866. Police instigated or exacerbated both disturbances, and each cost the lives of some fifty African Americans. Congress reacted by approving the FOURTEENTH AMENDMENT and sending it to the states for ratification. Alone among former Confederate states, TENNESSEE quickly assented to the amendment and was rewarded by Congress with readmission to the Union and the seating of its representatives in WASHINGTON, D.C.

In spite of his home state's ratification vote, Johnson publicly opposed the Fourteenth Amendment, which anchored African American citizenship in the Constitution and required all states to treat their citizens equally under the law. In an unprecedented move, Johnson toured the North denouncing the proposed amendment and calling for the election of conservatives. Southerners, heartened by Johnson's message, rejected the Fourteenth Amendment; northerners, repulsed by Johnson, elected moderates and so-called RADICAL REPUBLICANS to Congress.

Congressional Reconstruction

Even before new members arrived in Washington, Congress swung into action. In January, 1867, over Johnson's veto, Congress enacted legislation giving African American men in Washington, D.C., and in the nation's territories the right to vote. More significant still was Congress's effort, embodied in the RECONSTRUCTION ACT OF 1867, to put loyal U.S. citizens in the South, including African Americans, into power. The ten former Confederate states that had not yet ratified the Fourteenth Amendment were virtually required to do so. Additionally, these states had to write new state constitutions and enfranchise African American men in order to gain readmission to the Union.

Those Radical Republicans in Congress who wished to do more for African Americans were frustrated in their efforts. Senator Charles Sumner of Massachusetts wanted the national government to require integrated public schools and to do everything possible to assure blacks of full equality before the law. Representative Thaddeus Stevens of Pennsylvania, outraged at Johnson's forcing the Freedmen's Bureau to take back thousands of acres it had given to former slaves, called for new legislation to promote land redistribution. Most Republicans, however, were not willing to go as far as Stevens and Sumner, particularly after the Democrats, seizing on racial prejudice, did well in elections all across the North in 1867.

In the South, Republicans did much better, winning overwhelming majorities in all ten southern states that were electing constitutional convention delegates. The Republican coalitions that wrote the new state charters consisted of "scalawags," native southern whites who made up the largest group of delegates in the region as a whole; "carpetbaggers," northerners who had moved to the South; and African Americans, who, though underrepresented, won seats in all ten states and managed to gain a majority in South Carolina, one of the three states where they made up most of the population.

Black Lawmakers

African American delegates consistently took positions that helped produce constitutions that were more democratic than those they replaced. The new constitutions abolished imprisonment for debt, whipping as a punishment for crime, and property qualifications for holding public office. The new charters also provided for free public education, something the planter elite before the war had always opposed. The South Carolina constitution gave the state legislature the authority to set up a commission to buy land and resell it to former slaves. Lawmakers acted, and before Reconstruction ended, thousands of African Americans in South Carolina were able to buy land.

It was only in South Carolina that African Americans ever controlled a state house of representatives. No state elected an African American governor during Reconstruction, though P. B. S. PINCHBACK served as acting governor of LOUISIANA for forty-three days. Including Pinchback, six African Americans served as lieutenant governors. Three were speakers of state houses, including John LYNCH of Mississippi, who won his position in 1872 at the age of twenty-four. Mississippi sent two African Americans to the U.S. Senate, choosing Hiram R. REVELS in 1870 and Blanche K. BRUCE in 1875. Fourteen African Americans served in the U.S. House of Representatives before 1877, most of them representing districts in South Carolina and ALABAMA. African Americans also held local offices throughout the South. Though African

Americans remained underrepresented, their participation in elective government positions marked a significant break with the past.

Counterreconstruction

Members of such hate groups as the KU KLUX KLAN were particularly appalled at African American political successes. The Klan was organized in Pulaski, Tennessee, in 1865 or 1866 and quickly evolved into a terrorist organization that threatened, tortured, and murdered African Americans, especially those who were comparatively prosperous or politically active. Sometimes scalawags and carpetbaggers were Klan targets as well. Congress passed a series of enforcement acts in 1870 and 1871 that made crimes of the Klan federal offenses, but these laws were ultimately not enough to save a Reconstruction experiment against which most of the country was turning.

Reconstruction received a blow when historian James S. Pike charged in *The Prostrate State: South Carolina Under Negro Government* (1873) that African American politicians were corrupt and ignorant. Pike's book found a receptive audience, as even many reformers were turning their attention away from the former slaves. President Ulysses S. Grant intervened in 1874 to protect Reconstruction in Louisiana from violent opposition, and the resulting outcry, along with the REPUBLICAN PARTY's loss of the U.S. House of Representatives that year, was enough to convince Grant not even to try to save Reconstruction in Mississippi in 1875. Grant's successor, Rutherford B. Hayes, removed the last federal troops from the South two years later, and the remaining Reconstruction governments collapsed.

The U.S. SUPREME COURT, too, backed away from Reconstruction. In 1876 the Court narrowly interpreted the FIFTEENTH AMENDMENT, which had been ratified in 1870 and which prohibited discrimination on the basis of race in voting. In 1883 the Supreme Court struck down the Civil Rights Act of 1875, which had banned discrimination in public places.

Reconstruction was not a total failure. African Americans, if only for a time, held public office, helping to bring to the southern states permanent changes that included the addition of public schools. Moreover, the Fourteenth and Fifteenth Amendments became part of the Constitution, though it remained for a later generation to breathe new life into them.

—*Robert S. Porter*

Suggested Readings:

Cox, LaWanda, and John H. Cox, eds. *Reconstruction, the Negro, and the New South.* Columbia: University of South Carolina Press, 1973.

Foner, Eric, and Olivia Mahoney. *America's Reconstruction: People and Politics After the Civil War.* New York: HarperCollins, 1995.

_____. *Reconstruction: America's Unfinished Revolution, 1863-1877.* New York: Harper & Row, 1988.

Franklin, John Hope. *Reconstruction After the Civil War.* Chicago: University of Chicago Press, 1961.

Rabinowitz, Howard N., ed. *Southern Black Leaders of the Reconstruction Era.* Urbana: University of Illinois Press, 1982.

Richter, William L. *The ABC-CLIO Companion to American Reconstruction, 1862-1877.* Santa Barbara, Calif.: ABC-CLIO, 1996.

Stampp, Kenneth M. *The Era of Reconstruction, 1865-1877.* New York: Alfred A. Knopf, 1965.

Trefousse, Hans L. *Historical Dictionary of Reconstruction.* New York: Greenwood Press, 1991.

_____. *Reconstruction: America's First Effort at Racial Democracy.* Rev. ed. Malabar, Fla.: Krieger, 1999.

Williamson, Joel. *After Slavery: The Negro in South Carolina During Reconstruction, 1861-1877.* Chapel Hill: University of North Carolina Press, 1965.

Reconstruction Act of 1867: Legislation passed by the U.S. Congress concerning governance of the former Confederate states. The South had been devastated by the CIVIL WAR, which ended in 1865, and needed assistance to rebuild its institutions. Two of the most important needs of the South were a rebuilding of its economic system on a wage labor basis and integration of more than four million African Americans into southern social and political life. Republican political leadership was concerned that a Democrat-dominated South would return to the days of SLAVERY and believed that Congress could prevent this by taking an active role in the reconstruction of southern states.

The Reconstruction Act divided the South into five military districts controlled by the U.S. Army, proclaimed universal male suffrage, and required that all states seeking readmission to the Union ratify the FOURTEENTH AMENDMENT and write new state constitutions. The Reconstruction Act protected African Americans from official denials of fair employment, and it guaranteed them an education. This act set the South on a course toward social, political, and economic equality for African Americans.

The Reconstruction Act resulted in African Americans being elected to political offices in the South. During the military occupation of the South, nearly seven hundred thousand African Americans registered to vote. African American majorities in some states (ALABAMA, FLORIDA, LOUISIANA, MISSISSIPPI, and SOUTH CAROLINA) allowed numerous African Americans to be elected to political office.

President Rutherford B. Hayes began removing federal troops from the South one month after his inauguration in 1877, as part of a deal struck with southern Democrats in a disputed election between himself and Democrat Samuel Tilden. This effectively ended the monitoring of the Reconstruction Act as practiced in the South. Over the next two decades, African American politicians were removed from office, and African American citizens increasingly were disfranchised from the rights given by the U.S. Constitution. It was not until the Civil Rights Act of 1964 and the VOTING RIGHTS ACT OF 1965 that many of the rights guaranteed by the Reconstruction Act of 1867 were restored.

See also: Reconstruction.

Recording labels: Although at the end of the 1980's African American-owned businesses accounted for only 3 percent of all U.S. firms, some black entrepreneurs have achieved extraordinary success in the recording industry. There have been opportunities for independent record labels to carve out lucrative niches and, in some cases, challenge the major companies despite the fact that the industry is controlled by a few huge multinational corporations. Perhaps because their product is music developed in the black community, a number of African American businessmen have succeeded in this field and reaped both critical and financial reward.

Black Swan Records, 1921-1923
The first African American-owned company in the fledgling recording industry was Harry H. Pace's Black Swan label. Pace, a songwriter and former bank cashier, had been a partner in the MEMPHIS, TENNESSEE-based music publishing firm founded by famed blues songwriter W. C. HANDY in 1912. The Pace & Handy Music Company moved to New York City in 1918 and, thanks to the songwriting talents of Handy and to the combined business acumen of Pace and the Handy brothers, the firm became a major force in sheet-music sales.

Mamie SMITH's "Crazy Blues," a 1920 hit on the OKeh label, opened a nationwide market for what were then called "race records." In 1921 Pace left the sheet-music business and established the Pace Phonograph Corporation, with offices at 2289 Seventh Avenue in Harlem. With a board of directors including W. E. B. Du Bois and realtor John V. Nail, Pace engaged twenty-three-year-old pianist Fletcher Henderson as musical director, William Grant STILL as staff arranger, and Lester Walton as business manager. The label was named to honor the acclaimed African American concert artist Elizabeth Taylor GREENFIELD, who was billed on her international tours as "The Black Swan." Appealing to a sense of racial pride, Pace advertised his products in the magazine of the NATIONAL ASSOCIATION FOR THE ADVANCEMENT OF COLORED PEOPLE (NAACP), THE CRISIS, as "The Only Genuine Colored Record—Others Are Only Passing for Colored."

Black Swan's first hit was Ethel WATERS's "Down Home Blues." Other big sellers followed with "Trixie's Blues" and "Desperate Blues" by Trixie Smith. Blues diva Alberta HUNTER, who recorded "How Long, Sweet Daddy, How Long" in May, 1921, recalled the era's primitive technology. Accompanied by Fletcher Henderson on piano, she sang into a horn while a needle in the next room cut directly into a wax matrix. Disappointed that her recordings did not receive the same promotion that Ethel Waters had enjoyed, Hunter signed with powerful Paramount Records the next year.

Although popular female blues singers were responsible for the bulk of its sales, Black Swan Records also released classical and operatic works by performers such as Florence Cole Talbert; Pace believed that such releases would "uplift" the musical taste of African American record buyers. Off to a good start, with 1921 sales of more than $100,000, the company released more than 180 records by 1923, despite a lack of distribution deals with dime-store chains such as the major labels had. In 1924, however, competition and poor distribution forced Pace to sell the Black Swan catalog to Paramount Records.

While the major companies controlled recording in the late 1920's and 1930's, a 1942 recording ban by the American Federation of Musicians and wartime shortages of shellac created opportunities for independent record labels to make a strong reappearance in the late 1940's.

Rhythm and Blues Independents, 1940-1950

Otis Rene and his songwriter brother Leon Rene, whose "When the Swallows Come Back to Capistrano" was a hit for the INK SPOTS in 1940, operated the Excelsior and Exclusive labels in Los Angeles, recording musicians such as Joe Liggins, Big Jay NcNeely, and Jimmy Rushing. The Renes were the first to record Nat "King" COLE in 1944. Other California entrepreneurs included OAKLAND, CALIFORNIA's Bob Geddins, whose song "Tin Pan Alley," sung by Jimmy Wilson, scored a hit on Feddins's Big Town label in 1953 and became a classic among blues performers.

A typical smaller operation of the period was that of LOS ANGELES record-shop owner John Gratton Dolphin. His Lucky, Cash, Money, and Recorded in Hollywood labels produced records by important artists such as Pee Wee Crayton, Peppermint Harris, MEMPHIS SLIM, Jimmy Witherspoon, and Percy Mayfield in the early 1950's. Distribution of those records, however, was mainly through Dolphin's own store.

In HOUSTON, TEXAS, businessman Don Robey (1904-1975) founded Peacock Records in 1949 to issue music by Clarence "Gatemouth" Brown, the headliner at Robey's Bronze Peacock supper club. The label soon also released GOSPEL MUSIC recordings by the Reverend Cleohus Robinson, the DIXIE HUMMINGBIRDS, the Mighty Clouds of Joy, and the Five Blind Boys of Mississippi, among others. Robey bought Memphis-based Duke Records in 1954. With his partner, Evelyn Johnson, Robey operated Buffalo Booking Agency, which managed tours for B. B. KING and other acts, and Lion Publishing Company.

Other Robey labels included Songbird and Backbeat. The Duke-Peacock recording orchestra, led by Joe Scott, included session men such as tenor saxophonist Grady Gaines, Clarence Hollimon, and Teddy Edwards. Robey's songwriters included Peppermint Harris and the prolific Joe Medwick (1933-1992), whose "I Pity the Fool" provided a million seller for singer Bobby "Blue" BLAND. Other top artists in Robey's stable included Little Junior Parker, Johnny Ace, and Willie Mae "Big Mama" THORNTON. Bland alone accounted for more than forty top sellers. In 1973 Robey added to his already considerable fortune when he sold the Duke-Peacock catalog to ABC/Dunhill.

Vee Jay Records

In CHICAGO, ILLINOIS, record-store owners James Bracken and his wife, Vivian Carter, established Vee Jay Records in 1953 to record local gospel groups. Vivian Carter Bracken, a disc jockey at WGRY in Gary, Indiana, soon expanded the company's repertoire, and Vee Jay's 1954 release of "Goodnight Sweetheart Goodnight" by the Spaniels became a top RHYTHM-AND-BLUES hit; the company earned huge royalties when the McGuire Sisters' pop cover version of the song sold more than a million copies. Vee Jay soon grew into the country's largest African American-owned record company. The orchestra, led by Al Smith, included top JAZZ musicians such as saxophonist Red Holloway and guitarist Lefty Bates; arrangers included Von Freeman and Riley Hampton. Among the most popular Vee Jay artists were Jerry Butler, Curtis MAYFIELD and the Impressions, and Gene Chandler, who scored Vee Jay's own million seller with "Duke of Earl" in 1962. The Staples Singers, the Highway QCs, and the Swan Silvertones were among Vee Jay's gospel artists, and the company's jazz-oriented Falcon label featured Eddie Harris, Wynton Kelly, and Lee Morgan.

Vee Jay operated successfully in the same market as the major companies and, in fact, introduced the British rock group the Beatles to the United States in 1962. The release of the Beatles' "I Want to Hold Your Hand" resulted in a territorial battle between Vee Jay, the multinational EMI, and Capitol Records (EMI's American subsidiary). Litigation eventually overwhelmed the company and its founders. Though Vee Jay Records grossed $15 million in 1964, it succumbed to bankruptcy in 1966.

The Motown Era

By the time of Vee Jay's demise, a company founded in Detroit by former boxer and record-shop owner Berry GORDY, Jr., had almost matched it as a major African American-owned firm. Gordy's MOTOWN Records included the Motown, Gordy, Tamla, VIP, and Soul labels and the Jobete Music Publishing Company. Started in 1958 with singer William "Smokey" ROBINSON and Gordy family members, Motown achieved its first hit with the Miracles' "Shop Around" in 1960. Motown artists, local performers discovered and coached by Gordy, included Diana Ross and the SUPREMES, Stevie WONDER, MARTHA AND THE VANDELLAS, Marvin GAYE, the FOUR TOPS, the Jackson 5, and the Temptations. With a recording orchestra led by Gil Askey that was often augmented by string players from the Detroit Symphony, Motown created a fresh rhythm-and-blues style that the company advertised as "The Sound of Young America" and that reached a wide cross-section of record buyers in the United States and abroad.

Motown actually became one of the recording industry "majors" and was doing business in excess of $50 million a year when Gordy, while retaining his position as chairman of the board, sold a large interest in the company to MCA in 1984. By that time, Motown Industries, relocated to Los Angeles, had expanded into motion picture and television production; its 1972 feature *Lady Sings the Blues*, starring

Diana Ross and Billy Dee Williams, had been a box-office success that had earned five Academy Award nominations.

During the 1950's and 1960's, a number of African American musicians established their own labels. These included Sam COOKE's SAR, Ray CHARLES's Tangerine, and Otis REDDING's Jotis label. Jazz musicians Charles MINGUS and Max ROACH founded Debut Records in 1952; its catalog of historically unmatched live recordings of early BEBOP performances by Charlie PARKER and others has been reissued by Fantasy Records. Among the most successful of these artist-owned labels was Curtis Mayfield's Curtom, founded in March, 1968. By 1976 the label, distributed nationally by Warner Brothers, grossed $10 million annually. Mayfield closed the company in 1980. Composer Quincy JONES's Qwest label, with performers such as Tevin Campbell, operates (as did Curtom) more as a large independent than as a typical artist-owned label.

The Rap Revolution
As the sudden popularity of blues in 1920 had boosted the fortunes of record companies, the emergence of a new style among inner-city youth presented an opening for new entrepreneurs. Neighborhood disc jockeys, influenced by radio personalities such as Jocko Henderson, developed a style of rhyming repartee while spinning records. The clever patter became known as "RAP." In 1969 Sylvia and Joe Robinson's New Jersey-based Sugar Hill Records achieved one million sales with "Rapper's Delight," a novelty version of this style performed by the Sugar Hill Gang. More authentic rappers such as GRANDMASTER FLASH AND THE FURIOUS FIVE were also recorded on the Sugar Hill label. By 1984 a rap group from Hollis, New York, called Run-D.M.C., produced by twenty-six-year-old Russell Simmons, had become national stars and headliners of a $3.5-million, twenty-seven-city tour.

Simmons's Def Jam label, artist management agency, and Rush-Groove publishing company became prominent forces in the music industry with artists such as L.L. COOL J., Kurtis Blow, and PUBLIC ENEMY. By 1991 Rush Communications grossed $35 million annually and was listed by *Black Enterprise* magazine as thirty-second among the nation's top one hundred African American-owned businesses. As Gordy had done earlier, Simmons expanded his activities into television, producing music videos and a comedy series in association with the Home Box Office cable television network.

Since the creation of Harry H. Pace's Black Swan label in 1921, African American-owned recording companies have ranged from local and regional labels such as Bobby Robinson's Harlem-based Fury, Red Robin, and Fire during the 1950's to giants such as Philadelphia International (run by songwriter Kenny Gamble and arranger Leon Huff in the 1970's). The history of past successes and ever-changing musical fashion make the recording industry continually attractive to black entrepreneurs.

—*Lorenzo Thomas*

Suggested Readings:
Early, Gerald L. *One Nation Under a Groove: Motown and American Culture*. Hopewell, N.J.: Ecco Press, 1995.
George, Nelson. *The Death of Rhythm and Blues*. New York: Pantheon Books, 1988.
_____. *Where Did Our Love Go? The Rise and Fall of the Motown Sound*. New York: St. Martin's Press, 1985.
Gordy, Berry. *To Be Loved: The Music, the Magic, the Memories of Motown*. New York: Warner Books, 1994.
Govenar, Alan. *The Early Days of Rhythm and Blues*. Houston, Tex.: Rice University Press, 1990.
Pruter, Robert. *Chicago Soul*. Urbana: University of Illinois Press, 1991.
Shaw, Arnold. *Honkers and Shouters: The Golden Years of Rhythm and Blues*. New York: Collier Books, 1978.

Vaughn, Christopher. "Pumping Up the Jam for Profits." *Black Enterprise* (December, 1991): 50-58.

Whitall, Susan. *Women of Motown: An Oral History*. New York: Avon Books, 1998.

Redding, Otis (September 9, 1941, Dawson, Georgia—December 9, 1967, Lake Monona, near Madison, Wisconsin): SOUL MUSIC singer. One of the most popular soul singers of the 1960's, Redding was famous for his energetic live performances.

Redding was also a musical arranger who helped created the Memphis sound, a style of SOUL MUSIC produced at Stax Records in MEMPHIS, TENNESSEE. The Memphis sound became the chief rival of the MOTOWN sound in the black popular music of the 1960's.

Redding grew up in Macon, GEORGIA, where he sang GOSPEL MUSIC in church and began a secular music career in local clubs. In 1962 he received a recording contract from Stax and over the next five years turned out a series of hit records, including "These Arms of Mine," "Pain in My Heart," "I've Been Loving You Too Long," "Respect" (also recorded by Aretha Franklin), "Try a Little Tenderness," and "Tramp," a duet with Carla Thomas.

Soul music combined RHYTHM AND BLUES with vocals that used gospel singing techniques. Various black artists in the 1950's developed this style, including LITTLE RICHARD, Sam COOKE, Jackie WILSON, Ray CHARLES, and James BROWN. Redding's early recordings show the influence of all these artists as well as the influence of Elvis Presley, the white creator of rockabilly music.

At Stax, Redding developed a unique style derived from several sources. He used a grainy voice, an African singing technique that he took from African American gospel music. He employed melisma, a gospel technique in which a single syllable is stretched out over several musical notes. Solomon

Singer Otis Redding was noted for his unusual grainy voice. *(AP/Wide World Photos)*

Burke's recording "Cry to Me" inspired Redding's use of vocal stutters. Redding took the phrase "got-ta" from Sam Cooke's recording "Shake" and began to use the phrase frequently in his records as a kind of vocal signature.

Redding became known as "Mr. Pitiful" (the title of one of his songs) because of the begging and moaning he did on his records. He characteristically did vocal ad libs at the end of his songs. As a musical arranger, Redding created distinctive horn lines for his recordings. Stax producers began to use similar horn lines on recordings by other artists done at Stax, including Wilson Pickett and Sam and Dave. These horn lines came to be the main distinguishing characteristic of the Memphis sound.

Among black audiences in the 1960's, Redding was second in popularity only to

James Brown. In 1967 Redding appeared at the Monterey Pop Festival and gained a white following as well. Redding began to study recordings popular with young whites, including the Beatles' *Sergeant Pepper* album and Bob Dylan's recordings, with the idea of adapting his music to hold this new audience.

Redding's change in musical style was evident in his final recording, "Dock of the Bay." In December, 1967, Redding died in a plane crash while traveling to a performance. "Dock of the Bay," released posthumously, reached the number-one position on the popular music charts.

—*Donald M. Whaley*
See also: Gospel music and spirituals.

Suggested Readings:
Guralnick, Peter. *Sweet Soul Music: Rhythm and Blues and the Southern Dream of Freedom.* New York: Harper & Row, 1986.
Wexler, Jerry, and David Ritz. *Rhythm and the Blues: A Life in American Music.* New York: Alfred A. Knopf, 1993.

Redemption: Movement of conservative southern whites that restored DEMOCRATIC PARTY political dominance to the South after RECONSTRUCTION. The movement toward this "redemption" began in the late 1860's as Union troops began gradually withdrawing from the South. Democrats organized locally to reclaim state legislatures and governorships; by 1877 all eleven states of the former CONFEDERACY were controlled by conservative redeemer Democrats. Redeemers sought to secure control of land, capital, and political power for white southerners by advocating smaller government, repudiation of debt owed by southern states, expanded rights for landlords, more investment by northerners, modern business methods, and white supremacy.

Under redeemer state governments, the small advances that African Americans had attained under Reconstruction were systematically reversed. The voting rights of southern blacks were first nullified through electoral fraud and later restricted by poll taxes, literacy tests, and "grandfather clauses" that prevented all but a handful of blacks from voting. SHARECROPPING, encouraged by redeemer policies, defined economic life for increasing numbers of blacks and poor whites in the South during the last two decades of the nineteenth century. Violence against African Americans escalated throughout the redemption period; by the 1890's, LYNCHINGS of black men had become commonplace in many southern localities. By the end of the nineteenth century, JIM CROW LAWS made possible by the U.S. SUPREME COURT'S PLESSY V. FERGUSON (1896) decision had given legal sanction to segregation and a racial caste system that would shape southern society well into the twentieth century.

—*Michael H. Burchett*
See also: Grandfather clause.

Redistricting: The U.S. Constitution provides that each state will have two senators in the U.S. Senate, but that the number of seats each receives in the U.S. House of Representatives will be determined by population (with each state guaranteed at least one seat). The apportionment of seats in the first House of Representatives was listed in the Constitution with the provision that seats be reapportioned every ten years following a national census. State legislatures then carve up their respective states into U.S. congressional districts to reflect population shifts and lost or gained seats, with each district electing one representative.

State legislatures quickly learned that district boundary lines could be drawn to favor partisan interests. The state legislature of Massachusetts was persuaded in 1812 by Governor Elbridge Gerry to create an odd-shaped district that one observer noted resembled a

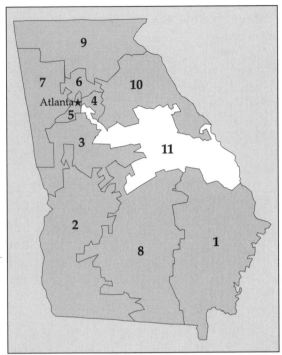

Challenged on constitutional grounds in the Supreme Court's decision in *Miller v. Johnson*, Georgia's predominantly black 11th Congressional District had its boundaries redrawn later in a plan issued by a panel of three federal judges in December of 1995.

1965 (renewed and expanded several times since), which sought to eliminate voting restrictions used to discriminate against blacks and other minorities. As a result of amendments to the Voting Rights Act adopted in 1982, the U.S. Justice Department urged states following the 1990 census to "gerrymander" so as to maximize the voting power of minority groups—to create districts with a "majority minority."

The 1992 congressional election produced probably the most racially diverse results ever. The number of blacks elected to Congress went from twenty-five to thirty-nine. Increased representation of Latinos and Asian Americans also contributed to this cultural diversity. In order to ensure minority dominance in a district, however, congressional districts were redefined with odd-shaped boundaries. Congressional districts with black majorities had been created in Florida, Georgia, Louisiana, North Carolina, Texas, and other states in the South. The Fourth Congressional District in Louisiana resembled a thin "Z"; the Twelfth District in North Carolina, another narrowly drawn district some 165 miles long that followed Interstate 85, prompted local residents to joke that a car driving down the interstate highway with both doors open would kill most of the voters in the district. Some challenges to redistricting have caused divisions within state Democratic Party leadership, since black-majority districts have tended to diminish the strength of the party's support in adjacent districts, leaving some incumbent white Democrats vulnerable to Republican challengers (as seen in the 1994 Republican landslide).

In its 1993 ruling in *Shaw v. Reno*, the U.S. Supreme Court examined the NORTH CAROLINA congressional districts and issued a ruling that challenged the "bizarre" shapes of districts. In its 1994 ruling in *Miller v. Johnson*, the Court struck down race-based districting in Georgia, saying that the government must

salamander. Another observer said that it should be called a "Gerrymander." The term was soon applied generally to partisan and unfair districting. There are various forms of GERRYMANDERING, but a common technique is to concentrate an opponent's strength in one district while watering it down in surrounding districts.

A history of "creative" districting, with one district sometimes having many times the population of a neighboring district, was confronted by the U.S. SUPREME COURT in 1962 (*Baker v. Carr*) in a Tennessee case. That case, and a host of others in the 1960's, focused on the equal protection clause of the FOURTEENTH AMENDMENT as a vehicle for ensuring that state legislatures would protect the principles of fair elections and equal representation. Congress enacted the VOTING RIGHTS ACT OF

In 1995 Louisiana representative Cleo Fields took his fight to save his congressional district from being ruined by redistricting to the Supreme Court. *(AP/ Wide World Photos)*

treat citizens as individuals and not as simply the component of some kind of class—racial, religious, or other. These Court rulings unsettled both newly defined minority districts and surrounding districts benefiting electorally from the concentration of minority voters. Observers predicted both the Court and Congress would be busy sorting out redistricting issues in a number of states.

Redman, Don (July 29, 1900, Piedmont, West Virginia—November 30, 1964, New York, New York): Alto saxophonist, composer, arranger, and orchestra leader. A prodigious student of music, Donald Matthew "Don" Redman played clarinet, saxophones, and other band instruments. Redman came from a musical family in which his mother was a

contralto and his father an instrumentalist in a brass band.

Redman began playing trumpet at the age of three, and he had begun performing publicly by the time he was six. He studied theory, harmony, and composition during his youth and at the age of twenty graduated from Storer College in Harpers Ferry, WEST VIRGINIA. He also attended the Boston Conservatory and the Detroit Conservatory. Redman performed with Billy Paige's Broadway Syncopators in Pittsburgh, Pennsylvania, and later with Fletcher Henderson, whom he joined at the Club Alabam in 1923. Redman played a major role in the development of big band orchestral jazz. In addition, Redman made early recordings with Bessie SMITH (1924), Louis ARMSTRONG (1928), and the Chocolate Dandies (1928-1929).

Redman's arrangements for Henderson include "Shanghai Shuffle" (1924), "Go 'Long Mule" (1924), and "Copenhagen" (1924). After leaving the Henderson Orchestra in 1927, Redman became musical director of McKinney's Cotton Pickers, which recorded such Redman arrangements as "Gee, Ain't I Good to You?" (1926), "Cherry" (1928), and "Rocky Road" (1930). In 1931 Redman, with the assistance of Horace Henderson, the brother of Fletcher Henderson, organized an ensemble that included Benny Morton and Harlan Lattimore. The group recorded and toured until 1940. Redman's orchestra was one of the first black swing-era bands to be sponsored for a radio series and was considered to be one of the premier orchestras of the day. Among Redman's recordings as a leader were "Chant of the Weed/Shakin' the African" (1931), "Got the Jitters" (1934), and "Sweet Sue" (1937). Redman wrote arrangements for Count Basie, Paul Whiteman, and Jimmy Dorsey as well as for NBC's *Lower Basin Street* program. He toured Europe from 1946 to 1947.

During the 1950's, Redman served as musical director for vocalist Pearl BAILEY and appeared with Bailey in the Broadway production *House of Flowers* (1954). Redman's later years were devoted to composing longer pieces rather than to performance.

Red Summer of 1919: Refers to an escalation of interracial violence that occurred in 1919. At the end of WORLD WAR I, unemployment and the necessity of absorbing returning soldiers into the economy created economic uncertainty. In 1919 patriotism aroused in the war combined with nationalist, nativist, and anticommunist sentiments to generate the Red Scare. The GREAT MIGRATION of African Americans from the South as well as immigration from Europe and elsewhere added to economic and political tension. Some saw developments in Russia as a threat to the American political and social system. White hostilities were directed toward African Americans, whom many saw as trying to advance themselves at the expense of white people, as well as toward immigrants. These hostilities erupted in a series of assaults, LYNCHINGS, and race riots. Riots occurred in more than twenty-five communities during the summer of 1919.

In CHICAGO, ILLINOIS, racial tension was heightened by economic competition between the white population of the city and rural black migrants. In addition, political tension was caused by Republican voting patterns among African Americans that challenged the DEMOCRATIC PARTY machine. Prior to the Chicago riot in July, the entrance of African Americans into white residential housing areas resulted in several incidents of bombing. The final riot precipitant occurred when a black teenager accidentally crossed an invisible "segregation line" on a Lake Michigan beach. In the ensuing riot, twenty-three African Americans and fifteen whites were killed. More than five hundred people were injured, and more than three thousand African Americans lost their homes.

Another major riot occurred in WASHINGTON, D.C., another popular destination of migrants from the rural South. Rumors that black soldiers had had sexual relations with white French women increased racial tensions in the city. Immediately prior to the riot, a series of attempted rapes, only one of which was completed, was attributed to a black assailant. The precipitating event for the riot occurred when a white woman married to a serviceman was jostled by two black men. In response, a white mob of servicemen and civilians began attacking black people.

In both the Chicago and Washington, D.C., RACE RIOTS, African Americans grouped together and attempted to defend themselves. Despite resistance against white violence, property damage in black areas was extensive. This pattern was repeated in the many other cities affected by rioting.

Reed, Ishmael (b. February 22, 1938, Chattanooga, Tennessee): Author. Reed's essays, poems, and satiric novels challenge accepted beliefs about society, politics, and the way literary works should be written. Born in TENNESSEE, Reed was the son of Henry Lenoir and Thelma Coleman, who later married Bennie Stephen Reed. In 1942 Reed and his mother moved to Buffalo, NEW YORK. He graduated from high school in 1956 and attended the University of Buffalo, where he was encouraged to write fiction and to value the African American vernacular. He worked on a Buffalo newspaper and cohosted a radio show on which he interviewed Malcolm X.

From 1962 through 1967, Reed lived in NEW YORK CITY, where he was editor of a weekly newspaper, *Advance*. He moved to Berkeley, California, in 1967 and taught at the University of California. Although he was denied tenure in 1977, that decision was reversed in 1988. He founded Yardbird Publishing Company in 1971 and established the Before

Ishmael Reed. *(James Lerager)*

Reed's essays, collected in *Shrovetide in Old New Orleans* (1978), *God Made Alaska for the Indians* (1982), and *Writin' Is Fightin': Thirty-seven Years of Boxing on Paper* (1988), cover a variety of controversial social, political, and literary subjects. He writes appreciations of Richard Wright and Chester Himes, debates with feminists, and describes his neighborhood in Oakland, California, and the devastating changes in it caused by crack-cocaine dealers. Consistently arguing for diversity of opinion, his overriding political goal is to exercise free speech and oppose the tyranny of uniformity.

Columbus Foundation in 1976. Both of these ventures sought to expand the American literary canon to include a multiplicity of ethnic groups and perspectives. Reed was married to Priscilla Rose (1969-1970), then married Carla Blank in 1970.

Beginning with his first novel, *The Free-Lance Pallbearers* (1967), Reed challenged the belief that social realism best expresses the African American experience. Instead, he wrote books that are mosaics of various forms. For example, in *Flight to Canada* (1976), he depicts a protagonist defying the limitations of both time and space when he describes Raven Quickskill's escape from slavery on a jet airplane. In *Mumbo Jumbo* (1972), he writes a novel with illustrations, notes, and a bibliography as a parody of the documentary impulse of the realistic novel. As he says in *Yellow Back Radio Broke-Down* (1969), "No one says a novel has to be one thing. It can be anything it wants to be, a vaudeville show, the six o'clock news, the mumblings of wild men saddled by demons." Reed's art has a playful element that toys with the reader's aesthetic expectations.

Reed, Jimmy (September 6, 1925, Dunleith, Mississippi—August 29, 1976, Oakland, California): BLUES musician. James "Jimmy" Mathis Reed was one of ten children of SHARE-CROPPERS on a MISSISSIPPI plantation. As a child, he sang in local church choirs. From age seven, he was raised with Eddie Taylor and learned guitar from him. He dropped out of school to work as a farmer.

From 1940 to 1943, Reed sang with the Pilgrim Rest Baptist Church choir in Meltonia, Mississippi. He was in the U.S. Navy from 1943 to 1944. When he got out, he moved to Gary, Indiana, then to ILLINOIS, playing in CHICAGO clubs and on the streets for tips. Eddie Taylor began playing with him around 1949. They continued to play together through the 1960's.

By the late 1950's and early 1960's, Reed constantly was releasing hits on the Vee Jay label, with songs that crossed over into popular music. His first hit was "You Don't Have to Go," recorded in 1955. Meanwhile, older musicians such as Muddy WATERS, Elmore James, and HOWLIN' WOLF, who were playing considerably more complex and rough ghetto blues in local clubs, were recording few, if any, pop hits.

Reed played guitar and harmonica at the same time, playing loose but catchy boogie-woogie beats. He slurred his words when he sang, an echo of the lazy sound of the LOUISIANA swamp blues of Lightnin' Slim, Lonesome Sundown, Slim Harpo, and Lazy Lester.

Reed's wife wrote most of his songs, and most of his nine children became musicians. By the 1970's, he was performing concerts and recording in California. Although he had eleven hits between 1956 and 1961 that reached the top twenty on the rhythm-and-blues charts, none of his later recordings met with much success. Reed is known as one of the few successful 1950's blues musicians and as the teen idol who sang "Big Boss Man."

Reformed Methodist Union Episcopal Church: Religious denomination. Delegates to the General Conference of the African Methodist Episcopal Church in 1883 who were dissatisfied with how some delegates were chosen met in 1885 under the leadership of William E. Johnson in Charleston, SOUTH CAROLINA. They organized the Independent Methodist Church and disavowed episcopacy but reversed that decision when they took their final name in 1896. In 1983 the denomination reported eighteen churches with about 3,800 members.

Reformed Zion Union Apostolic Church: Organized in 1869 at Boydton, Virginia, by AFRICAN METHODIST EPISCOPAL ZION CHURCH elder James R. Howell of New York. Church doctrines are similar to those of the Methodist Episcopal Church. The organization had more than fifty churches and a membership of about 16,000 as of the late 1980's.

Reggae: Musical style formed from the traditional JAMAICAN sounds of ska and rock steady. It is as much a social phenomenon as it is a musical genre. Reggae grew out of Jamaican RASTAFARIANISM, a religion based on a belief in the martyred king of Ethiopia, Haile Selassie, as a black God sent to lead displaced African people back to their homeland, a theory highly publicized by Marcus GARVEY's back-to-Africa movement in the early twentieth century. Reggae translates loosely as "the king's music" and is a highly charged and spiritual musical form.

Reggae began to evolve in the mid-1960's from ska, a Jamaican adaptation of NEW ORLEANS RHYTHM AND BLUES in which guitars scratched out "skat" rhythms furthered by the chug-a-lug tempo of horns and saxophones. Through the West Indian population of London, ska was introduced into the British scene. The 1964 hit for Millie Small, "My Boy Lolli-

Jamaican reggae singer Jimmy Cliff in a New York recording studio in 1986. *(AP/Wide World Photos)*

One of Bob Marley's original Wailers, Peter Tosh became a solo reggae star until he was murdered in 1987. *(AP/Wide World Photos)*

the Sheriff." The reggae movement as a whole ran the full gamut from nonviolence to more radical and violent means of expression.

British punk rockers of the 1980's (notably the Clash) often fused reggae with their own unique energy and subsequently introduced reggae to a more diverse audience. With a much wider appeal, reggae continued to seek sociopolitical change as it attracted people with diverse backgrounds.

pop," was in fact a ska novelty song which would also bring the form some attention in the United States. Rock steady marked a continuation of the chug-a-lug tempo of ska but was more derivative of James BROWN-type soul, utilizing more upbeat and heavier guitar and electric bass sounds in its format. A 1966 Alton Ellis hit, "Rock Steady," provided this style with its label. By the end of the decade, future reggae stars such as Jimmy Cliff and Bob Marley had released tracks which were steeped in ska and rock steady styles.

In the 1970's, Marley and his group, the Wailers, which featured another influential artist, Peter Tosh, abandoned the lighter, more traditional Jamaican sound for the Rastafarian-rooted reggae, a term which first appeared in 1968 on the Maytals' "Do the Reggay." This new wave of Jamaican artists embraced the sociopolitical struggles of their people and decried their poverty and oppression, opting for a radically different look and lifestyle while singing songs about freedom. They wore their hair in dreadlocks, long thick ringlets left uncombed, smoked marijuana "spliffs," and sang songs such as "Rasta Revolution" and "I Shot

Reitman v. Mulkey: U.S. SUPREME COURT discrimination case in 1967. In 1964 the California electorate passed Proposition 14, an initiative that amended the state constitution in a way that effectively repealed the state's anti-HOUSING DISCRIMINATION laws. Mr. and Mrs. Lincoln Mulkey, an African American couple, sued Neil Reitman in a state court, claiming that he had refused to rent them an apartment because of their race. They argued that Proposition 14 was invalid because it violated the equal protection clause of the FOURTEENTH AMENDMENT. After the Mulkeys won in California, Reitman appealed to the Supreme Court of the United States.

Justice Byron White's opinion for the five-justice majority held that Proposition 14 was unconstitutional. White admitted that mere repeal of an antidiscrimination statute would not be unconstitutional. In this case, however, the California supreme court had held that Proposition 14 encouraged private racial discrimination. This encouragement amounted to "state action" that violated the equal protection clause of the Fourteenth Amendment.

—*Robert Jacobs*

During the 1990's some African Americans, such as these Harlem residents, turned to traditional Yoruba religious practices in a search for their roots. *(Library of Congress)*

Religion: African American religion developed within the larger contexts of SLAVERY in the antebellum South, the caste-like system of racial relations in the South following the Civil War, and industrialization and urbanization in both the North and the South. In *The Negro Church in America* (1974), E. Franklin FRAZIER argues that African American religion historically has functioned as a "refuge in a hostile white world." At another level, however, African American religion has served as a form of self-expression and resistance to a white-dominated society.

The development of African American religion, particularly during the twentieth century, took many interrelated paths. Through religion, African Americans found a voice to speak not only of their spiritual quest but also of their earthly trials and tribulations and so-

cial aspirations. As a result, African American religion has always contained, sometimes subdued and at other times explicit, a political orientation that sought to address the injustice experienced by peoples of African ancestry over the course of American history.

African Roots
Many scholars have debated the extent to which African American religion draws upon African religion in its variegated forms. Given the diversity of African societies, particularly in West Africa and Central Africa, from which the first slaves came, it is evident that no single African culture or religion could have traveled intact to North America. African religious concepts and rituals, such as ancestor worship, initiation rites, spirit possession, healing and funeral rituals, magical rituals for obtain-

ing spiritual power, and ecstatic ceremonies enlivened by rhythmic dancing, drumming, and singing, are found in African American religion but generally in syncretized ways, blended with diverse Euro-American elements. Many scholars, for example, argue that the call-and-response pattern between the preacher and the congregation and the chanting style of delivering a sermon found in many African American churches were derived from African religion.

Slave Religion

Prior to the American Revolution, very few slaves were Christian, other than in a nominal sense. A shortage of missionaries resulted in only a small number of slaves being instructed by representatives of the Society for the Propagation of Faith, an organization established by the Church of England in 1701. Most planters initially were reluctant to proselytize or allow others to proselytize their slaves because they suspected that Christianity would provide their subjects with an egalitarian ideology and a thirst for freedom. In time, with assurance from missionaries, many slaveholders came to believe that a selective interpretation of the Gospel would foster docility and subservience in the slaves. Slaveholders were only partially successful in utilizing Christianity as a mechanism of social control, for the slaves transformed it into a religion of resistance.

Some blacks joined the evangelical churches—METHODISTS, BAPTISTS, and PRESBYTERIANS—during the First Awakening (1720-1740). The Second Great Awakening (1790-1815), with its camp meetings, attracted many slaves and free black people to evangelical Protestantism. The Methodists initially opposed slavery but began to downplay this

Camp meetings were an important manifestation of evangelical faiths during the nineteenth century. *(Library of Congress)*

stance after the General Conference of 1784. The Baptists never opposed slavery with the fervor of the Methodists, and in time they also came to accept it as they evolved into a mainstream southern denomination. The growing strength of the northern abolitionist movement prompted many southern evangelical ministers to offer religious instruction as evidence that slaveholders respected the humanity of their slaves.

The Methodists emerged as leaders in the development of religious instruction among slaves. Upon its creation in 1845, the Southern Baptist Convention instructed its Board of Domestic Missions to provide religious outreach to black people. The Baptists in particular may have been able to make inroads among the slaves because baptism by immersion resembled initiation rites associated with West African cults. Just as the water spirits induced devotees to jump into a stream, lake, or river, the Holy Spirit occasionally prompted a Christian convert to shout for joy as he or she emerged from the baptismal waters.

The slaves worshiped in a wide variety of congregations, including with whites, with free blacks, exclusively with fellow slaves, and in private. Slaveholders often took house slaves to religious services at white churches, where they were required to sit in separate galleries or in balconies and were instructed to obey their masters. Whites came to find the numerical predominance and emotional exuberance of blacks in many congregations distracting and often encouraged the establishment of separate black churches. Given the racism of white Christians, the movement toward religious separatism was welcomed by both free blacks and slaves. Although white ministers often presided over services for the slaves, the latter often chose instead to hold meetings in their quarters, "praise houses," or "hush arbors," or even deep in the woods, swamps, and caverns. Slave religious gatherings sometimes provided a cover for various forms of re-

sistance, including slave revolts and individual escapes. Some slaves continued to adhere to traditional African beliefs or Islam.

The Black Church Independence Movement
Although black people in North America never enjoyed complete religious autonomy during the antebellum period, relatively independent African American congregations and religious associations emerged during this time. Some scholars point to a slave congregation established in 1758 on the plantation of William Byrd III near Mecklenburg, VIRGINIA, as the first independent black church in North America. Others give this distinction to another Baptist congregation, the Silver Bluff Church in SOUTH CAROLINA, established sometime between 1773 and 1775. Other early independent black Baptist congregations were established in Savannah, GEORGIA, and in various parts of Virginia during the late eighteenth century. Early northern Baptist churches, such as the Joy Street Baptist Church (established in 1805) in BOSTON, MASSACHUSETTS, and the ABYSSINIAN BAPTIST CHURCH (established in 1808) in New York City, appear to have emerged as protests to discrimination in racially mixed congregations.

Black Baptist churches in the Midwest were the first to organize separate regional associations. In September, 1835, six black Baptist congregations made up of former slaves formed the Providence Baptist Association, which merged in 1853 with the Wood River Association into the Western Colored Baptist Association. Membership in independent black Baptist churches increased dramatically after the Civil War. The first of the national Baptist associations, the NATIONAL BAPTIST CONVENTION OF AMERICA, finally was formed in 1895.

Black Methodists also established independent congregations and associations during the antebellum period, although primarily in the North. A group of free blacks belonging to

Since the early nineteenth century, churches have been mainstays of African American communities. *(Library of Congress)*

the FREE AFRICAN SOCIETY, a mutual aid society within St. George's Methodist Episcopal Church in PHILADELPHIA, PENNSYLVANIA, severed ties with the parent body sometime between 1787 and 1792 in response to discriminatory practices of the church's white members. The majority of the schismatics formed St. Thomas's African Episcopal Church, under the leadership of Absalom JONES, in 1794.

A minority contingent under the leadership of Richard ALLEN established the BETHEL AFRICAN METHODIST EPISCOPAL CHURCH two weeks later. Mother Bethel became the founding church for the AFRICAN METHODIST EPISCOPAL CHURCH, the largest of the black Methodist denominations. The racially mixed St. John's Street Church in New York City served as the focal point for the development of what eventually became the second major black

Methodist denomination, the AFRICAN METHODIST EPISCOPAL ZION CHURCH. Although these two denominations made substantial inroads in the South following the Civil War, the white-controlled Methodist Episcopal Church, South, created the structure for the Colored (later Christian) Methodist Episcopal Church.

The Black Rural Church

At the beginning of the twentieth century, more than 90 percent of African Americans still resided in the South. In 1910 about 80 percent of African Americans lived in rural areas. Consequently, the vast majority of churchgoing blacks were attending relatively small churches in the countryside, towns, and small cities of the South. The GREAT MIGRATION of African Americans from the rural South to the cities of both the North and the South had a significant impact on the black rural church during the first half of the twentieth century. Most black churches in the countryside relied on circuit preachers or upon deacons as ceremonial leaders when the former were not present.

Most black rural churches were and still are either Missionary Baptist or Methodist, but black Primitive Baptist and Holiness Churches began to appear in the countryside in the late nineteenth century. Some of these, such as the CHURCH OF GOD IN CHRIST, evolved into PENTECOSTAL sects, which emphasized glossolalia, or speaking in tongues, as the most explicit manifestation of sanctification, in the wake of the interracial Azusa Street Revival in Los Angeles from 1906 to 1909. Although a fair amount of cooperation and visiting occurs between Missionary Baptist and Methodist congregations in small communities, most Holiness-Pentecostal (usually referred to collectively as Sanctified) churches and Primitive Baptist congregations hold themselves and are held at a distance by the conventional churches.

In the typical rural African American congregation, the monthly or bimonthly preaching service is a social gathering that permits members and visitors to reestablish social ties and to share information and gossip. Women wear their finest dresses, hats, hose, and jewelry. Men generally wear suits, even on hot, humid summer days, although some of the young men and adolescents may forgo jackets. The preaching service almost invariably includes prayers, hymn singing, testimonies, "penny" and regular collections, the sermon, and the benediction. On those Sundays when the minister is absent, or during the week, church auxiliaries or deacons conduct prayer meetings and special events, such as suppers and musical programs.

Revivals constitute an important part of the annual ritual cycle and often serve as a home-coming, with former inhabitants of the community returning to their place of origin. Ecstatic behavior in the form of shouting and dancing is much more common during regular religious services. In the Baptist churches, baptisms by immersion at the bank of a river may occur as an aftermath of the revival. Funerals are extremely significant religious occasions which often prompt more ecstatic behavior than do preaching services or even revivals. For many church members, a proper burial constitutes the most valued goal of life.

Historically, the black rural church has constituted the principal center of sociability and a major repository of African American culture. In the past, churches often operated schools, and churches continue to serve religious educational functions. In contrast to the somber tone of many white evangelical churches, black churchgoers find no contradiction in having a good time at religious services. Particularly during the Jim Crow era, black rural churches often played an accommodative role by providing their adherents with a cathartic outlet for coping with the vagaries of racism and the frustrations associated with poverty and economic exploitation. Although the Civil Rights movement was based primarily in urban churches, some rural churches played a supportive role in it.

Religious Diversification

African American religion underwent a further process of diversification in the early decades of the twentieth century as an increasing number of blacks began to migrate from the rural South to the cities of the North and the South. By this time, the National Baptist and the black Methodist denominations had become the "mainstream" churches of African American communities in the large and medium-sized cities of both the South and the North. Congregations affiliated with these denominations exhibited considerable class variation, both from congregation to congregation and within congregations. In contrast, black congregations affiliated with white-controlled EPISCOPALIAN, Presbyterian, and Congregational Churches catered primarily to elite African Americans.

Many mainstream churches created social welfare and employment services for rural migrants from the South. The most notable example of these was the Institutional Church and the Social Settlement of Chicago, which was established in 1900 by Reverdy Ransom, a staunch proponent of Christian socialism who later became a leading bishop in the African Methodist Episcopal Church. Many migrants apparently found niches in the large, well-established Baptist and Methodist congregations. These churches, however, often did not have the resources to meet the material needs of overwhelming numbers of migrants. Furthermore, many migrants who had enjoyed positions of leadership and responsibility in rural churches found themselves relegated to the sidelines in large urban congregations.

As a consequence, many migrants established storefront and house churches, many of which eventually became affiliated with one of the black-controlled mainstream denominations. Often, however, the migrants were attracted to the new "gods of the metropolis," the charismatic prophets and messiahs of a wide array of Holiness, Pentecostal, Spiritual, Islamic, Judaic, and other syncretistic sects such as the AFRICAN ORTHODOX CHURCH and FATHER DIVINE's Peace Mission movement. By the 1920's, HARLEM offered migrants houses of worship such as the Metaphysical Church of the Divine Investigation, Mt. Zion Pentecostal Church, St. Matthew's Church of the Divine Silence and Truth, Congregation of Beth B'Nai Abraham, the Temple of Luxor, Sanctified Sons of the Holy Ghost, and Live-Ever-Die-Never Church.

The GREAT DEPRESSION accelerated the process of religious diversification. As Gayraud Wilmore observes in *Black Religion and*

Black Radicalism (1983), the black community by the end of the 1930's was literally glutted with churches of every variety. Regardless of their religious orientation, storefront churches represented an effort on the part of migrants to re-create the communal ethos of the black rural church. Many storefronts evolved into substantial congregations and the foundations of a wide array of unconventional African American sects. Many of them folded as their founders died or moved to other cities.

Most African American religious groups fit into one of several types: mainstream denominations, messianic-nationalist sects, conversionist sects, and thaumaturgical sects. These four types will be discussed in turn.

Mainstream Denominations

The mainstream denominations are committed, at least in theory, to a reformist strategy of social action that will enable African Americans to become better integrated into the economic, political, and social institutions of American society. Although many of their congregations conduct expressive religious services, churches affiliated with mainstream denominations often exhibit a strong commitment to instrumental activities, such as supporting various protest demonstrations, social uplift programs, and college scholarships. Members of mainstream denominations tend to accept the cultural patterns of the larger society and seek to share in the American Dream. Most mainstream congregations are affiliated with one of the following historically black denominations: the NATIONAL BAPTIST CONVENTION, U.S.A.; the National Baptist Convention of America; the PROGRESSIVE NATIONAL BAPTIST CONVENTION; the African Methodist Episcopal Church; the African Methodist Episcopal Zion Church; and the Christian Methodist Episcopal Church. Other black-controlled mainstream denominations include the African Union Methodist Protestant Church, the Union American Methodist

Episcopal Church, and the Second Cumberland Presbyterian Church in the U.S.A.

About 90 percent of churchgoing African Americans belonged to black-controlled religious organizations during the 1990's. The remaining 10 percent or so belonged to white-dominated religious bodies, but most were affiliated with predominantly black congregations within the larger white bodies. Some blacks affiliated with white-controlled religious groups belonged to sects, such as the JEHOVAH'S WITNESSES, Seventh-day Adventists, Christian Scientists, or Bahai, Nichiren Buddhist, and Unity sects, but most of them belonged to white-controlled mainstream denominations such as the Episcopalian, Presbyterian, and Congregational Churches and, particularly in more recent decades, the ROMAN CATHOLIC Church, the United Methodist Church, the Southern Baptist Convention, and the CHURCH OF JESUS CHRIST OF LATTER-DAY SAINTS (the Mormons).

Black Roman Catholics in the United States numbered close to two million in 1990, a figure that resulted in large part from Caribbean immigrants and upwardly mobile African Americans who had children in parochial schools. Some middle-class African Americans belonged to both a white-controlled denomination and a National Baptist or African Methodist congregation. Although the majority of churchgoing blacks attended services at a congregation affiliated with a mainstream denomination, many others belonged to a variety of black-controlled religious sects.

Messianic-Nationalist Sects

These sects generally are founded by charismatic individuals who are regarded by their followers as messiahs who will deliver black people from white oppression. In their early stages, messianic-nationalist sects often repudiated "Negro identity" and created a new conception of ethnic identity that regarded black people as the original human beings.

They have expressed strong criticism of white racism and have stressed the creation of alternative communities, businesses, and schools that will serve to prepare for the coming of a new golden age for black people.

African American messianic-nationalism has exhibited Judaic, Islamic, and Christian streams. Congregations calling themselves "Black Jews" appeared around 1915 in Washington, D.C., Philadelphia, New York, and other cities, although there is evidence of such groups even earlier, including in the South. Messianic-nationalist sects drawing upon Judaism include the Church of the Living God, the Pillar Ground of Truth for All Nations, the Church of God and Saints of Christ, and the Original Hebrew Israelite Nation.

The best-known messianic-nationalist sects are those that subscribe to Islam. The first of these was the Moorish Science Temple established by Noble Drew Ali in Newark, New Jersey, around 1913. Although remnants of the Temple still exist, its main thrust was picked by the Nation of Islam, initially under the leadership of Wallace D. Fard, an individual who reportedly was of Middle Eastern extraction, and later under Elijah Muhammad. The Nation of Islam grew rapidly, a result in part of the charisma of Malcolm X, the minister of the Harlem temple during the 1960's. Rapid growth did not check schismatic tendencies that led to the appearance of numerous splinter groups, including the Ahmadiya Moslem movement of Chicago, the Hanafis of Washington, D.C., and the Ansaru Allah community of Brooklyn. After the death of Elijah Muhammad, Wallace D. Muhammad, one of his sons, led the transformation of the Nation into the World Community of Islam in the West and still later into the American Muslim Mission, which adopted an orthodox Islamic orientation and even admitted whites into its ranks. Louis Farrakhan established a reconstituted Nation of Islam that he claimed would preserve the original teachings of Fard and of Elijah Muhammad.

The smallest wing of messianic-nationalism remained within the Christian fold. The best known of these groups was the AFRICAN OR-THODOX CHURCH under the leadership of George Alexander McGuire, a former Episcopalian priest from Jamaica. This body grew out of Marcus GARVEY's Universal Negro Improvement Association, the largest mass organization in African American history, and promoted the veneration of the Black Madonna and the Black Christ. A later variant of Christian messianic-nationalism was developed by Albert B. Cleage as the Shrine of the Black Madonna, headquartered in Detroit, Michigan. Cleage, a former minister in the United Church of Christ and a pivotal figure in the Black Theology movement, began to assert in the 1960's that Jesus had been a black revolutionary who came to free peoples of color from white oppression.

Conversionist Sects

These sects characteristically adopt expressive forms of social activity, emphasizing the importance of various ritual activities such as shouting, ecstatic dancing, and glossolalia as outward manifestations of "holiness" or "sanctification." They stress a puritanical morality involving avoidance of carnal pleasures such as drinking, smoking, dancing, gambling, theater-going, and premarital and extramarital sex. Conversionist sects often are other-worldly and apolitical, although some congregations have been known to participate in social activism. After the mainstream churches, the conversionist sects, which encompass a multitude of Holiness-Pentecostal (or Sanctified) sects and smaller Baptist organizations, constitute the largest religious category among African Americans.

The Church of God in Christ, headquartered in MEMPHIS, TENNESSEE, has grown into the largest black Pentecostal body in the world and claimed to have some 3.7 million members as of the early 1990's (this figure is proba-

bly highly inflated). Although it still manifested many conversionist elements, the church began a process of denomination-alization and mainstreaming in the middle of the twentieth century. Many congregations within the Church of God in Christ have substantial numbers of middle-class and prosperous working-class members. Other conversionist bodies include the Church of Christ (Holiness) U.S.A., Christ's Sanctified Holy Church (Holiness), the Pentecostal Assemblies of the World, and the Primitive National Baptist Convention. Although the more established conversionist bodies prohibit women from serving as bishops and pastors, many others have female pastors and even overseers of associations.

Thaumaturgical Sects

These sects maintain that the most direct way to achieve socially desired objectives, such as financial prosperity, prestige, love, and health, is to engage in various magico-religious rituals. Acquiring esoteric knowledge and developing a positive attitude provide an individual with spiritual power. Thaumaturgical sects generally accept the cultural patterns, values, and beliefs of the larger society but tend to eschew social activism as a strategy for attaining goals.

Spiritual churches began to appear in various large cities, particularly Chicago, New Orleans, and Detroit, in the 1910's. They constitute the most common example of the thaumaturgical sect. These groups blend elements from American Spiritualism, Roman Catholicism, African American Protestantism, and voodoo. Depending on the specific association or congregation, thaumaturgical sects may incorporate various other religious traditions. In large part, African Americans in these groups modified Spiritualism to fit into their own experience and began to refer to their churches as "Spiritual" rather than "Spiritualist" by the 1930's and 1940's. Spiritual churches often urge their members to obtain salvation in the earthly world, rather than in an ill-defined afterlife, by burning candles before images of Jesus, the Blessed Virgin, or the saints, obtaining messages from prophets and mediums, and taking ritual baths.

Most Spiritual churches are small and are located in storefronts or converted dwelling units, but some are housed in substantial edifices and cater to relatively affluent working-class and professional people. Even more so than Sanctified churches, Spiritual churches allow women to rise to positions of leadership that they are denied in the Baptist churches. Most Spiritual congregations are affiliated with larger associations such as the METROPOLITAN SPIRITUAL CHURCHES OF CHRIST (established in 1925 in Kansas City), the Universal Hagar's Spiritual Church (established in 1923 in Detroit), the Mt. Zion Spiritual Temple, the Universal Ancient Ethiopian Spiritual Church, or the SPIRITUAL ISRAEL CHURCH AND ITS ARMY.

Although not a part of the Spiritual movement per se, the United Church and Science of Living Institute probably is the best known of the African American thaumaturgical sects. It was founded in 1966 by the Reverend Frederik Eikenrenkoetter II, better known as REVEREND IKE. Reverend Ike teaches that the lack of money is the root of all evil and urges his followers to obtain "green power" through visualization.

Social Activism

From its very beginnings, African American religion has exhibited a contradictory nature. On one hand, slave masters attempted to use Christianity as a mechanism of social control and encouraged their slaves to seek their salvation in a nebulous afterlife. On the other hand, peoples of African ancestry shaped Euro-American Christianity in its various forms, as well as in some cases Judaism and Islam, to meet their own needs and to serve as the single social institution that, historically, they have been able to call their own. Like religious groups in the larger society, black churches provide their adherents with a sense of community and cultural identity, emotional release from the uncertainties of modern life, and philosophical answers to existential questions. Like other subordinate groups in complex societies, African Americans have used religion as a response to their status within the context of the American political economy and social structure.

Many black churches based in the antebellum North were active in the abolition movement. During various periods, black ministers served as federal and state officials, state legislators, and members of the U.S. Congress. George Washington Woodbey, a black Baptist preacher, served as a delegate to the Socialist Party conventions of 1904 and 1908. Some black mainstream ministers, such as Adam Clayton Powell, Jr., worked for social reform in the ghetto alongside COMMUNIST PARTY-sponsored organizations during the 1930's and 1940's. African American religious congregations with activist leaders often serve as local organizational and resource bases for supporting a larger protest movement. At the denominational level, however, political involvement on the part of black mainstream churches tends to focus more on ecclesiastical politics than on the politics of liberation. The organizational structure of the mainstream denominations, especially that of the National Baptists, however, does allow ministers, lay members, and constituent congregations considerable flexibility in choosing whether to participate in social activism.

Although most black congregations stood on the sidelines of the events following the U.S. SUPREME COURT *Brown v. Board of Education* desegregation decision of 1954, many black ministers, particularly ones affiliated with the mainstream denominations, joined the Civil Rights movement. Martin Luther King, Jr., a young middle-class Baptist minister with an affinity for the Social Gospel and Gandhian nonviolence, became a pivotal figure. King's SOUTHERN CHRISTIAN LEADERSHIP CONFERENCE served as a political arm of the black church. In his last years, King became an outspoken critic of American foreign policy in Southeast Asia and expressed concern for the economic plight of black working-class people.

In the wake of the BLACK POWER MOVEMENT, progressive African American clergy created the National Conference of Black Churchmen (NCBC) and black caucuses in the National Council of Churches and many white-controlled denominations. Although the NCBC continued to convene into the 1980's, by 1972 it had lost much of its momentum. Various black clerics involved in the Civil Rights and Black Power movements began to develop the Black Theology project in the late 1960's. Despite their differences, many black theologians agree that Jesus Christ acted as a liberator against human oppression. Although most black theologians remain uncritical of class stratification in American society and of U.S. foreign policy, some proponents of Black Theology, such as Cornel West and James Cone, engaged in a Marxist-Christian dialogue with liberation theologians in the Third World and called for the development of an African American revolutionary Christianity. Despite its roots in African American social activism, Black Theology remains by and large an academic pursuit of black scholars teaching in white-controlled seminaries and universities.

The RAINBOW COALITION under the leadership of the Reverend Jesse JACKSON, a minister affiliated with the Progressive National Baptist Convention, emerged in the 1980's as yet another activist manifestation of African American religion. Although Jackson's agenda was largely reformist in a social democratic vein rather than a revolutionary one, many progressives among whites, Hispanics, Asian Americans, and Native Americans as well as African Americans rallied around his bids for the U.S. presidency in 1984 and 1988. As they did in the Civil Rights movement, black churches served as a vital support base. Jackson's political rallies were well attended by black ministers and were conducted in a style modeled after African American religious services.

In contrast to the generally relatively moderate posture of the mainstream churches, messianic-nationalist sects historically have provided the most vehement African American religious critique of institutional racism. Toward the end of his life, MALCOLM X became an outspoken critic of American foreign policy and capitalism, a posture that contributed to the rift between him and Elijah MUHAMMAD. Over time, these sects generally have modified their radical theological and political stances, a process manifested in the NATION OF ISLAM's transformation into the American Muslim Mission under the leadership of Wallace D. MUHAMMAD.

Although conversionist sects often manifest a posture of political fatalism, some Holiness-Pentecostalist congregations, particularly those affiliated with the Church of God in Christ, have become involved in social activism since the 1960's. That church provided the headquarters for the Memphis sanitation workers' strike, which was punctuated by the assassination of Martin Luther King, Jr., in 1968. Black Pentecostals have won seats on city councils and in state legislatures, and they have been appointed to minor cabinet positions in the executive branch of the federal government.

Thaumaturgical sects appear to be accommodative in terms of their strong tendency to substitute individualistic magico-religious rituals for social activism in an effort to solve the problems of their adherents. Nevertheless, Spiritual churches in particular express protest to existing social relations in a variety of subtle ways, including their rejection of the Protestant work ethic as a sufficient means for obtaining material prosperity and their criticism of "pie-in-the-sky" religion. Certain Spiritual groups have even incorporated elements of messianic-nationalism, and some Spiritual pastors occasionally comment critically upon business practices, politics, and racism in American society.

In addition to exemplifying the richness of African American culture, religion provides significant insights into the social condition of people of African ancestry in American society. Although African American religion underwent some institutionalization during the antebellum period, its development in the form of a wide array of organized denominations and sects occurred after the Civil War and concurrent with the development of industrial capitalism in both the North and the South.

In addition to their status as houses of worship, black churches function as centers of social life, primary vehicles of communication, and mutual aid societies in the African American community. African American religion has been characterized by a dual consciousness in that it has fostered both accommodation and protest to institutional racism and social stratification in American society. Conservative tendencies within black faiths reach for spiritual liberation rather than material and earthly goals, whereas the radical consciousness within the black faith concerns itself with the immediate conditions of black people. Perhaps more than any other institution, religion illustrates the diversity of strategies that African Americans have adopted in attempting to address racial and social injustice. As in the past, African American religion undoubtedly will continue to manifest both accommodative and activist qualities, but its more progressive expressions can be expected to be part of any effort for radical social transformation emanating from the black community.

—*Hans A. Baer*

Suggested Readings:

Baer, Hans A., and Merrill Singer. *African-American Religion in the Twentieth Century: Varieties of Protest and Accommodation*. Knoxville: University of Tennessee Press, 1992.

Chapman, Mark L. *Christianity on Trial: African-American Religious Thought Before and After Black Power*. Maryknoll, N.Y.: Orbis Books, 1996.

Curry, Mary C. *Making the Gods in New York: The Yoruba Religion in the African American Community*. New York: Garland, 1997.

Fulop, Timothy E., et al. *African-American Religion: Interpretive Essays in History and Culture*. New York: Routledge, 1997.

Haney, Marsha S. *Islam and Protestant African American Churches: Responses and Challenges to Religious Pluralism*. San Fransisco: International Scholars Publications, 1999.

Johnson, Paul E., ed. *African-American Christianity: Essays in History*. Berkeley: University of California Press, 1994.

Lawrence, Beverly H. *Reviving the Spirit: A Generation of African Americans Goes Home to Church*. New York: Grove Press, 1996.

Lincoln, C. Eric, and Lawrence H. Mamiya. *The Black Church in the African American Experience*. Durham, N.C.: Duke University Press, 1990.

McCloud, Aminah B. *African American Islam*. New York: Routledge, 1995.

Murphy, Larry, J. Gordon Melton, and Gary L. Ward, eds. *Encyclopedia of African American Religions*. New York: Garland, 1993.

Nelsen, Hart M., and Anne K. Nelsen. *Black Church in the Sixties*. Lexington: University Press of Kentucky, 1975.

Pinn, Anthony B. *Varieties of African American Religious Experience*. Minneapolis, Minn.: Fortress Press, 1998.

Raboteau, Albert J. *A Fire in the Bones: Reflections on African-American Religious History*. Boston: Beacon Press, 1995.

_____. *Slave Religion: The "Invisible Institution" in the Antebellum South.* New York: Oxford University Press, 1978.

Turner, Richard B. *Islam in the African-American Experience.* Bloomington: Indiana University Press, 1997.

Wilmore, Gayraud S. *Black Religion and Black Radicalism: An Interpretation of the Religious History of African Americans.* 3d ed. Maryknoll, N.Y.: Orbis Books, 1998.

Wynia, Elly M. *The Church of God and Saints of Christ: The Rise of Black Jews.* New York: Garland, 1994.

Religious publishing: The majority of African Americans are concentrated in black Protestant churches. BAPTISTS and METHODISTS account for more than 75 percent of these churchgoers, with the other 25 percent distributed among other Protestant churches (EPISCOPAL, Lutheran, PRESBYTERIAN), the ROMAN CATHOLIC Church, and other religious sects (including NATION OF ISLAM, Pentecostal, Yahweh, and more). Most of the religious publishing aimed at African Americans has come out of the Baptist and Methodist Churches.

Black churches developed quite differently from their white counterparts, growing out of a need for African Americans to find a sense of relevance and dignity that had been denied them in the white churches. For the most part, white churches evidenced little or no interest in the critical needs of black people and tended to perpetuate a doctrine of black inferiority. It was inevitable, then, that African Americans should establish their own churches and ultimately their own religious publishing houses.

Black Church Origins

During the colonial period and early years of the American republic, the Baptist and Methodist churches in the northern and southern states treated their black congregants with indifference and often open hostility. In the South, where discrimination was the greatest, the black Baptists were the first to break with the white Baptist churches. African Americans organized the first black Baptist churches in the South as early as 1758—the African Baptist Church in Virginia and the Silver Bluff Baptist Church in Georgia. In 1840, however, the first convention of black Baptists met in New York City to form the American Baptist Missionary Convention. An offshoot from this organization was the National Baptist Convention of the U.S.A., which established the National Baptist Publishing Board.

The first black Methodist churches developed in the North as a result of the discriminatory practices in the white Methodist churches. In breaking with the white Methodists, the black Methodists established three distinct sects: the African Methodist Episcopal (AME) Church, the African Methodist Episcopal Zion (AMEZ) Church, and the Christian Methodist Episcopal (CME) Church.

The first of the AME churches—St. Thomas African Episcopal Church and Bethel Church of Philadelphia—were established in 1787, after a group of black congregants was expelled from St. George's Methodist Episcopal Church in Philadelphia for sitting in pews reserved for whites. In NEW YORK CITY in 1796, as a result of discrimination against black members and refusal to ordain black ministers, several African Americans broke with the St. John Street Methodist Church to form the African Chapel, which later became the AME Zion Church. The Christian Methodist Episcopal Church originated from a split with the Southern Methodist Episcopal Church, whose discriminatory practices had long relegated its black parishioners to positions of subservience and segregation. In 1870 the CME Church was formally established, with the blessings of the Southern Methodists. The first Methodist publishing house was founded by the AME Church in 1890.

Black Church Publishing

By the end of the nineteenth century, these major black denominational publishing houses had been established and had begun publishing church materials for their congregations. As early as the mid-nineteenth century, a number of ministers—especially black ministers—had begun to publish independently. These ministers discovered that the press was extremely powerful, much freer than the pulpit, and that it reached far more people. As a result, they were able to influence the attitudes and opinions of black Christians throughout the United States. Journals such as *The Sunbeam* and *The National Monitor* (1870), published by the Reverend Rufus Perry for the "moral, spiritual, and educational advancement of the race," are distinctive among such publications.

State and national organizations also aided in the development of black church publishing, as these conventions, conferences, and associations saw the need for official journals and began to adopt many independent journals to fulfill these needs. Thus, *The Baptist Companion* became the official organ of the Virginia State convention; *African Missions* became the official journal for the Baptist Foreign Mission Convention of the United States. *The National Baptist Magazine*, the literary journal of the National Baptist Convention, published some of the best Baptist minds and gave birth to the National Baptist Publishing Board. By 1896 this organization had become the largest black publishing concern in the United States. Its primary responsibility was the publication of all church and Sunday school literature (Sunday school books, home and foreign mission guides, Bible commentaries, hymnals, and other works) to which it had exclusive rights. The National Baptist Publishing Board saw as its mission the production of books by authors who could interpret African American feelings, needs, and aspirations.

The black Methodist church focused its earliest publishing efforts upon church literature, particularly the publication of the proceedings of the Methodist conferences (*General Conference Minutes*) as well as the doctrines and disciplines of the faith (the *Discipline*). Later, the literary efforts were expanded to include church periodicals, hymnals, Sunday school literature, histories, and miscellaneous writings by members of the Methodist faith. Like the black Baptist publishing house, the black Methodist publishing houses allowed African Americans to participate more fully in the production of study materials for the black Methodist churches. One of its major publications, *The Quarterly Review*, was founded in 1890. It had as its stated purpose the representation of the history, character, religious thought, and development of the black churches of the United States.

The publication of religious materials in the black church has not, however, been exclusively the province of black denominational publishing houses. During the 1960's, several of the major white church publishers began to take an interest in publishing materials for the black churches, some even developing special sections for ethnic publications. Some publishers—including Judson Press, Broadman Press, and Orbis Books—have been more aggressive in publishing some of the more controversial religious works than have the black church presses. Such works included Afrocentric versions of the Bible (*The Original African Heritage Study Bible*, 1993), Bible commentaries (*Examining the Record: An Exegetical and Homiletical Study of Blacks in the Bible*, 1994; *Black Theology: A Documentary History*, 2 vols., 1993), and collections of Afrocentric sermons and sermons by women preachers (*Best Black Sermons*, 1972; *Those Preachin' Women: Sermons by Black Women Preachers*, 2 vols., 1985-1988). Other publishers have brought out various study aids and devotional works targeted at black readers. Recognizing the emergence of this untapped market, these publishers have capitalized on the emerging notion that Bible reading and spiritual education should be tailored to an individual's personal experience and cultural background.

Impact of Black Church Publishing

Black church publishing grew out of a need to participate in the creation of religious study materials for black churches. Before establishing their own publishing houses, African Americans had been restricted from making contributions to the very Sunday school lessons that they used in their churches. Thus, the major black denominations determined that they could never be able to fulfill their own unique needs as black church members until they were able to control the written word and thus produce their own religious literature. In some degree, the literature produced by the black churches has served as a medium of religious and cultural exchange among African Americans in various regions of the United States.

Most types of religious publishing done by black churches—primarily Sunday school lessons, lesson commentaries, and missionary works—have not differed radically from those produced by white churches. Because the writers of most of these religious publications have relied on standard lectionaries or commentaries and have rarely taken the opportunities to adapt those materials specifically to the realities of the black experience, there is a certain similarity between their works and those of their white counterparts. Although this similarity may be the result of these authors' adherence to orthodox Christian conservatism, it may also be attributable to the fact that many of the authors are members of the black church clergy who were educated in white theological seminaries.

—*Gladys J. Washington*

Suggested Readings:

Fitts, Leroy. *A History of Black Baptists*. Nashville, Tenn.: Broadman Press, 1985.

Lincoln, C. Eric. *The Black Muslims in America*. Boston: Beacon Press, 1961.

Lincoln, C. Eric, ed. *The Black Experience in Religion*. Garden City, N.Y.: Anchor Books, 1974.

Lincoln, C. Eric, and Lawrence Mamiya. *The Black Church in the African American Experience*. Durham, N.C.: Duke University Press, 1990.

Lovett, Bobby Lee. *A Black Man's Dream: The First One Hundred Years: Richard Henry Boyd and the National Baptist Publishing Board*. Jacksonville, Fla.: Mega, 1993.

Richardson, Harry V. *Dark Salvation: The Story of Methodism Among Blacks in America*. Garden City, N.Y.: Doubleday, 1976.

Remond, Charles Lenox (February 1, 1810, Salem, Massachusetts—December 22, 1873, Boston, Massachusetts): Remond was born free. He joined the MASSACHUSETTS Anti-Slavery Society in 1838 as its first black lecturer and became one of the most famous and outspoken figures in the ABOLITIONIST MOVEMENT. One of four delegates to the World's Anti-Slavery Society meeting in 1840 at London, England, he was received enthusiastically by audiences throughout the British Isles. When he returned to the United States, he carried a petition signed by hundreds of Irish people demanding an end to slavery.

Reparations: Compensation for damage of some sort. Claims for reparations are lodged against the oppressor—whether it is an individual, a group, or a state—or, if the damage occurred far enough in the past, against a successor to the actual oppressor. In practice, claims for reparations are most often made against large businesses or against governments, as those bodies are the ones able to pay significant economic reparations. As applied to the African American experience, there have been discussions and proposals for reparations payments to be made in compensation for the deprivations of slavery and for the many years of discrimination and economic oppression that followed.

An important reparations precedent was set by the payment of nearly one billion dollars to Israel by the former Federal Republic of Germany as compensation for Nazi atrocities against Jews. In the United States, reparations claims made by several Native American nations resulted in financial settlements. The Civil Liberties Act of 1988 provided both an apology and financial restitution to Japanese Americans who had been interned during WORLD WAR II. The reparations consisted of $1.5 billion, to be used to provide tax-free payments of $20,000 to each surviving internee and to create a foundation to study the causes of discrimination against Japanese Americans.

In the unique case of African Americans, efforts to obtain reparations have been led by black nationalists. In the "anti-depression program" drafted by the REPUBLIC OF NEW AFRICA in June, 1972, a formal request was made to Congress to authorize $300 billion for reparations, along with providing a sizable tract of land in the U.S. Southeast. The monetary figure was based upon calculations of losses resulting from SLAVERY as well as from systematic discrimination against African Americans during the post-slavery era.

More moderate proposals for reparations suggest that a formal apology could be made for slavery, with reparation payments made to African American institutions such as community organizations, educational funds, and cultural institutions. In December, 1988, Massachusetts state senator William Owens introduced a bill to negotiate reparations for damages caused by slavery to state residents "of African descent." In April, 1989, the Detroit city council unanimously approved legislation urging Congress to establish a $40 million

educational fund for the descendants of African slaves. Democratic U.S. representative John CONYERS of Michigan subsequently drafted a bill to study the need for reparations to African Americans and the appropriate means by which reparations could be paid.

Republican Party: The relationship between African Americans and the Republican Party has a checkered history. When the Republican Party was created in the mid-1850's it did not advocate abolishing SLAVERY where it already existed; however, the party did oppose the extension of slavery. As early as 1856, African American members of the ABOLITIONIST MOVEMENT in BOSTON supported the Republican presidential ticket. In 1860, after an initial period of reluctance, black abolitionist leader Frederick DOUGLASS supported the Republican Party and its presidential candidate, Abraham Lincoln. African Americans subsequently strongly supported the party of Lincoln. African American support for the Republican Party was reinforced by Lincoln's EMANCIPATION PROCLAMATION (1863) during the CIVIL WAR, although some black leaders were upset at Lincoln's cautious approach; the proclamation freed slaves in areas in rebellion against the Union but not slaves in Union territory.

Reconstruction and Southern Republicans
The Civil War ended in 1865, and in the postwar era the Republican congressional plan for RECONSTRUCTION reinforced African American support for the Republican Party. Reconstruction mandated the establishment of new governments and constitutions in states in the former Confederacy. Reconstruction resulted in the election of Republicans, both white and black, to public office throughout the South. In addition, Republicans in the U.S. Congress were instrumental in securing the passage of the FIFTEENTH AMENDMENT in

1870, which gave African Americans the right to vote.

Following the Compromise of 1877, officially ending Reconstruction, and the return of all-white governments in the South, the Republican Party began to decline there. While a few southern whites continued to support the party of Lincoln, its primary southern base consisted of African American voters. In the 1890's, southern states disfranchised African American voters. The Republican Party virtually disappeared in the South until the 1960's. Because the DEMOCRATIC PARTY was responsible for DISFRANCHISEMENT and segregation in the South, those few African Americans who were able to continue participating in politics in southern states did so as Republicans.

In the North, African Americans continued to support the Republican Party during the first two decades of the twentieth century. These voters gradually became a more important voting bloc in urban centers of industrial states as more blacks migrated to the North. The Republican Party gave some recognition to the importance of African Americans to its electoral success. For example, President William Howard Taft appointed William Lewis, an African American, as assistant attorney general of the United States.

Decline of African American Support
Some defections from the Republican Party occurred in 1924 when presidential candidates for both the Democratic and Progressive parties pledged to make no distinctions based on race if they were elected president. Then, in 1928, the Republican Party attempted to build its southern base with white leadership, ignoring those African Americans who previously had served as convention delegates from these states. On the other hand, that same year, Oscar DEPRIEST was elected to Congress from the First Illinois Congressional District as a Republican, the first African American from the North elected to Congress.

In 1932 more African Americans began to desert the Republican Party because of frustration over the effects of the GREAT DEPRESSION; however, a large majority still voted Republican. Then Democratic president Franklin D. Roosevelt's New Deal programs, conceived to combat the Depression and give people hope, had a significant economic impact on black Americans in the 1930's. The New Deal led to vastly increased black support for the Democratic Party. Roosevelt also began to establish ties to African American organizations and leaders. Finally, Roosevelt's wife Eleanor established close ties with African American women, most notably Mary McLeod BETHUNE, the president of the NATIONAL COUNCIL OF NEGRO WOMEN. In 1934 a black Democrat, Arthur MITCHELL, was elected to Congress, defeating black Republican incumbent Oscar DePriest in Illinois. Mitchell, the first black Democrat in Congress, illustrated the movement by African Americans away from the Republican Party.

Throughout the 1930's and 1940's, African American voters tended to be divided between the two parties. Northern blacks in urban centers became important swing voters in presidential elections and were courted by both parties. In the South, African Americans were most frequently associated with the Republican Party, in part because white southern Democrats excluded them from the Democratic Party, which was by far the more dominant party in the South. In 1948 the national Democratic Party adopted a strong CIVIL RIGHTS plank in its party platform. In that election 81 percent of African Americans voted Democratic.

The movement away from the Republican Party by African Americans continued as the national Democratic Party became the supporter of civil rights. In 1952 only 21 percent of African American voters voted for Republican presidential candidate Dwight D. Eisenhower. Eisenhower's support from

African Americans did increase significantly in 1956, when he received 39 percent of the vote. In 1960 Republican presidential candidate Richard M. Nixon discussed appointing an African American to his cabinet if he were elected president. Despite this tactic, Nixon received only 32 percent of the black vote.

African American movement away from the Republican Party was most pronounced in the 1960's. Democratic president Lyndon B. Johnson pushed the landmark Civil Rights Act through Congress in 1964, and the next year he obtained passage of the Voting Rights Act. In the 1964 election, the conservative Republican presidential candidate, Barry Goldwater, openly solicited the votes of southern whites by emphasizing states' rights. (The phrase "states' rights" generally stood for states' claimed right to resist federal integration efforts.) In contrast, Johnson promoted his Great Society programs, his WAR ON POVERTY, and civil rights legislation. Only 6 percent of African Americans voted Republican in the presidential election of 1964.

After 1964

African American support for the Republican Party was minimal after 1964, because a large majority of African Americans perceived the Republican Party as opposing their economic interests and opposing or being indifferent to their civil rights. The Republican NIXON ADMINISTRATION (1969-1974) made many African Americans suspicious, with its appeals to what it called the "silent majority" and promising them a return to "law and order"—these phrases were widely interpreted as being code words for white crackdowns on urban black unrest and even on black civil rights demonstrators.

The Ronald REAGAN ADMINISTRATION (1981-1989) was extremely conservative; it cut back funding for government agencies involved in protecting civil rights and opposed affirmative action. The administration drew criticism from both the NATIONAL URBAN LEAGUE and the SOUTHERN CHRISTIAN LEADERSHIP CONFERENCE (SCLC) for intensifying racial polarization; other black organizations also felt that the administration offered little to the majority of African Americans.

The George H. W. BUSH ADMINISTRATION (1989-1993) was somewhat less unpopular with blacks than the Reagan administration had been. Bush, however, vetoed a 1990 civil rights bill, and his lackluster support for the 1991 Civil Rights Act offended many African Americans. In 1992 he praised the judicial system after four white Los Angeles policemen were acquitted of beating black motorist Rodney King. The acquittal so outraged Los Angeles blacks that it led to days of rioting, and Bush's support for the verdict intensified feelings that the Republican Party had no understanding of the African American community.

In 1996 Democrat Bill Clinton outpolled Republican Bob Dole among African Americans 84 percent to 12 percent. In 1994 African Americans supported Democratic congressional candidates over their Republican counterparts by a 92 to 8 percent margin. In 1997 only one of the thirty-eight African American members of Congress, J. C. WATTS of Oklahoma, was a Republican.

In the 1990's the Republican Party began attempting to recruit more African Americans to its ranks. One African American, Persian Gulf War hero General Colin POWELL, considered running for president in the 1990's as a Republican. The Republican Party's success has been greatest among African Americans who are upper class or who are political or religious conservatives. Overall, fewer than 10 percent of African Americans identify themselves as Republicans.

—*William V. Moore*

See also: Eisenhower administration; Lincoln administration; Politics and government.

Suggested Readings:

Barber, Lucius J., and Mack H. Jones. *African Americans and the American Political System.* Englewood Cliffs, N.J.: Prentice-Hall, 1994.

Pohlmann, Marcus D. *Black Politics in Conservative America.* 2d ed. New York: Longman, 1998.

Walton, Hanes, ed. *Black Politics and Black Political Behavior.* Westport, Conn.: Praeger, 1994.

Republic of New Africa: Revolutionary nationalist group. The RNA was formed on March 31, 1968, in DETROIT, MICHIGAN. Declaring that U.S. SLAVERY had forcibly created a new African nation out of various African nationalities, the RNA claimed, by right of REPARATIONS, land entitlement to Mississippi, Louisiana, Alabama, Georgia, and South Carolina. The RNA emulated African collectivist principles and accepted the necessity of armed struggle to defend the nation-building process. Seven RNA members, including President Imari OBADELE, were convicted in 1973 of charges stemming from a shootout in Jackson, Mississippi, in 1971.

Restrictive covenants: Private agreements to discriminate on the basis of color or other characteristic. The term has been applied most often to agreements among whites not to sell property or houses to other groups, such as African Americans, or among Christians not to sell to Jews. Restrictive covenants began to be used in urban areas of the United States in the late nineteenth century as a means of keeping African and European Americans separated. They were most common in the northern states, including many areas—such as ILLINOIS and MICHIGAN—where segregation was technically illegal.

In SHELLEY V. KRAEMER (1948), the U.S. SUPREME COURT ruled that although a restrictive covenant itself was not illegal, it was unconstitutional for a government agency to enforce one. Later, in JONES V. ALFRED H. MAYER COMPANY (1968) the Court held that any HOUSING DISCRIMINATION against blacks (whether in sale or rental, whether public or private) was illegal.

See also: Racial discrimination; Segregation and integration.

Revels, Hiram Rhoades (September 27, 1822, Fayetteville, North Carolina—January 16, 1901, Aberdeen, Mississippi): RECONSTRUCTION era politician. Revels played prominent roles in the Christian church, in education, in the Civil War, and in politics. Born free, he was educated at the Quaker seminary in Liberty, Indiana, and Knox College in Galesburg, Illinois. He was ordained a minister in the AFRICAN METHODIST EPISCOPAL CHURCH in BALTIMORE in 1845. For several years, he served churches in a number of states, including Missouri, Ohio, Illinois, Indiana, Maryland, and Kentucky. He combined teaching and lecturing with his pastoral ministry. From 1858 to 1863, he served as the first African American pastor of Madison Street Presbyterian Church in Baltimore.

While in Baltimore in 1863, Revels helped organize one of two African American regiments of the Union army. In the same year, he moved to St. Louis, Missouri, where he founded a school for freedmen. He taught at the school for two years, then moved to Vicksburg, Mississippi, and assisted with education efforts of the Freedmen's Bureau. He organized churches and schools in Jackson, and the African Methodist Episcopal Church appointed him presiding elder of the Natchez District.

Revels launched his political career in 1868, when he was appointed as an alderman in Natchez. He won election to the Mississippi state senate in 1869. When Jefferson Davis va-

After former Confederate president Jefferson Davis was forced to resign his seat in the U.S. Senate, Hiram Rhoades Revels succeeded him. *(Library of Congress)*

cated his U.S. Senate seat, the Mississippi legislature elected Revels in 1870 to fill Davis's unexpired term of one year. He thus became the first African American to serve in Congress. After his Senate term, he was named the first president of ALCORN College, near Lorman, Mississippi. He served from 1871 to 1873 and from 1876 to 1882. For a brief period beginning in 1873, he served as Mississippi secretary of state. He spent the latter years of his life with the church, variously serving as editor of the church's *Southwestern Advocate* and as district supervisor in Holly Springs. He died while attending a meeting of the Mississippi conference of the African Methodist Episcopal Church.

Reverend Ike (Frederick Joseph Eikerenkoetter II; b. June 1, 1935, Ridgeland, South Carolina): Clergyman. Reverend Ike attended the American Bible School, where he obtained a bachelor's degree in theology in 1956. After graduation, he served as a chaplain in the U.S. Air Force, from 1956 to 1958, as a BAPTIST. His interest in full-time evangelism and faith healing soon blossomed. In 1962 he left the Baptist ministry to become the founder and president of the United Christian Evangelistic Association.

From the United Christian Evangelistic Association grew the United Church and Science of Living Institute, for whose doctrine and philosophy Reverend Ike is most often remembered. The church holds that God's desire is that humankind should prosper and that it is not money but the lack of it that gives root to evil behavior and mischief among human beings. Reverend Ike taught the positive use of mental power and strength, and he urged his followers to be resourceful and productive spiritually and materially instead of looking for a reward only in the afterlife. Followers were encouraged to think of God working inside them, not outside them. With this attitude of working with God, they would be capable of succeeding in their undertakings. Reverend Ike's teaching included a blessing plan for humanity that stresses faith, charity, and abundant life. His attitude emphasized triumph over spiritual and material adversity.

Reverend Ike lectured frequently at colleges and universities. He broadcast extensively on the radio and television on the East and West Coasts of the United States in the early 1990's. He became a lifetime member of the NATIONAL ASSOCIATION FOR THE ADVANCEMENT OF COLORED PEOPLE (NAACP) and was the recipient of the World Service Award for Outstanding Contributions to Mankind (1975). Reverend Ike's two main headquarters for his operation were in New York City and Boston, Massachusetts. The periodical *Action* was launched as the principal publication of the United Church and Science of Living Institute.

Reverse discrimination: The term "reverse discrimination" was coined to describe what some people believe to be one outcome of AF-FIRMATIVE ACTION programs. Affirmative action consists of giving preferential treatment (as in hiring, awarding contracts, or admitting students to a university) to members of a group that has historically suffered from discrimination. It has been argued that affirmative action, in its attempt to rectify a history of injustice, creates a present injustice in that it does not treat people equally. Instead of discriminating against a minority, this argument holds, it discriminates against the dominant group or majority—hence the name reverse discrimination.

Affirmative action programs must be able to demonstrate the necessity of subordinating the rights of individuals belonging to a traditionally privileged group in order to advance the greater good of the state. Where justification cannot be shown, the U.S. Constitution is considered to have been violated. A number of court cases have dealt with affirmative action and charges of reverse discrimination. The most famous of these is the BAKKE CASE (*Regents of the University of California v. Bakke*), a 1978 U.S. SUPREME COURT case. In the 1990's, U.S. courts handed down a number of rulings that restricted or forbade some types of affirmative action, indicating that federal judges, including the Supreme Court justices, were taking the concept of reverse discrimination seriously regardless of whether they used that particular phrase.

Revolutionary Action Movement: Militant group organized in Detroit, Michigan, in 1963. The movement was dedicated to the overthrow of the capitalist system in the United States and the installation of socialism. Robert F. WILLIAMS, a former president of the REPUBLIC OF NEW AFRICA, is credited with being the movement's leader. Max Stanford founded the group's nationalist journal, *Black America*, in 1963. The group was one of the first to advocate armed struggle.

Reynolds, Barbara Ann (b. August 17, 1942, Columbus, Ohio): Print and broadcast journalist. After graduating from Ohio State University with a bachelor of arts degree in journalism in the late 1960's, Reynolds landed her first newspaper job with *The Columbus Call and Post*, a hometown newspaper serving the black community. In 1968 she served as reporter for a metropolitan newspaper, the now-defunct *Cleveland Press*, then became assistant editor of *Ebony* magazine. In 1969 Reynolds began a twelve-year stint as writer for the *Chicago Tribune*.

While at the *Tribune*, Reynolds aired radio commentaries for an affiliate of the Columbia Broadcasting System. In 1974 she also began freelance writing for such magazines as *Essence, Playboy, The New Republic*, and *Black Family*. With a solid understanding of the publishing world, she cofounded *Dollars and Sense*, a magazine for black professionals. As a reporter assigned to cover the activities of Jesse Jackson, Reynolds became increasingly impressed with the man. In 1975 she published *Jesse Jackson: The Man, the Movement, the Myth*, a biography that focuses on Jackson's adult years and examines the Civil Rights movement. Her second book, *And Still We Rise: Interviews with Fifty Black Role Models* (1988), includes conversations with successful people, including writer Maya ANGELOU, talk show star and entrepreneur Oprah WINFREY, and historian John Hope FRANKLIN, who have made major contributions to society and helped to improve the image of African Americans worldwide. Other books by Reynolds are *Dorothy L. Sayers: Her Life and Soul* (1993) and *No, I Won't Shut Up: Thirty Years of Telling It Like It Is* (1998).

In 1983 Reynolds joined the editorial board of the newspaper *USA Today*. Among her many honors are a 1976 Nieman Fellowship at

Harvard University, a 1977 National Headliner Award for outstanding contributions to journalism, and the 1987 Southern Christian Leadership Conference's Drum Major for Justice Award. Reynolds is a member of Women in Communications and the National Association of Black Journalists.

Reynolds, Mel (b. January 8, 1952, Mound Bayou, Mississippi): ILLINOIS politician. Melvin J. "Mel" Reynolds was first elected to the U.S. House of Representatives as a Democrat from the Second District in Illinois in 1992 after a primary victory over Representative Gus Savage, whose racially divisive rhetoric had alienated many of the district's moderate black voters. Mel Reynolds was reelected in 1994 in an uncontested election amid an investigation of sexual misconduct and other charges involving a teenage campaign worker. Following a jury conviction in August of 1995, Reynolds was sentenced to serve five years in prison. He resigned his House seat effective October 1, 1995.

Reynolds v. Sims: Landmark 1964 U.S. SUPREME COURT case that extended the principle of one person, one vote to legislative districting. The original decision required ALABAMA to redraw its legislative voting districts. After *Reynolds v. Sims*, all states had to devise REDISTRICTING plans so their citizens would enjoy equal votes in elections, regardless of the legislative districts in which they resided. The decision had the effect of ending malapportionment in state legislatures that had favored lightly populated rural districts.

—*Christopher E. Kent*

Rhode Island: In 1997 Rhode Island had a total population of about 987,000, according to estimates of the CENSUS OF THE UNITED STATES. The state's African American population was about 47,000, or 4.7 percent of the total. One of the original thirteen states, Rhode Island ratified the federal constitution in 1790.

The earliest records of African Americans living in the nation's smallest state date back to 1652, when slaves were transported from the West Coast of Africa to Newport and Bristol. By 1750 these cities had become the leading slave ports in the country, a fact that dispels the myth that SLAVERY existed only in the southern states. Some black men were promised their freedom in exchange for fighting in the AMERICAN REVOLUTION. The FIRST RHODE ISLAND REGIMENT, an all-black platoon, fought valiantly in the Revolution. Slavery officially ended in Rhode Island in 1784, and most blacks settled in Providence, the state's largest city.

The first schools for African Americans in the state were started in Newport in 1763. In 1780 the first black self-help organization, the

Providence's Bethel African Methodist Episcopal Church was an important stop in the Underground Railroad. *(AP/Wide World Photos)*

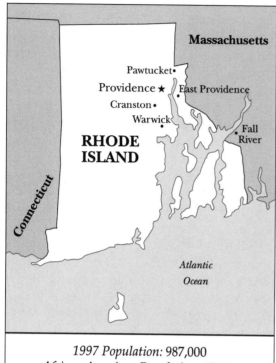

1997 Population: 987,000
African American Population: 47,000
African American Percentage of Total: 4.76

Newport, and the first black state senator came from Providence. Since then, state representatives and city councilmen have been elected. Several appointments were also made at the judiciary level, including the first black female judge, appointed in 1997. In Providence a successful black weekly newspaper began publishing in 1985.

From 1990 to 1997, the state's black population grew by 9 percent, to 47,000. In 1996 its median age was only 25.8, with 85 percent of the population under the age of fifty. Nearly 99 percent lived in urban areas, with the largest concentration in Providence. Unemployment among blacks was 12.6 percent, almost double the rate for the state's population as a whole. Twenty-three percent lived below the poverty line, compared with about 10 percent for all Rhode Islanders.

—*L. Norrine Simpson*

African Union Society, was established. Blacks built a number of churches between 1819 and 1824, and some remain today. Several blacks made significant contributions as philanthropists. Painter Edward BANNISTER and his Native American wife founded the Providence Art Club and the famous Rhode Island School of Design. Bannister's wife helped raise funds for equal pay for black soldiers, and she opened a home for the aged, which was still serving Providence's black community at the end of the twentieth century. At the beginning of the twentieth century, several short-lived black periodicals sprouted in Rhode Island. From these seedlings grew *The New England Chronicle*, which reported black achievement and had generated more than one hundred self-help organizations by 1930.

The 1970's brought particularly significant strides for African Americans in Rhode Island. The state's first black MAYOR was elected in

Rhythm and blues: The musical term "rhythm and blues" (commonly abbreviated R&B) resists easy definition. In that sense the term is less like the fairly well-defined genre of BLUES and more like the category SOUL MUSIC, which also has been used a number of different ways, some much more broad than others.

Rhythm and blues most specifically refers to the styles of African American music that became popular in the 1940's, primarily after WORLD WAR II. At this time the large swing bands of the 1930's and early 1940's were being replaced by smaller groups—partly because tastes were changing and partly because it was too expensive to travel and perform with a big band. These smaller groups usually had a rhythm section with piano, guitar, bass, and drums in addition to a small horn section.

The classic rhythm-and-blues era lasted about fifteen years, from the late 1940's to the early 1960's. The players and songwriters in these bands combined elements of swing,

(continued on page 2158)

Notable Classic Rhythm and Blues Groups

Chantels (Arlene Smith, Lois Harris, Sonia Goring, Jackie Landry, and Rene Minus). The Chantels adapted their group's name from that of a rival high school, St. Francis de Chantelle, in 1956. Two years later, their hit singles included "I Love You So" and "If You Try." They became the first successful all-female vocal group.

Coasters (Carl Gardner, Bobby Nunn, Billy Guy, and Leon Hughes). Doo-wop quartet. The Coasters built a reputation on wisecracking doo-wop hits, many written by the songwriting team of Mike Leiber and Jerry Stoller, that told humorous stories about teenage life and love. Their hits included "Yakety Yak" (1958), "Charlie Brown" (1959), "Along Came Jones" (1959), "Poison Ivy" (1959), and "Love Potion Number Nine" (1971).

AP/Wide World Photos

Drifters. Formed in 1953, the Drifters combined gospel-style vocals with rhythm and blues, helping to create soul music. The original Drifters (the group got its name from the fact that its members had "drifted" from group to group) featured Clyde McPhatter and turned out such hits as "Money Honey" and "Honey Love." In 1954 McPhatter left the group, which continued to perform with various lead vocalists until 1958, when manager George Treadwell replaced all the remaining members of the group. The new group featured Ben E. King, who was later replaced by Rudy Lewis, and then by Johnny Moore. The new Drifters featured vocal harmonizing, a Latin beat, and lush string orchestrations. Beginning with "There Goes My Baby" in 1959, the Drifters had a series of hits that included "Save the Last Dance for Me" (1960), "On Broadway" (1963), and "Up on the Roof"

AP/Wide World Photos

(1963). "Under the Boardwalk" (1964) was the group's last major American hit.

Impressions (Curtis Mayfield, Jerry Butler, Sam Gooden, Fred Cash, and Arthur and Richard Brooks). Vocal/instrumental soul group. Formed in 1957, their first hit single was "For Your Precious Love" (1958). By 1961 only Mayfield, Gooden, and Cash remained. Mayfield became the group's leader and helped it to become one of the most popular vocal groups of the 1960's.

Isley Brothers (O'Kelly, Rudolph, Ronald, Erine and Marvin Isley, and Chris Jasper). Among the group's early hits were the gold record "Shout" (1959) and "Twist and Shout" (1962). The Isley Brothers achieved crossover success with "It's Your Thing," "Love the One You're With," "Fight the Power," "Harvest for the World," and "Summer Breeze" in the 1970's. After their 1983 hit, "Between the Sheets," they broke into two groups, the Isley Brothers and Isley/Jasper/Isley. In 1992, the Isley Brothers were inducted into the Rock and Roll Hall of Fame.

Junior Walker and the All-Stars (Vic Thomas, Willie Woods, James Graves, and Autry DeWalt Walker, Jr.). In 1965 the group put four singles on the charts, including "Shotgun," which made it to number one on the soul charts. Similar success came the following year, with "How Sweet It Is (to Be Loved by You)" and a cover of Bo Diddley's "(I'm a) Road Runner," in addition to the *Soul Session* and *Road Runner* albums. Other hit singles included "Pucker Up, Buttercup" (1967), "What Does It Take?," and "These Eyes." In the 1970's pop hits included "Do You See My Love (for You Growing)?," "Take Me Girl, I'm Ready," "Way Back Home," and "Holly Holy"; soul hits included "Walk in the Night" and "Gimme That Beat."

Little Anthony and the Imperials. *See main text entry.*

Lymon, Frankie, and the Teenagers. *See main text entry.*

Orioles (Sonny Til, George Nelson, Alexander Sharp, Johnny Reed, and Tommy Gaither). The group attained some renown as the Vibronaires in

(continued)

the mid-1940's. The Orioles' first single was backed by "It's Too Soon to Know" (1948), which made the top ten on the rhythm-and-blues charts. Other top-selling songs include "What Are You Doing New Year's?" and "Forgive and Forget" (1950), "Baby, Please Don't Go" (1952), and "Crying in the Chapel" (1953).

Platters (Tony Williams, David Lynch, Herbert Reed, Alex Hodge, and Zola Taylor; later, Paul Robi). Doo-wop group. The Platters sold fifty million re-cords to become the most successful African American doo-wop group in the history of rock music. In 1955 million-sellers "Only You" and "The Great Pretender" were released. Between 1955 and 1960, the Platters had four number-one songs and earned sixteen gold records. Their recordings include "The Magic Touch" and "My Prayer" in 1956, "Twilight Time" and "Smoke Gets in Your Eyes" in 1958, and "Harbor Lights" in 1960. In addition, the Platters appeared in two 1956 rock films, *The Girl Can't Help It* and *Rock Around the Clock*.

blues, JAZZ, and BOOGIE-WOOGIE; they made the rhythmic element of the music prominent and played their music faster than traditional blues tempos to ensure that the music worked for dancing.

Much broader definitions of rhythm and blues have also been used. The term has sometimes been used as an umbrella term encompassing most types of African American pop music from the 1950's onward. In this sense it is used something like the earlier recording industry term "race music," used through the 1940's to denote music by blacks that was marketed to black audiences. The later term "soul music" was similarly used in a broad sense for a time in the 1960's and early 1970's to refer to popular dance music by African Americans.

To complicate matters more, in the 1980's and 1990's, the term rhythm and blues—here almost always abbreviated R&B—began to be applied to a highly produced and polished form of black pop music that emphasized singing skills and often featured considerable vocal embellishment of the melody.

The Classic R&B Era

Among the earliest rhythm-and-blues styles was "jump blues," an outgrowth of swing that was played by Louis Jordan, Wynonie Harris, Roy Brown, and others. Other early R&B performers included blues singer Big Joe Turner and saxophonist Illinois Jacquet. Soon har-mony singing groups, drawing upon such early influences as the Ink Spots, began performing rhythm and blues. Among the classic R&B vocal groups were the Orioles, Hank Ballard and the Midnighters, the Chords, the Platters, and the Drifters. The vocal style known as DOO-WOP can be considered a rhythm-and-blues style. Rhythm-and-blues solo singing ranged from the "shouting" style of singers such as Big Joe Turner to the smoother approach of Charles Brown and, later, Sam COOKE.

Other R&B performers of the classic era include Ruth BROWN, LaVern Baker, Etta JAMES, T-Bone WALKER, Big Mama THORNTON, Screamin' Jay Hawkins, and Ike Turner. A type of R&B known generally as New Orleans R&B was played by Fats DOMINO and Lloyd Price.

Rhythm and blues was an urban music, and its lyrics reflected the concerns and day-to-day experiences of black Americans of the time. Lyrics were sometimes sentimental but often wryly humorous, and they sometimes contained in-jokes, double meanings, and sly sexual references. Another significant aspect of rhythm and blues is that it gave rise to a number of independent RECORDING LABELS, including Sun, Chess, Specialty, and King; another label that released R&B recordings, Okeh, had already been around for many years.

In the mid-1950's, some rhythm-and-blues artists moved in directions that emphasized

(continued on page 2160)

Notable Classic Rhythm and Blues Musicians

Adams, Faye (Faye Scruggs, b. 1936?). Faye Adams's first single, "Shake a Hand" (1953) was the Herald label's first recording and sold more than one million copies. Her follow-up singles, "I'll Be True" and "Hurts Me to My Heart," both reached number one.

Baker, LaVern. *See main text entry.*

Berry, Chuck. *See main text entry.*

Brown, Roy (Sept. 10, 1925, New Orleans, La.—May 25, 1981, Pacoima, Calif.). Brown is regarded as being among the pioneer performers of rock and roll in the late 1940's and 1950's. He reached the pinnacle of his career with the 1947 release of "Good Rockin' Tonight."

Brown, Ruth Weston. *See main text entry.*

Butler, Jerry (b. Dec. 8, 1939, Sunflower, Miss.). With Curtis MAYFIELD, Sam Gooden, and Arthur and Richard Brooks, Butler formed a rhythm-and-blues group called the Impressions and released a hit single, "For Your Precious Love," in 1958. His own singles "Hey, Western Union Man" (1968) and "Only the Strong Survive" (1969) both reached number one. His albums include *The Ice Man Cometh*, *Ice on Ice*, and *Ice and Hot* (1982).

Charles, Ray. *See main text entry.*

Checker, Chubby. *See main text entry.*

Clark, Dee (b. November, 1938, Blythesville, Ark.). Rhythm-and-blues singer. When LITTLE RICHARD quit his music career in 1957, Delectus "Dee" Clark inherited his backup band, the Upsetters. His first hit, "Nobody But You," reached the top ten in 1958. In 1959 "Just Keep It Up" and "Hey, Little Girl (in the High School Sweater)," reached the top twenty. "Raindrops" (1961) reached the number two spot.

Diddley, Bo. *See main text entry.*

Domino, Fats. *See main text entry.*

James, Etta. *See main text entry.*

King, Ben E. (Benjamin Earl Nelson; b. Sept. 28, 1938, Henderson, N.C.). Soul balladeer and songwriter. In 1956 King joined a singing group called the Five Crowns. George Treadwell, a manager who owned the name "Drifters" after the original group of that name had disbanded, signed the Five Crowns as the New Drifters in 1959. In 1960, King co-wrote and sang lead for the group's first hit, "There Goes My Baby," and led it to the top of the charts with "Save the Last Dance for Me." King went solo that year. His 1960's hits include "Spanish Harlem," "Stand by Me," "Don't Play That Song," and "Seven Letters." In the mid-1970's, King released the album *Supernatural Thing, Part 1*. He collaborated with the Average White Band for *Benny and Us* in 1977, and continued performing during the 1980's.

AP/Wide World Photos

King Curtis. *See main text entry.*

Little Richard. *See main text entry.*

McPhatter, Clyde (Nov. 15, 1933, Durham, N.C.—June 13, 1972, New York, N.Y.). Singer, songwriter, and bandleader. By 1950, McPhatter was the lead tenor of the enormously popular vocal group the Dominoes. In 1953, McPhatter formed the Drifters. McPhatter's solo hits include "A Lover's Question," "Ta-Ta" (1960), and "Lover Please" (1962). He was inducted into the Rock and Roll Hall of Fame in 1987.

Price, Lloyd (b. Mar. 9, 1933?, New Orleans, La.). Singer, songwriter, and businessman. Price recorded his first hit, "Lawdy Miss Clawdy," in 1952. For the next two years, Price was one of the most popular and successful recording stars of the day, releasing hits such as "Oooh-Oooh-Oooh," "Restless Heart," and "Ain't It a Shame." His 1958 recording of "Stagger Lee" was his only release to reach number one on the pop charts.

(continued)

Thornton, Big Mama. *See main text entry.*

Turner, Ike (b. Nov. 5, 1931, Clarksdale, Miss.). Rhythm-and-blues instrumentalist and vocalist. By 1951, Turner was playing with his own rhythm-and-blues band, the

Kings of Rhythm. The band's "Rocket '88" (1951) is regarded by many as the first identifiably rock-and-roll record. Although Turner and the Kings of Rhythm recorded many records as backup musicians to Elmore James, HOWLIN' WOLF, and others, and even though Turner himself was an accomplished talent scout for Modern Records and the Memphis Recording Studio, he is best known for his work with his former wife, Tina TURNER.

Walker, T-Bone. *See main text entry.*

Heavily produced pop singers such as Erykah Badu were representative of the new breed of R&B recording artists in the late 1990's. *(AP/Wide World Photos)*

aggressive piano playing and electric guitar. This type of R&B—as played by Chuck BERRY (who was strongly influenced by Louis Jordan), LITTLE RICHARD, and Bo DIDDLEY—led directly to the birth of rock and roll, which is often considered the meeting of rhythm and blues and white country or "hillbilly" music.

By the early 1960's, the classic rhythm-and-blues era had faded. Many black performers were consciously adapting their music to appeal to white tastes. The 1960's saw rhythm and blues evolve into soul music and Motown-style pop. Moreover, the "British invasion" of the Beatles, Rolling Stones, and dozens of other groups wrought major changes in American pop music. In the arena of dance music, funk and then disco emerged in the late 1960's and 1970's.

A number of artists who began their careers known as rhythm-and-blues artists continued long enough to no longer be primarily associated with the genre. Prime examples are Ray CHARLES and James BROWN; Brown today is most often called a soul or FUNK performer.

Modern R&B

In the 1980's and 1990's, R&B came to refer to the heavily produced pop music of such artists as Toni Braxton, Luther Van-

Mary J. Blige, one of the emerging R&B stars of the late 1990's. *(MCA Records)*

dross, Anita Baker, Babyface, Bobby Brown, Soul II Soul, TLC, the Tony Rich Project, Mary J. Blige, Brandy, R. Kelly, and Erykah Badu. It also continued to be applied to the later work of such long-established artists as Ray Charles, Aretha Franklin, and Chaka Khan. In the 1990's some R&B artists began merging R&B with rap and hip-hop elements.

—McCrea Adams

Suggested Readings:

George, Nelson. *The Death of Rhythm and Blues.* New York: Pantheon Books, 1988.

Guralnick, Peter. *Sweet Soul Music: Rhythm and Blues and the Southern Dream of Freedom.* New York: Harper & Row, 1986.

Jones, LeRoi. *Blues People: Negro Music in White America.* New York: William Morrow, 1963.

Keil, Charles. *Urban Blues.* Chicago: University of Chicago Press, 1966.

Shaw, Arnold. *Honkers and Shouters: The Golden Years of Rhythm and Blues.* New York: Macmillan, 1978.

Ward, Brian. *Just My Soul Responding: Rhythm and Blues, Black Consciousness, and Race Relations.* Berkeley: University of California Press, 1998.

Rice, Condoleezza (b. November 14, 1954, Birmingham, Alabama): Educator and foreign policy expert. An honors student who was also an accomplished pianist, Rice graduated from high school early and entered the University of Denver when she was only fifteen years old. She originally intended to major in piano performance, but later switched to political science instead. She graduated magna cum laude with a bachelor's degree in 1974. Rice went on to earn a master's degree in 1975 before returning to the University of Denver for doctoral studies. Rice specialized in Soviet affairs while studying for her Ph.D. and was an intern with the State Department in 1977. She went on to complete an internship at the Rand Corporation in Santa Monica, California, in 1980.

After receiving her Ph.D. in international studies in 1981, Rice was hired to teach as an assistant professor of political science at Stanford University. While at Stanford, Rice served as assistant director of the school's arms control program until 1989. From 1989 to 1991, Rice served as a director and later as a senior director of Soviet and East European Affairs with the National Security Council. In this capacity, she served as a strategic adviser to the Joint Chiefs of Staff. President George H. W. Bush appointed Rice at the recommendation of Brent Scowcroft, his assistant for national security affairs.

In 1990 Rice sat at the bargaining table when Bush met Soviet premier Mikhail Gorbachev at a summit meeting held in Malta. She also worked as an analyst at a summit between the two leaders held later that same year in Washington, D.C. Her background in Soviet military affairs and strategic nuclear policy made Rice an ideal candidate to advise

Bush as he negotiated a peace plan to cope with the changing post-Cold War environment. Issues raised at the U.S.-Soviet summits included the future of arms control, the prospect for expanded trade ties between the two countries, and accommodation of the democratic movements emerging in Eastern bloc countries bordering the Soviet Union.

In 1991 Rice returned to Stanford as an associate professor; that same year, Governor Pete Wilson named Rice as a member of a bipartisan committee responsible for creating new congressional and state legislative districts in CALIFORNIA. In that same year, she was elected to fill posts on the boards of directors for Chevron and Transamerica Corporation. Rice became a full professor at Stanford in 1992 before being named to the post of provost in 1993. With this appointment, she became the first African American chief academic officer and budget officer at Stanford and was one of the highest-ranking black college administrators in the entire nation. As provost, Rice was ranked second in authority under the university's president. She served as Stanford provost until 1999. That year she became a foreign policy adviser to Republican presidential candidate George W. Bush. She was recommended by Brent Scowcroft, her associate from her days with the elder George Bush's administration.

Rice's academic honors include appointments as a fellow with the Ford Foundation and as a fellow of the Hoover Institute at Stanford from 1985 to 1986. She also served as a member of the Council on Foreign Affairs and received an award for excellence in teaching while at Stanford. Her books include *The Soviet Union and the Czechoslovakian Army, 1948-1983* (1985) and *Germany Unified and Europe Transformed* (1996, with Philip Zelikow).

Richards, Lloyd (b. 1922, Toronto, Ontario, Canada): THEATER stage director. Richards's direction of the premiere of Lorraine HANSBERRY's *A Raisin in the Sun* (1959) gave him the distinction of being the first African American Broadway director. Richards's work with the play was widely hailed by critics.

Beginning in 1969, as artistic director of the National Playwrights Conference, he helped develop the work of more than two hundred dramatists. He served as artistic director of the conference until 1999. He also held a number of teaching posts through the years, including positions at Hunter College and the Yale School of Drama; he was appointed dean of Yale's drama school in 1979, retiring in 1991. As artistic director of the Yale Repertory Theater, beginning in 1979, he directed the premiere productions of major works by August WILSON, starting in 1982 with *Ma Rainey's Black Bottom*. In 1986 Richards received a Tony Award for his direction of Wilson's *Fences*.

Director Lloyd Richards posing next to an advertisement for his Broadway play *Fences* in 1987. *(AP/Wide World Photos)*

Judge Scovel Richardson on the bench of the U.S. Customs Court in 1957. *(AP/Wide World Photos)*

Richardson, Scovel (b. February 4, 1912, Nashville, Tennessee): JUDGE. Richardson received his law degrees from Howard University (J.D., 1937) and Lincoln University (L.L.D., 1973). He pursued a legal career as a lawyer and as a professor and dean of the law school at Lincoln University. He was among the very few African Americans to receive national-level recognition in the 1950's. In 1954 during the Dwight D. EISENHOWER ADMINISTRATION, he became the chairman of the U.S. Board of Parole. In 1957 he was made a judge on the U.S. Customs Court for New York State.

Ricks, Willie (b. c. 1943): Activist. Ricks was the moving force behind the Student Organization for Black Unity and had formerly been affiliated with the STUDENT NONVIOLENT COORDINATING COMMITTEE. He joined the CIVIL RIGHTS movement while in high school in Chattanooga, TENNESSEE. During the demonstrations in MONTGOMERY, ALABAMA, on March 7, 1965, he is reported to have tried to organize small-scale impromptu marches, against the desires of Martin Luther KING, Jr., who wanted larger, more organized marches.

Riggs, Marlon T. (1957, Fort Worth, Texas—April 5, 1994, Oakland, California): Filmmaker, poet, and gay activist. Almost singlehandedly, Marlon Riggs blazed new territory for African American filmmakers, confronting black indifference to black gay male experience as well as the general society's reliance on stereotype and caricature in its representations of blacks as a whole. A 1978 graduate of Harvard who went on to earn a master's degree in journalism at the University of California, Berkeley, in 1981, Riggs translated his own concerns with black sexual and racial identity into a stunning series of films and videos which examine the relationships between race, sexuality, and political resistance.

With *Ethnic Notions* (1987), *Color Adjustment* (1991), and *Black Is . . . Black Ain't* (1995, featuring Angela Davis), Riggs investigated the racial landscape of representation and identity constructions of African Americans based on the evidence of nineteenth-century COLLECTIBLES as well as television broadcasts from the 1950's to the 1990's. Riggs received Emmy Awards for best documentary from the National Academy of Television Arts and Sciences for *Ethnic Notions* and *Color Adjustment* (which aired on the PBS television series *P.O.V.* in 1992). He also received grants from the National Endowment for the Humanities and National Endowment for the Arts.

Riggs was a pioneer of black gay male expression in film. *Anthem* (1988), *Tongues Untied* (1989), *Affirmation* (1990), and *No Regrets*

(1992) broke entirely new ground in the field of independent cinema. They honestly and sometimes boldly represented black gay experiences of love, rejection, lust, and acceptance. Riggs's films present the expressions, experiences, and aspirations of African Americans who had been rendered invisible and silent by the community. Incorporating poetry, confession, dance, and song, he eventually links these emerging expressions to the history of struggle and resistance shared by all African Americans.

Of these films, *Tongues Untied*, which featured Essex Hemphill, set off a firestorm of national controversy about the limits of free speech and expression over the government-funded airwaves. Yet *Tongues Untied* is Riggs's most personal and autobiographical work. His poem, which provided the film's title, recurs throughout the film and introduces different segments of the study—boyhood, adolescence in the big city, love, community—that, together, describe a process of "coming home." The final frames of the film suggest that such a return of the sons who have been denied and rejected by the black community can reconcile gay identity with black identity by aligning the two groups' struggles. *Tongues Untied* won numerous international prizes, including Best Documentary at the Atlanta Film Festival, Berlin International Film Festival, and Cleveland International Film Festival. It stands as the strongest example of the ways in which Riggs sought to construct a process of communal and personal identity for the filmmaker and for his audience.

Whether he concerned himself with relationships within or outside of the African American community, Riggs addressed black experience broadly and critically, rejecting one-dimensional ideas of blackness in favor of diversity and multiplicity. This rejection of monolithic blackness places his work in the forefront of late twentieth-century reconstructions of black identity.

Suggested Readings:

Beam, Joseph, ed. *In the Life: A Black Gay Anthology.* Boston: Alyson, 1986.

Harper, Phillip B. "Marlon Riggs: The Subjective Position of Documentary Video." *Art Journal* 54 (Winter, 1995): 69-72.

Hemphill, Essex, ed. *Brother to Brother: New Writings by Black Gay Men.* Boston: Alyson, 1991.

Price-Spratlen, Townsand. "Negotiating Legacies: Audre Lorde, W. E. B. Du Bois, Marlon Riggs, and Me." *Harvard Educational Review* 66 (Summer, 1996): 216-230.

Riles, Wilson (June 27, 1917, Alexandria, Louisiana—April 1, 1999, Sacramento, California): Educational administrator. Orphaned as an adolescent, Riles received his bachelor's (1940) and master's (1947) degrees from Ari-

Wilson Riles, the first African American elected to statewide office in California. *(Library of Congress)*

zona State University. He served as an administrator and teacher for the ARIZONA public school systems (1940-1954). In the 1960's he became the chairman of the U.S. Commission on Urban Education during the presidency of Lyndon B. Johnson. In 1970 the charismatic Riles became the first African American to be elected to statewide office in CALIFORNIA, being selected by voters as the state's superintendent of public instruction. Riles held the post for twelve years.

Ringgold, Faith (b. October 8, 1930, New York, New York): Artist, writer, and educator. Ringgold is known for her work in nontraditional materials, such as her soft sculpture and quilts. She uses these media to express her experiences as an African American woman. A twenty-five-year retrospective of her work was exhibited at the Museum of African American Art in 1991. She was one of the founders of Women Students and Artists for Black Liberation, devoted to ensuring equal space for male and female artists at exhibitions of African American work.

Riperton, Minnie (November 8, 1947, Chicago, Illinois—July 12, 1979, Los Angeles, California): Pop singer. Riperton, who studied opera as a child, reached the apex of her career in 1974 with her transatlantic hit "Lovin' You." The number-one pop song was recorded on her album *Perfect Angel* (1974), on the Epic label.

Known for her ability to sing in five different octaves, Riperton began her career with Chess Records, where she worked as a receptionist. Later, she became a backup singer for such rhythm-and-blues notables as Fontella Bass and Etta James. After much hard work, Riperton became one of the lead vocalists at Chess for a psychedelic pop group known as Rotary Connection. When this group dis-

Minnie Riperton in 1976. *(AP/Wide World Photos)*

banded in 1970, after producing four albums, she cowrote and produced *Come to My Garden* (1970) with her husband, Richard Rudolph, on the Janus label.

Riperton sang with Stevie WONDER's band, Wonderlove, before signing with Epic Records in 1974. Wonder produced two tracks on her *Perfect Angel* album. Her next albums, *Adventures in Paradise* (1975), *Stay in Love* (1977), and *Minnie* (1979), were not well received. During this period, Riperton was stricken with breast CANCER. She became a spokeswoman for the American Cancer Society before her death in 1979.

Love Lives Forever (1980), a collection of Riperton's previously unreleased vocal tracks with new backing music, was produced posthumously and made it to the top ten as an album.

Jazz percussionist Max Roach performing at the Newport Jazz Festival in 1978. *(AP/Wide World Photos)*

Roach, Max (b. January 10, 1925, Elizabeth City, North Carolina): One of the first outstanding BEBOP drummers. Roach formed a famous quintet with trumpeter Clifford Brown and saxophonists Sonny ROLLINS and Harold Land. A pioneer in his use of modern choral backgrounds, his career suffered when he became involved with the CIVIL RIGHTS movement of the 1960's. Roach's later career included work with BREAK DANCING and RAP groups, documentary films, plays, and videos. His daughter Maxine Roach plays classical viola and formed the Uptown Swing Quartet.

Roberts, Deborah A. (b. September 20, 1960, Perry, Georgia): Broadcast journalist. Setting her sights on a journalism career, Roberts chose to major in broadcast journalism at the University of Georgia. After graduating with her bachelor's degree, she started her career at television station WTVM in Columbus, GEORGIA, in 1982. At WTVM, Roberts focused many of her reports on public education in the state and on activities in the Georgia state legislature. In 1984 she accepted a job at station WBIR in Knoxville, TENNESSEE, as a general assignment editor and then moved to ABC affiliate WFTV in Orlando, FLORIDA, in 1987.

As a field anchor in Orlando, Roberts covered space shuttle launches and other stories connected with the Kennedy Space Center and the National Aeronautics and Space Administration (NASA). Roberts was later hired by NBC News in June of 1990, and was assigned to work at the network's ATLANTA bureau as a general assignment correspondent. During her stay in Atlanta, Roberts was assigned to cover stories on the PERSIAN GULF WAR and reported from Saudi Arabia in 1990 and 1991. She was also one of several network reporters who provided coverage of the 1992 Summer Olympics held in Barcelona, Spain. Roberts was invited to join the staff of the network's popular newsmagazine, *Dateline NBC*, in 1992. In 1995 she moved to the network's *20/20*; later that year she married Al Roker, NBC talk-show host and *Today Show* weatherman.

Robertson, Oscar (b. November 24, 1938, Charlotte, Tennessee): Basketball player. Oscar Palmer Robertson, a star guard for both the Cincinnati Royals (1960-1970) and the Milwaukee Bucks (1970-1974), has been regarded as one of the game's most versatile players of all time. On the court, he was a guard who rebounded like a forward, a brilliant ball handler and playmaker, and the highest-scoring guard in the National Basketball Association (NBA).

By the time Robertson graduated from the all-black Crispus ATTUCKS High School in Indianapolis, INDIANA, his reputation as a basketball wizard had spread throughout the state and much of the country. He was offered scholarships by more than a hundred colleges. It was not only his athletic ability that attracted top schools: A member of the National Honor Society, Robertson had graduated sixteenth in a class of more than 150. In order to stay near his mother in Indianapolis, he chose the University of Cincinnati.

At Cincinnati, Robertson set fourteen collegiate scoring records and was named college player of the year in each of his three varsity seasons. After being graduated in 1960, he became cocaptain of the gold medal-winning U.S. Olympic team. During that same year, he was drafted by the Cincinnati Royals, who signed him to an unprecedented deal for a rookie that guaranteed him more than $30,000

Oscar Robertson, playing against the Los Angeles Lakers' Jerry West (left) in 1961. *(AP/Wide World Photos)*

a year as well as a percentage of the gate receipts. Establishing himself immediately in the NBA, Robertson won rookie of the year honors for the 1960-1961 season and was named the most valuable player of the all-star game. Nicknamed "the Big O," Robertson kept the Royals in contention throughout the 1960's, but an NBA championship eluded him until he was traded to Milwaukee. With Kareem ABDUL-JABBAR as a teammate, he took the Bucks to an NBA championship in 1971.

Robertson was named the NBA's most valuable player in 1964, and was the most valuable player of the all-star game three times. He held the league record for career assists until Magic JOHNSON broke his mark in April, 1989. Robertson was inducted into the NBA Hall of Fame in 1979. He became president and chief executive officer of a chemical company in 1981.

Robertson, Stanley (b. Los Angeles, California): Television and FILM executive. Robertson began his career at NBC television in 1957, as a page. By April of 1971, he was vice president for motion pictures for television, and by the late 1970's, he was director of programs. He created a pilot for *Harris and Company* in 1977. In the mid-1980's, Robertson was senior vice president of worldwide productions for Columbia Pictures.

Robeson, Eslanda Cardozo Goode (December 15, 1896, Washington, D.C.—December 13, 1965, New York, New York): CIVIL RIGHTS activist. Robeson's great-grandfather, Isaac Nunez Cardozo, whose family emigrated to the United States in the late 1700's, was of Jewish-Spanish ancestry and had married a slave in SOUTH CAROLINA. Francis Lewis Cardozo, her grandfather, was a graduate of Glasgow University, a pioneer of black education in the South, an advocate of African

American rights, and the treasurer in South Carolina during Reconstruction. Eslanda Goode, his daughter and Robeson's mother, was a smart, fashionable, and independent Victorian woman who was admired by WASHINGTON, D.C.'s brightest African Americans. Robeson was also a brilliant young woman who, at age sixteen, completed high school in CHICAGO with highest distinction in the class of 1912. She placed third in statewide exams and was awarded a full-tuition scholarship to the University of Illinois, where she majored in chemistry. With eyes set on a medical profession, she transferred to Columbia University after her junior year. She stood out in her sorority, Delta Sigma Theta, and graduated with a B.S. in 1920.

The self-styled "girl scientist" became the first African American on the staff at Presbyterian Hospital of Columbia University as a histological chemist. While at the hospital, she met and married actor Paul ROBESON. In her classic biographies, *Paul Robeson, Negro* (1930) and *African Journey* (1945), she records moving episodes of the successes and struggles of her black husband in white America and their enlightening safari on the African continent. She studied photography in London while touring with her husband and was a moving force behind her husband's success in acting. She encouraged him to accept important roles in *Taboo* (1922), *The Emperor Jones* (1933), and other films.

Robeson had an active political career as well. After World War II, her writings focused on the issue of colonialism. She saw the United Nations as a potential mediator between the European powers and their colonies, and in 1945 she attended the founding convention of the United Nations as a representative of the Council on African Affairs. She covered United Nations activities as a journalist in the 1950's. She drew attention for her criticism of U.S. foreign policy and favorable view of the Soviet Union.

Robeson, Paul (April 9, 1898, Princeton, New Jersey—January 23, 1976, Philadelphia, Pennsylvania): Singer, FILM actor, and social activist, Paul Robeson was a genuine American hero. A true Renaissance man, he excelled in a wide variety of areas: in sports, earning twelve varsity letters while at Rutgers University by starring in football, baseball, basketball, and track, and later entering professional football; in academics, graduating from Rutgers University Phi Beta Kappa and valedictorian of his class, graduating from Columbia University Law School, and, during his lifetime, learning more than twenty languages; in music, giving concerts around the world for most of his life; in acting, appearing on stage and screen and rendering immortal performances in such plays as *The Emperor Jones* and *Othello* and such films as *Show Boat* (1936); and in the black cause, dedicating much of his time and energy to fighting for equality for blacks in America and for freedom for African nations against European colonial powers.

A gifted singer, actor, and athlete, Paul Robeson was persecuted by the government for his outspoken political beliefs. *(Library of Congress)*

Background

Paul Robeson was born to William Drew Robeson—who had been born a slave in NORTH CAROLINA and who, after receiving his freedom, attained a college degree and became a minister—and to Maria Louisa Bustill Robeson. Paul had three older brothers, William, Reeve, and Ben, and a sister, Marian. The Reverend Robeson instilled in his children a sense of dignity, courage, and, according to Paul, the belief that "the Negro was in every way the equal of the white man." After graduating with honors from Somerville High School in 1915, he won an academic scholarship to Rutgers University where, in spite of racist attitudes that confronted him at every turn, he excelled in many areas.

Robeson won major oratorical contests four years in a row and earned America's highest scholastic honor, the Phi Beta Kappa key, in his junior year; was named twice to the All-American football team; participated in the Rutgers Glee Club; and in 1919 graduated with the highest grade-point average in his class. He entered Columbia Law School in 1920 and played professional football on weekends while also coaching basketball. In 1921 he married Eslanda Cardozo Goode, who had graduated from Columbia University and was the first black analytical CHEMIST working at Columbia Medical Center. They had one son, Paul, Jr.

Beginning Acting Career

While pursuing his law degree, Robeson appeared in an amateur production of a play at the HARLEM YMCA and was seen by members of the Provincetown Players and by the director Augustin Duncan, who was readying a

Paul Robeson (right) as Brutus Jones, with Dudley Diges, in *The Emperor Jones* (1933). *(AP/Wide World Photos)*

play to tour England in the summer of 1922. It was in Duncan's play, *Voodoo*, that Robeson's acting and singing gifts were first recognized abroad. After completing his law degree and working for a few months in a prestigious law firm, which he soon quit because of his encounters with RACIAL DISCRIMINATION, he was introduced in 1924 to Eugene O'Neill, who immediately cast him as Jim in *All God's Chillun Got Wings*. Because of the controversy surrounding this play, in which a black man and a white woman are shown as husband and wife, the Provincetown Players decided to revive O'Neill's *The Emperor Jones*, with Robeson in the role of Brutus Jones, while waiting to open the other play. After the productions of *The Emperor Jones* and *All God's Chillun Got Wings*, Robeson's acting and singing talents were widely recognized in the United States.

Musical Career Begins

In 1925 a chance encounter between Robeson and Larry Brown, an arranger and historian of black folk music, launched Robeson's concert career. The two gave a concert of Negro spirituals at the Greenwich Village Theatre under the auspices of the Provincetown Players, and Robeson's astounding voice was described by one reviewer as a voice in which "deep bells ring." For the next four years, Robeson and Brown gave performances all across the country, with phenomenal success. In 1927 the musical *Show Boat* opened in London to great acclaim, with Robeson singing "Old Man River," a song with which he would be identified for the rest of his career. In 1930 Robeson made history again by being the first black actor since Ira Aldridge in the nineteenth century to play the lead in *Othello*. During this period, Robeson began to study African culture, languages, and music and to develop the idea that blacks should take pride in their African heritage.

International Travel

After a brief encounter with Nazi racism at a Berlin, Germany, train station in 1934, Robeson traveled on to the Soviet Union, where he was received with great enthusiasm. In 1937 he and his wife visited Spain to support the Loyalist troops in the civil war there, and he sang for the International Brigade. In 1939 the couple returned to the United States, where Robeson appeared on a CBS radio program to sing "Ballad for Americans," which drew the greatest audience response since Orson Welles's famous 1938 broadcast of *The War of the Worlds*. A recording of the song sold thirty thousand copies, and the Republican Party chose it as the theme song for its national convention in 1940. Meanwhile, Robeson continued giving concerts to overflow crowds across the nation and made numerous films, including the film versions of *The Emperor Jones* (1933), *Show Boat* (1936), *Sanders of the River* (1935), *The Song of Freedom* (1937), and *King Solomon's Mines* (1937). He also continued to study and deepen his understanding of human civilization and to develop views of universal brotherhood and world peace.

Return Home

After a decade of living abroad, Robeson returned to the United States and immediately made history with his production of *Othello*, with Uta Hagen playing Desdemona and Jose Ferrer as Iago. After touring East Coast cities in 1942, *Othello* opened on Broadway at the Schubert Theatre in the fall of 1943, where it was hailed by some as one of the most memorable events in the history of the theater. After ten months in New York, a record for a Shakespearean play, the production traveled across the United States and Canada, finally closing in 1945. Robeson had become the most famous black person in America, and his portrayal of Othello placed him among the ranks of history's greatest Shakespearean actors.

Black Rights

While continuing to crisscross the United States in the late 1940's giving concerts, Robeson became increasingly vocal about the treatment of blacks, eventually meeting with President Harry S Truman to urge him to do something about the LYNCHINGS of blacks in the South. His candidness drew the condemnation of some who attempted to brand him as "un-American." In 1947 he made the announcement at a concert in Salt Lake City that he would suspend public concerts after the current tour, which itself ran into difficulties with local authorities as it continued. The House Committee on Un-American Activities called on Robeson to testify, but he refused to cooperate, citing his "constitutional right to say that my political beliefs are nobody's business." To the committee, he said: "My father was a slave, and my people died to build this country and I am going to stay here and have a part of it just like you. And no fascist-minded people will drive me from it. Is that clear?"

In 1949 he began another successful European concert tour; in Paris at the World Peace Conference, he spoke out once more against the treatment of blacks in America. As a result, he became an important voice in the fight for the constitutional rights of blacks as well as the object of attack by some whites. The hostility culminated in a riot at a Robeson concert scheduled in Peekskill, New York, in August of 1949. Shortly thereafter, the State Department revoked his passport. Throughout the 1950's, Robeson traveled extensively throughout the United States, singing and encouraging blacks to fight for equality. Under ever-increasing pressure, Robeson stood firm for his principles. In 1957 he published his autobiography, *Here I Stand*.

As the pressures of the Cold War lessened in the late 1950's, Robeson began a new series of highly successful concerts both in the United States and, after a 1958 U.S. SUPREME COURT ruling restored his passport, abroad in England, Russia, Australia, and New Zealand. In 1959 he again appeared as Othello at Stratford-on-Avon in England.

By 1960, with the onset of health problems, Robeson's official performance career came to an end. He died on January 23, 1976, at the age of seventy-seven.

The Man

Paul Robeson was an imposing human being, of large and impressive physical stature, a deep and resonant voice, a brilliant and agile mind, and a spirit filled with dignity, self-worth, and the burning desire to fight for human rights and oppose hatred and narrow-mindedness. Robeson could have had an even more successful career had he chosen to remain silent, but he could not. Instead, at the pinnacle of his career, he spoke out so vociferously against the degradation of black people that efforts were made to vilify and silence him. Eventually, though, he triumphed, and his life stands as a mighty symbol to all people, black and white, of human integrity and moral courage.

—*Tony J. Stafford*

Suggested Readings:

Brown, Lloyd L. *The Young Paul Robeson: On My Journey Now*. Boulder, Colo.: Westview Press, 1997.

Davis, Lenwood G. *A Paul Robeson Handbook: Everything You Want to Know About Paul Robeson*. Kearney, Nebr.: Morris, 1998.

Duberman, Martin Beuml. *Paul Robeson*. New York: Alfred A. Knopf, 1989.

Graham, Shirley. *Paul Robeson, Citizen of the World*. New York: Julian Messner, 1946.

Hamilton, Virginia. *Paul Robeson: The Life and Times of a Free Black Man*. New York: Harper & Row, 1974.

Hoyt, Edwin P. *Paul Robeson: The American Othello*. Cleveland: World, 1967.

Robeson, Paul. *Here I Stand*. London: D. Dobson, 1958.

Robeson, Susan. *The Whole World in His Hands: A Pictorial Biography of Paul Robeson*. Secaucus, N.J.: Citadel Press, 1981.

Stewart, Jeffrey C. *Paul Robeson: Artist and Citizen*. New Brunswick, N.J.: Rutgers University Press, 1998.

Robinson, Aubrey E., Jr. (b. March 30, 1922, Madison, New Jersey): Civil rights attorney and judge. He received his B.A. and LL.B. degrees from Cornell University (1943 and 1947). He practiced law in Washington, D.C., from 1948 to 1965. In 1965 he was appointed to the bench, on the juvenile court. He became a U.S. district court judge in 1966. In addition to being a federal judge, he became involved in several legal and social service agencies in varied capacities.

Robinson, Bill "Bojangles" (Luther Robinson; May 25, 1878, Richmond, Virginia—November 25, 1949, New York, New York): Dancer and actor. Robinson was one of the first entertainers to overcome the color barrier and become a star of stage and screen. He quickly lost the name "Luther" by changing names with his brother, Bill. "Bojangles" was a nickname given to him by a friend, Des Williams, meaning "happy-go-lucky."

From the age of six, he danced for nickels and dimes at the Richmond beer gardens. In 1886 he hitchhiked to Washington, D.C., and worked odd jobs while dancing in the streets. His first steady job was in a minstrel show called *The South Before the War*. Prohibited by white show managers from performing solo, he worked in VAUDEVILLE with a variety of partners, eventually forming a duo with George Cooper. An agent named Marty Forkins saw the two perform, signed them, and then persuaded Robinson to go solo.

In 1915 he was featured at Henderson's in Coney Island. By the 1920's, Robinson had be-

Bojangles Robinson with Shirley Temple in the 1935 film *The Little Colonel*. (AP/Wide World Photos)

come a regular at the Palace and began billing himself as "The Dark Cloud of Joy." Among his many steps, he created the famous Stair Dance, making a different sound with his feet on each step. He is credited with bringing the flat-footed "buck and wing" up on its toes.

He starred in the all-black musical *Blackbirds of 1928* and the Broadway success *Brown Buddies* (1930). Between 1930 and 1943, he was featured in twenty-one motion pictures, including three box office hits with child actor Shirley Temple—*The Little Colonel* (1935), *The Littlest Rebel* (1935), and *Rebecca of Sunnybrook Farm* (1938). *The Hot Mikado* (1939) marked Robinson's return to the stage. He continued to perform in films and played the lead in *Stormy Weather* (1943).

Unofficially, Robinson was called the "mayor of HARLEM." On April 29, 1946, Mayor William O'Dwyer of New York City proclaimed Bill Robinson Day. Three years later, millions gathered along his funeral route while a band in Times Square played "Give My Regards to Broadway." In his eulogy, Mayor O'Dwyer said, "Without money, just good manners and decency, you got into places no money can buy. You got into the heart of all America."

Robinson, Frank, Jr. (b. Aug. 31, 1935, Beaumont, Texas). The first African American to manage a major league baseball team, Robinson was both an infielder and an outfielder during his 21-season playing career. He began with the Cincinnati Reds in 1956 and led them to the National League pennant in 1961, while batting .323, with 37 home runs, 124 RBIs, and 22 stolen bases. That year he was voted National League MVP. After being traded to the Baltimore Orioles in 1965, he led the American League with a career-high 49 home runs, 122 RBIs, and a .316 batting average. He also led the Orioles to a World Series championship and was named American League MVP,

Robinson, Jackie (January 31, 1919, Cairo, Georgia—October 24, 1972, Stamford, Connecticut): BASEBALL player. Jackie Robinson earned lasting fame by breaking major league baseball's color line. Before Robinson took the field as the Brooklyn Dodgers' first baseman on April 15, 1947, no twentieth-century African American player had participated in a major league baseball game.

Boyhood and Young Adulthood

When Jackie Roosevelt Robinson was six months old, his father, Jerry Robinson, deserted his wife, Millie, and their five children. A year later, Mrs. Robinson moved her family into an all-white neighborhood in Pasadena, California. She took on domestic work, and her children attended school and participated in sports. (Jackie's older brother, Mack, would become a world-class sprinter and finish second to Jesse Owens in the 200-yard dash in the 1936 Olympics.)

As a youth, Robinson fell in with a group of neighborhood troublemakers. He later credited a local pastor and his love of sports for saving him from juvenile delinquency. By the time he reached John Muir Technical High School, he was a skilled athlete, and he earned varsity letters in football, basketball, baseball, and track.

Robinson received no scholarship offers after high school graduation, so he attended nearby Pasadena Junior College. After leading the school to conference championships in basketball, football, and baseball, Robinson was awarded a scholarship by the University of California at Los Angeles (UCLA). He enrolled there in September, 1939, and became the school's first four-sport athlete. As a halfback on the football team, he received All-American honors; he twice led UCLA's basketball conference in scoring; and he won the national championship in the long jump. He also starred at shortstop on the Bruins' baseball team.

Frank Robinson, the first African American manager of a major league baseball team. (*National Baseball Library, Cooperstown, New York*)

thereby becoming the only player named MVP in both leagues.

Robinson continued playing with Baltimore through the 1971 season, helping his team win pennants in 1969, 1970, and 1971, and the World Series in 1970. Robinson played for the Los Angeles Dodgers in 1972, the California Angels in 1973 and part of 1974, and the Cleveland Indians from 1974 to 1976. His final two seasons were as playing manager. He continued as Cleveland manager through part of the 1977 season and later managed the San Francisco Giants and Baltimore Orioles. While with the Giants in 1982, he was named manager of the year. Robinson finished his playing career with 2,043 career hits, 586 home runs, 1,812 RBIs, 204 stolen bases, and a .294 batting average. In 1982 he was elected to the Baseball Hall of Fame.

Despite his achievements at UCLA, Robinson decided to leave college before earning his bachelor's degree. In 1941 he quit school and took a job as an athletic director with the National Youth Administration. A year later, he was drafted into the U.S. Army.

Army Experience

Before 1948 the American armed forces were still segregated, and Robinson had difficulty coping with the Jim Crow conditions. At Fort Riley, Kansas, for example, Robinson and several other African American soldiers were denied entry to Officer's Candidate School (OCS)

After playing several years in the major leagues, Jackie Robinson returned to his minor league Montreal uniform to play himself in *The Jackie Robinson Story* in 1950. *(AP/Wide World Photos)*

because of their race. Robinson sought help from Joe Louis, the heavyweight boxing champion, who was also stationed at Fort Riley, and Louis used his influence to see that his fellow African American soldiers were admitted to OCS. Robinson completed the course and was awarded the rank of second lieutenant.

Later, at Fort Hood, Texas, Robinson was forced to face a military court-martial for refusing to move to a rear seat on an army bus. Charges were dropped, however, because shortly before the incident, Joe Louis and Sugar Ray ROBINSON, another famous African American prizefighter, had convinced the Army to end discrimination aboard military vehicles. Robinson received an honorable discharge from the Army in November, 1944, and he returned to civilian life in Pasadena.

Early Baseball Career

Before 1947 an unwritten agreement among major league baseball owners prevented African Americans from playing on major league clubs. Moses Fleetwood Walker and a handful of other African Americans had played on major league teams in the 1880's, but by 1890 the color barrier was firmly in place. African Americans who sought professional baseball careers were limited to the teams in the Negro Leagues. The playing conditions on the NEGRO LEAGUE BASEBALL circuit were often deplorable, and the salaries were less than half major league salaries, but the Negro Leagues still produced such standout performers as Buck Leonard, Josh Gibson, and Satchel PAIGE.

In 1945 Robinson was signed by the Kansas City Monarchs of the Negro American League. He became an immediate star, batting close to .400 and impressing Negro League players and fans with his remarkable speed and solid defensive play. Particularly impressed was Branch Rickey, the president of the National League (NL) Brooklyn Dodgers. Rickey, who had been scouting Negro League players for several seasons, had been informing baseball people that he was planning to form the Brooklyn Brown Dodgers, a team of African American players who would play at his team's home park, Ebbets Field, when the Dodgers were on the road. In reality, Rickey was planning to integrate major league baseball.

Rickey arranged to meet Robinson in New York on August 18, 1945. At that meeting, Rickey offered Robinson a contract to play for the Dodgers' top minor league team in Montreal. Robinson accepted, but the news was withheld from the public until October 23, when Rickey and Robinson held a press conference in Montreal to announce that major league baseball's color barrier was about to fall.

Robinson played the entire 1946 season for Montreal. In his first game, on April 18, against the Jersey City Giants at Roosevelt Stadium, Robinson had four hits, scored four times, drove home four runs, and stole two bases. He went on to lead the International League with a .349 batting average and help Montreal to a victory in the Little World Series, the minor league championship playoff. Shortly after the season, Robinson and his wife, Rachel Isum Robinson (a nursing student whom he had met at UCLA and married in the winter of 1946), had the first of their three children, Jack, Jr.

Success as a Brooklyn Dodger

In 1947 Robinson earned a spot on the Brooklyn Dodgers as the team's starting first baseman. (He would move to second base the following year.) He went hitless in his first game, but he soon proved himself ready for major league competition. He finished the season with a .297 batting average, led the NL with twenty-nine stolen bases, and helped the Dodgers win the NL pennant. For his performance in 1947, Robinson was named the major league rookie of the year.

Robinson's success opened doors for other African American players. On July 4, 1947,

By any measure, Jackie Robinson's comparatively brief career in the major leagues was remarkable. *(National Baseball Library, Cooperstown, New York)*

Larry Doby made his debut with the Cleveland Indians, and within a short time, other major league teams began signing African American players.

Robinson's first few seasons were difficult. Opposing players yelled racial slurs at him, pitchers threw at his head, and fans sent hate mail and death threats. At first, Robinson quietly tolerated these insults, but he later became more aggressive on the field and more outspoken off it. If an opposing player spiked Robinson while sliding into his base, Robinson retaliated the next time he reached base. If a pitcher threw at his head, Robinson bunted the ball toward the first baseman and slammed into the pitcher as he tried to cover first base. Always a skilled base stealer, Robinson took long leads off the bases and intimidated pitchers with his defiant glare.

Robinson's fiercely competitive play inspired his teammates. The Brooklyn Dodgers of Robinson's era were a talented group of players who responded to the challenge of integration. The team, which was fondly profiled in sportswriter Roger Kahn's best-selling book *The Boys of Summer* (1972), included all-stars Pee Wee Reese, Gil Hodges, Roy Campanella, Duke Snider, and Carl Furillo. They won NL pennants in 1947, 1949, 1952, 1953, 1955, and 1956, yet the team seemed ill-fated. The Dodgers lost close pennant races in 1950 and 1951, and only once, in 1955, were they able to beat the New York Yankees in the World Series.

Robinson played for Brooklyn through the 1956 season. After that year's World Series, the Dodgers traded him to the New York Giants. Rather than play for his former crosstown rivals, Robinson retired from baseball. He left the game with a .311 lifetime batting average and 197 stolen bases. His best season came in 1949, when he batted a league-leading .342, drove in 124 runs, and stole 37 bases. For his achievements that season, Robinson was voted the NL most valuable player. He was elected to the Hall of Fame in 1962.

Life After Baseball

After retiring from baseball, Robinson accepted a public relations position with the Chock Full O'Nuts restaurant chain. He also served as a fund-raiser and spokesman for the NATIONAL ASSOCIATION FOR THE ADVANCEMENT OF COLORED PEOPLE (NAACP). He participated in the organization's marches, and he supported Martin Luther KING, Jr.'s desegregation efforts.

In 1964 Robinson left Chock Full O'Nuts to help Nelson Rockefeller in his unsuccessful attempt to become the Republican Party's nominee for president. After the campaign, Robinson helped establish FREEDOM NATIONAL BANK, a HARLEM-based institution that financed African American businesses.

Robinson's final years were marked by bitterness and tragedy. He became a sharp critic of major league baseball because of its team owners' refusal to hire an African American manager. In 1967 his oldest son, Jack, Jr., was wounded in the VIETNAM WAR. A year later, Jack, Jr., was arrested on drug charges. He overcame his addiction and later worked as a counselor in a drug rehabilitation program, but on June 17, 1971, he lost his life in an automobile accident.

Robinson's health deteriorated after his son's death. By then, he had developed diabetes and heart problems and had lost most of his eyesight. He died from heart failure on October 24, 1972, at his home in Stamford, Connecticut, where he had lived the last several years of his life. Shortly before his death, he published an autobiography, *I Never Had It Made* (1972).

—*James Tackach*

Suggested Readings:

Chadwick, Bruce. *When the Game Was Black and White: The Illustrated History of Baseball's Negro Leagues.* New York: Abbeville, 1992.

Dorinson, Joseph, and Joram Warmund, eds. *Jackie Robinson: Race, Sports, and the American Dream.* Armonk, N.Y.: M. E. Sharpe, 1998.

Falkner, David. *Great Time Coming: The Life of Jackie Robinson from Baseball to Birmingham.* New York: Oxford University Press, 1995.

Peterson, Robert. *Only the Ball Was White.* Englewood Cliffs, N.J.: Prentice-Hall, 1970.

Rampersad, Arnold. *Jackie Robinson: A Biography.* New York: Alfred A. Knopf, 1997.

Robinson, Jackie. *I Never Had It Made.* New York: G. P. Putnam's Sons, 1972.

Robinson, Jackie, and Jules Tygiel, eds. *The Jackie Robinson Reader: Perspectives on an American Hero.* New York: E. P. Dutton, 1997.

Robinson, Rachel, and Lee Daniels. *Jackie Robinson: An Intimate Portrait.* New York: Harry N. Abrams, 1996.

Robinson, Sharon. *Stealing Home: An Intimate Family Portrait by the Daughter of Jackie Robinson.* New York: HarperCollins, 1996.

Stout, Glenn, and Dick Johnson. *Jackie Robinson: Between the Baselines*. San Francisco: Woodford Press, 1997.

Tygiel, Jules. *Baseball's Great Experiment: Jackie Robinson and His Legacy*. Rev. ed. New York: Oxford University Press, 1997.

Robinson, James (c. 1753-1868): Soldier. Robinson continued to serve his country despite his ill-treatment. After winning a gold medal for valor at Yorktown during the AMERICAN REVOLUTION, Robinson was denied the freedom that he had been promised and was forced to return to SLAVERY. During the WAR OF 1812 Robinson volunteered to fight with Andrew Jackson's forces at the Battle of New Orleans. He was returned to slavery after the battle. He lived to see the EMANCIPATION PROCLAMATION and died a free man.

Robinson, Jo Ann Gibson (b. April 17, 1912, near Culloden, Georgia): CIVIL RIGHTS activist and educator. As a youngster, Robinson moved to Macon, GEORGIA, where she graduated from the city's all-black high school as valedictorian. Robinson earned a bachelor's degree from Fort Valley State College, becoming the first member of her family to secure a college education, and taught in the Macon public schools. Later, she earned a master's degree in English from ATLANTA UNIVERSITY. In 1949 she accepted a position in the English Department at Alabama State College in Montgomery.

Robinson was a principal organizer of the MONTGOMERY BUS BOYCOTT. An experience aboard a city bus had acquainted her personally with the system of segregation that existed on bus lines throughout the South—a system in place for many years. Soon after her arrival in Montgomery, she boarded a bus to the airport. Robinson, who was unfamiliar with the segregated coach and preoccupied with her own thoughts, took a seat reserved for white riders. She was shaken when the white driver stood over her and demanded that she move from the white section of the vehicle. She left the bus hastily and never forgot the incident.

Having learned that her experience was not unique, Robinson was convinced that the Women's Political Council (WPC), a local organization of African American women who were denied membership in the League of Women Voters, should address the deplorable treatment accorded black city bus patrons. The arrest of Rosa PARKS, a black woman, for refusing to yield her seat to a white passenger was the catalyst that moved Robinson and her club members to concrete action.

Determined to see Parks vindicated, along with the countless unknown black victims of discrimination, members of the WPC, many of whom taught at Alabama State College, ventured out at night, meeting at the college. They drafted protest letters and coordinated plans for a bus boycott. On December 5, 1955, African Americans began to boycott the Montgomery city buses in protest. Approximately one year later, federal authorities ordered integration on the buses. Robinson and the women of the WPC had been instrumental in bringing about the change. Robinson published her account of the boycott, *The Montgomery Bus Boycott and the Women Who Started It*, in 1987.

Robinson, Max C. (May 1, 1939, Richmond, Virginia—December 20, 1988, Washington, D.C.): Television newscaster and brother of TRANSAFRICA founder Randall Robinson. At one time, Max Robinson was the only African American prime-time network news anchor. He was one of three anchors on the American Broadcasting Company's (ABC) *World News Tonight* from 1978 to 1983.

Robinson studied at OBERLIN COLLEGE in 1957 and 1958, then at Indiana University in

1959 and 1960. He became a cameraman for CHICAGO television station WTOP in 1965 and worked as a correspondent for WRC-TV from 1965 to 1969. He won a national Emmy Award in 1967 along with the journalist of the year award from the Capital Press Club. WTOP put him on its *Eyewitness News* local news program in 1969.

Robinson taught television production and communicative arts at Federal City College from 1968 to 1972. In June of 1978, ABC chose him as the Chicago anchor of *World News Tonight*. Washington, D.C., and Richmond, Virginia, each proclaimed a Max Robinson Day that year. Robinson won the Capital Press Club's national media award in 1979 and another Emmy Award in 1981, for election coverage.

After Frank Reynolds, one of the *World News Tonight* coanchors, died in 1983, ABC made Peter Jennings the sole anchor of the

Television broadcaster Max C. Robinson in 1984. *(AP/ Wide World Photos)*

show, leaving Robinson with few responsibilities. Robinson appeared on weekend reports for several months. While at the network, Robinson spoke out about racism and accused the media of being a "cracked mirror" in which white America viewed itself. He helped found the Association of Black Journalists, which encouraged African Americans in the field of journalism. The pressure of being a role model had led to drinking problems for Robinson.

In February, 1984, Robinson became coanchor of the evening news show on station WMAQ, but he soon left the station. He died of complications related to ACQUIRED IMMUNO-DEFICIENCY SYNDROME (AIDS). In accordance with his wishes, his family requested that his death be an occasion for discussing education about AIDS. Robinson never talked about the disease publicly or revealed to family members how he had contracted it.

Robinson, Randall (b. July 6, 1941, Richmond, Virginia): CIVIL RIGHTS activist and brother of television broadcaster Max ROBINSON. Randall Robinson founded and became executive director of TRANSAFRICA, a Washington, D.C., human rights organization focused on securing civil and political rights for black Africans in South Africa. Because he grew up before the Civil Rights movement, Robinson himself experienced the type of segregation that he battles through TransAfrica. Robinson, a graduate of Harvard Law School, where he sat next to a white student for the first time, worked on the congressional staff of Charles DIGGS (a Michigan Democrat) before 1977, when he began focusing on white-ruled Rhodesia (future Zimbabwe) by organizing protests of U.S. policies toward Rhodesia.

Robinson founded TransAfrica in 1977. Under his leadership, the organiztion grew and accomplished a great deal in the realm of protest against the South African apartheid system. Relying on some of the tactics used by

Randall Robinson, the director of TransAfrica. *(© Roy Lewis Archives)*

By the mid-1990's, South Africa had undergone profound changes and had finally abandoned apartheid; Nelson Mandela was elected as the country's first black president. The economic sanctions imposed on South Africa by the U.S. government were lifted. Within a few years, Robinson's efforts had been a factor in the transformation of the South African political system, the U.S. government response to South Africa, and public awareness of the importance of individual political and civil rights.

In the mid-1990's Robinson lobbied the government to change its policies toward the government of Nigeria. In 1994 he went on a hunger strike in an attempt to urge the U.S. government to assist in returning Jean-Bertrand Aristide to power in Haiti and to give fleeing Haitians refugee status. Robinson published a memoir, *Defending the Spirit: A Black Life in America* in 1999, and *The Debt: What America Owes to Blacks* in 2000.

U.S. civil rights organizations in the 1950's and 1960's, such as picketing and sit-ins at official government offices, Robinson's organization earned the support and participation of a large cross section of the American population. Among those arrested in demonstrations organized by TransAfrica have been U.S. congresspersons, entertainers, and public figures. TransAfrica claimed about eighteen thousand members in 1990.

TransAfrica's demonstrations, lectures, and lobbying efforts throughout the United States were influential in government decisions on sanctions imposed on South Africa by the Ronald REAGAN ADMINISTRATION. Robinson's ability to rally a multicultural base of individuals and groups into peaceful and effective opposition was credited by some members of Congress as being a factor in garnering their support for economic sanctions against South Africa.

Robinson, Rubye (April 25, 1942, Atlanta, Georgia—October 7, 1967): CIVIL RIGHTS activist. Rubye Doris Smith Robinson played a key role in the student-led civil rights protests of the 1960's. At the age of seventeen, she sat in and was arrested at a segregated restaurant at the Georgia state capital. In 1960 she participated in the Rock Hill, SOUTH CAROLINA, protest and was one of the first young people to serve a sentence under the "jail, no bail" policy of the STUDENT NONVIOLENT COORDINATING COMMITTEE (SNCC). She worked with SNCC in Georgia, Tennessee, Mississippi, Alabama, and South Carolina. In 1966 she became SNCC's executive secretary; she died of leukemia a year later.

Robinson, Smokey (b. February 19, 1940, Detroit, Michigan): Singer and songwriter. William "Smokey" Robinson, Jr., founder and lead singer of the Miracles, songwriter, producer, and executive for MOTOWN Records, figures prominently in the history of African American music as it evolved from the 1940's through the 1980's. As a producer of black music, he contributed to the unparalleled growth of Motown Records, the most successful black-owned RECORDING COMPANY ever launched in the United States and the starting point for many of the leading black musicians who emerged during the 1960's. Robinson was among the first black recording artists of popular songs whose music appealed across color lines.

Early Years

Born in DETROIT's predominantly black inner city, Smokey Robinson grew up in the Brewster Projects at a time when music and the entertainment business were fast becoming attractive goals for a considerable segment of the city's black youth. As a child, Robinson developed a strong love for music, and in the early 1950's, while a freshman at North Parker High School, he formed a singing group called the Matadors. The group's original members were Robinson's schoolmates: Sonny Rogers (guitar), Pete Moore (bass vocals), Bobby Rogers (tenor), and Ronald White (baritone). Claudette Rogers, who married Robinson in 1959, became a temporary member of the group after her brother Sonny left in 1959. Sonny was soon replaced by Marvin Tamplin, a guitarist whom Robinson recruited from the Supremes in 1960. Until Robinson's departure from the Miracles in 1973, there were no additional changes in the group's personnel.

Robinson's innate organizational and artistic talents in music were evident from the very start. His ambitious plans kept the group together all through high school, and the Matadors performed regularly at local and school events. When Robinson and the others finished school, the group turned professional, and they began to appear steadily in local Detroit nightclubs. Their repertoire in this early stage of their career primarily consisted of songs written by Robinson or by Robinson in collaboration with other group members. A prolific songwriter by the time he had reached his teens, Robinson had, by the late 1950's, already written a hundred songs. His musical tastes, influenced by black jazz, rhythm and blues, and white-oriented pop music, veered toward anguished love songs and fast dance music.

Motown

Having achieved an impressive measure of celebrity as a local singing and dancing act, in 1958 young Robinson and his group came to the attention of Berry GORDY, Jr., a part-time record producer and songwriter scouting young talent for his fledgling music enterprise, soon to become Motown Records. A keen judge of talent, Gordy instantly recognized Robinson's worth as both a singer and a songwriter. As a result of their meeting, he quickly signed Robinson's group, which he renamed the Miracles, to a recording contract. Their first record with Gordy, "Got a Job," became a popular hit for the group.

Clearly, Gordy and Motown Records benefited from this timely association with Robinson. Gordy, a lifelong entrepreneur, had in the late 1950's begun to focus his ambitions on the music business, hoping to penetrate the lucrative white-dominated pop music market that catered to postwar adolescents, both black and white. The Miracles, with their lyrical, beat-driven pop music, provided Gordy with an entry into this market, and Smokey Robinson, with his breathy falsetto and striking good looks, the mastermind of his group's sound and performance style, would become the key to Motown's calculated "crossover" strategy. Thus, in 1959, when Gordy formed the Tamla label at Motown, he inaugurated it by producing another Miracles song, "Shop Around," which earned a gold record. From that point on, Robinson occupied a dual position at Motown, operating not only as a performer but also as a producer of company talent, a model as well as a facilitator of Berry Gordy's entrepreneurial vision.

Producer and Songwriter

As Gordy's protégé, Robinson rose to a unique position at Motown. He was the only singer and the only person outside the Gordy family at Motown permitted to produce other artists, to audition them, and to write songs for them. When the Supremes, then known as the Primettes, first approached Motown in 1960, Robinson was their first contact; he appraised their singing and subsequently arranged their decisive meeting with Gordy. Over the years, he also produced and wrote songs for such singers as Mary Wells ("My Guy"), the Temptations ("My Girl," "Get Ready," "The Way You Do the Things You Do"), and Marvin GAYE ("Ain't That Peculiar" and "I'll Be Doggone"), among many others. With these artists, Robinson was responsible for toning down any overtly gospel or rhythm-and-blues roots so that the music would engage white listeners as well as black ones. The collaboration between Robinson and Gordy was a great success. By 1962 Robinson was officially a vice president of Motown, and by the mid-1960's, Motown was firmly established as a major force in the pop music recording industry.

Between 1960 and 1975, Smokey Robinson and the Miracles led Motown as one of its premier singing acts and were among the earliest crossover performers on any record label to bridge black and white musical tastes. Robinson and the Miracles increasingly performed before sizable, racially diverse audiences. During this period, the group had more than forty songs on the record charts, with more than half of those making top-forty lists. Such songs as "You've Really Got a Hold on Me" (1962), "Mickey's Monkey" (1963), "Going to a Go-Go" (1965), "The Tracks of My Tears" (1965), and "I Second That Emotion" (1967)

became hits on both the rhythm-and-blues and national pop charts. With "The Tears of a Clown" (1970), the group extended its popularity to Great Britain. Appearances on such popular teen shows as *American Bandstand, Hullabaloo,* and *Shindig* solidified the Miracles' appeal as a mainstream pop group and, in addition, served to show other Motown acts how to widen their marketability beyond the black community.

Post-Miracles Career

In the late 1960's and early 1970's, when baby boomers became immersed in the hippie culture, the VIETNAM WAR, acid rock, and social-message songs, many of the black pop acts produced by Motown and other record companies began declining in popularity. Motown, too, began to change, having grown from a small "mom-and-pop" record company into an entertainment corporation with new concerns in filmmaking. During this tran-

Smokey Robinson in 1989. *(AP/Wide World Photos)*

sitional period, Motown lost many of the acts responsible for its success; many groups left to pursue their careers away from the tightly controlled management of Gordy's empire. In 1973 even Robinson left the Miracles to devote himself full-time to his burgeoning administrative responsibilities at Motown, though he continued to perform periodically as a soloist throughout the 1970's and 1980's. Though the Miracles managed several hits after Robinson left, by the mid-1970's the group's popularity had begun to fade, and by the 1980's the Miracles had crossed into the realm of memorable nostalgia acts.

Honors and Awards

Despite the changes in musical styles from the 1950's to the 1990's, Robinson became one of the few performers to boast hits that covered four decades. In 1986 he was inducted into the Rock and Roll Hall of Fame and into the Songwriter's Hall of Fame, honors that reflect Bob Dylan's tribute to Robinson as the greatest living poet in America. In 1987, as a soloist, he won a Grammy Award for "Just to See Her." In 1989, he published an autobiography, *Smokey: Inside My Life*, which contained frank disclo-

sures about his life and career, most notably about the breakup of his marriage and his brief dalliance with and recovery from drugs.

—*Tana R. McDonald*

Suggested Readings:

Early, Gerald L. *One Nation Under a Groove: Motown and American Culture.* Hopewell, N.J.: Ecco Press, 1995.

George, Nelson. *The Death of Rhythm and Blues.* New York: E. P. Dutton, 1985.

———. *Where Did Our Love Go? The Rise and Fall of the Motown Sound.* New York: St. Martin's Press, 1985.

Gordy, Berry. *To Be Loved: The Music, the Magic, the Memories of Motown.* New York: Warner Books, 1994.

Hochman, Steve, ed. *Popular Musicians.* 4 vols. Pasadena, Calif.: Salem Press, 1999.

Robinson, Smokey, and David Ritz. *Smokey: Inside My Life.* New York: McGraw-Hill, 1989.

Singleton, Raynoma Gordy, with Bryan Brown and Mim Eichler. *Berry, Me, and Motown: The Untold Story.* Chicago: Contemporary Books, 1990.

Stambler, Irvin. *Encyclopedia of Pop, Rock, and Soul.* New York: St. Martin's Press, 1974.

Robinson, Spottswood W., III (b. July 26, 1916, Richmond, Virginia): Judge and lawyer. Robinson pursued a steady legal career after receiving his B.A. degree in 1936 from Virginia Union University and an LL.B. in 1939 from the HOWARD UNIVERSITY Law School. He acted in diverse roles in the law field as a practicing attorney, a faculty member, a dean of the Howard University Law School, and a district court judge. In 1966 he was appointed as a circuit court

Lawyers in the NAACP Legal Defense Fund team in 1954 included, left to right, Louis L. Redding, Robert L. Carter, Oliver W. Hill, Thurgood Marshall, and Spottswood W. Robinson. *(AP/Wide World Photos)*

judge. He served as an active member and counsel for the Legal Defense and Educational Fund of the NATIONAL ASSOCIATION FOR THE ADVANCEMENT OF COLORED PEOPLE (NAACP) and on the U.S. COMMISSION ON CIVIL RIGHTS.

Robinson, Sugar Ray (Walker Smith, Jr.; May 3, 1921, Detroit, Michigan—April 12, 1989, Culver City, California): Boxer. Born Walker Smith in DETROIT, MICHIGAN, Robinson used the Amateur Athletic Union card of a retired boxer named Ray Robinson in his first fight and eventually became known by that name. Later, he legally changed his name to "Sugar Ray Robinson."

Sugar Ray Robinson raises his arm in victory after taking the middleweight title from Jake Lamotta in early 1951. *(AP/Wide World Photos)*

In 200 professional bouts, from the 1940's to 1965, Robinson won 175 times, lost 19 times, and had 6 draws; he won 110 fights by knockouts. He dominated the middleweight division, defeating opponents such as Jake LaMotta and Rocky Graziano and taking the world title a record five times (1951, 1952, 1955, 1957, and 1958). Many modern boxing authorities regard him, pound for pound, as the most skilled boxer of all time. He was inducted into the International Boxing Hall of Fame in 1990.

Rodgers, Johnathan A. (b. January 18, 1946, San Antonio, Texas): Broadcast executive. When Rodgers was named the president of the stations division of CBS Television, in 1990, he became one of the highest-ranking African Americans in broadcast management.

Rodgers received a bachelor's degree in journalism from the University of California at Berkeley in 1967. He began his journalism career as an intern at *Time* magazine. In 1966

he took a job as a writer-reporter for *Sports Illustrated*. From 1968 to 1972, Rodgers worked as a reporter and then associate editor at *Newsweek*. While at *Newsweek*, Rodgers took time off to serve in the U.S. Army, and he received a master's degree in communications from Stanford University.

After completing his degree at Stanford, Rodgers decided to pursue a career in broadcast journalism. His first broadcast job was as a producer at WNBC-TV in NEW YORK CITY. He left his position behind the scenes to take a job in front of the camera as a reporter at WKYC-TV in Cleveland, Ohio. Rodgers's career continued to flourish in 1976 after he became the assistant news director at WBBM-TV, a CBS network affiliate in CHICAGO. Two years later, he moved to the LOS ANGELES affiliate KNXT-TV (later KCBS-TV), where he rose through the ranks from executive producer to news director and finally to station manager. In 1983 Rodgers moved back to New York to work for the CBS network as executive producer for CBS *Nightwatch*. He later served as executive producer of the weekend CBS *Even-*

ing News and then took on the same duties for the CBS *Morning News.*

In March of 1986, Rodgers was offered the position of vice president and general manager of Chicago's WBBM-TV. Station management had been under attack by many individuals in the local African American community because of its decision to demote its black male weekday anchor in favor of a white male journalist.

Rodgers later told a *Chicago Tribune* reporter that he almost did not take the job because people might think he had been offered it "to solve CBS's problems with Jesse JACKSON and OPERATION PUSH." Rodgers went on to note that he had been the second individual approached for the position and knew that the station's first candidate had been white. That knowledge reassured Rodgers that the station was not looking "for just any black guy." After successfully increasing the Chicago station's profits and ratings and improving its relations with the community, Rodgers was called back to network headquarters as president of the stations division in August of 1990. In this position, he was responsible for overseeing CBS-owned television stations in several cities, including New York (WCBS), Los Angeles (KCBS), and Chicago (WBBM).

In 1996 Rodgers was named president of the Discovery Networks. In his new post, he was responsible for overseeing operations of the Discovery Channel and the Learning Channel from the cable network's headquarters in Bethesda, Maryland. Rodgers married broadcast journalist Royal Kennedy.

Rodman, Dennis (b. May 13, 1961, Trenton, New Jersey): Professional BASKETBALL player. Earning many rebounding titles in the National Basketball Association (NBA), Rodman played on five championship NBA teams. Popularly nicknamed the "Worm," he also became well known for his "bad boy" behavior.

Rodman did not play high school basketball, but he grew nine inches after high school. Eventually, he won an athletic scholarship to Southeastern Oklahoma State. He was signed as a second-round draft pick of the Detroit Pistons in 1986. As a Piston, Rodman was named a member of the NBA all-star team twice. With his rebounding and defensive skills, the Pistons earned back-to-back NBA championships in 1988 and 1989.

In 1995 Rodman joined the Chicago Bulls. Along with Michael JORDAN and Scottie Pippen, he helped form the nucleus of one of the greatest basketball teams of all time. The team won an unprecedented seventy-two games during the 1995-1996 regular season and won NBA championships in 1996, 1997, and 1998.

Known as well for his off-court activities as his basketball, Dennis Rodman has often dressed flamboyantly—as when he appeared on television's *Tonight Show* in early 1997. *(AP/Wide World Photos)*

Rodman became known for his lavish lifestyle, and as his career progressed he grew increasingly outrageous in his appearance and brazen in his statements to the press. He regularly colored his hair multiple colors, covered his body with tattoos, and generally treated the world, including the basketball court, as his stage. With Michael Silver, he wrote a raucous autobiography, *Bad as I Wanna Be* (1996). In 1997 he was suspended for eleven games for kicking a courtside cameraman in the groin. By 1998 his behavior was increasingly making him a liability. Nevertheless, Rodman had become a pop-culture fixture and parlayed his fame into roles in films, including the film version of *Bad as I Wanna Be* (1998) and *Simon Sez* (1999).

In 1999 Rodman played briefly for the Los Angeles Lakers, but he was soon cut because of his unreliability and unpredictable behavior. Later in 1999 he and his wife, model Carmen Electra, were arrested after having a noisy and disruptive fight in a hotel in Miami, where Rodman was acting in a film.

—*Alvin K. Benson*

Rodney, Walter (1942, British Guiana—June 13, 1980, Georgetown, Guyana): Guyanan scholar. Rodney graduated from the University of the West Indies, Jamaica, and London University, where he received a Ph.D. in history. He authored *A History of the Upper Guinea Coast, 1545-1800* (1970) and *The Groundings with My Brothers* (1969). Known as a scholar of the concept of the underdevelopment of Africa, he wrote *How Europe Underdeveloped Africa* (1972). He was a leader in the Working Peoples Alliance. He died in a car bomb explosion in Guyana.

Rogers, Joel A. (September 6, 1883, Jamaica—March 26, 1965, New York, New York): Historian and war correspondent. In 1935 Rogers

$4.95

WORLD'S GREAT MEN OF COLOR

"A richly pioneering work that commends itself to all who are interested in black men whose lives have enriched mankind."—Benjamin Quarles

VOLUME I

Asia and Africa, and historical figures before Christ, including:

Akhenaton, Aesop, Hannibal, Cleopatra, Zenobia, Askia the Great, the Mahdi, and Samuel Adjai Crowther

J.A.ROGERS

First published in 1946, J. A. Rogers's *World's Great Men of Color* has gone through many editions. *(Arkent Archive)*

became the first African American war correspondent when he covered the invasion of Italy for the *Pittsburgh Courier*, for which he also wrote a weekly feature on African American history.

Rogers wrote many books, including several on black history. His titles include *From Superman to Man* (1917), *World's Greatest Men and Women of African Descent* (1935), *Your History from the Beginning of Time to the Present* (1940), and *As Nature Leads: An Informal Discussion of the Reason Why Negro and Caucasian Are Mixing in Spite of Opposition* (1919). Rogers's histories of African Americans were more widely read than those written by other African Americans of the mid-twentieth century.

Rogers, John W., Jr. (b. March 31, 1958, Chicago, Illinois): Investment broker and financier. Rogers grew up in a financially secure, middle-class black family in CHICAGO. His father, John W. Rogers, Sr., was a judge, and his mother, Jewel Stratford Lafontant-Mankarious, was an attorney. An accomplished high school basketball player, Rogers attended Princeton University, where he was captain of the school's basketball team and completed a bachelor's degree in economics in 1980. After graduation, he began his career in the world of finance as a stockbroker for William Blair & Company and remained at the company for two and a half years.

In 1983 Rogers decided to start his own investment firm. He founded Ariel Capital Management, Inc., with one major account: the endowment fund of Howard University. The company went on to become one of the most successful money management firms owned by an African American. The company's staff had grown from two to twenty-five employees by the mid-1990's, and it was responsible for managing more than $1 billion in assets. Ariel's major clients included companies and organizations such as Revlon, Clorox, and the UNITED NEGRO COLLEGE FUND. The firm also worked for the Calvert Group, an investment fund noted for its socially responsible goals. Ariel became involved in managing more than thirty pension funds, which represent a lucrative segment of the financial market. African Americans have more than $75 billion invested in pension funds, the largest repository of black-owned assets.

Unlike many money managers, Rogers did not aim for a diversified portfolio, choosing instead to deal solely in stocks. He developed an investment style and financial objectives involving a conservative, value-oriented strategy of seeking stocks of lesser-known companies that were selling for less than ten times earnings. Relying on extensive research, Rog-

ers applied his strategy of looking for undervalued stocks and patiently timing his acquisition of these stocks. His strategies were successful, and Ariel frequently outperformed the Standard & Poor index. Ariel's growth in its first decade prompted its fourth-place ranking among fifty small company funds tracked by Lipper Analytical Services, a leading investment analysis service.

The success of Ariel brought Rogers to the attention of the media and of the business world. Articles about him appeared in periodicals such as *The Wall Street Journal*, *Black Enterprise*, *Fortune*, *Barron's*, *Business Week*, and *The New York Times*. Rogers made guest appearances on the PBS television program *Wall Street Week* and was invited to speak at various academic institutions, including Howard University, the Wharton School of Business, Harvard Business School, and the Kellogg School.

Among his honors and awards, Rogers received special recognition in 1988, when he was named mutual fund manager of the year by *Sylvia Porter's Personal Finance Magazine* and entrepreneur of the year by Arthur Young and *Venture Magazine*. He became known as a prominent civic leader in his hometown of Chicago, serving as director of the Chicago Urban League, president of the Board of Commissioners of the Chicago Park District, board member of the Chicago Symphony Orchestra, and trustee of Rush-Presbyterian-St. Luke's Medical Center. He also served as director of the National Association of Securities Dealers and on several corporate boards.

Rollins, Sonny (b. September 7, 1930, New York, New York): Free-style JAZZ saxophonist, recording artist, and producer. Tenor saxophonist Theodore Walter "Sonny" Rollins, influenced strongly by Coleman HAWKINS, began recording in 1949 and began recording albums under his own name in 1951, launching a career that spanned more than fifty years. Rollins is widely regarded as one of the great sax players of all time.

He came to prominence in the 1950's, performing with such jazz greats as Earl "Bud" Powell, Thelonious MONK, Max ROACH, Clifford Brown, Miles DAVIS, and Charlie PARKER. After the late 1950's, he focused almost exclusively on leading his own group.

Many critics regard his 1950's recordings to be his most outstanding work; among them are *Vintage Sessions* (1951), *Taking Care of Business* (1955), *Saxophone Colossus* (1956), and *Way Out West* (1957). His prominence continued in the 1960's, when his playing became freer, perhaps under the influence of Ornette COLEMAN. Albums of the 1960's include *What's New* (1962) and *East Broadway Rundown* (1966); Rollins also recorded the music for the film *Alfie* (1966).

Rollins's work in the 1970's and beyond drew mixed reactions, partly because he drifted away from pure jazz and incorporated fusion and rhythm-and-blues elements into his work. He continued playing and recording through the 1980's and 1990's.

Roman Catholics: While U.S. Catholicism often has been characterized as a white immigrant or ethnic religion, the North American Roman Catholic Church has included African Americans since its colonial foundations. After centuries of ambivalent membership, partial segregation, and recurrent evangelization, more than 1.5 million blacks represent a strong and visible minority among the nation's 55 million Catholics. Catholicism also represents the third-largest denomination in the black Christian community, after BAPTISTS and METHODISTS.

African American Catholic history has been marked by dramatic shifts among both congregants and their predominantly white leaders. After emancipation, for example, many slaves left the Catholic Church. Yet other blacks soon were converted through education and outreach programs through which white bishops and clerics slowly transformed both opportunities and attitudes in the Catholic Church. Still, accommodation to southern norms kept blacks from religious authority in most cases until after the end of the nineteenth century, a state of affairs that caused black leaders to attack Catholicism as a white man's religion.

In the twentieth century, the black Catholic Church migrated with its parishioners to northern industrial cities while maintaining traditional southern bases. The Civil Rights movement promoted a new awareness of black values, needs, and leadership that coincided with increased pluralism in Catholicism prompted by the Second Vatican Council. Black bishops, priests, nuns, and lay leaders have taken forceful stands on social as well as religious issues within the church, although both criticism and challenges continue to shape black Catholic life.

The First Centuries
Catholicism was established among blacks in the Americas by missionaries in Latin America and in French territories such as LOUISIANA. The first black Catholics within the boundaries of the modern United States were baptized in Spanish St. Augustine, FLORIDA, in the sixteenth century and worshiped thereafter alongside whites in that city's sanctuary. The North American Catholic colony of MARYLAND also fostered some conversions among slaves.

Although both slave and free black Catholics practiced their religion in antebellum cities from NEW YORK to NEW ORLEANS, congregations were limited by general restrictions on black life that the white Catholic hierarchy rarely disputed (in part because of the denomination's ambiguous status as a "foreign" religion). For example, James Augustine HEALY, America's first black priest and the bishop of

Portland, MAINE, after 1875, was sent north by his Irish father and slave mother in order to get an education. He was ordained in France in 1854; several siblings followed him in religious life. Yet no black priest was ordained in the United States until 1891, while many white Catholics accepted SLAVERY and, later, acquiesced to segregation.

Despite the defection of slave Catholics from the church after the CIVIL WAR, American bishops saw emancipation as an ideal opportunity for evangelization through missions and schools. They also saw themselves as competitors with Protestants, who offered different forms of liturgy and leadership. Although these RECONSTRUCTION programs were eclipsed in importance to the Catholic Church by the needs of newly arrived European immigrants, the programs set the pattern for the reemergence of black Catholicism. Despite the presence of preexisting black congregations in Louisiana and other areas, many black Catholic churches emerged after the war under the aegis of orders of white priests and nuns, who were often immigrants.

The Most Reverend Joseph L. Howze, the first African American bishop to head an American diocese during the twentieth century, is seated at his Biloxi, Mississippi, diocese in June, 1977. *(AP/Wide World Photos)*

Black Catholic Orders

Black orders for women had already existed in slave days. The OBLATE SISTERS OF PROVIDENCE formed in BALTIMORE in 1829, and the SISTERS OF THE HOLY FAMILY began in New Orleans in 1842. Another women's teaching order, the Franciscan Handmaids of the Most Pure Heart of Mary, began in Savannah, GEORGIA, in 1916. Yet these often were overshadowed by white-run orders such as the Blessed Sacrament Sisters for Indians and Colored People and the Franciscan Sisters of the Immaculate Conception, Missionary. Through the work of these orders, schools were established in black neighborhoods that were primarily Protestant and that often lacked public schools. These schools, in fact, often preceded the establishment of separate or integrated congregations.

Through the mid-twentieth century priests assigned to black parishes generally were also white. Many came from the English Mill Hill Fathers (later St. Joseph's Society of the Sacred Heart, or Josephites, founded in 1866), the Divine Word Missionaries (founded in 1875), and the Society of African Missions (founded in 1856), which began its work in the United States in 1907. Black priests faced difficulties in gaining ordination and acceptance from both whites and blacks, and such difficulties embittered the experiences of early black priests. Despite attempts by white orders and some bishops to recruit blacks for the priesthood, sustained results were only achieved by the Divine Word Fathers through their seminary in Bay St. Louis, MISSISSIPPI, during and after the 1920's. By the 1990's, thirteen black bishops and roughly 250 black priests, as well as some 550 black nuns, were serving the church in the United States. Many permanent lay deacons worked with them as members of local communities.

Catholicism's hierarchical character should not overshadow the important roles of lay leadership among African Americans. In antebellum Louisiana, for example, Catholicism took on its own character because of the strength of African customs and the development of color differences within the black community. In the North, Pierre Toussaint (1766-1853), born in HAITI, became known in New York after 1787 for his charity to blacks and whites; he has been proposed as a candidate for sainthood. After the Civil War, some blacks demanded their own parishes; the long-term effects of such a segregation were debated for a century thereafter. Black associations also emerged, whether local mutual-aid societies or the KNIGHTS OF ST. PETER CLAVER, founded under Josephite patronage in 1909. Perhaps the high point of early lay involvement came with the Congresses of Colored Catholics of 1889-1894.

Nevertheless, there were limits on turn-of-the-century black participation in the church. Catholic universities, seminaries, and fraternal organizations, such as the Knights of Columbus, rejected African Americans. Moreover, while blacks were never barred from white churches, they were often discouraged from attending white congregations, forced to sit in the backs of churches or in choir lofts, and received communion at mass after the whites.

Catholic priest officiating over the Mass at the Our Mother of Africa Chapel in 1997; the Washington, D.C., chapel was funded by black Roman Catholics throughout the country. *(AP/Wide World Photos)*

The Twentieth Century

When the Jesuit John Gillard published his *Catholic Church and the American Negro* (1930), he found strong black churches meeting challenges not only among traditionally Catholic populations in the South but also in northern urban centers of black migration such as New York, Chicago, and Detroit. Meanwhile, Thomas Wyatt TURNER emerged as an active spokesman with the Federated Colored Catholics (founded 1925), while Father John LaFarge's Interracial Council began its activities at the same time. New Orleans's Xavier University also was established as a college for black Catholics by 1925. Yet many parishes remained segregated, poor, and staffed by white missionary clergy.

Changes came to black Catholics with the gains of the CIVIL RIGHTS movement. Catholic schools in the South slowly desegregated between the 1950's and the 1970's. While the Catholic Church was involved in the Civil Rights movement, it was not in the vanguard, which led to recriminations from blacks. In other cases, blacks also complained that their churches and schools were consistently closed in order to integrate white parishes.

During this time, the Catholic Church itself underwent reorganization through the deliberations of world bishops in the Second Vatican Council (1962-1965). Council reforms included the changing of the mass from Latin to vernacular, the liberalization of rules, and the encouragement of more individually thoughtful and culturally sensitive worship. Subsequent debates over the limits of reform in such areas as the admission of married and female clergy, abortion, and social justice caused more convulsive changes and declines in the numbers of priests and nuns.

With these social and religious changes, black Catholics explored renewed cultural options in their religious and community expression, ranging from African contributions to prayer, song, and dance to black theology. The National Office for Black Catholics began its work in 1970, along with organizations of black clergy and seminarians. Many questions of black and Catholic heritage were considered at length in the 1984 letter written by U.S. black bishops entitled *What We Have Seen and Heard*, which celebrated the history, spirituality, community, and joy of the black Catholic tradition. In this letter, however, as well as in other statements, the bishops also raised critical concerns about the problems of black men, women, and families; about the need for the Catholic Church to address poverty, inequality, and crime in black neighborhoods; and about discrimination in the church. These themes also have been issues in the departure of blacks from the Catholic Church.

Black Catholics have emerged as well-educated and sometimes critical voices within both the black and Catholic communities. Prominent African American Catholics include U.S. SUPREME COURT Justice Clarence THOMAS, liturgists Clarence Rivers and Sister Thea BOWMAN, and historian Cyprian Davis. Periodicals, studies, and conferences foment awareness of history and prospects while raising questions concerning Catholic commitments to the inner city, to integration, to education, and to leadership.

—*Gary W. McDonogh*

Suggested Readings:

Baer, Hans A., and Merrill Singer. *African American Religion in the Twentieth Century: Varieties of Protest and Accommodation.* Knoxville: University of Tennessee Press, 1992.

Bowman, Thea, ed. *Families: Black and Catholic, Catholic and Black.* Washington, D.C.: U.S. Catholic Conference, Commission on Marriage and Family Life, 1985.

Brown, Joseph A. *To Stand on the Rock: Meditations on Black Catholic Identity.* Maryknoll, N.Y.: Orbis Books, 1998.

Davis, Cyprian. *The History of Black Catholics in the United States.* New York: Crossroad, 1990.

Hayes, Diana L., and Cyprian Davis, eds. *Taking Down Our Harps: Black Catholics in the United States.* Maryknoll, N.Y.: Orbis Books, 1998.

Irvine, Jacqueline J., and Michele Foster, eds. *Growing Up African American in Catholic Schools.* New York: Teachers College Press, 1996.

MacGregor, Morris J. *The Emergence of a Black Catholic Community: St. Augustine's in Washington.* Washington, D.C.: Catholic University of America Press, 1999.

McDonogh, Gary W. *Black and Catholic in Savannah, Georgia.* Knoxville: University of Tennessee Press, 1993.

Ochs, Stephen J. *Desegregating the Altar: The Josephites and the Struggle for Black Priests, 1871-1960.* Baton Rouge: Louisiana State University Press, 1990.

Shuster, George, and Robert M. Kearns. *Statistical Profile of Black Catholics.* Washington, D.C.: Josephite Pastoral Center, 1976.

Roosevelt administration, Franklin D.: Franklin D. Roosevelt's tenure in the White House, from 1933 to 1945, spanned the GREAT DEPRESSION and WORLD WAR II, eras that brought hardship and opportunity to African Americans. Because CIVIL RIGHTS posed a potential political liability during his years in the White House, Roosevelt proved unwilling to serve as an advocate for African American interests. He saw little gain in aiding black Americans in their quest for equal rights, and he knew that such a position would create a significant loss of support from southern members of Congress. The president's attitude shaped the attitudes of most other members of his administration, who did not show particular interest in working with black leaders. Nonetheless, African Americans supported Roosevelt, because they received some economic relief from New Deal programs and because First Lady Eleanor Roosevelt and a few other administration officials showed an interest in African American affairs.

Prior to the Great Depression, most African American voters supported the Republican Party. DEMOCRATIC PARTY politicians, including Franklin Roosevelt, did not seek the black vote and offered no assistance to African Americans. During the 1932 presidential election, African Americans saw little reason to vote for Roosevelt, and they did not defect from the REPUBLICAN PARTY in large numbers. As a result, Roosevelt owed black voters nothing when he entered the White House, and he did not speak out against RACIAL DISCRIMINATION. Although African Americans held more government positions under Roosevelt than they had in any previous administration, they did not hold any prominent or prestigious offices.

Some members of Roosevelt's administration, among them Interior Secretary Harold Ickes, did show concern for the well-being of African Americans. First Lady Eleanor Roosevelt was the most prominent administration advocate of civil rights. Although her efforts were in vain, she urged her husband to support antilynching legislation being debated in Congress during the 1930's. At public events she mixed with African Americans, a departure from the norms of the day that earned her the admiration of blacks—and the enmity of some whites—throughout the nation. Behind the scenes she worked to ensure that African Americans shared in the benefits of New Deal programs. When the Daughters of the American Revolution (DAR) refused to allow singer Marian ANDERSON to perform in Constitution Hall in 1939, Eleanor Roosevelt resigned from the organization and played a role in having Anderson perform for thousands in front of the Lincoln Memorial.

Roosevelt appointed some prominent civil rights activists to positions in the government, and he selected William HASTIE for a federal judgeship; Hastie was the first African American to be appointed a federal judge. African

In 1937 Roosevelt appointed William. H. Hastie judge of the Virgin Islands—a post that made Hastie the first African American judge in the federal judiciary. *(Library of Congress)*

American Mary McLeod BETHUNE was a director in the National Youth Administration (NYA), a New Deal program. The NYA held a 1937 conference on the Problems of the Negro and the Negro Youth. Many observers viewed the conference, the first of its kind, as at least a tentative step forward. The NYA aided black secondary schools and universities. To decrease discrimination against black workers, another New Deal agency, the Public Works Administration (PWA), established a quota system that allowed at least some African Americans to enter southern construction industries. Large numbers of African Americans also benefited from government-sponsored literacy programs. Roosevelt met occasionally with a group nicknamed the "black cabinet"

or "black brain trust" as well as with other leading black professionals.

Despite such efforts, the Roosevelt administration had a poor record on facing civil rights issues squarely. Nonetheless, New Deal programs provided African Americans with some relief during the long economic crisis of the Depression, and black voters strongly supported Roosevelt in the 1936 and 1940 elections. With the threat of war growing after 1940, many African Americans hoped that Roosevelt would battle discrimination in the workplace. However, the president placed a higher priority on preparing for war than on engaging in a potentially divisive struggle on behalf of African Americans. Only after black leaders resorted to public pressure, threatening a march on Washington if the president did not act, did Roosevelt relent. In 1941 he issued EXECUTIVE ORDER 8802 banning discrimination in defense agencies and industries.

—*Thomas Clarkin*

Suggested Readings:

Ashmore, Harry S. *Hearts and Minds: The Anatomy of Racism from Roosevelt to Reagan.* New York: McGraw-Hill, 1982.

Natanson, Nicholas. *The Black Image in the New Deal: The Politics of FSA Photography.* Knoxville: University of Tennessee Press, 1992.

Sitkoff, Harvard. *A New Deal for Blacks: The Emergence of Civil Rights as a National Issue.* New York: Oxford University Press, 1978.

Weiss, Nancy J. *Farewell to the Party of Lincoln: Black Politics in the Age of FDR.* Princeton, N.J.: Princeton University Press, 1983.

Ross, Diana (b. March 26, 1944, Detroit, Michigan): Singer and FILM actor. With the SUPREMES, Diana Ross helped pioneer the MOTOWN sound, and as a solo performer she became recognized as a singing superstar around the world. She recorded more than fifteen singles that reached number one on the U.S. charts.

Since Ross's parents both sang in DETROIT's Olivet Baptist Church choir, she grew up surrounded by music. She and her sisters sang in the junior choir at church. By the age of six, Diana had decided that she wanted to be a professional singer. Because of her high grade point average in junior high school, she was accepted into the prestigious Cass Technical High School, one of the best high schools in Detroit.

While in high school, Ross and some of her friends formed a singing group named the Primettes. They performed at various local events and signed their first recording contract with LuPine Records. After graduation from high school, the Primettes signed with Hitsville Records, which later became Motown Records. Eventually they were renamed the Supremes, and during the 1960's, they recorded twelve number one hits with Ross as lead vocalist.

In 1967 the group became known as Diana Ross and the Supremes; in 1970 Ross left the group to pursue an independent career. Her first solo single, "Reach Out and Touch Somebody's Hand," ensured her continued success in the music industry. Her 1980 hit, "Upside Down," earned a platinum record. In 1981 Ross left Motown and signed with the Recording Corporation of America (RCA), but she returned to Motown in 1989 as a partner and artist. Ross also starred in several films, including *Lady Sings the Blues* (1972), *Mahogany* (1975), *The Wiz* (1978), and *Out of Darkness* (1994).

Ross has received many awards, including the National Association for the Advancement of Colored People (NAACP) IMAGE AWARD for entertainer of the year (1970) and a Grammy Award for best contemporary vocal performance by a female singer for "Ain't No

Diana Ross (center) with Nipsey Russell and Michael Jackson in *The Wiz* (1978), an all-black adaptation of L. Frank Baum's classic *The Wizard of Oz*. The fact that Ross was thirty-three years old when she played the child Dorothy contributed to the film's failure. *(AP/Wide World Photos)*

Diana Ross performing at a Carnegie Hall benefit in New York City in 1996. *(AP/Wide World Photos)*

President Lyndon B. Johnson's Youth Opportunity Program and for her contributions to the SOUTHERN CHRISTIAN LEADERSHIP CONFERENCE (SCLC).

—*Alvin K. Benson*

Rowan, Carl Thomas (b. August 25, 1925, Ravenscroft, Tennessee): Journalist, COLUMNIST, and author. Rowan's first job paid only a dollar a week, but his determination to succeed, evident at a young age, saw him graduate from Barnard High School in 1942 as class president and valedictorian. In 1944 Rowan became one of the first fifteen African Americans to earn a commission in the Navy. He then received a bachelor's degree from OBERLIN COLLEGE in 1947 and a master's degree in journalism from the University of Minnesota. In 1948 he joined the *Minneapolis Tribune* as a copyreader, becoming a general

Mountain High Enough" (1970). She received an Academy Award nomination for her role as Billie HOLIDAY in *Lady Sings the Blues* and a Tony Award for her one-woman show *An Evening with Diana Ross* (1977). Ross was inducted into the Rock and Roll Hall of Fame in 1988 and was subsequently awarded a star on the Hollywood Walk of Fame.

In addition to singing and acting, Ross established a successful business career. She founded Diana Enterprises, a record production company, in 1977. Some of her other ventures included Anaid Films, a production company; Just For Fun Enterprises, which focuses on merchandising; Rosco, an advertising firm; Rosstown and Rossville, publishing companies; and the Diana Ross Foundation, which cares for charitable interests. She received citations for her efforts on behalf of

Carl Rowan, testifying before a Senate committee in 1964. *(AP/Wide World Photos)*

reporter in 1950. His series *How Far from Slavery?*, written about the black experience in the South, elicited the largest volume of mail in the paper's history.

In 1952 *Look* magazine reprinted portions of *How Far from Slavery?* Rowan then wrote a book, *The Pitiful and the Proud* (1956), about his experiences in India and Southeast Asia. Another book, *Go South to Sorrow*, was published in 1957. He was named deputy assistant secretary for public affairs by the U.S. Department of State in 1961, and he served until 1963. He then became ambassador to Finland, serving in 1963 and 1964. Rowan directed the U.S. Information Agency from 1964 to 1965. His book *Wait Till Next Year: The Life Story of Jackie Robinson* was published in 1960, followed by *Just Between Us Blacks* in 1974. His memoirs, *Breaking Barriers*, were published in 1991. Rowan began his long-running column for the *Chicago Sun* in 1965 and additionally produced a syndicated national affairs radio commentary, *The Rowan Report*. He served as a commentator for the Post-Newsweek Broadcasting Corporation and was a frequent panelist on television's *Meet the Press*.

Rudolph, Wilma (June 23, 1940, St. Bethlehem, Tennessee—November 12, 1994, Brentwood, Tennessee): TRACK AND FIELD athlete. The fifth of eight children born to Ed and Blanche Rudolph, Wilma Glodean Rudolph overcame physical handicaps and racial prejudice to become one of the greatest track stars in U.S. history.

A victim of childhood illnesses that restricted the use of her left leg until she was eight, Rudolph became a sports superstar at Burt High School in Clarksville, TENNESSEE, breaking the state basketball scoring record for girls and remaining undefeated in all of her

Wilma Rudolph. *(AP/Wide World Photos)*

track meets. Her ability interested Tennessee State University's women's track coach Ed Temple, who convinced her to participate in a summer track program at his school and to train for the 1956 Olympics. Rudolph returned from the Melbourne, Australia, Games with a bronze medal for the 400-meter relay and with determination to train for the 1960 Olympics.

She attended Tennessee State University, where she excelled as a member of the track team and received a degree in education. In July, 1960, she set the world record for the 200-meter run. Rudolph's performance at the Rome Olympics in 1960 earned her the title of the world's fastest woman. She won three gold medals, the first woman to do so, in the 100-meter dash and 200-meter dash (an Olympic record), and as anchor for the 400-meter relay (a world record). She won the title of Associated Press U.S. female athlete of the year (1960), the Helms World Trophy Award (1960), and the James E. Sullivan Memorial Trophy (1961).

After retiring from competition in 1962, Rudolph coached track at the University of California and at DePauw University in Indiana; taught elementary, junior high, and high school; participated in an Americans Abroad program in Mali and Senegal, where she taught teenage girls how to race; served as assistant director of athletics for the Mayor's Youth Foundation in Chicago; founded the Wilma Rudolph Foundation, an Indianapolis-based organization to promote amateur athletics, in 1981; and served as director of human resources at the Commerce Union Bank in Nashville, Tennessee.

For many years after her track career ended, Rudolph continued to receive honors for her stirring Olympic performances. In 1974 she was inducted into the National Track and Field Hall of Fame, and she received similar honors in 1983 from the U.S. Olympic Hall of Fame. Along the way she was inducted into the Women's Sports Foundation Hall of Fame and the Black Athletes Hall of Fame. Her alma mater, Tennessee State University, named an indoor track in her honor. In 1990 she became the first woman to receive the National Collegiate Athletic Association's Silver Anniversary Award.

In July of 1994, Rudolph nearly fainted during a speaking engagement in Atlanta, Georgia. She consulted with physicians and was diagnosed with a malignant brain tumor. The CANCER spread quickly, and she died only four months later at her home in Brentwood, Tennessee, near Nashville. A funeral procession of ten limousines and more than 130 automobiles—carrying her four children, several grandchildren, and her many siblings, cousins, nieces, nephews, and other relatives—commenced at Tennessee State University and drove to her gravesite. Her funeral was also attended by numerous track stars—contemporaries who had competed with her as well as later champions who had been inspired by her example.

Married first to William Ward and later to Robert Eldridge, she had four children. She was a popular lecturer on physical fitness and wrote two books: *Wilma: The Story of Wilma Rudolph* (her autobiography, 1977) and *Wilma Rudolph on Track* (a training book for children, 1980).

Rudolph's career served as an inspiration to many individuals, from members of the African American community to young people and adults who were physically challenged. A tall, graceful woman who was fiercely competitive on the athletic field and equally dedicated to community service, Rudolph set an important example for many African American female athletes who followed, including Evelyn Ashford, Jackie JOYNER-KERSEE, and Florence GRIFFITH-JOYNER.

—*Updated by James Tackach*

Ruggles, David (March 15, 1810, Norwich, Connecticut—December 26, 1849, Northampton, Massachusetts): Businessman, abolitionist, and journalist. Born a FREE BLACK in Connecticut, Ruggles dedicated his life to the ABOLITIONIST MOVEMENT.

Ruggles opened a New York City grocery in 1829 and the first African American bookstore in New York in 1834; the store was burned by anti-abolitionists a year later. Ruggles founded the first black press in the United States, which he used to publish abolitionist pamphlets, and the first black magazine, *Mirror of Liberty*, which printed antislavery speeches and accounts of slave and freeman kidnappings. He ended his career as a prosperous hydropathist (hydropathy attempted to use water to cure disease).

Ruggles began his antislavery work in 1830 by seeking revolutionary war hero Marquis de Lafayette's endorsement of abolition. Ruggles was a traveling speaker for the *Emancipator*, the New York antislavery newspaper, and a COLUMNIST for the *Emancipator* and *The Colored*

American. He was a founder of the Garrison Literary and Benevolent Association and the New York Vigilance Committee, which protected free blacks from kidnapping. He was a New York City Temperance Union leader and an UNDERGROUND RAILROAD conductor, harboring Frederick DOUGLASS and more than one thousand other escaping slaves traveling north to safety.

Ruggles's writings include the *Slaveholders Directory* (1839), which identified politicians, lawyers, and police serving as slave catchers or kidnappers of freemen, and *The Abrogation of the Seventh Commandment by the American Churches* (1835), appealing to northern women to shun wives of slaveholders.

—*Gordon Neal Diem*

Run-D.M.C. performing at a free concert in New York City in May, 1996; Joseph Simmons is at left, Daryl McDaniel at right. *(AP/Wide World Photos)*

Run-D.M.C.: Rap trio composed of Joe "Run" Simmons, Darryl "D.M.C." McDaniels, and Jay "Jam Master Jay" Mizell. Simmons and McDaniels were childhood friends from Queens, New York. Simmons became involved in RAP through his brother, Russell Simmons, whose Rush Productions Company helped launch the careers of such early rap groups as Kurtis Blow and GRANDMASTER FLASH AND THE FURIOUS FIVE.

Simmons began performing raps with Kurtis Blow in the late 1970's, when he was fifteen, and began his own rap career in the early 1980's in collaboration with McDaniels. Simmons, who was studying mortuary science at LaGuardia Community College, came up with a verse for his first rap hit while working in a lab. He shared it with McDaniels, who was then attending St. John's University.

The duo recorded its first single, "It's Like That," in 1983. The single sold more than 250,000 copies by the end of 1983 and was later acknowledged as the first rap song with a truly political message. "It's Like That" was followed by the equally successful "Hard Times." The debut album *Run-D.M.C.* was released in 1984 by the independent label Profile Records.

Joined by deejay Jay Mizell and working under the management of Russell Simmons, the group developed its distinctive visual style. Members used tough-talking street lyrics and a gangster image—all-black outfits consisting of warm-up suits, gold chains, Adidas tennis shoes, and Kangol hats—to get across their antidrug, antigang message. *King of Rock* was their second hit album. *Raising Hell*, their third album, was released in 1986. It featured the first rap crossover single, "Walk

This Way," a remake of the rock band Aerosmith's 1970's hit. Aerosmith performed on the single and video with Run-D.M.C., and the video received considerable airplay on the Music Television (MTV) cable channel. *Raising Hell* reached number three on the pop charts on the strength of such popular singles as "My Adidas" and "Proud to Be Black," and it sold more than three million copies. The group's 1988 album, *Tougher than Leather*, featured songs that fused rap and heavy metal themes. The group borrowed the album's title for its 1988 rap film, which included an appearance by the Beastie Boys, the white opening act for Run-D.M.C. The film was not a success.

At a Run-D.M.C. concert in Long Beach, California, thirty-seven fans were injured when a riot broke out between rival Bloods and Crips gang members before the group even took the stage. Journalists blamed the rap group for inciting the violence, but Simmons spoke out about the unfair connection being made between rap shows and violence. He cited the social conditions and economic situation faced by African Americans as producing the behavior rather than their admiration for rap lyrics that might be seen as promoting violence. Run-D.M.C.'s popularity declined with the advent of early hard rap and gangsta rap groups such as N.W.A. and 2 LIVE CREW, but in 1993 they had a hit with the Christian-themed *Down with the King*.

Runyon v. McCrary: U.S. SUPREME COURT discrimination case in 1976. *Runyon v. McCrary* involved a claim by a private school that refusing admission on the basis of race was legal. The parents of a student seeking admission argued that this policy violated CIVIL RIGHTS law. In 1972 the parents of Michael McCrary attempted to enroll him in Bobbe's School, a private school in Arlington, Virginia, operated by Russell and Katheryne Runyon. When he was refused admission because he was African American, his parents successfully sued the school.

When the case reached the U.S. Supreme Court, the Court decided that the Civil Rights Act of 1866 made RACIAL DISCRIMINATION in private contracts illegal, including those made by private schools. Although this decision applied only to nonsectarian schools, the Court later decided, in *Bob Jones University v. United States* (1983), that discriminatory religious schools could lose their tax-exempt status.

—*Rose Secrest*

Rush, Bobby L. (b. November 23, 1946): ILLINOIS politician and radical activist. Active in the BLACK PANTHER PARTY during the late 1960's, Rush surrendered to Jesse JACKSON in 1969 when law enforcement officers were trying to arrest him. Rush went on to earn his bachelor's degree from Roosevelt University

Representative Bobby L. Rush. *(© Roy Lewis Archives)*

Christopher Rush. *(Library of Congress)*

began serving in the 103d Congress. Running against Republican opponent William J. Kelly in 1994, Rush was reelected to Congress in a landslide victory. He was reelected again in 1996 and 1998.

Rush, Christopher (1777-1872): Successor to James Varick, the first bishop (1822) of the New York-based AFRICAN METHODIST EPISCOPAL ZION CHURCH. Rush became bishop in 1828. He never married, and he lost his sight in 1852. Among his publications is *A Short Account of the Rise and Progress of the African Episcopal Church in America* (1843).

Rushing, Jimmy (August 26, 1903, Oklahoma City, Oklahoma—June 8, 1972, New York, New York): JAZZ and BLUES singer. Rushing's career is most closely linked with that of pianist and bandleader Count BASIE. In the late 1920's, both men were with the Blue Devils, a band led by bassist Walter Page, and then with one led by pianist Bennie Moten. Upon Moten's death in 1935, Basie assumed leadership, which he maintained until his death almost half a century later.

Rushing was an important member of the Page, Moten, and Basie bands. His rough-textured voice was ideal for singing the blues. His natural exuberance and great rhythmic sense enhanced his performances considerably. He had the good fortune or good sense to perform and record with some of the major instrumentalists of the time. Among them, early in his career, were saxophonists Chu Berry, Ben WEBSTER, and Lester YOUNG. For example, when Rushing recorded "New Orleans" with Moten in 1932, Webster's dynamic solo set up

in Chicago in 1974. He worked as a financial planner, served as associate dean of Daniel Hale Williams University, and later worked as a successful insurance salesman with Prudential Insurance Company before winning a seat as an alderman on the CHICAGO city council in 1983.

During his tenure on the city council, Rush was chair of the Environmental Protection, Energy, and Public Utilities committee and served on other important committees. After nine years as an alderman, Rush campaigned as a candidate for ILLINOIS's First Congressional District in 1992. After winning the Democratic primary, Rush was victorious in the November election and was one of the large group of black freshman representatives who

Blues singer Jimmy Rushing (right) with jazz trumpeter Dizzy Gillespie in 1959. *(AP/Wide World Photos)*

Russell, Bill (b. February 12, 1934, Monroe, Louisiana): Basketball player. Russell starred at the center position for the Boston Celtics of the National Basketball Association (NBA) from 1956 through 1969. During those thirteen seasons, Boston won eleven NBA championships. When he retired, he held the career rebounding record, with 21,620. Wilt CHAMBERLAIN later topped that mark.

Russell grew up in DETROIT, MICHIGAN, and OAKLAND, CALIFORNIA, where he became a high school basketball star. By the time of his high school graduation in 1952, he had almost reached his NBA playing height of six feet, ten inches. Seeing his promise, the University of San Francisco offered him a scholarship, and he led the university to National Collegiate Athletic Association championships in 1955 and 1956. During his college career, he averaged more than twenty points and twenty rebounds per game.

Russell's outstanding collegiate performance resulted in an invitation to join the 1956 U.S. Olympic team. At the Olympic Games in Melbourne, Australia, Russell helped his basketball teammates win the gold medal.

After the Olympic victory, Russell declined an offer from the HARLEM GLOBETROTTERS and signed with the Celtics. In his first professional season, 1956-1957, he led Boston to its first NBA championship. He also established himself as the league's best defensive player. He stopped opponents from driving to the basket and used his long arms to block shots, grab rebounds, and start the feared Boston fast break.

Besides the team championships, Russell won five most valuable player awards, played

Rushing's vocal and enhanced the entire performance.

After leaving Basie in 1950, Rushing continued his frequent recording, mostly for Vanguard Records and Columbia Records. Although he always performed at a high artistic level, "Harvard Blues" (1958) stands out as one of his more engaging recordings of the late 1950's. In addition to appearing on the notable television program *The Sound of Jazz* (1957), he performed at recording sessions led by clarinetist Benny Goodman (1958), pianist Duke ELLINGTON (1958 and 1959), and pianist Dave Brubeck (1960). Rushing's last recording, *The You and Me That Used to Be* (1971), illustrates that at the end of his career he was as forceful and effective as ever.

Bill Russell during his rookie season with the Celtics. *(AP/Wide World Photos)*

in twelve all-star games, and set several rebounding records. During his last three Celtics seasons, he also coached the team, becoming the first African American to serve as an NBA head coach. With Russell in charge, Boston won two NBA championships. When his playing career ended, Russell also coached the Seattle SuperSonics and the Sacramento Kings. In 1974 he was elected to the Naismith Memorial Basketball Hall of Fame. In 1980 basketball writers voted Russell the greatest player in the history of the NBA. In 1996 an NBA panel named him one of the fifty greatest players of the league's first half century. Even after Chicago Bulls star Michael JORDAN announced his retirement in early 1999, there were still many pundits and fans who regarded Russell as the greatest player of all time.

Both during and after his playing career, Russell was an outspoken proponent of equal rights for African American athletes. Although he was always a favorite with Celtics fans, Russell claimed that the city of BOSTON was inhospitable to its African American athletes. Russell's experiences on and off the court are recorded in his 1979 autobiography, *Second Wind: The Memoirs of an Opinionated Man.*

Russell, Herman (b. December 23, 1930, Atlanta, Georgia): Business proprietor and executive. Russell graduated from the Tuskegee Institute. His numerous businesses included land development, apartment management, mortgage brokerage, banking, and sports management. He served on the boards of directors of many professional and civic organizations. *Black Enterprise* magazine gave him its annual achievement award in 1978.

Russwurm, John Brown (October 1, 1799, Port Antonio, Jamaica—June 17, 1851, Liberia): Journalist. Born in JAMAICA, Russwurm was the son of a Jamaican mother and a white American father, John Russwurm. Until he was about eight years old, Russwurm was treated as free, even though he was a slave, and he stayed in Jamaica with his father. As was common at the time for MULATTO children, he was sent abroad for an education, first in Canada and then in the state of Maine. Up until that time, he was known by the name of John Brown. His father settled in 1812 in Port-

Born in Jamaica, John Brown Russwurm was one of the first African Americans to graduate from a four-year college. *(Associated Publishers, Inc.)*

land, MAINE, and in 1813 married Susan Blanchard, who insisted that Russwurm be given the family name and treated as a member of the family. Russwurm's father died in 1815, and Russwurm stayed with his mother.

Russwurm was one of the first African Americans to graduate from an American college. Accounts differ as to whether he was the first, second, or third to do so. He earned his bachelor's degree from Bowdoin College in Maine in 1826, and in 1829 he earned a master's degree.

Shortly after his arrival in NEW YORK CITY, he founded the first black weekly newspaper in the United States, *Freedom's Journal*. His partner in this venture was the Reverend Samuel Cornish of the African Presbyterian Church, who handled business matters for the paper. Russwurm and Cornish were prompted to found the paper by the appearance in New York City of an antiblack publication that ridiculed free African Americans and defended slavery.

The first issue of *Freedom's Journal*, published on March 16, 1827, stated objectives that its editors hoped to achieve. These included emancipation of all slaves, full civil and political equality for black people, an end to racist publicity, and promulgation of truth about Africa. Among the reporters or agents for the paper was David WALKER, who first published his provocative "Walker's Appeal" in *Freedom's Journal*. Other agents wrote from England, HAITI, and Canada.

At first, Russwurm declared in the paper that he was a black nationalist, but later he switched to promoting the COLONIZATION MOVEMENT as the best chance for survival for black Americans. That led to a dispute with Cornish that ended in dissolution of their partnership. Cornish had for several years devoted his time to the ministry and had not taken an active part in the paper. The last issue of *Freedom's Journal* appeared on March 28, 1829. Cornish soon restarted the paper under a new name, *Rights of All*. That paper failed, as did his later effort, the *Weekly Advocate*.

Russwurm traveled to the colony of LIBERIA, founded by the AMERICAN COLONIZATION SOCIETY, in 1829. He edited the *Liberia Herald* from 1830 to 1835, eventually resigning his editorship in protest against efforts by the American Colonization Society to control the paper. Russwurm served in a number of official capacities while in Liberia, including superintendent of schools and colonial secretary. As governor of the province of Maryland, he was the first black person to hold such a position in the colony.

Bayard Rustin (left) helps James Baldwin attach an armband commemorating the Birmingham children's crusade as they prepare for a New York City rally to protest police brutality in Alabama. *(AP/Wide World Photos)*

Rustin, Bayard (March 17, 1910, West Chester, Pennsylvania—August 24, 1987, New York, New York): CIVIL RIGHTS activist. Rustin was a primary organizer of the 1963 MARCH ON WASHINGTON, and he drew up founding plans for the SOUTHERN CHRISTIAN LEADERSHIP CONFERENCE (SCLC). Rustin was a committed worker for civil rights and a strong believer in pacifism. He believed in integration and favored multicultural coalitions in social and political organizing. More specifically, Rustin favored a coalition made up of the African American community, white liberals, religious groups, and labor unions. Rustin's preference for pacifism, which was the foundation of the nonviolent strategies pursued by civil rights activists such as Martin Luther King, Jr., is rooted in his upbringing. Rustin was reared

by his grandparents, and his grandmother was a devout Quaker.

Rustin studied literature and history at Cheyney State and Wilberforce colleges, and by 1941 he had become a youth organizer for a projected march on Washington under the guidance of A. Philip RANDOLPH. This undoubtedly influenced his later strategy in organizing the 1963 march. In subsequent years, Rustin was involved in a number of causes, including efforts to restrict nuclear armaments and to support African independence movements. He was one of the early members of the CONGRESS OF RACIAL EQUALITY and the Fellowship of Reconciliation. He was one of the first to participate in FREEDOM RIDES in the South in an attempt to enforce desegregation rulings. During WORLD WAR II, he was imprisoned for more than two years as a conscientious objector.

Rustin began his affiliation with Martin Luther KING, Jr., and the SCLC in 1955, serving as a special assistant to King until 1960. The 1960's ushered in a troubling time for Rustin. His intense belief in nonviolence was put to the test by an increasing militancy among African American youth, who were becoming dissatisfied with the nonviolent strategy favored by the SCLC and traditional civil rights activists. Rustin continued to preach nonviolence and spoke at several gatherings, many in cities that were in the throes of urban riots. Sometimes, he was booed and hooted off the stage. Rustin then began to focus his efforts on economic platforms and proposals designed to improve conditions for the poor and underprivileged of all races. From 1966 to 1979, he served as president of the A. Philip Randolph Institute, where he was able to utilize his organizational skills and belief in a coalition type of political action to solve political, social, and economic problems. He was cochair of the institute from 1979 until his death.

S

Salem, Peter (1750, Framingham, Massachusetts—August 16, 1816, Framingham, Massachusetts): AMERICAN REVOLUTION war hero. Salem was among the five thousand African Americans who served in the Revolutionary War. He had been a slave in Framingham but was freed so that he could serve in the Continental army. Only freed blacks were allowed to serve.

Salem was a member of the First Massachusetts Regiment, one of the more disciplined units of the Continental army. He participated in early battles at Lexington, Concord, and Bunker Hill. He is credited with firing the shot that killed British General John Pitcairn at Bunker Hill on June 17, 1775. He received a special commendation for this act from the Massachusetts General Court. Salem continued to serve in the Continental army until hostilities ended in 1783. He settled in Leicester, Massachusetts, and took up the trade of basketweaving. He eventually returned to his native city.

Salem is pictured in John Trumbull's famous painting, "Battle of Bunker's Hill." A small section of that painting, including Salem's likeness, was used on the commemorative six-cent postage stamp issued in memory of Trumbull in 1968.

Sampson, Edith (October 13, 1901, Pittsburgh, Pennsylvania—1979): JUDGE and diplomat. Sampson became, in 1927, the first woman to receive an LL.M. degree from Loyola University of CHICAGO, ILLINOIS. She also was, in 1950, the first African American to be appointed as a member of the U.S. delegation to the United Nations. Before being appointed as an assistant state's attorney in 1947, she estab-

Edith Sampson, the first African American woman to be elected as a judge. *(AP/Wide World Photos)*

lished a private law practice and served on the Cook County, Illinois, juvenile court. She served as a judge on Chicago's municipal court before becoming the first African American woman to be elected as a judge in 1964. She served as an associate judge of the Circuit Court of Cook County.

Sanchez, Sonia (Wilsonia Driver; b. September 9, 1934, Birmingham, Alabama): Poet, playwright, and educator. Sanchez is one of the major poets to arise from the Black Arts movement of the 1960's. Her strong voice and political commitment helped to define that movement.

2205

Poet Sonia Sanchez, addressing a panel of the Congressional Black Caucus. (© Roy Lewis Archives)

Sanchez's mother, Lena, died when Sonia was one, and Sonia lived with various relatives as a child. When she was nine, she moved with her father, Wilson Driver, to HARLEM, New York. After she received her B.A. degree in 1955 from Hunter College, she studied poetry at New York University with Louise Bogan. From a shy ALABAMA girl who stuttered, she became one of the most forceful voices of the "second black renaissance" of the 1960's and 1970's.

Her early books of poetry—*Homecoming* (1969), *We a BaddDDD People* (1970), and *It's a New Day: Poems for Young Brothas and Sistuhs* (1971)—were all published by Dudley Randall's Broadside Press of DETROIT, MICHIGAN, the most influential publisher of African American poetry during the period. Influenced by the chiding voice of MALCOLM X, her early poems are characterized by a militant critique of America and the promotion of alternative black values. She experimented with words, spellings, and typographical conventions; used dialect and profanity; and in public readings developed a dramatic style that in-

cluded screams, whimpers, and chants. Like other African American poets of the period, her goal was to make her work accessible to the young black masses who were impatient with intellectual exercises.

Sanchez matched her militant words with actions. She was part of movements to liberate AFRICA, to institute BLACK STUDIES programs in universities, and to influence nuclear disarmament. She befriended Etheridge Knight, who was imprisoned on drug charges, and later married him. The mother of three children, she wrote children's books such as *The Adventures of Fathead, Smallhead, and Squarehead* (1973) and *A Sound Investment and Other Stories* (1980) to educate children in a balanced and healthy way.

Sanchez not only fought against racism but also opposed sexism. In 1972 she joined the NATION OF ISLAM, but she objected to what she regarded as sexism within the organization. In the poetry volume *A Blues Book for Blue Black Magical Women* (1973), she criticized American society's indifference to the needs of black women. In her most popular play, *Sister Son/ji* (pb. 1969), she noted the contradiction of the black revolutionary movement's backward attitudes toward women. She left the Nation of Islam in 1975.

Sanchez taught at numerous universities, including San Francisco State College (1967-1969), the University of Pittsburgh (1969-1970), Rutgers University (1970-1971), Manhattan Community College (1971-1973), Amherst College (1972-1975), the University of Pennsylvania (1976-1977), and Temple University. Her poetry volume *homegirls & handgrenades* (1984) won the American Book Award in 1985. Later books of poetry include *Under a Soprano Sky* (1987), *Wounded in the House of a Friend* (1995), and *Like the Singing Coming Off the Drums: Love Poems* (1998). Sanchez also continued to write drama; her *Black Cats Back and Uneasy Landings* was produced in 1995. Her work has been widely anthologized, appearing in collections ranging from *Black Fire: An Anthology of Afro-American Writing* (1968) to *Every Shut Eye Ain't Asleep: An Anthology of Poetry by African Americans Since 1945* (1994) and *Celebrating America: A Collection of Poems and Images of the American Spirit* (1994).

See also: Black feminism; Literature; Women.

Santería: Afro-Cuban RELIGION imported to the United States by Cuban immigrants. Santería, or "way of the saints," arose among Afro-Cubans. Santería consists of traditions brought by slaves imported from West Africa to the island of CUBA in the late eighteenth and early nineteenth centuries.

These newcomers blended their native African mythology, rituals, and practices with some features of Spanish ROMAN CATHOLIC churches. Ultimately, a variety of autonomous but closely related Santería cults developed. They differed according to the particular West African ethnic background of participants, the largest group being the YORUBA of Nigeria (this branch is called Lecumí in Cuba).

Santería became established in various ethnic communities of the United States, brought by the waves of Cuban immigration since the Fidel Castro's communist revolution took power in 1959. In the United States it has attracted converts among Latin Americans, African Americans, and some whites. Because of common misrepresentations by outsiders of this faith and confusion with the kindred syncretic religion of VOODOO, some Santería followers prefer other terms for their religion, such as Orisha, Lecumí, *la regla de orisha* (or-der of the orishas), or *la religión*.

The link between Catholicism and African religion was possible because of a similarity between the Yoruba pantheon of deities and the Catholic saints. This association is especially evident in the symbols used with each saint or spirit to represent the special area in which he or she exercises authority. Orishas are spirits of important deceased tribal chiefs or founders of tribes who serve as patron saints for the faithful. The spirits may be referred to either by the Spanish term *santos* (saints) or by the Yoruba word *orishas* (spirits). The spirits were often worshiped in the form of Catholic saints because of the belief that a saint (such as Saint Peter or Saint Barbara) and a particular orisha are manifestations of the same entity. This link with Catholicism probably helped keep endangered African traditions alive under a protective cover.

Homes of devotees may display plaster statuettes of these saint/spirits or colored prints on the walls with candles burning in front of them. Santería rituals may vary widely, ranging from a close imitation of Roman Catholic rites to an emotionally charged atmosphere involving spirit possession. Singing, drum-

Santería altar in a New York City home. *(Allan Clear/Impact Visuals)*

ming, and hymn singing in Yoruba are common features of Santería meetings.

Priests and priestesses lead worshipers in practices such as animal sacrifice, divination of spirits, and spirit possession. The lives of cult followers are governed by an intimate relationship with one's patron saint or orisha. The leader of the congregation dispenses advice and charms, and conducts divination ceremonies that call forth spirits to determine the source and solution of problems in the lives of believers.

In the ethnic neighborhoods of communities such as Miami, Florida, where the religion is active, Santeros maintain retail shops called *botánicas* where followers can purchase items such as healing herbs and cult statues or figurines. It appears that by the year 2000, the number of followers of Santería in the United States equaled or outnumbered those in Cuba.

—*David A. Crain*

Satcher, David (b. March 2, 1941, Anniston, Alabama): Physician. After graduating Phi Beta Kappa from Morehouse College in 1963, Satcher completed his medical degree and a Ph.D. in cytogenics from the Case Western Reserve School of Medicine in 1970. He went on to serve as director of the King-Drew Medical Center in Los Angeles, California, from 1972 to 1975, and as associate director of the King-Drew Sickle Cell Center from 1973 to 1975. Later, he served as a professor and chairman of the Department of Community Medicine and Family Practice at Morehouse College from 1979 to 1982. In 1982 he was named president of Meharry Medical College in Nashville, Tennessee,

and chief executive officer of Hubbard Hospital. Satcher came to national attention in January of 1994, when he became the first African American director of the Centers for Disease Control and Prevention (CDC), an Atlanta-based federal agency. A respected physician, Satcher also served as an adviser to Hillary Rodham Clinton's task force on health care reform.

See also: Health; Medicine; Meharry Medical School.

Savage, Augusta (February 29, 1892, Green Cove Springs, Florida—March 26, 1962, New York, New York): Sculptor and teacher. Savage trained in New York and Paris despite the obstacles of her race and POVERTY. She gained fame for her exploration of black subjects in works such as *Gamin* (1929), *Woman of Martinique* (1932), and *The Harp* (1939). She also was active for decades as a teacher in private classes and community studios, especially under the Works Progress Administration. The Schomburg Center exhibited her works in 1988 and 1989.

See also: Sculptors.

Surgeon General David Satcher (left) with Morehouse School of Medicine president Louis Sullivan in November, 1999. *(AP/Wide World Photos)*

Savage, Gus (b. October 30, 1925, Detroit, Michigan): U.S. representative from ILLINOIS. Augustus F. "Gus" Savage was born in DETROIT, but his family moved to Chicago when he was young and he graduated from high school there in 1943. He entered the Army after graduation and served as a corporal until he was discharged in 1946. When he returned to CHICAGO, Savage studied at Roosevelt University and received his bachelor's degree in 1951. He attended Chicago-Kent College of Law from 1952 to 1953 and began his career in journalism in 1954. Savage became editor and owner of Citizen Newspapers, a chain of independent weekly community papers, in 1965.

Congressman Gus Savage during his 1982 reelection campaign. *(AP/ Wide World Photos)*

Savage's first brush with politics came in 1948, when he served as an organizer for former Vice President Henry Wallace's Progressive Party. Savage was active in the CIVIL RIGHTS movement, fighting against discrimination in housing, employment, and labor unions. In the 1960's, he served as chairman of Chicago's South End Voters Conference and of Protest at the Polls and was campaign manager for the Midwest League of Negro Voters.

Determined to break the stranglehold of Chicago's DEMOCRATIC PARTY machine, Savage ran against incumbent William T. Murphy in the 1968 primary for Illinois's Third Congressional District seat, but he was unsuccessful in this race. When Morgan F. Murphy announced his retirement in 1979, Savage declared his candidacy for the Second Congressional District seat. He won the primary against three opponents and then went on to win the general election in a landslide victory.

Savage took his seat on January 3, 1981. He was appointed as a member of the House Committee on Public Works and Transportation, of which he later became chairman. He also was appointed to serve on the House Subcommittee on Economic Development and the House Committee on Small Business. He was instrumental in the passage of an amendment to the National Defense Authorization Act for Fiscal Year 1987 that imposed a set-aside program on federal defense contracts, enabling minority-owned businesses and HISTORICALLY BLACK COLLEGES and universities to compete for more than twenty-five billion dollars in military procurement contracts and defense research. Savage served in the House until January, 1993.

See also: Congress members; Politics and government.

Savoy Ballroom: NEW YORK CITY dance ballroom. The Savoy was opened on March 12, 1926, by Moe Gale (Moses Galewski), Charles Galewski, and a HARLEM, New York, businessman named Charles Buchanan. Buchanan

Dancers at the Savoy Ballroom in 1953. *(AP/Wide World Photos)*

foreign languages, including Greek, Latin, Hebrew, and Sanskrit, and was known as a scholar of languages. He joined the faculty at Wilberforce University after serving as president of a small denominational college in South Carolina. Scarborough became president of Wilberforce in 1908 and retired in 1920.

See also: Intellectuals and scholars.

Scat singing: Musical style. Scat is said to have been created by Louis ARMSTRONG after he dropped his lyric sheet while recording "Heebie Jeebies" in 1926. It is a vocal style in which a singer imitates any typical JAZZ instrument while sing-

served as the ballroom's manager. Occupying the second floor of a building that extended for a whole block between 140th and 141st streets, the Savoy, with its ten thousand square foot dance floor and retractable stage, was billed as the world's most beautiful ballroom. The Savoy rapidly became the most popular dance spot in Harlem, and many of the 1920's and 1930's dance crazes originated in that room. The ballroom's "battle of the bands" nights were a hit with patrons. It was not until well into the 1950's that the Savoy went into decline. Many of the biggest stars of the 1930's and 1940's had long associations with the Savoy, including Chick WEBB, Ella FITZGER-ALD, Al Cooper's Savoy Sultans, Erskine Hawkins, and Benny CARTER.

See also: Apollo Theater; Minton's Playhouse.

Scarborough, William Sanders (February 16, 1852, Macon, Georgia—September 9, 1926, Wilberforce, Georgia): Educator. Scarborough learned to read and write as a child, even though he was a slave. He studied numerous

Ella Fitzgerald, seen here singing in 1987, was known as the Queen of Scat. *(AP/Wide World Photos)*

ing nonsensical improvised syllables to the rhythm of the music. Since its inception, scat singing has been regarded as an art form in the jazz world, used by vocalists ranging from Ella FITZGERALD to Al Jarreau.

Schomburg, Arthur (January 24, 1874, San Juan, Puerto Rico—June 10, 1938, New York, New York): Librarian and bibliophile. Known as a world-class collector, Arthur Alfonso Schomburg tracked down and gathered a significant collection of African American memorabilia and created a global research center that continues his work.

The son of a German father and a West Indian mother, Schomburg grew up in PUERTO RICO. He migrated to NEW YORK CITY in 1891 and worked in the mail room at Bankers Trust Company from 1906 to 1929. Schomburg began collecting books, manuscripts, and works of art on African and African American history and culture in 1910. His collection became an invaluable resource to both historians and HARLEM RENAISSANCE artists.

In 1911 Schomburg cofounded the Negro Society for Historical Research, an archival institute that published several important papers on African American history. Three years later, he was inducted into, and later presided over, the AMERICAN NEGRO ACADEMY, which championed African American history and battled racism. The keystone of Schomburg's work was the world-renowned African American collection that he built over a period of fifteen years. Comprising thousands of SLAVE NARRATIVES, manuscripts, rare books, journals, artwork, and other pieces of African American history, Schomburg's collection was presented to the New York Public Library in 1926. The collection was curated by Schomburg between 1932 and 1938 and eventually became housed in the library in the SCHOMBURG CENTER FOR RESEARCH IN BLACK CULTURE. It is the largest and most important sin-

gle collection of African American cultural materials in the world.

—*Alvin K. Benson*

See also: Black History Month; Historiography; Moorland-Spingarn Research Center; Visual arts.

Schomburg Center for Research in Black Culture: Research library dedicated to the cultural and historical aspects of African-descended people in the African diaspora and AFRICA. Located on Malcolm X Boulevard and 135th Street in HARLEM, New York, the center collects and preserves books, art objects, photographs, prints, films, newspapers, periodicals, sheet and recorded music, video and audio tapes, and manuscripts. The library is open to the public and offers on-site access to items and reference help.

The center was named for Arthur SCHOMBURG, a mostly self-educated Puerto Rican of African descent. Schomburg moved to NEW YORK CITY as a young adult, living in Harlem during the HARLEM RENAISSANCE. He became well known in the community, serving as grand secretary of the all-black Prince Hall Masons Grand Lodge of the State of New York and as president of the AMERICAN NEGRO ACADEMY. Schomburg began collecting all sorts of books, clippings, art works, magazines, pamphlets, and other items relating to people of African descent, focusing on racial politics and cultural heritage.

Schomburg's goal was to document and make known the contributions of Africans and people of African descent and to show their influences on world history. He also hoped to instill pride in the African American community. Inside his home, Schomburg's personal collection grew to the size of ten thousand objects. In 1926 the New York Public Library purchased his collection, placing it in the 135th Street branch. Schomburg curated the collection from 1932 to 1938; in 1940 the collection was named for him. In 1972 the Schomburg Center became a research branch of the New York Public Library system and was given its full title.

Schomburg experienced frustrations. As a Puerto Rican, he sought to bring black Latino concerns to the forefront, an approach that was not highly favored by African American intellectuals. In addition, his humble, self-taught background set him apart from more wealthy, formally educated black intellectuals. Schomburg believed that he did not receive adequate respect or recognition for his work. The Schomburg Center, however, is testament to the continuing benefit of his work.

By the year 2000, the collection boasted more than five million items and was one of the few centers of its kind in the world and was serving the nearby community as well as visitors and scholars from overseas. The center houses five collections: art and artifacts; general research and reference; manuscripts, archives, and rare books; a moving image and recorded sound collection; and a photographs and prints collection.

In addition, the Schomburg Center offers a large array of performances and presentations. On-site exhibits feature literary and fine arts personalities and their works. Programming includes plays, lectures, dance, poetry, discussions, films, and book presentations. Online exhibits focus on topics such as the history of Harlem and provide accompanying study guides for educators. Digital Schomburg is a full-text electronic collection of African- and African diaspora-related books.

—*Michelle C. K. McKowen*

See also: African cultural transformations; African heritage; Diaspora, African; Museum programs.

Suggested Readings:

The Legacy of Arthur A. Schomburg: A Celebration of the Past, a Vision for the Future. New York: New York Public Library, 1986.

Pineiro de Rivera, Flor. *Arthur A. Schomburg: A Puerto Rican's Quest for His Black Heritage—His Writings.* San Juan, Puerto Rico: Centro de Estudios Avanzados de Puerto Rico y el Caribe, 1989.

Sinnette, Elinor Des Verney. *Arthur Alfonso Schomburg, Black Bibliophile and Collector: A Biography.* New York: New York Public Library, 1988.

Schuyler, George S. (February 25, 1895, Providence, Rhode Island—August 31, 1977, New York, New York): Writer. A journalist and essayist, George Samuel Schuyler was also a brilliant, iconoclastic satirist. Arguably the most important black newspaperman in the first half of the twentieth century, Schuyler wrote one brilliant satirical novel but ended his life as an often unpopular, extremely conservative voice.

Schuyler grew up in a middle-class family in Syracuse, New York. After service in the army from 1912 to 1920, he arrived in NEW YORK CITY as a young journalist just in time to observe and participate in the HARLEM RENAISSANCE. In 1924 he began a forty-two-year career (in New York) with the PITTSBURGH COURIER, one of the two most widely read African American newspapers. Schuyler wrote the *Pittsburgh Courier*'s editorials, contributed a wide-ranging weekly column, *Views and Reviews*, and, especially in the 1930's, filled many of its pages with serialized fiction.

Two of Schuyler's early works remain his best known. In true contrarian fashion, he attacked the Harlem Renaissance "vogue of the Negro" in a caustic essay, "The Negro-Art Hokum" (1926). He went so far as to deny the possibility of a distinctively African American art or LITERATURE. Against white racist assertions of fundamental differences between races—which, Schuyler argued, always end in the notion "that the blackamoor is inferior"—he insisted that "the Aframerican is merely a lampblacked Anglo-Saxon"—"your American Negro is just plain American." It is an extreme stand and is in some ways uncharacteristic of Schuyler.

Schuyler's most impressive work is the bitterly hilarious novel *Black No More* (1931), an American classic and the most powerful African American satire before the work of Ishmael REED. A story of a miraculous process that physically changes black people into white people, the novel sees clearly the idiocy of a worldview based on skin color and assigning all positive values to lighter shades. It brutally satirizes both the KU KLUX KLAN and black leaders from Marcus GARVEY (named "Santop Licorice") to W. E. B. DU BOIS ("Dr. Shakespeare Agamemnon Beard"). *Black No More* is intellectually uncompromising, stylistically astringent, and sometimes designed to shock; it is also memorably funny in depicting the black comedy that the satirist sees beneath the national tragedy of the American racial dilemma.

During the 1930's, Schuyler wrote—mostly under pseudonyms—more than four hundred stories and serial installments for the *Pittsburgh Courier* and other papers. The most important of his serials are "The Ethiopian Murder Mystery" (1935-1936), "The Black Internationale" (1936-1937), "Black Empire" (1937-1938), and "Revolt in Ethiopia" (1938-1939). These four serials are fantasies involving SCIENCE FICTION and the freeing of Africa from colonialism by brilliant and single-minded African Americans. Though Schuyler claimed to disdain such popular fiction as "hokum and hack work of the purest vein," these stories show his own pan-Africanist leanings. Under the editorship of Marcus Garvey Papers editors R. Kent Rasmussen and Robert A. Hill, the four serials were published in book form for the first time during the 1990's, in the Northeastern Library of Black Literature volumes *Black Empire* and *Ethiopian Stories*.

Schuyler's choice of a title for his 1966 autobiography summed up how radically his views had changed since the 1930's. *(Arkent Archive)*

After WORLD WAR II Schuyler became increasingly conservative politically and fiercely anticommunist; he may even have been a member of the arch-conservative John Birch Society. In the 1960's, along with publishing his autobiography, *Black and Conservative* (1966), he attacked not only MALCOLM X but also the CIVIL RIGHTS movement in general and Martin Luther KING, Jr.

—*George F. Bagby*

Schuyler, Philippa Duke (August 2, 1931, Harlem, New York—May 9, 1967, near Da Nang, Vietnam): Pianist, composer, and journalist. Schuyler was the daughter of well-known black journalist George S. SCHUYLER and white artist and writer Jody Cogdell. As a

Philippa Schuyler in 1963. *(AP/Wide World Photos)*

child she became nationally known as a musical prodigy, but as she grew too old to be considered a prodigy, the American public lost interest in her talent. She turned to performing around the world and developed new skills. Never settling in any one country, she spent most of her life traveling. She wrote four books of nonfiction and worked as a journalist. While covering the end of the VIETNAM WAR for the *Manchester Union Leader* she died in a helicopter crash. Her full story is told in Kathryn Talalay's *Composition in Black and White: The Life of Philippa Schuyler* (1995).

Science and technology: Most anthropologists agree that modern humans have early roots on the African continent. From AFRICA and the Middle East, civilization began and advanced to other continents. According to Herodotus and Homer, civilization, science, and technical skills in ancient Egypt and Ethiopia were well advanced for the period.

Imhotep, an Egyptian who lived about five thousand years ago, is often cited as the first scientist and physician. Modern physicians can trace their roots from him through Hippocrates and Asclepiades, Greek physicians who followed about twenty-five hundred years behind Imhotep.

Some of the scientific knowledge contributed by the ancient Greeks and Romans stemmed from earlier learning in Ethiopia, Egypt, and West Africa. This knowledge passed from the African countries to Europe, where it was extended.

There are numerous examples of early African science that matched that of early Europe. The Haya people of present Tanzania, for example, smelted iron. Africans on the west shore of Lake Victoria, possibly as early as the first century C.E., made carbon steel. In 300 B.C.E. the people of Kenya made an astronomical observatory, the African equivalent of Stonehenge, at a place called Namoratunga. This tradition of scientific achievement continued as Africans were taken as slaves to the New World.

Slave Inventors
Enslavement hampered much of the advancement of African Americans, who had, for example, brought from Africa knowledge of the medicinal value of herbs. Slave doctors and nurses using herbs helped their own families and other slaves, and sometimes were called on to heal the master's family. Slaves were restricted in communicating their knowledge to each other, and white owners often took credit for the knowledge. One medical practitioner, a slave named Papan, was so successful in the treatment of skin problems and venereal disease that he was freed. Another slave, named Caesar, devised a formula to treat rattlesnake bites. He too was freed to practice medicine.

Formal EDUCATION of slaves was minimal. Slaves were forbidden to learn to read and write, but some masters and other whites taught slaves these skills. Although few were formally educated, slaves nevertheless were very inventive, out of a practical need to reduce labor effort. When a slave did piece together an invention, the patent process did not protect his or her rights to it. Since slaves were not considered to be people, they could not acquire patents. Even FREE BLACKS were restricted in their protection through patents. One account describes, for example, slaves developing a machine similar to the cotton gin. The story claims that Eli Whitney discovered their invention, improved upon it, and patented it in his name.

Not all early white Americans took such credit for their slaves' inventions. For example, Jo Anderson, Cyrus McCormick's slave, has been credited with offering suggestions for improving McCormick's mechanical reaper. McCormick's company, which became International Harvester, did not forget Anderson's contribution. Possibly in recognition, it maintained a nondiscriminatory hiring policy.

Craft Training

Many early African American INVENTORS came from the ranks of skilled craftspeople. In the late 1700's, the centers for African American craftsmanship were Charleston, SOUTH CAROLINA, and NEW ORLEANS, LOUISIANA, in the South and PHILADELPHIA, PENNSYLVANIA, NEW YORK, NEW YORK, and BOSTON, MASSACHUSETTS, in the North. In the 1700's and 1800's, African Americans were found in nearly every craft, even though free African Americans found it difficult to gain craft skills. Until the 1800's, the apprenticeship system was the primary means by which craft work-

Eli Whitney's invention of the cotton gin revolutionized cotton production in the South in the early nineteenth century and had the ironic result of prolonging the life of slavery. Some scholars argue that Whitney got the idea for his gin from machinery invented by slaves. *(Associated Publishers, Inc.)*

ers learned their trade. It was not easy for many young men and women to obtain apprenticeships, but it was particularly hard for African Americans. The apprenticeship positions in the most prestigious and remunerative crafts such as printing, silversmithing, and goldsmithing also were those least accessible to African Americans. Less remunerative crafts such as tailoring and shoemaking were easier for African Americans to enter.

Rather than hiring themselves out for wages, craftspeople who invented new devices or discovered innovative techniques that improved the quality of their products or reduced the cost of producing them often went into business for themselves. This posed the problem of financing a business, as many crafts required a large capital outlay. Financing presented further difficulties for African Americans because of discrimination in financial markets. Once established, however, African American artisans and craftspeople tended to rise to positions of political and social leadership in the African American, and sometimes in the mainstream, community.

Many slaves found ways to hire out their services. With the money they earned, they bought their freedom. John Parker (1827-1900) was an inventor who came from the ranks of hired-out slaves. He was a craftsman who was able to buy his own freedom and use the skills he learned while a slave to start a successful business. Parker began working in the iron foundries of Mobile, ALABAMA, where he apprenticed as an iron molder. He earned enough to purchase his freedom for $1,800. He later escorted more than one thousand slaves to freedom on the UNDERGROUND RAILROAD. In 1884 Parker invented the tobacco screw press. His company stayed in operation until World War I.

Combating Racism
African American inventors were used as particularly potent propaganda in abolitionist attacks on SLAVERY. White people of the time believed that African Americans displayed virtuosity in music and dance and had such gifts as storytelling and oratory. Some African Americans had made achievements in the mechanical arts and even in some of the more refined handicrafts. Many white people believed, however, that African Americans were largely incapable of creative and inventive thought. This belief helped justify keeping slaves and free blacks in inferior social positions.

To the abolitionists, African American inventors were prized, as their existence would tear down this racist belief system and thereby eliminate one justification for slavery. Editors of abolitionist newspapers advertised for African American inventors so that they could make the point that black people could be just as creative as whites. Fairs and institutes organized by African Americans also promoted the accomplishments of black inventors. One of the earliest of these fairs, the Colored American Institute for the Promotion of Mechanical Arts and Sciences, was held in Philadelphia on April 12, 1851. Abolitionist newspapers lauded such fairs as glimpses of the future achievements of African Americans once they had been freed from slavery.

In the 1800's, it was possible for a free African American to obtain a patent. The first U.S. patent issued to an African American probably went to Henry BLAIR in 1834 for his seed planter. Thomas Jennings, who invented a dry cleaning process in 1821, may have received a atent, but his claim to be the first black patent holder is less clear. One reason for confusion regarding African American patents is that the "race" of inventors was generally not recorded. Moreover, U.S. Patent Office policy allowed only citizens to obtain patents. Although African Americans were not considered citizens by the Patent Office, some African Americans obtained patents before the CIVIL WAR.

Opportunities and Setbacks for Inventors

Some free African Americans emigrated to the western territories, where there often were more opportunities for those who were innovative and self-sufficient. An excellent example was George Peake (1722-1827), a native of Maryland who settled in Cleveland, Ohio. Peake patented a stone hand-mill that relieved pioneer families of labor intensive work involved in producing fine ground meal. Peake's family became one of the wealthiest in the region.

African Americans were prominent as maritime inventors. By 1840 there were about six thousand African American seamen. African Americans were especially prominent in whaling. About three thousand were part of whaling crews, many of which operated out of New Bedford, MASSACHUSETTS. Black whalers often were discriminated against in job category and wages, but even so, a few did become captains or mates of whaling vessels. The whaling ship *Loper*, for example, had a black captain, was navigated by African Americans, and had an almost entirely black crew.

The whaling industry was revolutionized by Lewis Temple, a New Bedford blacksmith who invented the toggle harpoon in the 1840's. This new commercial harpoon represented a qualitative improvement over other harpoons of the time. Temple's harpoon employed a toggle bar that locked into the whale, not allowing it to slip out. The device was used by prehistoric whale hunters, but the technology had been lost. Temple rediscovered the toggle harpoon but never patented it, so other blacksmiths could make them. Had Temple patented his invention, he would have been wealthy.

Reconstruction Inventors

During RECONSTRUCTION, the creativity of African Americans was recognized in patent awards. The U.S. Patent Act of 1790 was designed to promote innovation by making detailed information about inventions available to the public and by protecting inventors from unauthorized use of their inventions. Free black inventors could legally receive patent letters before the CIVIL WAR, but few actually received them. Discrimination within the Patent Office and the cost of filing for a patent discouraged many inventors. Emancipation ended any legal justification for discrimination, encouraging black inventors to protect their ideas through patents.

By 1895 the U.S. Patent Office was able to advertise a special exhibit of inventions patented by African Americans. Agricultural implements, devices for easing domestic chores, and devices related to the railroad industry were common. By 1900, even though 80 percent of African American adults were illiterate, African Americans had been awarded several hundred patents. These included patents for assorted equipment to lubricate machinery by Elijah McCoy (1872), a shoe lasting machine by Jan MATZELIGER (1883), a machine for making paper bags by William Purvis (1884), a railroad telegraph by Granville WOODS (1888), and an automatic railroad car coupler by Andrew BEARD (1897).

Later Inventors

The flow of patent activity among African Americans increased during the twentieth century. One of the more notable black inventors in the early part of the century was Garrett A. MORGAN. However, the world paid little attention to Morgan's inventions, which included a gas mask. Morgan won several awards for that invention but did not gain widespread recognition until 1916, when he and three volunteers wore his gas masks to rescue several workers trapped in a tunnel beneath Lake Erie. Morgan also invented an automatic traffic signal that General Electric later purchased from him.

Black women also began contributing more to the rich history of invention. Julia

Hammonds received a patent in 1896 for a device to hold yarn while knitting. Sarah E. GOODE patented a folding cabinet in 1885. Beatrice Kenner of Charlotte, North Carolina, is the first black woman to obtain five patents, including licensing rights for a carrier attachment for invalid walkers in 1976 and for a back washer mounted on the wall of a shower or bathtub in 1987.

African American Scientists

In the years of slavery and Reconstruction, the contributions of African American inventors were better known than those of African American scientists. Inventors made devices for practical daily needs, whereas there were few black scientists, and their work rarely touched daily lives. Into the twentieth century, the contributions and numbers of black American scientists grew. George Washington CARVER, an agricultural scientist, was the first to

George Washington Carver's research in agriculture enriched the lives of countless farmers and sharecroppers. *(National Archives)*

receive widespread recognition. African American scientists later contributed to the development of such important medical advances as open-heart surgery and cortisone. Black scientists have contributed to advances in all branches of science.

One of the outstanding black scientists in the medical field was Charles R. DREW. Drew disseminated information about the means of storing blood plasma for blood transfusions and preserving it for long periods of time. Drew graduated from medical school at McGill University in Canada with degrees in medicine and surgery. During his residency in surgery, he saw patients die because of insufficient blood supplies for transfusions. After his residency, he taught at HOWARD UNIVERSITY in Washington, D.C. He took leave to work during WORLD WAR II as medical director of the Blood for Britain program. As medical director, he studied blood more carefully and found ways to preserve blood plasma. This knowledge saved countless lives, as it made blood transfusions much more practical. Although Drew made no discoveries of his own, his synthesis and application of existing knowledge revolutionized medicine. His plans for blood storage became the model for blood banks around the world.

In 1876 Edward Bouchet received a doctorate in physics. Although he was a graduate of Yale University and the first African American member of Phi Beta Kappa, the only job he could find was teaching high school science. Prior to 1900, a total of only thirteen science doctorates were awarded to African Americans. The larger white universities that offered doctorates slowly began accepting black candidates for advanced degrees. By 1943 African Americans had earned 130 science doctorates.

The early black doctorate holders in science led a lonely existence. Most became professors at African American colleges, as industry and laboratories discriminated against them. In addition, many wanted to improve the science education offered at the HISTORICALLY BLACK COLLEGES. World War II presented more opportunities for work in laboratories and institutions with government contracts.

Education of Black Scientists

Howard University was founded by the FREEDMEN'S BUREAU in 1867 at the urging of Oliver Otis Howard. Howard, a general in the Civil War, became interested in the fate of African Americans freed by the EMANCIPATION PROCLAMATION. The university named for him, although it originally was open to students of all races, gradually attracted a primarily black student population. As one of the first colleges to accept black students, it pioneered in all areas of education, including scientific training. Soon, other schools opened. TUSKEGEE INSTITUTE offered primarily industrial training in its early years, but George Washington Carver taught there. FISK UNIVERSITY opened its MEHARRY MEDICAL SCHOOL in 1876.

By 1972 an estimated 850 African Americans had earned doctorates in the natural sciences. The once racially segregated universities of the South provided significant numbers of these degrees. Even so, African Americans held only about 1 percent of American science doctorates at that time.

The small number of black scientists with advanced degrees makes it unrealistic to expect enormous scientific accomplishments from the group as a whole. Approximately 75 percent of all African American science doctorate holders were employed in the early 1990's by predominantly black colleges and universities. These schools generally offered fewer opportunities for serious scientific research. The most notable contribution made by African American science doctorate holders, therefore, has been in teaching the sciences at predominantly black institutions of higher learning. By the 1990's, about three-fourths of all black science doctorate holders

had received their undergraduate training at these institutions.

Black college students began taking a greater interest in the sciences, as reflected in rising numbers of undergraduates pursuing science majors and African Americans entering graduate schools in scientific fields. Colleges and universities, including historically black ones, responded by extending curricular offerings in science and technology. Increasing numbers of black science graduates are choosing careers in science and technology in the corporate world, but many choose to stay in academia as professors or administrators, offering role models for the next generation of science students. Those outside academia have played important roles in the development of solid state electronics, high-powered laser technology, hypersonic flight, particle science, and many other fields. Black scientists and engineers are integral parts of the National Aeronautics and Space Administration (NASA) as well.

African Americans with NASA

Perhaps nowhere are the achievements of African American scientists more visible to the public than in NASA. The black scientists and engineers employed by NASA have made significant contributions in both managerial and research positions. Notable advances in engineering include those of Robert E. Shurney, who designed tires for the *Apollo* moon exploration vehicle. The "moon buggy" was used by astronauts to explore the lunar landscape beyond the landing craft. He also designed commodes used on the Skylab space laboratory and on the space shuttles. George CARRUTHERS designed an ultraviolet camera and spectrograph that was placed aboard Apollo 16 to determine the extent and composition of Earth's upper atmosphere. Carruthers received the NASA Exceptional Scientific Achievement medal for his work.

Perhaps the most visible of the African

American scientists with NASA are the astronauts who have flown on the space shuttle. Guion S. BLUFORD, Jr., was the first African American to fly in space, in August, 1983. He was a mission specialist whose primary responsibility was to deploy a satellite from the space shuttle *Challenger*'s cargo bay. His second mission was a cooperative mission with the Germans. Ronald E. MCNAIR was the second African American to fly on a space shuttle. He was a mission specialist on shuttle Mission 41-B, helping to launch satellites from the shuttle cargo bay. McNair was also one of the astronaut cinematographers for the production *The Space Shuttle: An American Adventure*, which won a gold medal in the International Film Competition in 1985. McNair's next mission was the ill-fated flight of *Challenger* in 1986, in which the shuttle exploded shortly after takeoff. Charles F. Bolden, Jr., and Frederick D. GREGORY also have been selected as space shuttle pilots. Gregory invented a throttle controller that can be operated with one hand.

Outlook in the Year 2000

Despite the relatively few African American science doctorate holders and the relative lack of research emphasis at black colleges and universities, noteworthy achievements have been made, and the future looks brighter. In the latter part of the twentieth century, the advances of science and the methods used in scientific research began to obscure the accomplishments of individual scientists and inventors. The individual inventor largely has been replaced by government and corporate research and development teams. Thus the individual, regardless of race, receives less recognition.

Still, there are individuals of all races with the creativity and ingenuity to invent new devices or make other discoveries. African American inventors have made significant contributions to the welfare of civilization, despite social and legal obstacles. For example,

the examination process of obtaining a patent, including government fees and an attorney, can take from two to five years and cost thousands of dollars.

To help African American scientists and inventors, the National Council of Black Engineers and Scientists formed in 1986. This group evolved from the Western Regional Black Engineering and Science Council, founded in 1977. After several years, it was determined that a national organization was needed to represent the interests of a broad sector of African American technical professionals. Thus, the National Council of Black Engineers and Scientists was founded. The group's main thrust is to help those who come from single-parent homes, economically depressed environments, or other disadvantaged backgrounds and are interested in entering technical fields.

African Americans have contributed greatly to the inventive and scientific realms of the nation, though they have had to overcome hardship. The National Technical Association, an organization of African American engineers and scientists, along with the National Patent Law Association, made a strong case for enshrinement of African Americans in the National Inventors Hall of Fame.

—*David R. Teske*

See also: Aviators and astronauts; Chemists; Engineers; Historically black colleges; Physicists.

Suggested Readings:

Goldsmith, Donald. *The Astronomers*. New York: St. Martin's Press, 1991.

Haber, Louis. *Black Pioneers of Science and Invention*. New York: Harcourt, Brace & World, 1970.

Harrison, Ira E., and Faye V. Harrison, eds. *African-American Pioneers in Anthropology*. Urbana: University of Illinois Press, 1999.

James, Portia P. *The Real McCoy: African American Invention and Innovation, 1619-1930*.

Washington, D.C.: Smithsonian Institution Press, 1989.

Jenkins, Edward S. *To Fathom More: African American Scientists and Inventors*. Lanham, Md.: University Press of America, 1996.

Kessler, James H., ed. *Distinguished African American Scientists of the Twentieth Century*. Phoenix, Ariz.: Oryx Press, 1996.

Massaquoi, Hans J. "Blacks in Science and Technology." *Ebony* (February, 1997): 172-175.

Pizer, Vernon. *Shortchanged by History: America's Neglected Innovators*. New York: G. P. Putnam's Sons, 1979.

Simmons, Vivian O. *Blacks in Science and Medicine*. New York: Hemisphere, 1990.

Science fiction: Although science fiction remains a genre dominated by white authors, in the second half of the twentieth century important African American authors and works dealing with African American issues began to appear.

Until the 1950's, American science fiction generally ignored African Americans or depicted them in stereotypical ways. Ray Bradbury wrote sympathetically about oppressed African Americans escaping to Mars in "Way in the Middle of the Air" (1950) and depicted a Mars controlled by African Americans who oppress whites in his satiric story "The Other Foot" (1951). That same year Mack Reynolds and Fredric Brown wrote about marriage between a modern white woman and a multiracial man from the future in "Dark Interlude." Mack Reynolds also produced a series of stories dealing with African Americans involved in the development of Africa in the near future, beginning with "Black Man's Burden" (1961).

With the development of "new wave" science fiction in the 1960's, an increasing number of stories began to depict African Americans in more realistic ways. Although many

First published in two newspaper serials during the 1930's, George S. Schuyler's novel *Black Empire* used the science fiction conventions of its era in a story about African Americans retaking Africa from its European colonizers. *(Arkent Archive)*

writers created futures in which race was no longer an issue, others dealt with racism more directly. In "The Day After the Day the Martians Came" (1967), Frederik Pohl compared prejudice against alien beings to prejudice against African Americans. *Black in Time* (1970) by John Jakes dealt with time travel and the Civil Rights movement. Richard A. Lupoff's novella "With the Bentfin Boomer Boys on Little Old New Alabama" (1972) was a satiric story of racial war in space in the far future. *Night of Power* (1985) by Spider Robinson was a realistic depiction of a revolution by African Americans in New York City in the near future.

Little science fiction was written by African Americans until the 1960's, when Samuel R. DELANY produced a series of acclaimed novels and stories. Delany went on to become one of the genre's most respected and controversial authors. In the 1970's Octavia E. BUTLER became the first African American woman to excel as a writer of science fiction. Her novels often depicted African American protagonists and dealt directly with racism.

In the 1980's Steven Barnes emerged as a popular and prolific African American writer of science fiction novels, often written in collaboration with noted white science fiction authors Larry Niven and Jerry Pournelle. In the 1990's new African American authors of science fiction continued to appear. One of the most promising was Nalo Hopkinson, winner of the Warner Aspect First Novel Contest for *Brown Girl in the Ring* (1998). In addition to science fiction, new African American authors won acclaim in the related fields of fantasy and horror, including Jewelle Gomez (*The Gilda Stories*, 1991); Gary Bowen (*Diary of a Vampire*, 1996); and Tananarive Due (*The Between*, 1994, and *My Soul to Keep*, 1997).

—*Rose Secrest*

Suggested Readings:

Johnson, Rebecca O. "African American Feminist Science Fiction." *Sojourner* 19, no. 6 (February, 1994): 12-14.

Moskowitz, Sam. "Civil Rights: Rockets to Green Pastures." In *Strange Horizons: The Spectrum of Science Fiction*. New York: Charles Scribner's Sons, 1976.

Scott, Bobby (b. April 30, 1947, Washington, D.C.): VIRGINIA politician. A graduate of Harvard University, Robert Cortez "Bobby" Scott went on to receive his law degree from Boston College Law School. Returning to his hometown of Newport News, Scott entered the private practice of law in 1973 before pursuing a political career.

In 1979 Scott was elected as a delegate to the Virginia state legislature. He later ran for office as a state senator and served in the Virginia State Senate from 1983 to 1993. Ever aware of the needs of his constituents, many of whom were employed in the area's naval shipyards, Scott worked to secure shipbuilding contracts for his district and focused his legislative priorities on the issues of health care, education, employment and job training, and crime prevention.

Scott was elected to the U.S. House of Representatives in 1992, serving the Third Congressional District of Virginia. He was one of fifteen African Americans (including Senator Carol Moseley BRAUN) who entered Congress as newly elected members in 1993. Scott was appointed to serve on the House Judiciary Committee and on two subcommittees: one on crime and the other on commercial and administrative law. He later served on the Education and Workforce Committees as well. He was reelected through the 1990's.

See also: Congress members; Politics and government.

Scott, Hazel (June 11, 1920, Port of Spain, Trinidad—October 2, 1981, New York, New York): Singer. She was brought to the United States at the age of four by her musician mother, who played in an all-woman band. Recognized as a prodigy, she studied at Juilliard, then appeared in Broadway musicals. She recorded many of her own BLUES and JAZZ compositions, playing the piano and accompanying small jazz groups. She had her own radio show and appeared in several films in the 1940's. She married Adam Clayton POWELL, Jr., in 1945 and divorced him in 1960.

Scottsboro cases: One of the greatest miscarriages of American justice involved nine young African American men who were arrested in Jackson County, ALABAMA, in 1931 and charged with raping two white women. The nine, tried and initially convicted in Scottsboro, were nicknamed by the press the "Scottsboro Boys." The nine were quickly convicted and sentenced to death, but that only began a fight for justice that was not to end for nearly twenty years.

Arrest and Initial Trial

On March 25, 1931, a freight train bound for Memphis carried a group of African American youths in search of new lives; they were Charlie Weems, Ozie Powell, Clarence Norris, Olen Montgomery, Willie Roberson, Haywood Patterson, Eugene Williams, and two brothers, Andrew and Leroy Wright. Their ages ranged from the early teens to the early twenties. Also on the train were a number of white male youths, as well as two young white women, Ruby Bates and Victoria Price.

At a train stop in Stevenson, Alabama, a white youth claimed a group of African Americans had tossed him and his companions from the train as it left the depot. A call to the sheriff of the next town was made; he was authorized to arrest all African Americans aboard the train. In Paint Rock, Alabama, the train was stopped; only nine African Americans, one white youth, and Bates and Price were found. As the African Americans were being questioned, the two women suddenly called a deputy over and said the nine African Americans had raped them. The white crowd that had gathered wanted an immediate LYNCHING, but the sheriff ordered the crowd dispersed and arrested the nine, who were taken to the county seat, Scottsboro, to be incar-

cerated. That night, a mob of more than two hundred white men gathered outside the jail and demanded the release of the nine so they could be hanged. The sheriff telephoned the governor, who then called in National Guard troops to keep the peace in Scottsboro.

On the morning of April 6, between five and ten thousand white spectators gathered in Scottsboro for the beginning of the trial. National Guard machine guns ringed the courthouse to keep the mob at bay. The trial itself was perfunctory; eight of the nine youths were convicted and sentenced to death, even though the testimony of Bates was shaky and that of Price was obviously embellished with lies. Further, the testimony of two doctors who had examined Bates and Price had established that neither woman had injuries consistent with gang rape. (The jury in Leroy Wright's case could not reach a decision, so the judge reluctantly declared a mistrial. Later, the charge was reinstated by the prosecutor.)

First Appeal

The battle for who would represent the nine was fought between the NATIONAL ASSOCIATION FOR THE ADVANCEMENT OF COLORED

Scottsboro defendant Clarence Norris (center) in court in April, 1933. *(National Archives)*

PEOPLE (NAACP) and the International Labor Defense (ILD), a COMMUNIST PARTY organization. The NAACP urged a cautious approach to the case, but the ILD succeeded in persuading the nine and their families that only a radical defense—one that could indict capitalism and racism—could possibly free them. The ILD consequently represented the nine, and the NAACP was forced to withdraw from active participation in the case.

Meanwhile, private investigators had uncovered evidence that both Bates and Price had worked as prostitutes in Chattanooga, Tennessee. This evidence was attacked by southern newspapers as slanderous; an appeal based upon the reports was denied. Shortly after these facts were made public, Bates disappeared.

The ILD prepared an appeal to the Alabama supreme court arguing that the nine had been unjustly convicted since they had not been given adequate legal representation, had not been convicted by a jury of their peers—since African Americans were automatically excluded from jury rolls in Jackson County—and had not been guaranteed an impartial jury, since it was obvious that all of Jackson County had read the inflammatory newspaper editorials and had seen the lynch mobs. Yet the Alabama supreme court on March 24, 1932, upheld the convictions of seven of the eight sentenced to death; Eugene Williams's conviction was overturned, since he had been younger than fourteen when the alleged crimes took place.

After a preliminary hearing five days later, the U.S. SUPREME COURT agreed to hear the case. On November 7, 1932, it overturned the nine's convictions on the grounds that they had not received the minimum legal representation required by the Constitution.

Second Trial

The ILD lawyers then asked for a venue change for the new trials, and the motion was granted; the trials would be held in Decatur, Alabama, beginning March 27, 1933. Soon afterward, the ILD hired Samuel Leibowitz, one of the most prominent defense attorneys in the nation. He immediately asked the new judge to dismiss the indictments on the grounds that African Americans would be excluded from the jury rolls. The motion was denied, and Haywood Patterson was ordered to stand trial.

Much of the early testimony in this trial was virtually identical to that presented in the Scottsboro trials; it strongly suggested that the nine had not committed the crime for which they stood accused. Leibowitz, too, had a surprise defense witness to bring forth near the end of the trial—Ruby Bates. The shocked courtroom listened as Bates related the events of that day on the train more than two years earlier. First, she testified that she and Price had had sex with two acquaintances immediately before hitching rides on the freight train; she then denied that either woman had been raped.

The whole idea, according to Bates, had been contrived by Victoria Price simply as a way to escape being charged with vagrancy. The prosecution, however, accused her of lying in order to gain a reward from the ILD; the charge flustered Bates, and she was unable to refute it convincingly. After closing arguments, the case went to the jury on April 8. The next day, the jury—to the horror of Leibowitz but to the satisfaction of the packed courthouse—returned a guilty verdict, with the recommendation that Patterson be executed. Many of the spectators, talking to the media after the trial, expressed views that the nine should be electrocuted to set an example of the penalty for raping a white woman.

Second Appeal

Because of the charged atmosphere in Decatur following the Patterson verdict, the trials that were to follow were postponed. Protests across the nation grew more heated, and for the first time, some southern newspapers suggested that the nine might be innocent. The judge, citing the evidence presented by the prosecution as obviously flawed, ordered a retrial. A new judge—one known to be very conservative—was appointed.

In late November, 1933, Patterson's retrial began, and three days after it started, he was again convicted and sentenced to death. Clarence Norris was then tried; just as swiftly, he too was found guilty and condemned to death. The sentences were appealed to the Alabama supreme court, which upheld the verdicts and sentences.

Crowd that gathered at the White House in 1933 to demand the federal government ensure that the Scottsboro defendants receive a fair trial in Alabama. *(National Archives)*

Two years later, however, the U.S. Supreme Court overturned the state decision, ruling that, since African Americans were excluded from Alabama jury rolls, Patterson and Norris had not received fair trials. The governor of Alabama received letters from all across the country begging him to pardon the nine, but he took no action. On May 16, 1935, the Alabama supreme court ordered new trials for Patterson and Norris.

Resolution

On January 20, 1936, the next round of trials began. Again, Patterson was found guilty, but this time his sentence was set at seventy-five years. Next, Norris stood trial and was also found guilty; his sentence was death, though it was later commuted to life imprisonment. Shortly afterward, Andrew Wright and Charlie Weems were found guilty and sentenced to ninety-nine years and seventy-five years, respectively. Rape charges were suddenly dropped against Olen Montgomery, Leroy Wright, Willie Roberson, and Eugene Williams, all of whom were freed. Rape charges were also dropped against Ozie Powell, though he pleaded guilty to charges of assaulting a police officer during an alleged escape attempt; he was sentenced to twenty years.

Weems was paroled in 1943, while Powell and Norris both gained release three years later. Patterson escaped from prison in 1948, but upon his capture in Michigan, the state of Alabama decided not to press for his extradition. Andrew Wright, the last of the nine, was paroled on June 9, 1950—more than nineteen years after he was pulled from a train in Paint Rock, Alabama, for the crime of being an African American man.

—*Jim McWilliams*

See also: Jury selection.

Suggested Readings:

Carter, Dan T. *Scottsboro: A Tragedy of the American South*. Baton Rouge: Louisiana State University Press, 1969.

Chalmers, Allan K. *They Shall Be Free*. Garden City, N.Y.: Doubleday, 1951.

Goodman, James E. *Stories of Scottsboro*. New York: Pantheon Books, 1994.

Kinshasa, Kwando M. *The Man from Scottsboro: Clarence Norris and the Infamous 1931 Alabama Rape Trial, in His Own Words*. Jefferson, N.C.: McFarland, 1997.

Norris, Clarence, and Sybil D. Washington. *The Last of the Scottsboro Boys: An Autobiography*. New York: G. P. Putnam's Sons, 1979.

Patterson, Haywood, and Earl Conrad. *Scottsboro Boy*. New York: Bantam Books, 1950.

Sculptors: The achievements of African Americans in the area of sculpture have been notable but often overlooked. African American sculptors have drawn upon an AFRICAN HERITAGE of excellence in sculpture that dates back hundreds, if not thousands, of years. This heritage is particularly evident in, but not exclusive to, the work of African Americans whose ancestors came from West AFRICA, where wood carving, bone carving, and bronze casting were quite well developed.

Edmonia Lewis

African American sculpture was largely ignored for several centuries by art connoisseurs and the art establishment. In the nineteenth century, most fledgling African American sculptors had to emigrate to Europe in order to seek training, gain commissions, and attain recognition; those who could not leave the country remained self-taught. One of the most famous African American sculptors of this period was Edmonia LEWIS. Of black and Native American heritage, Lewis was born in upstate New York and was educated at OBERLIN COLLEGE in Ohio. After graduating from Oberlin in 1863, Lewis moved to Boston, where she studied with Edmund Brackett. In 1865 Lewis moved to Rome, Italy, where she lived and worked until her death in 1890. Her affinity for

historical subjects and mastery of the neoclassical style of sculpture is evident in such notable works as *Hiawatha, Madonna and Child, Hagar in the Wilderness,* and *The Death of Cleopatra.*

New Opportunities

Early black sculptors who managed to attain recognition were often self-taught and worked in the prevailing style of the time. These constraints often limited them to creating standard busts of wealthy patrons rather than experimenting and attempting to portray African American figures and experiences in their work. By the beginning of the twentieth century, however, it had become possible for African Americans to gain entry into the art establishment by studying under the tutelage of well-known sculptors in the United States and abroad. Soon the HARLEM RENAISSANCE gave further encouragement to many black artists, including sculptors. Through the support of organizations such as the Harmon Foundation and the interest of historically black colleges, African American sculptors were able to support themselves through their art and were encouraged to incorporate black history and themes into their works. Later, freedoms gained during the CIVIL RIGHTS movement and through the impetus of the Black Arts movement led to further development of African American sculpture.

In the early twentieth century, the situation for black sculptors improved somewhat as it became possible for African Americans to obtain formal art training in American schools or with American mentors. Philanthropic foundations, such as the William E. Harmon Foundation, and other organizations, such as Karamu House, developed that were aimed at fostering African American art. Two African American women who were able to take advantage of these opportunities received art training at the Philadelphia Academy of Art.

(continued on page 2228)

Notable Sculptors

Artis, William E. (Feb. 2, 1914, Washington, N.C.—1977). Artis studied at Chadron State College in Nebraska and Syracuse University, in addition to the New York State College of Ceramics, Pennsylvania State University, and the Art Students League (1933–1935). He later studied under August Savage and taught at the Harlem Young Men's Christian Association and Nebraska State Teachers College. His work is known for depictions of human aspiration.

Barthé, Richmond. *See main text entry.*

Billops, Camille J. (b. Aug. 12, 1933, Los Angeles, Calif.). Billops earned her B.A. at Los Angeles State College and her M.F.A. at Los Angeles City College. Her ceramic sculptures characteristically are combinations of wheel-thrown and hand-built forms. Billops also is recognized for her work as an art educator, lecturer, and filmmaker. She won numerous awards, including the James VAN DER ZEE Award in 1994.

Burke, Selma (Dec. 31, 1901, Mooresville, N.C.—Aug. 29, 1995, New Hope, Pa.). Burke earned a reputation for sculptures of American leaders and classical representations of the human body. In 1943 she designed the portrait of former president Franklin D. Roosevelt that appears on dime coins. Later, she won acclaim for a statue of Martin Luther KING, Jr. Burke received the 1987 Pearl S. Buck Award and a 1989 award from ESSENCE magazine.

Catlett, Elizabeth. *See main text entry.*

Chase-Riboud, Barbara. *See main text entry.*

Cummings, Michael A. (b. Nov. 28, 1945, Los Angeles, Calif.). Quiltmaker. A master quiltmaker, Cummings began to construct quilts around themes that depict stories of African American life. Cummings's works are displayed in the permanent collections of institutions such as the California Afro-American Museum in Los Angeles, the Atlanta Life Insurance Company, and the Studio Museum of Harlem.

Doyle, Sam (1906—1985, Saint Helena Island, S.C.). A self-taught artist, Doyle is known for a raw, highly expressive style typical of artists considered "na-tive." His work reflects the lore of the community, composed largely of descendants of freed slaves, where he spent his entire life. Enamel paintings imaginatively depict local personalities, and his wood sculptures re-create animals with regional as well as spiritual significance: turtles, snakes, and alligators.

Edmunson, William. *See main text entry.*

Edwards, Melvin E. (b. May 4, 1937, Houston, Tex.). Critics have characterized Edwards's sculptures as containing "black humor." Among his awards are a Los Angeles County Art Institute Fellowship, a John Hay Whitney Fellowship, and a Los Angeles County Museum Grant. He holds a B.F.A. from the University of Southern California and has trained at the University of California at Los Angeles as well as at the Chouinard Art Institute in Los Angeles. In 1996 a show of his welded metal sculptures was held at the CDS gallery in New York City.

Fuller, Meta Vaux Warrick. *See main text entry.*

Gilliam, Sam (b. Nov. 30, 1933, Tupelo, Miss.). In the early 1960's, Gilliam gave up figurative painting in favor of brightly colored abstract art. He specialized in enormous relief works that combine sculpture and painting, such as suspended paintings with geometric metal attachments projecting from the canvas. Among his awards are the Norman Walt Harris prize and two grants from the National Endowment for the Arts. One of his most striking pieces is the 1995 *Sesame, Sesame*, which is acrylic on paper and fabric and mounted on hinged wood panels.

© Roy Lewis Archives

Hathaway, Isaac (Apr. 4, 1871, Lexington, Ky.—?). Hathaway headed the ceramics department at Alabama State Teachers College in Montgomery. His most recognized works are portrait busts of Frederick DOUGLASS, Paul Laurence DUNBAR, and Booker T. WASHINGTON. He also was commissioned by the U.S. Mint to design memorial coins issued in honor

(continued)

of Booker T. WASHINGTON and George Washington CARVER.

Jackson, May Howard (1877, Philadelphia, Pa.—July 12, 1931, Long Beach, Long Island, N.Y.). Many of Jackson's works are portraits emphasizing characteristics that Jackson thought were part of the subject's social conditions. Her reputation was built on her busts of such notables as Paul Laurence DUNBAR and W. E. B. DU BOIS.

Johnson, Daniel LaRue (b. 1938, Los Angeles, Calif.). After receiving a Guggenheim Fellowship in 1965, Johnson moved to Paris to study with Swiss sculptor Alberto Giacometti. Johnson's early work identified with the Civil Rights movement, and his later minimalist sculptures contained overtones of the rhythms of American jazz and African music.

Johnson, Sargent. *See main text entry.*

Lewis, Edmonia. *See main text entry.*

Logan, Juan Leon (b. Aug. 16, 1946, Nashville, Tenn.). Nonfigurative in style, Logan's art explores such formal matters as the representation of volume by means of modern industrial materials. Like West African sculptors centuries before, Logan found metal to be an expressive and aesthetically gratifying medium. He has been credited with transforming hard steel into lyrical arrangements that interplay organically. In 1977 Logan received the Romare BEARDEN Award for Creativity for Innovation of Medium.

McCullough, Geraldine (b. Dec. 1, 1922, Kingston, Ark.). McCullough taught at Rosary College in River Forest, Illinois, and produced commissioned sculptures in Chicago. She has work in the permanent collections of the Oakland Museum and at HOWARD UNIVERSITY. In 1992 she produced the striking work entitled *Confrontation*, an ink resist on paper.

Outterbridge, John Wilfred (b. Mar. 12, 1933, Greenville, N.C.). An exponent of "junk" or "found" art, Outterbridge claimed that discarded materials "have related to human experience in a very profound way." His sculptural assemblages orchestrate varied materials into an artistically interesting whole. A major figure in the community arts movement, Outterbridge served as director of the Watts Towers Art Center until 1992. In 1995 he was an inaugural recipient of the Artist-Nominated Awards, voted on by artists throughout Los Angeles County.

Perkins, Marion (1908, Marche, Ark.—1961). Perkins studied under Cy Gordon. He exhibited at the Art Institute of Chicago, Howard University, Hull House (Chicago), and the American Negro Exposition in Chicago (1940). His work is in the permanent collection of the Art Institute of Chicago, where he received a purchase award in 1951.

Pierce, Elijah. *See main text entry.*

Ringgold, Faith. *See main text entry.*

Savage, Augusta. *See main text entry.*

Shelton, Christopher (b. 1933, New Orleans, La.). Seeking to individualize his imagery during the late 1960's and early 1970's, Shelton experimented with multidimensional sculpture, combining painting with the manipulation of space. His works form an artistic sequence under the title *Air Afrique*.

Warbourg, Eugene (c. 1825, New Orleans, La.—1867). Warbourg's most famous sculpture is a portrait bust of John Young Mason, a United States minister to France. Warbourg, who was trained as a stonemason, shared a studio with his brother, Daniel, in New Orleans. The jealousy of local white artists allegedly prompted Warbourg to leave the United States for Europe, where he resided until his death.

Meta Vaux Warrick FULLER was a PHILADELPHIA, PENNSYLVANIA, native who trained at the School of Industrial Art before studying at the Academy. She later studied sculpture with Charles Grafly and then moved to Paris to study with Auguste Rodin. Her most famous work, *The Wretched*, was exhibited during 1903 and 1904 by the William E. Harmon Foundation and other art organizations dedicated to fostering African American art. May Howard Jackson, another native of Philadelphia, was trained at J. Liberty Tadd's art school before studying at the Philadelphia Academy. She established her reputation as a sculptor of famous people and was able to open her own art studio in WASHINGTON, D.C., in 1902. She continued to maintain the studio until her death in 1931 and devoted much of the final two decades of her life to chronicling African American life in her art.

Another black sculptor gained fame in the West. Sargent JOHNSON was born in BOSTON, MASSACHUSETTS, in 1888 and studied at the Worcester Art School before moving to San Francisco in 1915. While there, he studied sculpture with Benjamin Bufano and Ralph Stackpole. Johnson created bas-relief murals, metal sculptures, and ceramics that portrayed the dignity and natural beauty of African Americans. Among his best-known works are the pieces *Sammy* and *Forever Free*. Johnson won numerous awards and prizes for his work, was a three-time recipient of the William E. Harmon Foundation Award for outstanding African American art, and was the subject of major exhibitions at such famous museums as the Art Institute of Chicago and the Baltimore Museum.

The Harlem Renaissance to Midcentury
During the 1920's, many black sculptors contributed to the artistic flowering that was called the Harlem Renaissance. As a result of this artistic development, HISTORICALLY BLACK COLLEGES and universities such as HOWARD UNIVERSITY started to collect and authenticate African American art, creating places to display and study African American art works that had been virtually excluded from the nation's great art museums. Augusta SAVAGE, a leading sculptor of the Harlem Renaissance period, was born in Florida and studied at Tallahassee State Normal School before training at New York's Cooper Union. Her work was included in the Harmon Foundation's first all-black exhibition in 1939. Known for works such as *Gamin*, *Black Women*,

and *Lift Every Voice and Sing*, Savage became the first black woman member of the National Association of Women Painters and Sculptors and received fellowships from the Carnegie and Rosenwald foundations.

Other sculptors gained fame in the Midwest. Richmond BARTHÉ moved from his native MISSISSIPPI to study at the Art Institute of Chicago from 1924 to 1928. He later studied under the tutelage of Charles Schroeder and Albin Polasek. Barthé's work includes busts of black personalities, such as TOUSSAINT-L'OUVERTURE and Henry O. TANNER, and portraits of black life, such as *The Singing Slave*. One of the first black sculptors to become a member of the American National Academy of Arts and Letters, Barthé had several works exhibited in New York's Metropolitan Museum of Art and other major museums. Marion Perkins, on the other hand, was a largely self-taught sculptor who developed his skills while tending a CHICAGO, ILLINOIS, newspaper stand. Later, Perkins studied with

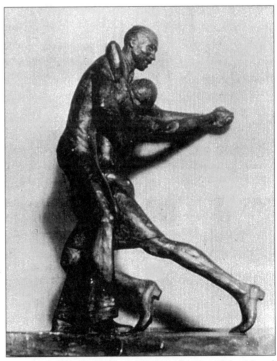

Richmond Barthé's *Rug Cutters. (National Archives)*

Simon Gordon and contributed works to exhibits at the Art Institute of Chicago. One of Perkins's best-known works, *Mother and Child*, became part of a major museum collection. Perkins was invited to be artist-in-residence at Jackson State College in Mississippi, and he founded a scholarship fund for black art students at the college.

Later sculptors received even further formal training. Elizabeth CATLETT was born in Washington, D.C., in 1919 and studied at Howard University. After completing her undergraduate work, Catlett attended the University of Iowa, where she earned a master's degree in fine arts. In 1946 she moved to Mexico and eventually took up residence in Cuernavaca. Catlett's strong and forceful works include *Black Unity, Target Practice*, and *Woman Resting*. Her works brought her several awards and prizes and have become part of the permanent collections of more than twenty museums in the United States and abroad. During 1998-1999, a traveling exhibition, "Elizabeth Catlett Sculpture: Fifty-Year Retrospective," made its way across America. Starting at the Neuberger Museum of Art in Purchase, New York, the exhibition traveled to Houston, Baltimore, Los Angeles, and Atlanta.

Civil Rights Movement and Beyond
By the late 1960's and early 1970's, African American galleries and museums such as Harlem's Studio Museum, the Just Above Midtown Gallery, the Cinque Gallery, the Museum of African Art, and the Hatch-Billops Studio had opened and were flourishing in New York and throughout the United States. One sculptor who came to prominence during this period was Richard Hunt. Hunt was born in Chicago in 1935 and studied at the Art Institute of the Art School of Detroit and John Huntington Polytechnic Institute. His best-known works include *Extending Horizontal Form* and *Linear Spatial Theme*, and many of his pieces are in-

cluded in the collections of the Museum of Modern Art, the Art Institute of Chicago, and the Cleveland Museum of Art. Hunt received numerous fellowships and awards, including a Guggenheim Fellowship, and became active in art education. In addition to serving as a commissioner at the National Museum of American Art, Hunt served on the board of governors at the School of the Art Institute of Chicago and on the advisory committee for the Getty Center for Education in the Arts.

One of the founding members of Harlem's Studio Museum was sculptor Betty Blaynton-Taylor. Blaynton-Taylor was born in Williamsburg, Virginia, in 1937, and received her bachelor of fine arts degree from Syracuse University. After graduation, she studied sculpture with Arnold Prince and Munoru Niizuma. Active in the New York art community, Blaynton-Taylor served as president of the Children's Art Carnival in Harlem and as director of the Printmaker's Workshop. In addition to her exhibits at the Studio Museum, Blaynton-Taylor's works have been displayed at the Metropolitan Museum of Art. She won the New York Governor's Award and received the Empire State Woman of the Year in Arts Award in 1984.

Although still underrepresented in most museum collections, black sculptors came to be much better known in the 1980's and 1990's, partly as a result of the efforts of black curators who joined the staffs of such famous institutions as the Guggenheim Museum and the Museum of Modern Art. African American sculpture has become a unique and powerful part of mainstream American art—a tribute to the great talent of its practitioners and the determination that enabled them to excel against great odds.

Since the 1970's, the number of African American sculptors who have gained recognition has increased. Using a variety of media, including woods, ceramics, glass, and rattan, these sculptors have attempted to appeal to a wider audience. Some of the contemporary sculptors go so far as to create whole sculptural environments. Sculptors such as David Hammons create "site-specific" installations in which the location and the viewer almost become part of the sculpture itself. Hammons also used "found" objects to create his sculptures. He scavenged for striking, ordinary, and unusual objects, and then organized these objects in such a way as to create an original work of art.

During 1992-1993, Martha Jackson-Jarvis created a series of ceramic assemblages called *Last Rites*. The sculptures of the series dealt with a variety of issues, including gender, cultural pluralism, and the natural environment. Site-specific installations became popular during the 1980's, and that popularity grew during the 1990's. The installations allow the viewer to become visually engaged with the work. When a site is changed, the nature of the work also changes. In 1997 a retrospective exhibition of the influential sculptor Noah Purifoy was held at the California African American Museum in Los Angeles. Titled "Noah Purifoy: Outside and In the Open," it was a reminder of how important Purifoy was to the development of the new forms of presenting sculpture that became popular in the 1990's.

—*Sanford S. Singer*
—*Updated by Jeffry Jensen*

See also: Painters and illustrators; Photographers; Visual arts.

Suggested Readings:

Dallas Museum of Art. *Black Art Ancestral Legacy: The African Impulse in African-American Art*. New York: Harry N. Abrams, 1989.

Dover, Cedric. *American Negro Art*. Reprint. Greenwich, Conn.: New York Graphic Society, 1969.

Fine, Elsa H. *The Afro-American Artist: A Search for Identity*. New York: Hacker Art Books, 1982.

Fitzgerald, Sharon. "Breaking the Mold." *Ms.* (September/October, 1996): 72-75.

Lippard, Lucy R. *Mixed Blessings: New Art in a Multicultural America*. New York: Pantheon Books, 1990.

Patterson, Lindsay. *International Library of Afro-American Life History: The Afro-American in Music and Art*. Cornwells Heights, Pa.: Publishers Agency, 1979.

Reynolds, Gary A., and Beryl J. Wright. *Against All Odds: African-American Artists and the Harmon Foundation*. Newark, N.J.: The Newark Museum, 1989.

Wolfe, Rinna. *Edmonia Lewis: Wildfire in Marble*. Parsippany, N.J.: Dillon Press, 1998.

Sea Islands: Coastal island chain stretching from SOUTH CAROLINA to FLORIDA. Some PLANTATIONS there were turned over to slaves after the CIVIL WAR. Isolation allowed the islands to become preserves for African American languages and traditional culture. This continuity had begun to face challenges from increasing contact, outmigration, and development by the late twentieth century.

The Sea Islands include James, Johns, Edisto, Port Royal, Parris, St. Helena, Hilton Head, and Daufuskie (in South Carolina); Tybee, Ossabaw, St. Catherines, Sapelo, St. Simons, Jekyll, and Cumberland (in GEORGIA); and Amelia (in Florida). Spanish missionaries contacted Guale Indians there in the sixteenth century. By the eighteenth century, highly successful English cotton plantations dominated the islands' economy, while the islands' name designated a variety of fine, long-staple cotton. By the start of the CIVIL WAR in 1861 the Carolina islands' population was 83 percent black.

After the Union capture of Beaufort in 1861, the islands became centers for independent black agriculture as well as RECONSTRUCTION education and politics. Whites had their land confiscated or abandoned it. In the 1870's, St.

Helena had a population of six thousand African Americans and seventy white people. The cotton economy, however, was undercut by wartime devastation, international competition, depressions, and the problems of small-scale farming, so men turned increasingly to the mainland. Storms and boll weevil infestations shifted the declining economy to farm-garden crops and fishing at the beginning of the twentieth century, as Jim Crow legislation eroded CIVIL RIGHTS.

In the twentieth century, folklore and ethnographic scholars have documented the complex life of the islands, which also have appeared in novels and films. The GULLAH language, a creole dialect combining African and European elements, endured for generations alongside spirituals, arts, and social structures that set Sea Islanders apart from nearby black and white populations. Over time, the islands became differentiated: Some are natural wildlife preserves or include historic centers, while Parris Island hosts Marine basic training. St. Simons Island and Hilton Head, among others, have become elite tourist sites.

The remaining black communities, many of which have lost members to migration, face constant threats from tourism and development as bridges and highways connect the islands to the mainland. These inroads have been challenged with campaigns for cultural preservation and rights which may well determine the islands' future.

Seale, Bobby (b. October 20, 1936, Dallas, Texas): Political activist. Seale was one of the most prominent black radicals of the 1960's. While a student at Oakland's Merritt College, Seale met Huey P. NEWTON and with him became involved in black student political activity in the San Francisco Bay Area in the mid-1960's. Inspired by the ideas put forth by MALCOLM X, upset by the miserable living

Former Black Panther leader Bobby Seale in March, 1999, during a visit to Rutgers University. *(AP/Wide World Photos)*

conditions of African Americans in OAKLAND, CALIFORNIA, and incensed by police mistreatment of and disrespect for blacks, Seale and Newton in 1966 founded the BLACK PANTHER PARTY for Self Defense. Newton took the title of "defense minister"; Seale became the chairman of the group. Joined by Eldridge CLEAVER, whose book *Soul on Ice* (1968) became a bible of the 1960's, and others, Seale and the Black Panthers quickly became the best-known—and most notorious—black radical group in the country. Strutting around Oakland in black leather jackets and berets and carrying shotguns in full view, the Black Panthers were a symbol of black revolutionary fervor.

As the organization spread nationwide, it became the target of FEDERAL BUREAU OF INVESTIGATION (FBI) surveillance and infiltration. Seale, the chairman of the party, was a particular target of persecution; he was arrested and charged with conspiring to riot during the 1968 DEMOCRATIC PARTY convention in Chicago. Seale was originally one of the Chicago Eight, a group of celebrated radicals brought to trial for disrupting the convention, but his case was separated from those of the others, who then became known as the Chicago Seven. Seale was also implicated in the murder of a turncoat Black Panther in New Haven, Connecticut. In both cases, Seale was acquitted of all charges. In 1970 Seale published *Seize the Time: The Story of the Black Panther Party and Huey P. Newton*. The Black Panther Party broke up in the early 1970's as a result of government harassment; rivalries among Seale, Newton, and Cleaver; and the party's failure to organize effectively the ghetto dwellers for whom it purportedly spoke.

Seale did not vanish with the collapse of the party. In 1973 he ran for mayor of Oakland and was defeated by a narrow margin. In 1978 he published *A Lonely Rage: The Autobiography of Bobby Seale*. In the 1980's, Seale resurfaced as a celebrity cook, promoting his own special barbecue recipes and sauce. He also worked as a minority recruiter and consultant for Temple University.

Sears-Collins, Leah Jeanette (b. June 13, 1955, Heidelberg, West Germany): JUDGE. The daughter of a U.S. Army colonel, Sears-Collins was born in West Germany and traveled around the world as a result of her father's assignments. After completing her bachelor's degree at Cornell University in 1976, Sears-Collins worked as a reporter for the *Columbus Ledger* newspaper in Columbus, Ohio. In 1980 she completed her law degree at Emory University in ATLANTA, GEORGIA, and passed the bar exam. From 1985 to 1988, she served as a judge in the City Court of Atlanta. After being elected to a judgeship on the Superior Court of

Leah Sears-Collins in 1992. *(AP/Wide World Photos)*

Fulton County (serving Atlanta) in 1989, Sears-Collins received an appointment to the Georgia supreme court from Governor Zell Miller in 1992. She was able to retain this post after being reelected for a six-year term to her superior court judgeship in July of 1992. One of the youngest judges to serve on any state supreme court, Sears-Collins joined fellow black judge Robert Benham on the seven-member Georgia supreme court. Dedicated to community service, she helped found the Battered Women's Project of Columbus, Georgia. Among her awards, Sears-Collins received a Distinguished Leadership Award for Outstanding Service in the Judiciary (1988) and a Community Service Award from the Atlanta chapter of the NATIONAL ASSOCIATION FOR THE ADVANCEMENT OF COLORED PEOPLE (NAACP).

Secondary education: The EDUCATION of African Americans became a national public-policy issue only after the CIVIL WAR. During RECONSTRUCTION, schools for the newly emancipated citizens, including a limited number of postprimary institutions, were sponsored throughout the South by various philanthropic groups and by the U.S. government-created FREEDMEN'S BUREAU. The close of Reconstruction, however, saw the emergence of a dual system of education separated by the color line. Government funding was reduced by the 1880's, leaving black public schools in terrible condition and limiting their expansion.

This dual system of education, condoned by the 1896 PLESSY V. FERGUSON U.S. SUPREME COURT ruling that approved "SEPARATE BUT EQUAL" public facilities for whites and blacks, limited the educational advancement of blacks. Many southern whites believed that secondary schooling would be wasted on African Americans, whereas others justified the separate systems as an economic and political necessity. Traditionally, schooling for the black masses focused on elementary levels of industrial education, teaching trades, and manual skills. For example, the first black high school did not open in Atlanta until 1924. These practices profoundly affected post-primary education for African Americans and continue to influence the education of black youth.

Reforms and Progress

Since the Supreme Court's 1954 BROWN V. BOARD OF EDUCATION decision, which reversed the 1896 decision and made school segregation illegal, there have been well-meaning efforts to reform public education to redress historical inequities in opportunities and access to secondary schools for African Americans. These efforts have resulted in much research to isolate school practices contributing to the educational problems faced by black youth and to suggest possible remedies. Most reform plans, however, have been compensatory in nature and have overlooked systemic societal problems—POVERTY and classism, for example—and structural underpinnings such as school financing, population growth, and

political ideology, which also affect the roughly three million blacks enrolled in secondary schools.

Nevertheless, minority enrollment in U.S. public schools grew from 24 percent in 1976 to 30 percent in 1986, and the U.S. Department of Education predicted that minority students would compose 46 percent of the secondary enrollment by 2020. Furthermore, the CENSUS OF THE UNITED STATES reported that the black population grew almost 14 percent during the 1980's; this growth was expected to bring new challenges to schools in the following decades.

Retention and Dropout Rates

A relatively high rate of African American students leave secondary school without earning their diplomas; however, this rate began to decline toward the end of the twentieth century. Of all racial and ethnic groups considered from 1970 to 1988, the dropout rate of blacks fell most dramatically, and between 1974 and

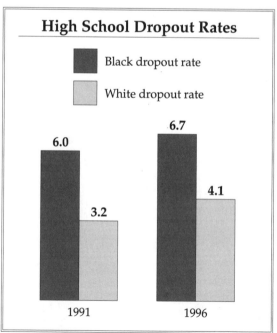

High School Dropout Rates

Black dropout rate

White dropout rate

Source: Newsweek, June 7, 1999.

Note: Percentage of tenth to twelfth-grade students who dropped out.

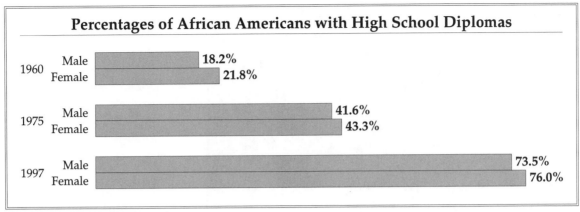

Percentages of African Americans with High School Diplomas

1960	Male	18.2%
	Female	21.8%
1975	Male	41.6%
	Female	43.3%
1997	Male	73.5%
	Female	76.0%

Source: U.S. Bureau of the Census.

Note: U.S. Census figures of people reporting having completed four years of high school or four years of high school plus additional education.

1989, the difference between black and white high-school completion rates was narrowed considerably. Furthermore, blacks in the North and the West had long been graduating at higher rates than their counterparts in the South; the U.S. Census indicated that there were no such regional differences in 1988.

It is important to note that a student may drop out of high school and yet receive a diploma or its equivalent in subsequent years. In 1979 roughly 69 percent of black nineteen- and twenty-year-olds had completed high school. Yet by 1989, when members of this group had reached age thirty, an additional 12 percent had earned their diplomas. Still, 20 percent of blacks never complete secondary school, which severely limits their employment opportunities. While the employment rate of dropouts differs greatly from that of high-school graduates for any ethnic group, the picture is particularly bleak for blacks who do not finish secondary school.

Achievement

For blacks who stay in high school, there was improvement in the realm of academic achievement in the 1980's and 1990's, although their test scores remain behind those of their white peers. For example, the reading scores of black seventeen-year-olds increased

almost 15 percent from 1971 to 1988; however, the U.S. Department of Education notes in 1991 that the average reading proficiency of black seventeen-year-olds was still only slightly higher than that of white thirteen-year-olds. In other academic subjects, including math and science, while the scores of black students were on the rise, in most cases they had yet to reach the level of scores achieved by white students. There are several possible explanations for this continued gap in achievement and school completion; among the most frequently discussed are poverty, modal grade, and lack of problems with discipline.

Risk Factors

Studies indicate that several factors are considered to place a student at risk of school failure. Such factors are often associated with poverty, such as a student's having a single parent, parents without a high-school diploma, or a sibling who has dropped out of school. A student with one risk factor is not necessarily in danger, but students with several of these attributes are often at high risk of school failure. In 1988 black students were at least twice as likely as white students to have more than two risk factors. Almost half of all black eighth-graders came from single-parent families, and as many came from fami-

Students at Manhattan Day and Night School in New York City, which caters to working and married students, prepare for graduation in 1997. *(Hazel Hankin)*

lies with incomes of less than $15,000.

The number of impoverished blacks increased through the 1980's: 45 percent of black children were considered poor in 1987, and the poverty rate for black children living with a single mother was found to be as high as 78 percent in 1988. A high-school student whose family lives below the poverty line is likely to attend a school with large classes and under-qualified teachers. Such students often lack energy as the result of poor nourishment, often do not have adequate space and resources at home to complete assignments, and are likely to be solicited to participate in illegal activities that may appear to be a quick way out of poverty. Black teenagers are likely to face a number of challenges that hinder school performance and may lead to their falling behind.

The modal grade is defined as "the grade in which most children of a certain age are enrolled." Research suggests that those below their modal grade are at greatest risk of dropping out. While during the 1980's, there was a significant increase in the percentage of individuals below modal grade across all ethnic groups, on average, black male students were most likely to be below modal grade. Forty-six percent of thirteen-year-old black male students and 36 percent of thirteen-year-old black female students were below modal grade in 1988. In other words, almost half of these black teenagers were one or more years behind their peers in school, a factor that posed a great risk to their completion of school.

Another risk factor is racial bias in the administration of discipline. A 1989 Office for Civil Rights study reported that black high-school students were disproportionately expelled—as many as eight times as often as whites. Another study reported that blacks were often punished for offenses allowed white students or given heavier penalties for similar offenses. The same study also concluded that suspensions were more likely to be given to black students than to white students and that such suspensions were generally lengthier. Other research suggests a link between these disparities in disciplinary practices and dropout rates of blacks and other minorities. Repeated suspensions can alienate students from schoolwork and staff and often result in students' falling behind, dropping out, or receiving expulsion. While it is important to maintain order in schools, discipline that is seen as unfairly distributed exacerbates the problems of academic performance and school completion for blacks.

Prognosis

African Americans have seen improvements in secondary education, a fact reflected by black students' increasing school-completion rates and improving test scores. Nevertheless, there remain many gaps to fill before the outcomes for black students are on par with those of their white peers. Considering the rates for poverty, enrollment below modal grade, and disciplinary action such as suspension and expulsion, it seems unlikely that the academic performance and completion rates of black teenagers will continue to improve much in the near future. Prospects seem even more dismal in light of the insufficient facilities of most urban schools, where the bulk of African Americans are enrolled, and the carryover effects of various practices in elementary schools: culturally biased tests, overrepresentation of black students in "lower ability" tracks, a curriculum that ignores or negates the achievements of African Americans, and other related factors. Moreover, black representation is needed on school boards and in key political positions if schools are to incorporate salient features of the black experience and better meet the needs of African American students.

While serious efforts have been made to comprehend the inequities faced by African American students and to bring about equal opportunity, the resulting policies and practices have only struck at the surface. *Brown v. Board of Education* and the subsequent efforts to desegregate schools and develop compensatory programs have made quality secondary education somewhat more accessible to African Americans. Yet, the education that blacks receive in secondary schools will not likely be adequate until more systemic social and political changes take place.

—*Claudine Michel and Louise Jennings*
See also: Education.

Suggested Readings:

Arnez, N. L. "Implementation of Desegregation as a Discriminatory Process." *Journal of Negro Education* 47 (Winter, 1978): 28-45.

Berry, Gordon L., and Joy K. Asamen, eds. *Black Students: Psychosocial Issues and Academic Achievement*. Newbury Park, Calif.: Sage Publications, 1989.

Blackwell, James E. *The Black Community: Diversity and Unity*. 3d ed. New York: HarperCollins, 1991.

Eyler, J., V. J. Cook, and L. E. Ward. "Resegregation: Segregation Within Desegregated Schools." In *The Consequences of School Desegregation*, edited by Christine H. Rossell and Willis D. Hawley. Philadelphia: Temple University Press, 1983.

Meier, Kenneth J., Joseph Stewart, Jr., and Robert E. England. *Race, Class, and Education*. Madison: University of Wisconsin Press, 1989.

National Center for Education Statistics. *Elementary and Secondary Education*. Vol. 1 in *The Condition of Education, 1991*. Washington, D.C.: U.S. Government Printing Office, 1991.

Pallas, Aaron M., Gary Natriello, and Edward L. McDill. "The Changing Nature of the Disadvantaged Population: Current Dimensions and Future Trends." *Educational Researcher* 18 (1989): 16-22.

Second Cumberland Presbyterian Church: The only predominantly African American denomination in the United States adhering to a Reformed theology in 1991. In 1869 freed slaves separated from the predominantly white Cumberland Presbyterian Church and formed the Colored Cumberland Presbyterian Church, later known as the Second Cumberland Presbyterian Church. A majority of the more than 150 congregations existing in 1990 were in TENNESSEE, TEXAS, ALABAMA, and KENTUCKY.
See also: Presbyterians.

Segregation and integration: During the 1950's and 1960's, the CIVIL RIGHTS movement brought changes in American race relations. For almost one hundred years after SLAVERY, the United States consisted, in essence, of two societies, one white and the other black. Although white and black Americans lived in the same country, American law and custom divided them under a system of segregation. They attended separate schools, drank from segregated water fountains, and sat in segregated waiting rooms at hospitals, clinics, and airports. The U.S. SUPREME COURT approved the policy known as "SEPARATE BUT EQUAL" in PLESSY V. FERGUSON in 1896. Segregated facilities, however, rarely were equal. For roughly a century after emancipation, African Americans fought to achieve integration in the United States so that they could enjoy equality.

In the battle to topple segregation, African Americans found few friends in the beginning. In 1909 a few northern whites concerned about race wars joined the movement for civil rights. Later, a few liberal Supreme Court justices also joined the crusade. By mid-century, the Court had reconsidered the morality of segregation in public education. Its decision in the BROWN V. BOARD OF EDUCATION case of 1954 declared segregation unconstitutional. The fight for desegregation and equality was not easy, however. Efforts to desegregate high schools and colleges often grew violent.

Historical Overview

Although legal segregation was most pervasive in the United States after the CIVIL WAR, it originated decades earlier. Legal separation of the races was not necessary under slavery. Slavery itself proscribed intimate relations between blacks and whites, and slavery effectively subjugated African Americans. Slaveholders could punish, sell, and control the mobility of enslaved blacks. After the AMERICAN REVOLUTION, northern states emancipated enslaved blacks. New institutions emerged to regulate black Americans who were no longer controlled by slavery. Legal segregation, therefore, began in the North. Some states first adopted a policy of exclusion,

making it illegal for an African American to participate in activities with whites. These activities included education, jury service, and voting.

Some states in the territory west of the Ohio River, including OHIO, INDIANA, and ILLINOIS, adopted BLACK CODES. They regulated the immigration of blacks by requiring large monetary payments from them before granting legal residency. They also required proof of freedom for employment and denied African Americans admission to common schools, participation in jury service, and the freedom to marry outside their race. These were exclusionary laws that denied African Americans citizenship rights. Exclusionary laws worked effectively for years, until the courts began to chop away at them. Some courts, for example, questioned whether the black laws should deny children of racially mixed backgrounds admission to white schools simply because they had some African blood in their backgrounds. The courts advanced a test to determine whether persons from mixed backgrounds should be denied access to institutions created for whites. The courts concluded that if a person was visibly white, he or she should be entitled to the privileges of being a white person. The visible admixture rule replaced the exclusionary rule.

In other parts of the North, where exclusionary rules were not strong, segregation developed. In these states, whites agreed that African Americans were at least entitled to basic rights such as educational training. This was the case in MASSACHUSETTS, a leader in abolishing racially segregated institutions. During the first half of the nineteenth century, the state made progress with its racial policy. Massachusetts began to desegregate its railroad cars, abolish miscegenation laws, and admit black children to white schools. Early desegregation in Massachusetts was not uniform, however. This was especially true in Boston, a city that rigidly segregated its educational system. African American leaders there assailed the legal system with petitions and resolutions, calling for desegregation. The experiences of Sarah C. Roberts enabled them to test the school policy in court.

Early Segregation in Education

Sarah was the five-year-old daughter of Benjamin F. Roberts, who lived in a school district reserved for whites. Segregated schools were available for blacks, but Sarah would have been required to pass by several white schools to attend a segregated school. She applied for admission to a white school four times, but the school district rejected her applications. Mr. Roberts hired Charles Sumner and Robert Morris, Jr., to carry the dispute to court. Sumner, a future champion of civil rights in Congress and author of the Civil Rights Act of 1875, and Morris, an African American lawyer, argued that state and federal law provided for the equality of all persons before the law. Segregation, Sumner said, created misunderstandings and produced harmful effects for blacks and whites. Sumner and Morris further explained that the school board denied Sarah admission solely on account of her race, and they urged the court to correct this wrong.

The state's supreme court had followed a liberal racial policy since 1783, when it had signaled the end to slavery in Massachusetts by freeing Quock Walker. Chief Justice Lemuel Shaw, speaking for the Massachusetts supreme court, explained that Massachusetts did not recognize slavery. The court thus appeared to be somewhat progressive, so the petitioners were optimistic when it agreed to review *Roberts v. City of Boston* (1849). Chief Justice Shaw, however, rejected the arguments of the plaintiff. Shaw explained that Boston had provided a school system for the children of both races. Since all children had an equal right to an education, separate facilities did not constitute a violation of state or federal law. The Shaw court announced its version of the "separate but equal" rule.

Efforts to desegregate the public schools of Ohio began in the 1830's. The Supreme Court first admitted racially mixed children to white schools. In *Williams v. School District* (1836), the Court admitted children whose color was visibly white to the public schools. The Supreme Court also defended the authority of a schoolmaster to admit children of any race to a private school, so long as the children's tuition

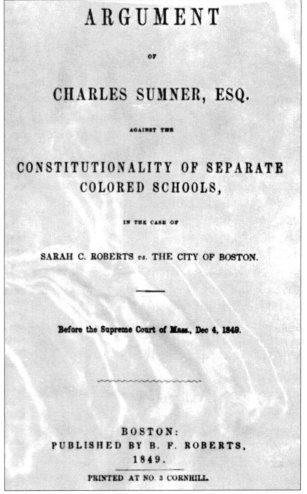

ARGUMENT

OF

CHARLES SUMNER, ESQ.

AGAINST THE

CONSTITUTIONALITY OF SEPARATE
COLORED SCHOOLS,

IN THE CASE OF

SARAH C. ROBERTS vs. THE CITY OF BOSTON.

Before the Supreme Court of Mass., Dec 4, 1849.

BOSTON:
PUBLISHED BY B. F. ROBERTS,
1849.

PRINTED AT NO. 3 CORNHILL.

Pamphlet published by Charles Sumner when he represented Sarah Roberts. *(Arkent Archive)*

was paid. Once the Ohio State supreme court had declared that children of African ancestry were entitled to a common school education, the legislature created a segregated school for African Americans, funded by black taxpayers. Buoyed by this growth in civil rights, African Americans pursued desegregation in Ohio. The case of *Van Camp v. Board of Education of Logan County* (1859), however, signaled the rise of legal segregation in Ohio.

In the *Van Camp* case, the plaintiff sued when the Logan school board denied admission to his children because of their African ancestry. The plaintiff contended that his children were more than one-half white and, under Ohio law, should be regarded as "white." The Court observed that legislative acts of 1848, 1849, and 1853 had provided for the education of African American children in separate schools. The statutes provided the schools, in addition to funds collected from African American taxpayers, with access to the common school fund. Ohio law, therefore, had provided for the education of all children within the state. It had also prescribed the separation of black and white children by constructing a segregated educational system. The Court concluded that black children were not entitled to admission to Ohio schools organized for the instruction of white youths.

In adjusting to the freedom of slaves in the North, whites excluded blacks from most institutions and practices. The courts forced the issue by admitting that "color" could not be used to deny African Americans access to services offered to whites. The exclusionary rule then gave way to segregation. By the outbreak of the Civil War, segregation was entrenched in the North. When the Union army organized against the Confederacy, for example, it was unthinkable to many whites that blacks would be enlisted. When the exigencies of war made enlistment of black soldiers necessary, the Army organized segregated units. The Union adopted a host of discrimina-

tory practices such as unequal pay and inadequate food, clothing, and training for African American soldiers. Segregation affirmed the idea that African Americans were inferior to whites.

Legislative Changes

The THIRTEENTH AMENDMENT abolished slavery in the South in 1865. Southern states quickly adjusted by adopting laws to replace slavery, the institution that had held African Americans in a separate and servile state. Congress attempted to protect African Americans by adopting civil rights legislation. The Civil Rights Act of 1866 declared that African Americans were citizens of the United States. As citizens, they were entitled to access to all public places including parks, theaters, and conveyances. Two years later, Congress adopted the FOURTEENTH AMENDMENT, which affirmed African American citizenship. Congress adopted a comprehensive Civil Rights Act in 1875. This law assured African Americans access to public places and prescribed penalties for persons who violated the statute. Meanwhile, the conservative U.S. Supreme Court undermined federal protection of civil rights.

The Court announced its most sweeping rejection of civil rights reform in the Civil Rights Cases of 1883, ruling that the federal government could protect only federal citizenship rights. It invalidated the Civil Rights Act of 1875 as making the federal government responsible for state citizenship rights. Only the states, the Court concluded, could protect state citizenship rights. Without restraint, the states in the South adopted a system of segregation.

Segregation in the South

Southern lawmakers copied the North when they designed their system of segregation. In schools, transportation facilities, restaurants, and other places where the races would likely come together, state laws separated blacks and whites. Southerners called these statutes JIM CROW LAWS, mimicking a satire about blacks. The Louisiana legislature produced a Jim Crow statute governing railroad travel, requiring separate railway coaches for black and white travelers.

African Americans frequently challenged segregation laws in the South, just as they had done in the North. Homer Plessy tested the legality of the Louisiana law when he boarded a railroad coach reserved for whites. The dispute reached the U.S. Supreme Court in 1896. In *Plessy v. Ferguson*, the Court offered no objections to racial segregation. Indeed, the Court approved the practice. Justice Henry B. Brown, speaking for the majority, concluded that separate but equal facilities for persons of both races satisfied American civil rights laws. The states had already applied this formula to most of their institutions. Emboldened by the opinion in the *Plessy* case, they extended this doctrine to other social practices and institutions.

The Supreme Court affirmed the Plessy doctrine in 1899 and applied it to public education when it reviewed CUMMING V. RICHMOND COUNTY BOARD OF EDUCATION. By 1945 legalized segregation was a way of life in the South as well as in many northern states. Eighteen states mandated the segregation of white and black schoolchildren. Six others approved the segregation policies of local school boards.

Desegregation
The separate but equal doctrine was only a fiction. American institutions were rigidly segregated but rarely were equal. Disparities were evident, especially in southern schools. Teacher pay, training, books, and other resources did not match those of white institutions. The justice system reflected this same bias; a black person rarely received a fair trial in a southern court. It is not surprising that African Americans challenged segregation.

The NAACP Role in Ending Segregation
The NATIONAL ASSOCIATION FOR THE ADVANCEMENT OF COLORED PEOPLE (NAACP) led the crusade against segregation. Organized in 1909, the NAACP petitioned the courts to defend the civil rights of African Americans. Its objectives included voting opportunities for African Americans, fairness in the judicial system, an end to LYNCHING and violent crimes against blacks, and desegregation of public places. The NAACP rejected the belief that individual prejudices should be made public policy.

Charles Hamilton HOUSTON developed the legal strategy of the NAACP. Houston was born in 1895 in WASHINGTON, D.C., to a middle-class African American family. He graduated from Amherst College and Harvard Law School. At Harvard, he studied with future Supreme Court justice Felix Frankfurter. A precocious legal scholar, Houston served on the editorial board of the *Harvard Law Review*. He joined the law firm of his father in 1924 and accepted a teaching appointment at HOWARD UNIVERSITY. Houston ultimately became dean of Howard Law School and developed its program into a fully accredited one. He was convinced that law could be used as a tool for social reform, and he trained students to participate in reform.

The NAACP recognized Houston's ability as a litigator and called on him to try difficult cases. Houston joined the NAACP full-time in 1935 as special counsel. He developed the strategy for the legal department. He planned to illustrate the fallacy behind separate but equal by insisting that separate facilities be tested for parity. He also challenged disparities in salaries for black and white schoolteachers.

The NAACP obtained financial backing early in its crusade against segregation. The Garland Fund provided the first significant contribution. In 1922 Charles Garland, a twenty-two-year-old white American, inherited a fortune from his millionaire father. Garland identified with liberal causes and anguished over his personal fortune, obtained solely because of his gifted birth. He established a foundation to address social issues and contributed $100,000 to the NAACP.

Houston and his colleagues launched an attack on graduate and professional schools that did not conform to the separate but equal doctrine. Donald Murray provided an opportunity for the NAACP to challenge segregation in 1934, when the University of Maryland law school denied him admission solely because of his race. Maryland did provide an out-of-state tuition program for African Americans interested in legal training. Thurgood MARSHALL, who also had been turned away by the university, represented Murray. Marshall argued that the state's tuition program did not constitute equality before the law and insisted that the practice violated the equal protection clause in the Fourteenth Amendment. The appellate court agreed and ordered the university to either admit Murray or provide equal facilities for African American students. The university admitted Murray in 1936.

The pattern of discrimination in Maryland prevailed elsewhere. The application of Lloyd Gaines to the University of Missouri provided another opportunity to challenge segregation in professional schools. Gaines met all of the qualifications for admission except race. The university denied admission to blacks, although the state provided scholarships for them to study in another state. The NAACP carried Gaines's petition to the courts. The Missouri supreme court upheld state law, which barred blacks from white schools in Missouri. The U.S. Supreme Court reviewed the case, MISSOURI EX REL GAINES, in 1938.

Houston handled this case personally, arguing that American law assured that African Americans would be entitled to the same opportunities available to whites. Missouri violated this dictum in legal education. The Supreme Court accepted this interpretation of equal protection under the law. Missouri, the Court declared, was bound to furnish all its citizens an equal opportunity to obtain legal training within the state. The Court offered Missouri an option, to admit Gaines or to build a law school for blacks. The state legislature accepted the latter and appropriated money to construct a law school at the all-black Lincoln University. The NAACP filed briefs to challenge this action. Before the case could proceed further, Gaines mysteriously disappeared.

The Murray and Gaines cases made cracks in the wall but did not topple segregation in professional schools. Actually, the decisions of the Supreme Court seemed to approve segregation. The Court only questioned whether separate but equal facilities were available to blacks. Any state that conformed to *Plessy* satisfied the Court, at least before WORLD WAR II.

Advances in the World War II Era
By the 1940's, some whites were becoming more responsive to calls for civil rights. A growing number of middle-class black voters in the North attracted the attention of politicians in urban centers such as Chicago, Philadelphia, and New York. Some politicians became responsive, hoping to win their vote. President Franklin D. Roosevelt, for example, created the Fair Employment Practices Commission in 1941. By executive order, the armed forces awarded African Americans commissions in desegregated military units. President Harry S Truman later desegregated the armed forces. Labor unions also admitted African American workers in larger numbers.

It is not surprising that victory in the campaign for desegregation came after World War II. Litigants found courts more willing to concede to civil rights reform. The Oklahoma case of *Sipuel v. Board of Regents*, decided in 1948, signaled the Supreme Court's growing

Segregation remained evident even as the nation pulled together during World War II; Oscar-winning actor Hattie McDaniel (center) was the chairperson of the "Negro Division" of the Hollywood Victory Committee. She is seen here with fellow African American entertainers preparing to stage a show at a military base. *(National Archives)*

commitment to equality before the law. Sipuel met all qualifications for admission to law school except race. The Supreme Court upheld the model set forth in the *Gaines* case: The university could either admit Sipuel or establish a school for the training of black lawyers. Unlike those in Missouri, Oklahoma lawmakers established such a school. The NAACP challenged this action in *Fisher v. Hurst* (1948). The Court denied relief to the plaintiff.

Victory in the battle for desegregation of professional schools came in 1950, in the case of SWEATT V. PAINTER. The University of Texas Law School denied admission to a qualified African American applicant. Texas lawmakers hastily established a separate law school for blacks in order to conform to previous Supreme Court decisions. Litigation had begun

before this action, and the Supreme Court had to consider whether such a school satisfied the law. The Court found that the newly created law school was unequal in every way: It lacked adequate facilities, staff, and the prestige enjoyed by the university. The new school could not furnish African American students equality in their professional training.

Professional schools did not desegregate enthusiastically. Some schools maintained a policy of DE FACTO SEGREGATION, although they admitted at least one black student. Classrooms, libraries, and school cafeterias were segregated. Many schools established separate areas exclusively for African American students. The University of Oklahoma maintained such a policy. Although the university admitted African Americans to its

The first African American student at the University of Missouri dines quietly in the school cafeteria in 1951. *(Library of Congress)*

graduate program, it segregated them in classrooms, libraries, and dining facilities. The students protested this treatment, and in McLAURIN v. OKLAHOMA STATE REGENTS (1950), the Supreme Court declared the scheme unconstitutional. These were lonely times for African American students, who frequently were ignored or taunted by white professors and students.

Segregation in Secondary Schools
The NAACP placed greater pressure on the Court to invalidate the precedent established in *Plessy v. Ferguson*. The Court considered this question in 1954, in *Brown v. Board of Education*. Discrimination and segregation were facts of life for African Americans at that time. It was an easy matter, therefore, for the NAACP to find school-aged children to participate in a suit against segregation. During the 1950's, plaintiffs from around the country initiated a class-action suit, complaining of discrimination in public education. The experience of an African American student in Topeka, Kansas, became the focus of the case. Parents had tried to enroll their daughter at a white school near her home. The school board denied her application even though the nearest black school was several miles away.

The dispute came before the U.S. Supreme Court in 1954. The Court had been transformed by the appointment of Chief Justice Earl Warren, former governor of California. His appointment strengthened the Court's liberal wing, although most of the justices were still uneasy about voiding segregation policies of the states. Warren carefully persuaded his colleagues to support desegregation. To him, segregation had become a moral issue.

Warren recognized that segregation was a long-standing practice in the nation and that any opinion short of a unanimous decision would send a mixed message to the nation. Consequently, he encouraged the Court to speak with a single voice. In the celebrated case of *Brown v. Board of Education*, the Supreme Court concluded that separate facilities were inherently unequal. School segregation, therefore, was rendered unconstitutional. The Court urged the states to desegregate with all deliberate speed.

Massive Resistance
Public schools throughout the South rejected the *Brown* decision. Some states resurrected the doctrine of interposition, claiming that a state could nullify a federal law. The first major test for desegregation came in 1955 in Charlotte, NORTH CAROLINA. Dorothy Counts, a young African American student, attempted to integrate Harding High School. Counts was a gifted student who had some contact with white teenagers when she attended retreats

with her church organization. She assured her parents that she had gotten along well and was convinced that she could handle the pressure desegregation would surely precipitate. Her parents agreed and enrolled her at Harding.

The first day passed without incident, although Counts experienced isolation in the classroom and taunts by whites who did not want her there. Two white girls even befriended her. Their behavior encouraged Dorothy, but when she saw them the next day, they appeared aloof. They had been threatened, and notes had been distributed referring to them as "nigger lovers." A white mob confronted Counts on her second day of school. After a few days, her parents withdrew her from Harding.

The most violent contest over desegregation broke out in the LITTLE ROCK CRISIS in Arkansas in 1957. Nine children, selected because of their ability and temperament, participated in a desegregation experiment.

When the teenagers appeared on the Central High School campus, a violent mob confronted them. Orval Faubus, the governor of the state, tried to block their admission. People came to Little Rock, many of them hoping to prevent desegregation. They overturned cars, taunted the children, and threw bricks at African American journalists who covered the story. Ultimately, President Dwight Eisenhower dispatched federal troops to restore peace. Troops patrolled Central High for a year, escorting the children to school and around campus.

Desegregation virtually collapsed by the 1960's, and school boards tried a number of schemes to nullify the effects of the *Brown* decision. Among the strategies adopted were pupil-placement laws. These statutes authorized school boards to move children around in school districts in a way that maintained segregation. Other states repealed compulsory attendance laws, so that white parents could legally withdraw children should the school district desegregate. Other states threatened to withhold funding or even close schools that desegregated. Still others adopted freedom-of-choice plans, whereby children could select their own schools. A few African Americans attended white schools; few school boards, however, desegregated their programs. During the early 1970's, when many southern states began to comply with desegregation, whites withdrew from public schools to form private academies. Others struggled to preserve neighborhood schools, many of which were racially homogeneous.

To integrate Central High School in Arkansas's state capital, Little Rock, in 1957, the federal government had to send in military troops to protect the school's new African American students. *(AP/Wide World Photos)*

Desegregation of Colleges

The battle over desegregation returned to college campuses by 1960. Although a few African Americans had been enrolled in professional schools, most campuses in the nation were still segregated, especially in the South. The University of Mississippi was among them. James MEREDITH challenged the practice in 1961. The U.S. Supreme Court backed Meredith's admission, confirming an order by a lower court. Governor Ross Barnett personally appeared on the campus to turn Meredith away, but President John F. Kennedy dispatched U.S. marshals to the campus to protect Meredith. Once students and the community in Oxford learned that Meredith was on campus that September, Oxford exploded into violence. President Kennedy's pleas to Governor Barnett that he restore order failed. Barnett wanted only to delay segregation, not to enroll Meredith. The president finally dispatched federal troops to restore order and enroll Meredith.

Public Facilities

The battle over desegregation went beyond education to include transportation and dining facilities. Cities throughout the nation had passed ordinances to segregate everything from elevators and parks to swimming pools and local transit systems. The city of MONTGOMERY, ALABAMA, was such a place. Segregation on city buses meant that seats in the front of a bus would be reserved for whites. Blacks could sit in the rear only, although a white could claim a seat in the section reserved for blacks. Drivers all were white, although the majority of passengers were black. They some-

When Alabama governor George Wallace (at doorway) tried to block the integration of the University of Alabama in 1963, President John F. Kennedy federalized the local National Guard, whose commander ordered Wallace to step aside. *(AP/Wide World Photos)*

times referred to blacks using derogatory terms, and occasionally a driver would take the fare from a black passenger, order him or her to board from the rear of the bus, and then pull away before the passenger could enter.

The Reverend Vernon JOHNS was among those determined to challenge segregation in Montgomery. Johns pastored the Dexter Avenue Baptist Church in Montgomery. He often challenged injustice, both in the pulpit and in confrontations with local officials. Johns threatened to resign his pastorship, hoping to coerce parishioners into supporting his militant activities. Church leaders accepted his resignation and began a search for a new pastor. Johns did not intend to resign; church leaders, however, had grown weary of him.

They offered the pastorship to Martin Luther KING, Jr., a doctoral candidate at Boston University. King and his wife, Coretta, had grown up in the South and were hesitant to move to such a rigorously segregated community. King nevertheless accepted the appointment. Dexter Avenue Baptist Church did not know that the new direction initiated by Johns would continue with the new pastor.

The events that thrust King into the movement to desegregate Montgomery began in December, 1955. Rosa PARKS, a seamstress and secretary for the NAACP, was arrested for violating the city's segregation laws by refusing to surrender her seat to a white patron. Her arrest symbolized the experiences of all African Americans, and they rallied to pressure the city to alter its segregation laws in public transit. Members of the newly formed Montgomery Improvement Association (MIA) selected King as their president. The MIA, however, did not demand desegregation initially. It asked the city to demand courtesy from bus drivers, and to employ a few black bus drivers, and to revise its segregation law to allow African Americans to keep their seats. When the city refused, the MIA launched a suit to achieve desegregation.

Meanwhile, the MIA launched a boycott against the transit authority. Its demonstration was a peaceful one, as urged by King. King, who had done extensive reading about civil disobedience, believed it was the only strategy to employ in a dispute when the oppressed were in the minority. Whites in Montgomery, however, were far from nonviolent. The KU KLUX KLAN and other secret white societies intimidated African Americans, and bombs exploded in King's home and at local churches. Whites taunted those who walked long distances and formed car pools during the boycott. The boycott went on. The Supreme Court eventually upheld a ruling that had declared Alabama's state and local segregation laws unconstitutional. The boycott ended, in triumph, on December 21, 1956.

The Sit-In Movement

Students from across the country also joined the movement to achieve desegregation. In February, 1960, students from North Carolina Agricultural and Technical College, one of the state's segregated colleges, launched the student SIT-IN movement. The students sat down for service at a lunch counter at the Woolworth store in Greensboro. They were refused service. They returned the next day and were joined by others. Within months, the sit-in movement spread across the country. Thousands were arrested; some, including college professors, were expelled from school or fired. Students formed the STUDENT NONVIOLENT COORDINATING COMMITTEE to organize student participation in the Civil Rights movement.

Before the decade ended, students participated in FREEDOM RIDES, in which they challenged segregation in interstate travel. Whites and blacks boarded a coach in Washington, D.C., for a tour through the South. They were confronted by violent mobs, and some barely escaped with their lives. The rides and the protests that surrounded them led to numerous injuries and several deaths.

Students also participated in the MARCH ON WASHINGTON in 1963, demonstrating the urgent demand for desegregation and civil rights for African Americans. The assault on children in BIRMINGHAM, ALABAMA, demonstrated to the nation the urgent need for civil rights reforms. The assassinations of President John F. Kennedy and his brother Robert aptly illustrate the climate of the times. In 1968 an assassin's bullet claimed the life of Martin Luther King, Jr. Ironically, in death, these American heroes continued to effect change. The Civil Rights Act, Voting Rights Act, and Great Society programs of President Lyndon Johnson were all responses, in part, to the senseless killings during the 1960's. The Civil Rights movement had placed the nation on the road to equality of opportunity and civil rights.

—*Stephen Middleton*

See also: Johnson administration; Montgomery bus boycott; Voting Rights Act of 1965.

Suggested Readings:

Branch, Taylor. *Parting the Waters: America in the King Years, 1954-63.* New York: Simon & Schuster, 1988.

_____. *Pillar of Fire: America in the King Years, 1963-65.* New York: Simon & Schuster, 1998.

Clark, E. Culpepper. *The Schoolhouse Door: Segregation's Last Stand at the University of Alabama.* New York: Oxford University Press, 1993.

Hampton, Henry, and Steve Fayer, with Sarah Flynn, comps. *Voices of Freedom: An Oral History of the Civil Rights Movement from the 1950's Through the 1980's.* New York: Bantam Books, 1990.

Jones, Leon. *From Brown to Boston: Desegregation in Education, 1954-1974.* Metuchen, N.J.: Scarecrow Press, 1979.

Kohn, Howard. *We Had a Dream: A Tale of the Struggle for Integration in America.* New York: Simon & Schuster, 1998.

Kluger, Richard. *Simple Justice: The History of Brown v. Board of Education and Black America's Struggle for Equality.* New York: Vintage Books, 1977.

Litwack, Leon F. *Trouble in Mind: Black Southerners in the Age of Jim Crow.* New York: Alfred A. Knopf, 1998.

Merchon, Sherie, and Steven Schlossman. *Foxholes and Color Lines: Desegregating the U.S. Armed Forces.* Baltimore: The Johns Hopkins University Press, 1998.

Rasmussen, R. Kent. *Farewell to Jim Crow: The Rise and Fall of Segregation in America.* New York: Facts on File, 1997.

Steinhorn, Leonard, and Barbara Diggs-Brown. *By the Color of Our Skin: The Illusion of Integration and the Reality of Race.* New York: E. P. Dutton, 1999.

Selika, Marie (Marie Smith; c. 1849, Natchez, Mississippi—May 19, 1937, New York, New York): Concert singer. Selika was one of several renowned African American concert singers of the nineteenth century. Few details are known about her early life. She apparently was moved to several cities before she came to the attention of a wealthy Cincinnati, OHIO, family. The family oversaw her education, which included music lessons. Sometime during the early 1870's, she moved to San Francisco, where she studied voice with Giovanni Bianchi. In 1876 she made her professional debut in that city. She then moved to Ohio, then to CHICAGO, where she studied with Antonio Farini. From there, she went to BOSTON in 1878.

It was in Boston that she adopted the stage name "Selika," the African princess from Giacomo Meyerbeer's opera *L'Africaine.* There are conflicting accounts as to whether she sang an entire performance of the opera from which she adopted her professional name. She became the first African American to sing at the White House, during the Hayes administration, in 1878. Her husband, Sampson Williams, whose stage name was Signor Velosko, also sang.

In 1882 she and her husband left for Europe. After a command performance for Queen Victoria at St. James Hall in 1883, she sang in several European countries, including Belgium, France, Germany, and Scotland. After returning to the United States in 1885, she sang in several cities, including Baltimore, Boston, Chicago, Cincinnati, Louisville, New York, and Philadelphia. She and Williams embarked on another tour of Europe between 1887 and 1892. During this period, she also sang in the WEST INDIES. After returning to the United States a second time, she and Williams established a vocal studio in Ohio. In 1911 they moved to Philadelphia. Selika retired in 1916 to teach at the Martin-Smith School of Music. Selika was promoted at the height of her career as the "Queen of Staccato" because of the precision of her coloratura.

Sellers, Cleveland, Jr. (b. November 8, 1944, Denmark, South Carolina): Political activist. Sellers met Stokely CARMICHAEL while a student at HOWARD UNIVERSITY. He had been interested in social activism even as a child, so he joined the Nonviolent Action Group on campus, to which Carmichael also belonged. Members of it were also unofficial members of the STUDENT NONVIOLENT COORDINATING COMMITTEE (SNCC).

Sellers was elected as SNCC program secretary in November, 1965, and held that position until May, 1967, when he did not run for reelection because Carmichael was stepping down as the head of SNCC. Sellers was the state coordinator for SOUTH CAROLINA for SNCC during the ORANGEBURG MASSACRE in February, 1968. He was convicted on September 28, 1970, of participating in the riot and sentenced to a year in prison. He was released on bail so that he could attend college. Sellers published his autobiography, *The River of No Return*, in 1973.

Selma to Montgomery march: CIVIL RIGHTS leader Martin Luther KING, Jr., organized the Selma to Montgomery march in March, 1965. Hoping to pressure the federal government into passing legislation protecting voting rights, King and other members of the SOUTHERN CHRISTIAN LEADERSHIP CONFERENCE (SCLC) planned a series of demonstrations in Alabama. King knew that angry racists would almost certainly disrupt the demonstrations with violence. He believed that Americans watching the events on national television would be shocked by the violence and would pressure the federal government into responding. The SCLC leaders chose Selma, a town in central Alabama and the seat of Dallas County, as the center of their demonstrations.

Selma Demonstrations

Selma was well known to civil rights activists. The population of Dallas County was 60 percent black, but only 335 of the county's ten thousand registered voters were black. County Sheriff James G. Clark was adamantly opposed to black civil rights, and voter registration drives in Selma had been met with violence in the past. Selma seemed a likely place to provoke a confrontation. The demonstrations began in early January of 1965, when King and other activists attempted to register black voters. Larger demonstrations were held in February. Although hundreds of protesters were arrested, the civil rights activists were convinced that they still needed an incident that would make the national news. Somewhat to their disappointment, Sheriff Clark kept a firm hand, and there was minimal violence.

On Saturday, March 6, King announced a march from Selma to MONTGOMERY, ALABAMA, the state capital. George C. Wallace, the governor of the state and an avowed segregationist, immediately issued an order banning the march. For a variety of political reasons King decided to cancel the march, but enthusi-

Selma, Alabama, 1965-1995

Five months after the Selma to Montgomery march, President Lyndon B. Johnson signed the Voting Rights Act of 1965, which eliminated literacy tests, poll taxes, and other restrictions that had been used to deny voting rights to African Americans in the South. In 1965 the number of African Americans living in Selma and surrounding Dallas County who were registered to vote stood at 250. Thirty years later, the county had 20,573 black registered voters out of a total black population of approximately 27,915 (58 percent of the area's 1990 Census population of 48,130).

In 1965 no African Americans served as members of the Selma city council, as commissioners for Dallas County, or as city or county school board officials. Thirty years later, there were five African Americans on the nine-member Selma city council and six African Americans on the eleven-member city school board. For Dallas County, there were two African Americans on the five-member county commission and three African Americans on the five-member county school board.

Source: Data from *Los Angeles Times*, March 6, 1995, p. A11

astic protesters ignored his instructions and met at the local church the following morning to begin the 54-mile trip to Montgomery.

Bloody Sunday

Hosea WILLIAMS, an SCLC leader, led a crowd of five hundred marchers toward Highway 80, the road to Montgomery. When they reached the Edmund Pettus Bridge on the outskirts of town, they met approximately two hundred sheriff's deputies and state troopers. The commander of the state troopers gave the marchers two minutes to turn around and then, without warning, ordered his troops to move on the protesters. The troopers and deputies entered the crowd swinging clubs, whips, and chains. Some were armed with electric cattle prods. Clouds of tear gas added to the confusion. The march collapsed under the furious attack of law enforcement officials.

Journalists caught the violence on film, and the images of the unarmed protesters being savagely beaten appeared on television and in newspapers. Hoping to keep tensions high so that the federal government would have to intervene, King announced another march to be held on March 9. A crowd of fifteen hundred blacks and whites crossed the bridge and encountered a line of state troopers. King refused to continue the march and led the protesters back to the church. Violence in Selma had not abated, however. That same day, a white minister in Selma who supported the march was beaten so badly that he died two days later on March 11.

March to Montgomery

The violence in Selma outraged many Americans, who pressured the federal government to act. On March 15, President Lyndon B. Johnson urged Congress to pass a voting rights bill. He also helped King obtain a permit to conduct the march. On March 21, King led more than three thousand marchers across the Edmund Pettus Bridge and down Highway 80 to Montgomery. They arrived in the state capital four days later, where thousands more gathered to listen to speeches and celebrate their victory.

The SCLC plan worked. The savage beating on the Edmund Pettus Bridge troubled the nation's conscience and built momentum for voting rights legislation. Congress passed the bill that summer, and President Johnson signed the VOTING RIGHTS ACT OF 1965 into law on August 5, 1965.

Anniversary March in 1995

Activists from across the United States gathered in Selma in 1995 to commemorate the thirtieth anniversary of the Selma to Montgomery march. Mayor Joe Smitherman, who had been mayor in 1965 and had supported segregation, this time offered the keys to the city to Hosea Williams and Congressman John LEWIS, both of whom had marched thirty years earlier. When the crowd of fifteen hundred marchers arrived at the Edmund Pettus Bridge, they met vendors selling snacks and souvenirs instead of armed troops.

Approximately one hundred people, including seventy-three-year-old SCLC president Joseph LOWERY, reenacted the entire 54-mile march to Montgomery. When the marchers reached the state capital, they were joined by civil rights activist Jesse JACKSON and Congressman Donald Payne, chairman of the Congressional Black Caucus. A crowd of more than a thousand people assembled to listen to speeches commemorating the first march.

An Unusual Appearance

The event that garnered the most media attention during the reenactment of the march was the appearance of former Alabama governor George Wallace. Thirty years before, Wallace had been a symbol of the South's resistance to black civil rights and had sent troopers to block the Edmund Pettus Bridge. In 1995, confined to a wheelchair and in poor health, Wallace had an aide read a statement in which he welcomed the marchers to Montgomery and praised their cause. Many of the marchers thanked Wallace and forgave him for past deeds; others assumed that the aging Wallace was merely trying to salvage his reputation or soothe his own conscience.

—*Thomas Clarkin*

Flanked by Ralph and Juanita Abernathy and Ralph Bunche at his right and by his own wife, Coretta Scott King at his left, Martin Luther King, Jr. (in front of flag) leads marchers across the Alabama River toward Montgomery on March 21, 1965. *(AP/Wide World Photos)*

Suggested Readings:

Bragg, Rick. "Emotional March Gains a Repentant Wallace." *The New York Times* (March 11, 1995): 1.

Fager, Charles. *Selma, 1965*. New York: Charles Scribner's Sons, 1974.

Garrow, David J. *Protest at Selma: Martin Luther King, Jr., and the Voting Rights Act of 1965*. New Haven, Conn.: Yale University Press, 1978.

Harrison, Eric. "Blacks Celebrate Gains as Selma March Revisited." *Los Angeles Times* (March 6, 1995): A1.

Sitkoff, Harvard. *The Struggle for Black Equality, 1954-1992*. Rev. ed. New York: Hill & Wang, 1993.

Taylor, Branch. *Pillar of Fire: America in the King Years, 1963-65*. New York: Simon & Schuster, 1998.

Seminole wars: Three Seminole wars (1817-1819, 1835-1842, 1855-1858) were fought by Seminole Indians and their African American allies to retain FLORIDA land holdings.

The Seminole are a Native American tribe whose villages were situated in northern Florida. As part of the southeastern cultural group, they derived most of their nourishment from the products of their farmlands and cattle herds. For years, relations between the Seminole and whites in Spanish-owned Florida were good. However, conflicts arose in the late 1700's when American southerners began allowing their cattle to graze through Seminole fields and hunting grounds. The Seminoles worried about American desires for their land, and the Americans complained that the Seminole stole their cattle.

Seminoles further antagonized American southerners by assisting escaped slaves. Runaway slaves were welcomed in Florida and found freedom there. They established MAROON forts and villages near Seminole towns. Seminoles and African Americans traded and hunted together, intermarried, and fought against common enemies.

The first Seminole war began in 1817 when U.S. forces successfully attacked a "black Seminole" stronghold at Fort Negro. Seminole and African Americans fought together against American forces, but General Andrew Jackson quickly captured key Spanish towns. The resulting Spanish defeat gave Florida to the United States.

American settlers quickly moved into northern Florida and onto Seminole holdings. Property disputes arose, and settlers petitioned the government to remove Native Americans from the area. In 1823 the Seminole agreed to move to reservation lands in central Florida in exchange for 24 million acres of land and a $5,000 annuity.

Contemporary illustration decrying the alliance of Indians and blacks in the Seminole wars. *(Library of Congress)*

However, the reservation lands were not as fertile. Americans complained that hungry Seminoles were raiding cattle from nearby PLANTATIONS and were hampering the efforts of slave hunters trying to retrieve runaways. Southerners also feared that the existence of free African American towns in Florida encouraged runaways, and they disliked negotiating with African American advisers and interpreters for the Seminole nation.

In 1830 the U.S. Congress passed the Indian Removal Act. All Native Americans east of the Mississippi River were given land in Indian Territory (roughly present-day Oklahoma) in exchange for their eastern holdings. They would be transported west and given funds to begin a new life in Oklahoma. In the 1832 Treaty of Payne's Landing, the Seminole agreed to move in exchange for $80,000. While many left Florida immediately, others protested the treaty and urged resistance.

Verbal protests turned to violent skirmishes, and the U.S. Army marched into Florida to squelch the uprising and force the Seminole west. Tribal chief Osceola led Seminole and African American allies in a persistent guerrilla war against American forces in the second Seminole war. The United States eventually abandoned the war in 1842 but at a cost of approximately $30 million and fifteen hundred men. Most Seminole and African Americans were forced to move west.

A few Seminoles remained in hiding in Florida's everglades. During the 1850's they made selected attempts to regain their lands in the third Seminole war. Though they numbered fewer than three hundred persons by 1858, Florida Seminoles numbered almost two thousand by 1996. Through legal battles they eventually acquired hundreds of thousands of acres of reservation lands.

—*Leslie A. Stricker*

Suggested Readings:
Covington, James W. *The Seminoles of Florida.*

Gainesville: University of Florida Press, 1993.
Metzler, Milton. *Hunted Like a Wolf: The Story of the Seminole War.* New York: Farrar, Straus and Giroux, 1972.

Sengstacke, John (b. November 25, 1912, Savannah, Georgia): Publisher. Sengstacke inherited a publishing company from his uncle, Robert Sengstacke ABBOTT, having served as vice president and general manager. He also acquired the *Courier* newspapers of Pittsburgh and Miami and the *Chronicle* in Detroit. He directed the NATIONAL NEWSPAPER PUBLISHERS ASSOCIATION, founded the Negro Newspaper Publishers Association, and was appointed to committees by Presidents Truman, Kennedy, and Johnson.
See also: Black press.

Sentencing Project Report of 1995: A study of young African Americans and the criminal justice system released in October of 1995 by the Sentencing Project, an organization based in WASHINGTON, D.C. The report's authors were Marc Mauer, the project's assistant director, and Tracy Huling, a criminal justice consultant. Previous reports by the Sentencing Project were entitled *Dilemma of Black Male Youth.* The expanded 1995 report documented a worsening situation in which one in three young male African Americans were found to be under criminal justice jurisdiction.

Summary of Findings
The study's major proposition was that public policies developed to control crime and SUBSTANCE ABUSE contributed in numerous ways to the growing racial disparity in the criminal justice system while having minimal effect on the problems they were designed to remedy. The principal findings of the 1995 study were as follows:

1. Almost one in three (32.2 percent) young African American MEN between the ages of twenty and twenty-nine was under criminal justice supervision on any given day—in prison or jail, on probation, or on parole.

2. The cost of criminal justice control for these 827,440 young African American men averaged $6 billion per year.

3. In the five years between 1989 and 1994, African American WOMEN experienced the greatest increase in criminal justice supervision of all demographic groups, with their rate of supervision rising by 78 percent.

4. During that same period, drug policies constituted the single most significant factor contributing to the growth of the criminal justice population, with the number of incarcerated drug offenders having risen fivefold (510 percent) from 1983 to 1993. The number of African American women incarcerated in state prisons for drug offenses increased more than eightfold (828 percent) from 1986 to 1991.

5. While the national arrest rate of African Americans for violent crimes—45 percent—was disproportionate to their representation in the larger American population, this proportion had not changed significantly for twenty years. For drug offenses, however, the African American proportion of arrests went up from 24 percent in 1980 to 39 percent in 1993, well above the African American proportion of drug users nationally.

6. Almost 90 percent of offenders sentenced to state prisons in the early 1990's for drug possession were African American and Hispanic.

These findings prompted the authors of the report to predict that the high rates of criminal justice control for African Americans were likely to worsen considerably during the next few years. Moreover, they noted, the impact of "get tough" policies would inevitably lead to continuing increases in criminal justice control rates and increasing racially disparate impacts.

Explanations

A number of explanations may be offered for the study's findings. First, the growth of the criminal justice system coincided with a number of economic disruptions and changes in social policy that have had significant effects on income distribution, employment, and family structure. Since the 1970's, the decline of manufacturing, the expansion of low-wage service industries, and the loss of a significant part of the middle-class tax base in many urban areas led to a decline in real wages for most Americans, with a widening of the gap between rich and poor. In the case of African American male high school dropouts in their twenties, this has meant a significant decline in annual earnings by a full 50 percent from 1973 to 1989.

Compounding the problem is a decline in social service benefits: Mental health services and other forms of support have generally declined, while the social problems they were designed to address have been exacerbated. The impact of these changes on the African American community is said to have resulted from the intersection of race and class effects. The outcomes of these social problems are much more profound among African Americans because they are disproportionately represented in low-income urban communities.

Second, decisions made by prosecutors to increase the severity of the impact of drug policies on minorities has aggravated the racial disparity in arrest patterns. While federal prosecutors claim that they target high-level traffickers, many African Americans charged in federal court have been low-level dealers or accomplices in the drug trade. This prosecutorial discretion has had serious consequences for African Americans charged with such crimes, since federal mandatory sentencing laws require five- and ten-year minimum sentences even for first offenders.

Third, a succession of media images and racially divisive political campaigns in the late 1980's and early 1990's fostered the widespread public perception of an extremely violent young African American male community. These images contradict the fact that the typical African American man in the criminal justice system is not a violent offender. Considering the combined population of African Americans supervised by the four components of the criminal justice system—prison, jail, probation, and parole—approximately three-fourths of these individuals have been convicted of nonviolent offenses. The image of the violent African American man, while indicative of some disturbing trends, is quite inaccurate in its overall impact. Nevertheless, these media images have had some far-reaching effects on public policy, including the adoption of harsh federal sentencing policies for cocaine possession and distribution.

Finally, as increasing numbers of young African American men are arrested and incarcerated, their life prospects are seriously diminished. A corollary to this development is that gang or crime group affiliations are reinforced in prison and emerge even stronger once the individuals are released back to the community. These ubiquitous former offenders and gang members emerge as the community's role models in light of the fact that few African American men in the urban underclass have stable ties to the labor market.

Recommendations

The report's authors made a number of recommendations that they believed would help to reverse the rise of criminal justice control rates for African Americans. They suggested that national spending priorities should be revised with an eye to expanding drug treatment and other programs within the criminal justice system. Such treatment programs should be tailored to the needs of the prison population and should address the multiple and specific needs of women. The authors believed that there should be a renewed national dialogue concerning drug policy with an eye to considering the racial inequity resulting from "three strikes" laws and other mandatory sentencing measures. As a step toward eliminating the disparity in sentencing policies, judges and juries should be provided with a broader array of sentencing options for nonviolent offenders who would otherwise be sentenced to prison. Finally, the federal government should be required to prepare racial/ethnic impact statements concerning proposed legislation and should establish long-range crime control policies and strategies.

The Sentencing Project's report of October, 1995, clearly highlighted various strategies that could lead to the improvement of sentencing practices and to the development of sentencing programs that promote alternatives to incarceration, particularly for indigent defendants. The strength of the report hinges on the way it systematically analyzes empirical data on several levels of government to call for change in a manner that is consonant with American thinking about crime and punishment.

—*Abdul Karim Bangura*

See also: Crime and the criminal justice system; Gangs.

Suggested Readings:

Gest, Ted. "A Shocking Look at Blacks and Crime." *U.S. News and World Report* 119 (October 16, 1995): 53-54.

Massey, Douglas S., and Nancy A. Denton. *American Apartheid: Segregation and the Making of the Underclass.* Cambridge, Mass.: Harvard University Press, 1993.

Mauer, Marc. *Young Black Americans and the Criminal Justice System: A Growing National Problem.* Washington, D.C.: The Sentencing Project, 1990.

Mauer, Marc, and Tracy Huling. *Young Black Americans and the Criminal Justice System: Five Years Later.* Washington, D.C.: Sentencing Project, 1995.

Tonry, Michael H. *Malign Neglect: Race, Crime, and Punishment in America.* New York: Oxford University Press, 1995.

Separate but equal: Refers to segregation with a stated intent of keeping opportunities and conditions equivalent between or among the separated groups. The U.S. SUPREME COURT gave its approval to "separate but equal" facilities for blacks and whites in the 1896 decision PLESSY V. FERGUSON. As the decision applied to the southern Jim Crow segregation laws of the late 1800's, blacks and whites were to have access to the same quality of public facilities. This did not, in fact, happen. The facilities were separated, but they were far from equal; everything from white railroad cars to white schools were significantly superior to facilities available to blacks. In 1954 the U.S. Supreme Court finally ruled in BROWN V. BOARD OF EDUCATION that separate but equal facilities in education were unconstitutional.

See also: Jim Crow laws; Segregation and integration.

Symbols of the passing of the era of "separate but equal" are the segregation signs removed from the Montgomery, Alabama, municipal airport in 1962. *(AP/Wide World Photos)*

Sepia: Magazine. A monthly general-interest black magazine published from 1952 to 1982, *Sepia* followed the format of *Life* and aspired to compete with EBONY. George Levitan, a wealthy entrepreneur and owner of Good Publishing Company in Fort Worth, Texas, published *Sepia* and five other black magazines until his death in 1976.

In its eighty to one hundred pages per issue, *Sepia* covered news, FASHION, sports, and entertainment of interest to African Americans; highlighted black people of achievement; and explored in depth such issues as prejudice and violence against blacks, CIVIL RIGHTS, the importance of black churches, and support for HISTORICALLY BLACK COLLEGES. Levitan often talked of making *Sepia* a serious rival to *Ebony*. His consistent understaffing, heavy use of part-time employees, severe economizing, tight editorial control, and reluctance to seek subscriptions were all deterrents to that goal.

Sepia is perhaps best known for publishing John Howard Griffin's account of traveling through the South in 1959 posing as a black man. Griffin took a drug and used a sunlamp to darken his skin. His account of life as a "tenth-class citizen," with photographs by Don Rutledge, was published in *Sepia* from April through September, 1960, as "Journey into Shame." Griffin had received six thousand letters about his series by June, 1960. The full account of his experiences was published as a book, *Black Like Me*, in 1961.

During the VIETNAM WAR, *Sepia*'s column "Our Men in Vietnam" published stories and letters describing black soldiers' reactions to fighting the war and accounts of RACIAL DISCRIMINATION within the MILITARY.

—*Glenn Ellen Starr Stilling*

See also: Black press.

Serrano, Andrés (b. August 15, 1950, New York, New York): Photographer and conceptual artist. Born to an Afro-Cuban mother and a Honduran-born white father, Serrano was influenced as much by his Latino heritage as by his African roots. As an adolescent growing up in NEW YORK CITY, Serrano dropped out of high school at the age of fifteen and enrolled briefly in art school at age seventeen. By the age of twenty, Serrano had become a drug addict and drug dealer; he had also married and fathered a daughter with artist Julie Ault. It took Serrano eight years to conquer his drug addiction.

Serrano joined the radical arts collaborative Group Materials when he was twenty-eight. Although influenced by the group's artistic philosophy, he chose to work alone. As something of an artistic renegade, Serrano attempted to transform repulsive and shocking still-life images into works of art. Serrano's work often incorporates Roman Catholic imagery, and he decorated his apartment with vestments and sacramental chalices from around the world.

Serrano gained national notoriety in 1989 as the result of reactions to a photograph entitled *Piss Christ*, depicting a crucifix suspended upside down in a jar filled with golden fluid, identified by the artist himself as urine. The award-winning photograph was among several by Serrano that were chosen to appear in the Awards in the Visual Arts touring exhibition sponsored by the Southeastern Center for Contemporary Art (SECCA) in 1989. The three-city tour received part of its funding from the National Endowment for the Arts (NEA).

The photograph's title and imagery placed Serrano in the midst of political controversy. Senator Jesse Helms and other conservative politicians were outraged that federal funds had been used to promote an exhibition containing images they considered to be blasphemous and pornographic. Many curators and artists responded by supporting Serrano's right to free artistic expression and stating that loss of NEA funding for his work constituted a form of government censorship. This furor over artistic expression had significant political repercussions. Senator Helms suggested that the federal government make cuts in the NEA budget, and a bill was later introduced in Congress to eliminate the NEA altogether.

Serrano became a well-established artist despite the harsh criticism his work has received. He received a fellowship from the NEA in 1986, and his work was featured in eighteen solo exhibitions between 1990 and 1993. A retrospective exhibition entitled "Andrés Serrano: Works 1983-1993" was presented at New York City's prestigious New Museum of Contemporary Art in 1995. In 1997 his exhibition "A History of Andrés Serrano/ A History of Sex" was shown in the Netherlands and England.

A considerable amount of Serrano's photography is concerned with depicting bodily fluids in both realistic and abstract ways, and many photographs are sexually explicit. While acknowledging the disturbing (and, to some, distasteful) nature of Serrano's subject matter, many members of the art community have protested efforts to silence or censor works such as Serrano's that explore the debasement and exploitation of spiritual beliefs and values.

See also: Photographers; Visual arts.

Shabazz, Betty (May 28, 1936, Detroit, Michigan—June 23, 1997, Bronx, New York): Com-

Betty Shabazz, immediately after identifying the slain body of her husband, Malcolm X, in February, 1965. *(Library of Congress)*

munity affairs activist. A political activist, Hajj Bahiyah Betty Shabazz tried to continue the work begun by her husband, CIVIL RIGHTS leader MALCOLM X, who was assassinated in 1965.

Betty Shabazz was well educated and socially conscious. A registered nurse with a nursing degree from the Brooklyn State Hospital School of Nursing and a B.A. in Public Health Administration from Jersey City State College, Shabazz earned a master's degree in public health, writing a master's thesis on SICKLE-CELL ANEMIA. She was granted her Ph.D. in education by the University of Massachusetts at Amherst.

The mother of six children, Shabazz, after her husband's death, worked on the Sickle-Cell Anemia Telethon Board and was director of the African-American Foundation, the Women's Service League, and the Day Care Council of Westchester County, New York.

She was director of institutional advancement at Medgar EVERS College in New York City and chaired the forty-first NATIONAL COUNCIL OF NEGRO WOMEN Convention. A cultural center at Mount Holyoke College was named for her.

Shabazz's life came to a terrible end when a troubled grandchild, Malcolm Shabazz, angered at having to live with his grandmother because his mother, Qubilah SHABAZZ, was having legal difficulties, soaked her home with gasoline and set it afire on June 1, 1997. Severely burned, Shabazz survived until June 23. Malcolm was subsequently sentenced to eighteen months in a facility in Lenox, Massachusetts, that specializes in rehabilitating young arsonists.

—*R. Baird Shuman*

Shabazz, Qubilah Bahiyah (b. December 25, 1960, New York, New York): Accused conspirator. The second of six daughters of MALCOLM X and Betty SHABAZZ, Qubilah Shabazz was named for Kublai Khan, the Mongol emperor of China.

On January 12, 1995, Shabazz was arrested for hiring Michael Fitzpatrick, a former high school acquaintance, to assassinate Louis FARRAKHAN, the spiritual leader of the NATION OF ISLAM. Fitzpatrick, an informant for the FEDERAL BUREAU OF INVESTIGATION (FBI), gave authorities information that led to Shabazz's arrest. The alleged assassination plot was intended as revenge against Farrakhan's purported involvement in the 1965 assassination of Malcolm X. Farrakhan and Betty Shabazz overcame their long-standing antagonism in order to rally public support for Qubilah Shabazz. William Kunstler, a noted civil rights defender, was hired as Qubilah's defense attorney. Revelation of Fitzgerald's criminal record and countercharges of entrapment resulted in plea bargaining arrangements. Qubilah admitted responsibility for her actions but not guilt, absolved the government of blame, and agreed to undergo psychiatric and chemical dependency treatment at a facility in Texas.

Shadd, Mary Ann (October 9, 1823, Wilmington, Delaware—June 5, 1893, Washington, D.C.): Teacher, journalist, abolitionist, and lawyer. Shadd was the oldest of thirteen children born in Delaware to a free black shoemaker and his wife. Her father was active in the ABOLITIONIST MOVEMENT and served as president of the National Convention for Improvement of Free People of Color in the United States in 1833. Shadd was educated in a Quaker-run school for FREE BLACKS in PENNSYLVANIA. Upon completion of her studies, she returned to Delaware to organize and teach at a private school for blacks in 1839.

In 1851 Shadd moved with her brother Isaac to Windsor, Canada West (present-day Ontario), where they taught in a local segregated school for blacks supported by the AMERICAN MISSIONARY ASSOCIATION of New York. The entire Shadd family eventually joined them, and they later moved to Chatham, the key destination of the UNDERGROUND RAILROAD. In 1852 Shadd published a booklet based on her experiences as an African American on the Canadian frontier entitled *A Plea for Emigration, or Notes on Canada West, in Its Moral, Social and Political Aspects.*

Abolitionist Samuel Ringgold WARD hired Shadd to work as a subscription agent for his newspaper, *The Provincial Freeman,* published in Windsor beginning in 1853. By 1854 Shadd was serving as the paper's chief editor and published essays and news articles of interest to the black communities of the Canadian provinces. In 1855 she toured through Michigan, Ohio, Pennsylvania, and Illinois, lecturing to audiences on the benefits of black emigration to Canada. In 1856 she married Thomas F. Cary of Toronto. She became a

staunch advocate of integration in opposition to Henry Bibb and other emigrationists, who believed that segregated communities provided the best hope for the survival of blacks in Canada. The *Provincial Freeman* struggled financially, in part as a result of the illiteracy of Canada's growing black refugee population and because many who could read were unable to afford the cost of a newspaper subscription, and it ceased publication in 1858.

At the beginning of the CIVIL WAR, Shadd was teaching in MICHIGAN and remained there for a brief period in 1862 before returning to Chatham. After the EMANCIPATION PROCLAMATION was issued in 1863, she returned to the United States and accepted a commission to recruit black volunteers for the Union army. She became a regular contributor to several leading black newspapers, including Frederick DOUGLASS's *New National Era* and John Wesley Cromwell's *The Advocate.*

Near the end of the war, Shadd settled in WASHINGTON, D.C., where she was employed as a schoolteacher and a principal. She joined the National Woman Suffrage Association, successfully registered to vote in the District of Columbia, and founded the short-lived Colored Women's Progressive Franchise Association in 1880. Shadd became the first woman to enroll in the law department at HOWARD UNIVERSITY and was the third woman to graduate from the school when she received her LL.B. degree in 1883. She entered private practice as an attorney and had a successful career well into her sixties. Shadd suffered from rheumatism and other symptoms, possibly the result of cancer, which eventually led to her death at the age of sixty-nine.
See: Quakers and slavery.

Shakur, Assata Olugbala (JoAnne Deborah Byron, later Chesimard; b. July 16, 1947?, New York, New York): Political activist. Shakur was convicted on March 25, 1977, as an accomplice in the murder of NEW JERSEY state trooper Werner Foerster and of atrocious assault with intent to kill another state trooper, James Harper. Those charges stemmed from a shootout that occurred on the New Jersey Turnpike on May 2, 1973. Shakur, along with Zayd Malik Shakur, was a passenger in a car driven by Sundiata Acoli. Harper stopped the car, allegedly for having defective taillights.

All three of the car's passengers were known activists, and the COUNTER INTELLIGENCE PROGRAM (COINTELPRO) program of the FEDERAL BUREAU OF INVESTIGATION (FBI) suggested that activists be stopped for minor infractions of the law. Evidence indicates that Shakur had been a target of the COINTELPRO program as far back as 1971, and at the time of the turnpike incident she was accused of a number of serious crimes. Harper called in Foerster to assist with his stop. In an ensuing gun battle, Foerster was killed, as was Zayd Malik Shakur. Assata Shakur received serious wounds that temporarily paralyzed her right arm.

Even though medical evidence indicated that Shakur had not fired a gun and that her wounds would have prevented her from doing so, she was convicted on the two charges. Acoli was convicted of Foerster's murder at a separate trial. At the time of her arraignment, Shakur stood accused of various crimes in the media and was on the FBI's Most Wanted List in connection with a bank robbery. Prior to the turnpike incident, she had not been arraigned on any of those other charges, which included bank robbery, kidnapping, and attempted murder. She later was charged with some of those crimes, but eventually all charges except those connected with the turnpike incident were dismissed, were dropped for lack of evidence, or resulted in acquittal at trial.

Shakur's parents divorced shortly after her birth. She lived with her mother, an aunt, and her grandparents in Jamaica, New York, until the age of three, then in Wilmington, North Carolina. By the third grade, she was back in Queens, New York. In *Assata: An Autobiography* (1987), she recalls being the only black child in her class. She ran away from home as an adolescent, living with strangers for several months. Eventually she was taken in by her aunt, Evelyn Williams, who later served as her lawyer.

Shakur attended Manhattan Community College after holding a series of low-wage jobs. She intended to study business but was drawn to history, psychology, and sociology. While in college, she became involved in student politics and was attracted to socialist ideas. It was during this period that she took her new name. "Assata" translates as "she who struggles," "Olugbala" means "love for the people," and "Shakur," or "the thankful," was chosen out of respect for Zayd Malik Shakur and his family.

Shakur investigated various activist groups, looking for the appropriate one to join. She met with the Black Panthers during a trip to OAKLAND, CALIFORNIA, and later joined their Harlem branch. When the Black Panthers became more defensive in the face of COINTELPRO operations, she left. She then connected with elements of the BLACK LIBERATION ARMY. Some accounts list her as leader of that group, but in her autobiography, she describes it as consisting of many different groups, often not in communication with each other and having no formal leadership. It was after Shakur joined the Black Liberation Army that the turnpike incident occurred.

In 1979 Shakur escaped from prison, allegedly with the aid of members of the Black Liberation Army. She fled to CUBA and was granted political asylum. Her autobiography was written while she was in Cuba.

Shakur, Tupac (June 16, 1971, New York, New York—September 13, 1996, Las Vegas, Nevada): RAP performer and actor. Tupac Amaru

Shakur was the son of Afeni Shakur, a single mother. Since Shakur's mother had great expectations for her son, she named him for an Inca chief. In the Inca language, Tupac Amaru means "shining serpent," referring to wisdom and courage; the name Shakur is the Arabic word for "thankful to God."

Shakur grew up without knowing his father; and even his mother was uncertain who his father was. Instead, Shakur grew close to a man named Legs, whom his mother had dated. Legs had a history of dealing drugs; when Legs was sentenced to prison, Afeni Shakur moved the family to Baltimore. In Baltimore, Tupac Shakur entered and won his first rap contest. Soon after moving to Baltimore, the Shakur family heard the devastating news of the death of Legs from crack cocaine. The Shakur family eventually moved to Mann City, California. There Tupac Shakur dropped out of high school and began to sell drugs. Shakur later admitted that his life took a wrong turn when he left school.

Shakur's contacts with the underground rap scene in and around the Northern California community of OAKLAND eventually rekindled his desire to be a rap singer. Shakur auditioned for Shock-G, the leader of Digital Underground; the group later hired him to work as a roadie. While on tour with the group, Shakur eventually made an appearance onstage by dancing with a rubber doll.

Shakur's first solo album, 2Pacalypse Now, was released in 1991, and it sold well. As Shakur's career began to skyrocket, however, he amassed a growing record of arrests. In 1991 he faced charges for jaywalking and resisting arrest in Oakland. Later, in 1992, he was sued by a woman who claimed that the young black man who killed her husband had been influenced to do so by Shakur's music. That same year, Shakur faced criminal charges for attacking a limousine driver. In 1994 a warrant was issued for Shakur's arrest in connection with the shooting of two off-duty police offi-

Tupac Shakur in 1993. (AP/Wide World Photos)

cers in ATLANTA, GEORGIA. Although many of these charges related to Shakur's own actions, he was not always the perpetrator of the violence that followed in his wake.

In 1995, in the lobby of a New York recording studio, Shakur was shot five times, including once in the head. At the time there was in intense rivalry between West Coast and East Coast rappers. Police could not determine who was involved in the shooting, but Shakur himself blamed the incident on New York rappers such as the Notorious B.I.G. and Sean "Puffy" Combs.

In 1995 Shakur began serving a prison term of eighteen to fifty-four months for sexual assault. In court, he apologized to the victim but added that "I'm not apologizing for a crime" and "I hope in time you'll come forth and eventually tell the truth." The conviction stemmed from an incident that occurred in a New York hotel on November 18, 1993. Shakur met a young woman in a club who eventually returned with him to his hotel room. She later accused Shakur of sexual assault. The woman admitted that she had consented to some sexual acts but not to others. Several of Shakur's associates were also implicated and convicted based on testimony given in the trial. Despite his conviction, Shakur contended that the lawsuit was based on his lack of romantic interest in the young woman.

In the midst of these legal troubles, Shakur managed to complete several films and release an album. He appeared in films such as *Above the Rim* (1994), directed by Jeff Pollack; *Juice* (1992), directed by Ernest Dickerson; and *Poetic Justice* (1993), directed by John Singleton.

Shakur's third album, *Me Against the World* (1995), became a number-one seller while he was in prison serving time for the 1995 sexual assault conviction. His fourth album, *All Eyez on Me* (1996), was recorded after his release. It sold about five million copies, and once again Shakur's career looked promising. In September, 1996, Shakur was in Las Vegas with Suge Knight, head of Death Row Records, which had released *All Eyez on Me*, to see a Mike Tyson boxing matching. While he and Knight were driving on the Las Vegas strip, Shakur was shot by unknown assailants. He died from his wounds a few days later. Shakur remained controversial in death; rumors swirled about who had killed him and why, and a number of lawsuits were filed against his estate.

Shange, Ntozake (Paulette Williams; b. October 18, 1948, Trenton, New Jersey): Playwright. Shange is a feminist whose innovative plays and fiction of the 1970's and 1980's explored with painful honesty the lives of black women undervalued by society. Shange changed her name to two Zulu words meaning "she who comes with her own things" (NTOZAKE) and "she who walks like a lion" (SHANGE). Her father, Paul T. Williams, was a surgeon, and her mother, Eloise, a psychiatric social worker. Shange entered Barnard Col-

Ntozake Shange during the mid-1980's. *(Jules Allen)*

lege in 1966 and graduated with a B.A. degree in 1970. She received an M.A. from the University of Southern California in 1973. Depressed by her separation from her first husband in 1967, Shange attempted SUICIDE. According to a 1976 interview, she tried to commit suicide several other times because of her rage over the limitations imposed on her life because she was a black woman. From 1972 to 1975, she taught women's studies and Afro-American studies courses at Sonoma State College and Mills College in OAKLAND, CALIFORNIA. During this period, she performed her poetry in bars in Berkeley, San Francisco, and NEW YORK CITY. In 1977 she married David Murray, her second husband.

Shange's most famous work is *for colored girls who have considered suicide/ when the rainbow is enuf*, a "choreopoem" produced on Broadway in 1976. A collection of twenty poems acted out by seven female actors, the play protests black women's mistreatment at the hands of black men and celebrates the black woman's ability to survive and maintain a sense of self-worth. A very popular play, it was nominated for a number of awards and won an Obie Award. Shange thought the play was the victim of media exploitation, and she frequently expressed dissatisfaction with productions of it.

Serving as artist-in-residence at the New Jersey State Council on the Arts and as creative writing instructor at City College of New York, Shange wrote several experimental works in poetry, drama, and fiction. *Sassafrass* (1976), a novella, is the story of two sisters with opposite outlooks on their roles as women in relation to men. *Nappy Edges* (1978) is a book of poetry devoted primarily to the concerns of women. *Three Pieces* (1981) is a book of three plays that attempt to fuse poetry, drama, and music to reflect African Americans' "interdisciplinary culture." Other publications include *A Daughter's Geography* (1983), the play *From Okra to Greens: A Different Kinda Love Story* (pr. 1984, pb. 1985), a collection of her writings about her work entitled *See No Evil: Prefaces, Essays, and Accounts, 1976-1983* (1984), *I Live in Music* (poetry, 1994), and *Liliane* (novel, 1994).

Sharecropping: For many newly freed slaves, the farming system known as sharecropping evolved into an odious pattern from the wreckage of plantation SLAVERY. The wealthy landowners and their oppressed tenant farmers were, for several generations, the most prominent symbols of the American perception of the South. The former planters were paternalistic and exploitative of their tenants, and this class arrangement lasted well into the 1930's as a main way of life for millions of African Americans and whites in the South.

Historical Background

The disintegration of PLANTATION agriculture led to tenancy, a two-tier agricultural system that employed labor for the primary benefit of a landowning class, especially those who controlled estates. One tier of tenancy consisted of independent cash renters; the other tier, the larger of the two, comprised share tenants and sharecroppers. These two tiers were defined by the amount of farm tools, seeds, fertilizer, and mules contributed by tenants in order to produce a staple crop, usually cotton, and by the amount of support given by landowners to their tenants during crop season. Landowners supported their tenants by extending credit for seeds, fertilizers, and tools. In most cases, food and clothing were also provided by the landowner. Credit was secured through a lien on the tenants' portion of the future crop.

Tenancy was a response to the need of the landowners to acquire farm laborers in an economy that was deficient in finance capital for wages and mechanization. The South was land-poor; that is, there was much land but little available money for landowners to borrow in order to pay wage labor and to invest in mechanization. The combination of landless African Americans and whites with only labor to offer and landowners with enormous amounts of land led naturally to a system of allowing these workers to farm plots of twenty to forty acres on a crop-sharing basis.

Share tenants often owned mules or equipment and might be able to provide some seeds and fertilizer. Their need for credit varied and generally determined the degree of the landowner's supervision of their work; it also determined the portion of crops owed to the landowner. The share tenants' portion of the crop could be as much as two-thirds or three-fourths, less advances and interests.

Sharecroppers usually contributed only labor. They were completely dependent on credit for nearly all living necessities and farming provisions, which were secured by a lien on the crop for at least 50 percent and from which all advances and interest were deducted by the landowner.

The supervision, or overseeing, of tenants was determined by their investment in the production of the crop. Share tenants had little supervision, and cash renters had none. Sharecroppers had much supervision, however, and were often mistreated by landowners. The landowner, especially in the South and if the sharecropper was African American, kept the books and set the interest rate. The domineering position of the landowner was enhanced by the fact that most sharecroppers were illiterate and did not have general access to the courts. In addition, the society at large was dominated by the landowner, and the judicial system customarily supported any exaction of debt from sharecroppers, regardless of the worthiness of the claim.

Servility

Tenancy in the South was a form of servile labor that, at its worst, was not very distinct from certain kinds of penal labor. The crop lien system spread in the chronically depressed southern agriculture of the late nineteenth and early twentieth centuries; tenancy rose as owners of small and medium-sized farms lost their land. Several crop failures could easily lead to foreclosures in a money-strapped economy. Land prices were extremely low, as there was little money and practically no demand for new farmland. Tenancy reached its

apogee in the 1930's, when there were 228,598 cash tenants, 772,573 sharecroppers, and 759,527 other tenants; most sharecroppers were in the thirteen southern and border states.

The rise of tenancy was connected with the expansion of crop production to offset declining commodity prices. In most southern states, the entire economy was linked with cotton—its production, ginning, marketing, shipping, and manufacturing. Cotton was more than a crop; it was a way of life that affected every aspect of southern society. The crop itself required much work: It had to be tilled, hoed several times a year, and harvested, which required an inflated work force from late summer to the middle of fall. Cotton exhausted the people who produced it. They had nothing to give to their families or to the community after they expended their energy on this demanding crop, which was called a "king" but which was actually a despot.

Race was a factor in the demographics of tenancy but not an absolute determinant of who would become a tenant; that fate was meted out almost equally to the two races. In 1937 African Americans constituted an estimated 65 percent of the tenants and sharecroppers in the cotton belt and the tobacco region. Two-thirds of southern tenants, however, were whites. Among sharecroppers, the lowest economic group in tenancy, the numbers of whites and blacks were about equal. All told, in the early 1930's, tenants made up nearly half of the southern farm population of 15.5 million.

Cotton dominated the southern economy well into the twentieth century, and most sharecroppers grew cotton. *(AP/Wide World Photos)*

Paternalism

The crop lien system, while a natural reaction to the disintegration of the monetary economy of the South in the aftermath of plantation slavery, was a calamitous and leechlike social and economic system. Tenancy, which nurtured all manners of exploitation, was racist and paternalistic.

Landowners charged exorbitant interest rates on advances and took their tenants' cotton for debts owed or not owed. The landowner was the power structure, or the dominant feature of it, and as such could cut deeply and at will into a tenant's share in order to meet obligations to banks and suppliers. Tenants who were closely supervised and manipulated by landowners were unable to develop independence and self-direction. Southern paternalism was opportunistic. Landowners made verbal contracts that lasted for one year at a time, leaving them free to dispossess their tenants at the end of any given year. Because of the surplus of unskilled labor throughout the South, landowners had little need to compromise with dissatisfied or unwanted tenants. As a result, tenants were highly mobile and easily overworked, undercompensated, and even sexually violated. The transience of tenant workers and their families prevented the formation of viable social and economic institutions within communities. Tenants were on the periphery of social and political life. They became merely the pawns of the landowners and other power brokers. Cooperation with other tenants was virtually nonexistent because landowners sought to play tenant farmers against one another, especially on the basis of race.

Decline of Tenancy

The GREAT DEPRESSION centered national attention on tenancy and the POVERTY that sprang from it. Ironically, it was too late to improve the conditions of tenancy, for the landowner was beginning to abandon it for a wage system in an effort to reduce costs. In addition, some of the New Deal programs encouraged the abandonment of the crop lien system. The Agricultural Adjustment Act (AAA) proposed taking acreage out of production in order to reduce crop production and to increase prices for farm commodities. The AAA's policy influenced landowners to dispense with tenancy and thus avoid sharing government payments with their tenants.

Tenancy continued on a smaller scale after the 1930's. It was doomed, however, by the social and economic changes brought on by WORLD WAR II, such as increased mechanization, especially the use of the cotton harvester, and the exodus of whites and African Americans to regions outside the cotton belt. Landowners were able to employ wage workers to meet their more limited demand for labor.

Tenancy, or the more popular term of "sharecropping," perpetuated the worst of rural life: isolation, ignorance, bigotry, religious escapism, and political ineffectualness. Tenant farmers lacked the requisites for political organization and were the prey of landowners and other powerful groups. It was easy for the power structure to manipulate the racial prejudice of both blacks and whites—a strategy of "divide and suppress." Tenants of the South lived a life of quiet desperation under miserable conditions of unpainted and windowless shacks, disease, drudgery, and violence. African American sharecroppers suffered more, for they had the additional burden of RACIAL DISCRIMINATION and segregation to bear. They were cheated and otherwise abused with impunity. Whites were subject to the same injustices, but less so.

While the tenancy system contained the seeds of its own destruction, its heritage lingers in the South. Poverty, ignorance, and race manipulation continue to offer the power structure the methods to dominate a whole region and a people for economic benefit.

—*Claude Hargrove*

See also: Southern Tenant Farmers' Union.

Suggested Readings:

Caldwell, Erskine, and Margaret Bourke-White. *You Have Seen Their Faces*. New York: Arno Press, 1975.

Conrad, David E. *The Forgotten Farmers: The Story of Sharecroppers in the New Deal*. Urbana: University of Illinois Press, 1965. Reprint. Westport, Conn.: Greenwood Press, 1982.

Grubbs, Donald H. *Cry from the Cotton*. Chapel Hill: University of North Carolina Press, 1971.

Jaynes, Gerald D. *Branches Without Roots: Genesis of the Black Working Class in the American South, 1862-1882*. New York: Oxford University Press, 1986.

Kester, Howard. *Revolt Among the Sharecroppers*. New York: Arno Press, 1969.

Riddle, Wesley A. "The Origins of Black Sharecropping." *The Mississippi Quarterly* 49 (Winter, 1995): 53-71.

Royce, Edward. *The Origins of Southern Sharecropping*. Philadelphia: Temple University Press, 1993.

Taylor, Roy G. *Sharecroppers: The Way We Really Were*. Wilson, N.C.: J-Mark, 1984.

Sharpton, Al (b. October 3, 1954): CIVIL RIGHTS activist. The Reverend Sharpton is best known for leading protests and demonstrations in response to injustices done to black people. He is the leader of the United African Movement and a supporter of the political campaigns of Lenora Fulani and her New Alliance Party. With Fulani and Louis FARRAKHAN, Sharpton wrote *Independent Black Leadership in America* (1990), a series of short articles that discuss the activities and goals of the three authors.

Sharpton acted as adviser to Tawana Brawley, a sixteen-year-old African American girl who claimed to have been abducted by a gang of white men in Wyspingers Falls, New York, on November 24, 1987. She was found naked in a garbage bag, with feces and racial slurs covering her body. The case became a focal point of protests and racial tensions throughout the state of New York. Sharpton, along with lawyers Alton H. Maddox, Jr., and C. Vernon Mason, advised Brawley not to cooperate with law enforcement agencies, whom they accused of trying to cover up the real story of the abduction. A grand jury later found no evidence of any abduction or racial or sexual attack, or of any other crime against Brawley.

In 1988 Sharpton led demonstrations related to the assault on three black men that took place in Queens, New York, in December of 1986. Michael Griffith was killed in the attack, which took place in a white neighborhood. Sharpton's protests occurred during the trial of one of the three white teenagers accused of the beatings.

On August 23, 1989, Yusef Hawkins, a sixteen-year-old African American, was shot

The Reverend Al Sharpton (right) with Nation of Islam leader Louis Farrakhan. *(© Roy Lewis Archives)*

to death in the predominantly white Benson-hurst section of Brooklyn, New York. He and three friends were responding to an ad placed by someone selling a used car. A group of at least thirty white people, who thought that the black youths were trying to visit a white girl, attacked them, killing Hawkins. Sharpton and other civil rights activists led two days of confrontational demonstrations through the largely Italian-American neighborhood. Sharpton also spoke at Hawkins's funeral. Only six of the white teenagers involved in the attack were charged.

On May 1, 1991, Sharpton led a crowd of 250,000 protesters to Buckingham Palace in London, England, to demand an audience with Queen Elizabeth II. He wanted to call attention to the case of Rolan Adams, a black teenager who had been stabbed to death, allegedly by a gang of white people. Sharpton had just spoken in front of the House of Commons, as the first foreigner to address Parliament.

Sharpton's activities often were at odds with law enforcement agencies. He was tried in 1990 on sixty-seven counts of fraud, larceny, and falsified business actions in connection with alleged misuse of funds of the National Youth Movement, a civil rights organization he had founded at the age of sixteen. Defense lawyer Alton H. Maddox, Jr., did not call a single witness. A jury acquitted Sharpton on all counts after only six hours of deliberation.

In 1990 and again in 1993 Sharpton served brief jail terms for his role in disorderly demonstrations. He ran unsuccessfully for the U.S. Congress in 1992 and 1994. In 1997 he entered the DEMOCRATIC PARTY primary as a candidate for mayor of New York. He won 32 percent of the vote.

Shaw, Bernard (b. May 22, 1940, Chicago, Illinois): Television journalist. When Shaw was a

Bernard Shaw's coverage of the Persian Gulf War in 1991 made him a national figure. *(Cable News Network/George Bennett)*

youth, renowned Columbia Broadcasting System (CBS) reporter Edward R. Murrow became his idol. Shaw served in the Marine Corps from 1959 to 1963, then began attending the University of Illinois at Chicago. His major was history, and he worked as a reporter for the college radio station, WNUS. He left before finishing his degree, however, to pursue journalism full time when Chicago radio station WIND, a part of the Westinghouse Group W network, offered him a promotion as its Washington correspondent in 1968.

Shaw worked for CBS News from 1971 to 1977 as a Washington reporter, then a correspondent. He moved to the American Broadcasting Company (ABC) in 1977, then to the Cable News Network (CNN) in 1980 when CNN offered him the job of Washington correspondent. He soon was CNN's chief Washington anchor. Breaking news covered by Shaw from the 1970's to the 1990's included the 1979 Nicaraguan revolution, the 1989 Tiananmen Square demonstrations and killings in Beijing, China, the 1991 PERSIAN GULF WAR, and the 1994 Los Angeles earthquake.

Shaw's moments of highest visibility occurred during events involving Iraq in 1990 and 1991. Shaw interviewed Saddam Hussein in Baghdad, Iraq, in 1990, when an international crisis developed after Iraq's invasion of Kuwait. In 1991, when the United States and its allies attacked Iraq in Operation Desert Storm, Shaw reported live for about sixteen hours from Baghdad's Al-Rashid Hotel as the city around him was being bombed.

Among Shaw's numerous awards and recognitions are a 1989 Emmy Award for outstanding coverage of a single breaking news story, the George Foster Peabody Broadcasting Award and Cable ACE Award for best newscaster of the year (both 1991), and the 1994 Walter Cronkite Award for excellence in journalism and telecommunication.

Shaw, Herbert Bell (b. 1908, Wilmington, North Carolina): Clergyman. Shaw was educated at FISK UNIVERSITY and at the HOWARD UNIVERSITY School of Religion. He was ordained an elder in the AFRICAN METHODIST EPISCOPAL ZION CHURCH in 1928. From 1943 to 1952, he served as presiding bishop of the Third Episcopal District. Shaw was a member of the board of trustees at Livingstone College, Clinton College, and Lomax Hannon College.

Shelley v. Kraemer: U.S. SUPREME COURT discrimination case in 1948. In this case the Supreme Court held that RESTRICTIVE COVENANTS—racially discriminatory clauses preventing the sale or rental of housing to non-

whites—may not be enforced by state or federal courts.

In 1911 thirty owners of property on Labadie Avenue in St. Louis, MISSOURI, signed an agreement which provided in part that no part of their properties could be occupied "by any person not of the Caucasian race." In 1945 the Shelleys, a black family, bought one of the houses covered by this restrictive covenant. Other neighborhood landowners brought suit to restrain the Shelleys. After an initial defeat on technical grounds in the trial court, the landowners won an appeal to the supreme court of Missouri. The Shelleys appealed to the U.S. Supreme Court.

Chief Justice Fred Vinson delivered the Supreme Court's unanimous opinion. Although the restrictive covenant in the deed was a private agreement and did not violate the U.S. Constitution in itself, its enforcement by the Missouri courts was "state action." State action must be consistent with the command of

Chief Justice Fred M. Vinson. *(Collection of the Supreme Court of the United States)*

the Fourteenth Amendment that "no state shall deprive any person within its jurisdiction of the equal protection of the laws." If Missouri were to enforce the restrictive covenant it would be using the state's power to perpetrate a forbidden RACIAL DISCRIMINATION. The decision of the Missouri court was overturned, and the Shelleys were permitted to move into the home they had bought.

The impact of *Shelley v. Kraemer* was immense. Although slowly at first, the old patterns of racial segregation in housing began to disappear. All racial discrimination in housing, even in private agreements, was later made unlawful by the CIVIL RIGHTS Act of 1964 and its later amendments.

—*Robert Jacobs*

Sherwood, Kenneth N. (August 10, 1930, New York, New York—July 28, 1989, Kingston, Jamaica): Business executive. Sherwood, the son of Jamaican immigrants, became the first African American to own a business in HARLEM's economic hub on 125th Street when he bought Reter's Furniture Store in 1965. He soon diversified his Kenwood Company (the name was a combination of Kenneth and Sherwood) into other areas, including liquor and supermarkets.

Sherwood graduated from the predominantly white Erasmus Hall High School in 1948 as valedictorian. He earned a bachelor's degree in business administration in 1951 from St. John's University. From 1952 to 1962, he worked as a credit manager for the Busch Corporation, a retailing firm. He became an executive vice president of Reter Furniture Corporation in 1962. When the white owner of Reter's Furniture Store retired, Sherwood used $20,000 of his own money and a $200,000 Small Business Administration loan to purchase the store.

Along with developing his business, Sherwood served in a variety of government and public service positions. He was director of the Harlem Self-Help Agency and a director of the NEW YORK CITY Public Development Corporation. He was a commissioner of the New York State Parks Commission from 1968 to 1973 and served as its treasurer. In 1972 Sherwood was appointed a commissioner of the New York State Athletic Commission, taking the place of Jackie Robinson and serving until 1975. Sherwood also was appointed to the Business Council for Urban Development and was a director of the United Mutual Life Insurance Company. In 1969 President Richard Nixon invited him, along with about forty other business executives, to the White House to discuss the national economy.

Sherwood moved to the predominantly white, upper-class suburb of Irvington-on-Hudson, New York, with his family. Neighbors objected to the presence of an African American family and burned Sherwood in effigy. The family moved to JAMAICA in 1976. In 1986 Sherwood was elected president of the American Chamber of Commerce in Kingston. He held the Burger King franchise for Jamaica and had built two restaurants by the time of his death, with plans made for a third. He died of injuries suffered during a burglary of his home.

See also: Business and commerce.

Shines, Johnny (April 26, 1915, Frayser, Tennessee—April 20, 1992, Tuscaloosa, Alabama): BLUES musician. Shines moved to Memphis in 1921. He lived as a sharecropper and didn't begin playing guitar until 1932. The first time he performed publicly was at the intermission of a HOWLIN' WOLF dance.

In 1934 Shines began traveling and playing blues. He met up with Robert JOHNSON, with whom he traveled through ARKANSAS, TENnessee, and MISSOURI, playing at country suppers and dances. Only months before Robert Johnson's tragic death in 1938, they split up.

Blues musician Johnny Shines. *(Joseph A. Rosen/Archive Photos)*

Shines continued playing around Memphis until 1941 when, like many other southern blues musicians, he moved to CHICAGO, ILLINOIS. He formed a small group and began playing in clubs on the outskirts of Chicago. Lester Melrose recorded the group in 1946, but the recordings were not released.

In 1950 Shines was recorded by the Chess Records label as Shoe Shine Johnny. Two years later, he was recording under his own name, but the releases did little for his career. Shines experienced the frustration with recording companies that many blues musicians faced, and he eventually disappeared from the music world. He was employed as a construction worker in the South and did not have much to do with music until the blues revival of the 1960's, when he played at JAZZ and blues festivals and at folk clubs. He preferred working in the Delta blues tradition rather than changing to suit popular fashion, which probably is why he experienced so much difficulty recording.

Shines is known as a highly skilled bottleneck guitarist. His music is rhythmic and emotionally intense, and his lyrics offer striking images reflecting a MISSISSIPPI theme. His style is primitive country blues. Shines spent most of his time after 1960 in Tuscaloosa, Alabama. He suffered a stroke, and, in March, 1992, had one leg amputated. Two of his more famous songs are "Blues to Texas" and "Moon Is Rising."

Shirelles: Girl group of the early 1960's. The group (Shirley Owens Alston, Micki Harris, Doris Coley Kenner, and Beverly Lee) was formed in 1958 in the members' hometown of Passaic, NEW JERSEY. The group's recording of "Tonight's the Night" in 1960 was its first million seller and launched the group into fame. That song was followed by a series of 1961 and 1962 hits that included "Dedicated to the One I Love," "Will You," "Mama Said," "Soldier Boy," and "Baby, It's You." The group disbanded in the late 1960's but reunited briefly in the 1970's to play revival concerts.
See also: Music.

Shorter, Wayne (b. August 25, 1933, Newark, New Jersey): JAZZ saxophonist, composer, and bandleader. Shorter was first attracted to the VISUAL ARTS. He won an all-city contest in grammar school and went to a high school specializing in art. He became interested in the BEBOP music of Bud Powell and Dizzy GILLESPIE while listening to a radio program entitled *Make Believe Ballroom* on WNEW. At age sixteen, he studied the clarinet, and he was playing it in a New Jersey big band during his senior year of high school. Shortly after this, he changed to tenor saxophone. Within a year, he was impressing some of the giants of jazz—among them Sonny STITT and Max ROACH—at various jam sessions. He also studied music at

New York University, where he received a B.A. in 1955.

He was playing with Horace Silver's band in 1956 when he was drafted into the U.S. Army. Although Shorter feared that his absence from the East Coast musical scene might mean that his career as a musician was over, after his discharge in 1958 he discovered that he had not been forgotten. Several bandleaders sought his talent. He joined Maynard Ferguson in 1958, was with Art BLAKEY's Jazz Messengers from 1959 to 1963, and worked with Miles DAVIS's renowned quintet from 1964 to 1970. He first took up the soprano saxophone in 1968 when a part of that group.

Although known primarily as a team player rather than a bandleader, Shorter was the writer of numerous original compositions (including the jazz classic "Footprints," recorded by Davis and dozens of other artists through the years), and his innovative saxophone playing became highly admired. Shorter recorded solo albums beginning in 1959, including *Juju* (1964) and *Odyssey of Iska* (1970).

In 1970 Shorter and pianist Joe Zawinul (who had played with Davis and Cannonball ADDERLEY) founded Weather Report, a jazz-rock fusion group with which Shorter remained until 1985. Weather Report was extremely successful in the 1970's, winning critics' and listeners' polls and releasing landmark albums such as *Mysterious Traveller* (1973) and *Heavy Weather* (1977), which contained "Birdland." Shorter's unique style on the soprano sax was an instantly recognizable part of the group's sound, and he contributed many compositions to its recordings as well.

Shorter was involved in other projects during Weather Report's existence. In 1974 he released the highly respected *Native Dancer* with Brazilian musician Milton Nascimento. Other work included playing with pianist Herbie Hancock's straight-ahead bebop group, *V.S.O.P.*, in the 1970's and recording with jazz-pop artists such as Joni Mitchell and Steely Dan.

Many jazz fans urged him to start his own group after he left Weather Report. He formed a new band and led it on a tour of Japan, Europe, and the United States. Shorter's recording career continued in the 1980's and 1990's and included the releases *High Life* in 1995 and, with Hancock, *One Plus One* in 1997.

Shorter's chief influences were John COLTRANE (early in his career) and Miles Davis (in the mid- and late 1960's). His later style is terse and simple, and it incorporates long periods of silence. His preference is for the understated: a short song or short improvisation with clear, simple phrases rather than a lengthy and complicated piece. He once noted that the simple song form is disappearing, being replaced by long, complex, sometimes formless pieces. In addition to the jazz of Coltrane and Davis, Shorter was influenced by SOUL MUSIC, rock, BEBOP, BLUES, and Latin American idioms. To Shorter, the term "fusion," which many used to describe Weather Report, simply meant a loss of the categories that tended to restrict and stereotype music.

Shuttlesworth, Fred L. (b. March 18, 1922, Montgomery, Alabama): CIVIL RIGHTS activist. A BIRMINGHAM, ALABAMA, minister, Shuttlesworth organized the Alabama Christian Movement for Human Rights (ACMHR) to fight for civil rights in Birmingham in response to the outlawing of the NATIONAL ASSOCIATION FOR THE ADVANCEMENT OF COLORED PEOPLE (NAACP) in 1956. From this organization, Shuttlesworth went on to be a major player in the civil rights demonstrations of the late 1950's and early 1960's.

In addition to being a confidant of Martin Luther KING, Jr., Shuttlesworth was one reason why much of the focus of the civil rights demonstrations was in Alabama. Shuttlesworth and the ACMHR worked closely with King and the SOUTHERN CHRISTIAN LEADERSHIP CONFERENCE (SCLC) to organize the many demonstrations aimed at attacking Birmingham's segregated facilities. One of the strategies was to use T. Eugene "Bull" Connor, Birmingham's chief of police, to the advantage of the demonstrators. Shuttlesworth knew that Connor was intolerant of activism by Birmingham African Americans and would react in a violent way to halt the Civil Rights movement in his city. That intolerance elicited sympathy from television news viewers across the country. One of the most violent acts, although not traced to the Birmingham police, was the bombing of Bethel Baptist Church, the meeting place for the ACMHR. Connor and the Birmingham police proved predictable in advancing nationwide support for the movement in Birmingham by hosing, beating, and calling police dogs on demonstrators.

After numerous encounters over a three-year period, Shuttlesworth, along with King and Ralph ABERNATHY, announced a Birmingham Truce Agreement. The agreement called for desegregation of lunch counters, restrooms, drinking fountains, and fitting rooms in downtown department stores within ninety days. Within sixty days, hiring practices were to be improved, granting consideration to African Americans for jobs previously closed to them.

In addition to his Birmingham activities, Shuttlesworth also served as the secretary of the SCLC. He gave the invocation at the MARCH ON WASHINGTON in 1963. He was president of the Southern Conference Educational Fund, a seventeen-state interracial civil rights group focusing on integration. In 1966 he moved to Cincinnati, Ohio, to become pastor of a Baptist church.

Sickle-cell anemia: It is estimated that one in every four hundred to five hundred African Americans is born with a form of the hereditary blood disorder sickle-cell anemia. In the United States, sickle-cell disease is found primarily in people of African ancestry; however, members of other groups, especially those coming from Mediterranean areas, the Middle East, and some parts of India, can also have the disorder. Sickle-cell anemia is caused by an abnormality of hemoglobin, the red protein in red blood cells that carries oxygen from the lungs to the tissues. The cause is the presence of a blood element known as hemoglobin S.

The abnormality of the hemoglobin creates an inability in a body's red blood cells to transport oxygen, forcing round red blood cells into a sickle shape. Sickle cells do not pass smoothly through the blood vessels, and they can completely block the capillaries. Such circulatory problems starve tissues, which then become painful and are unable to fight infection. The first documented case of sickle-cell anemia in Western medicine was diagnosed by James B. Herrick, a Chicago physician, in 1910.

The Reverend Fred L. Shuttlesworth (wearing hat) on a Birmingham bus the day after his house was bombed in December, 1956. *(Library of Congress)*

Some otherwise healthy individuals have what is called a sickle-cell trait, a condition characterized by the possession of a single sickle gene. Sickle-cell anemia is often confused with sickle-cell trait, which is the carrier state for sickle-cell anemia. Individuals with sickle-cell trait are not ill and require no special treatment; however, it is important for such people to know they have the trait, because sickle-cell anemia is an inherited disorder. In the United States, one in twelve African Americans carry the sickle-cell trait. In some areas of Africa and the Middle East, the proportion of the population with this trait can reach 30 percent. Researchers have learned that the presence of the sickle-cell trait provides protection from the parasite that causes malaria. As a result, the sickle-cell gene is found primarily in regions of the world where malaria is prevalent (particularly in Africa).

Inheritance Pattern

Sickle-cell anemia results when a child inherits two genes for sickle hemoglobin, one from the mother and one from the father. Each parent must carry at least one sickle gene for the offspring to have sickle-cell disease. If both parents have sickle-cell trait, the child will have a 25 percent chance of having sickle-cell anemia, a 25 percent chance of being normal, and a 50 percent chance of having sickle-cell trait. If only one parent has sickle-cell trait, the child will have a 50 percent chance of having sickle-cell trait, a 50 percent chance of being normal, and a 0 percent chance of having sickle-cell anemia. If one parent has sickle-cell trait and one has the disease, the child will have a 50 percent chance of having sickle-cell anemia and a 50 percent chance of having sickle-cell trait. If one parent has sickle-cell disease, the child will have a 100 percent chance of having sickle-cell trait and a 0 percent chance of having sickle-cell anemia. If both parents have sickle-cell anemia, the child will have a 100 percent chance of having sickle-cell anemia.

Typical of many carriers of the sickle-cell trait, this Texas mother and her husband were unaware they carried it until their fourth child (pictured) was found to have been born with the disease. *(AP/Wide World Photos)*

Persons at risk can have a simple blood test to determine whether they are carriers of the trait. Newborns can be tested and diagnosed at birth so that preventive treatment can be started. Persons with the disease can stave off symptoms by maintaining good health habits, avoiding exposure to cold, not exercising excessively, drinking plenty of fluids, and treating any infection promptly.

Effects of the Disease

Unless an afflicted child has been given a blood test to detect sickle-cell anemia at birth or has had a blood test later in life, families are usually unaware that the child is affected until the first signs and symptoms appear, which can be as late as three years after birth. Sickle-cell anemia is a highly variable disorder; some individuals are severely affected, and others are only mildly affected. Researchers in the fields of molecular biology and population genetics are working on defining the cause of the variability.

Episodic attacks of pain (referred to as "pain crises") are the most common symptoms of sickle-cell anemia. The pain most involves the bones and joints of the hands and feet, arms and legs, back and chest, or abdomen. The duration of these episodes averages three to five days, but episodes lasting a week or more can occur. A small percentage of patients have frequent, severe painful episodes requiring multiple hospitalizations within a year, while others have long pain-free periods. It is not uncommon for an individual to experience a series of pain crises within a short period, then not be bothered with a pain crisis for months or even years. A pain crisis can be so mild that an individual can continue normal activities or can be so severe that narcotic pain medication or even hospitalization is required. Although a pain crisis is not a life-threatening complication, it can be incapacitating.

Individuals with sickle-cell anemia are also more susceptible to infection and fever. Children with sickle-cell anemia have higher incidences of bacterial infection, particularly pneumonia and meningitis, than do children who do not have the disease. Bacterial infection is the primary cause of death in young children with sickle-cell anemia and accounts for much of the morbidity and mortality related to it. Children under the age of three are particularly at risk for potentially fatal infections.

Other Manifestations
Inability to concentrate urine is another manifestation of sickle-cell anemia. Damage caused by repeated pain crises can cause the kidneys to lose the ability to concentrate urine. The result is frequent urination and dehydration, especially during increased activity and hot weather. When fluids are also lost through other means, such as perspiration, diarrhea, or vomiting, dehydration results, and a pain crisis can follow.

Some children with sickle-cell anemia experience strokes, which tend to recur in afflicted patients. Most commonly, the effect of a stroke is weakness or paralysis affecting a limb or limbs on one side of the body, facial weakness on one side, or complete loss of speech or speech disturbance. Less frequently, there may be seizures, coma, or even death.

The most immediately life-threatening complication of sickle-cell anemia is a condition called splenic sequestration. The condition requires prompt emergency medical treatment. Large amounts of blood become trapped in the spleen, which then becomes grossly enlarged. The effect can be likened to a hemorrhage, with the blood going into the spleen. An individual experiencing splenic sequestration becomes weak and listless, has a swollen and painful abdomen, and perspires profusely. The patient's hemoglobin level drops drastically, and the individual can go into shock and die. This condition seldom occurs in individuals over the age of five, as by that time the spleen has usually been destroyed by sickling.

Some children with sickle-cell anemia experience delays in physical and sexual maturation. While newborns have normal birth weights, delayed growth becomes apparent in the first decade of life. In a few cases, the delay is extreme, and affected children may appear years younger than they actually are. A late catch-up usually occurs, and adults with sickle-cell anemia are generally as tall on average as other adults. Sexual maturation is delayed in both sexes, but fertility appears to be normal in both men and women. The delay in growth and sexual maturation may be particularly disturbing during adolescence, when young people are preoccupied with body image and pubertal changes.

Children in the School Setting
Except for some children who have had strokes with neurologic aftereffects, children with sickle-cell disease are not different intellectually from the normal population; however, many children with sickle-cell anemia do not do well at school. The primary reason for this is time lost from school. Absenteeism will vary from child to child and in individual children from year to year. A child can have a year of good health followed by a year plagued with infections and painful episodes, leading to the loss of many school days. Some children may lose as many as fifty school days a year as a result of sickle-cell anemia. Although absences may be frequent, they are seldom of such duration as to prevent an affected child from taking advantage of tutoring programs.

Because education is dependent upon a cumulative input of information, frequent absences usually result in low academic skill levels despite normal intelligence. Children forced to compete with peers without equal access to information can become easily frustrated. The child with a painful episode or infection may also feel too ill to work at home for the first few days. Much makeup work must be done after the child returns to school, either through tutoring sessions, during class with the help of peer tutors, or at home. Some parents and teachers find it useful to plan in advance for missed days to try to offset potential problems.

Treatment and Research in the 1980's and 1990's
Direct treatment of sickle-cell anemia has been limited primarily to giving patients transfusion therapy during a crisis. During the 1980's, however, physicians began testing the use of the chemical hydroxyurea in order to alleviate symptoms of sickle-cell anemia. The theory behind this testing dates back to 1948, when Brooklyn pediatrician Janet Watson noticed children at risk of developing sickle-cell disease generally did not manifest symptoms until they were several months old. During this time, these children were shown to have hemoglobin F, a different form of hemoglobin produced while the fetus is developing. As their bodies gradually began to replace hemoglobin F with hemoglobin S during their first year, these children began to manifest symptoms of sickle-cell anemia.

In 1984 researchers at Harvard University who were giving hydroxyurea to laboratory monkeys with anemia noticed that the monkeys developed genes that encode hemoglobin F. The scientists reasoned that giving hydroxyurea to patients with sickle-cell anemia might have the same result. In 1995 medical investigators from Harvard, Johns Hopkins University, and the National Institutes of Health administered hydroxyurea to three hundred volunteers who previously had suffered severe symptoms of sickle-cell anemia. Test results showed a reduction in the number of yearly crises and in the need for blood transfusions among the volunteers. Although these results require further study, researchers agree that hydroxyurea appears to represent a significant advance in the treatment of sickle-cell anemia.

—*Audwin Anderson*
—*Updated by Richard Adler*

Suggested Readings:
Edelstein, Stuart J. *The Sickled Cell: From Myths to Molecules.* Cambridge, Mass.: Harvard University Press, 1985.
Hobbs, Nicholas, and James M. Perrin, eds. *Issues in the Care of Children with Chronic Illness.* San Francisco, Calif.: Jossey-Bass, 1985.
Hobbs, Nicholas, James M. Perrin, and Henry T. Ireys. *Chronically Ill Children and Their Families.* San Francisco, Calif.: Jossey-Bass, 1985.

Hurtig, Anita L., and Carol T. Viera, eds. *Sickle-Cell Disease: Psychological and Psychosocial Issues*. Urbana: University of Illinois Press, 1986.

Hwang, Mi Young. "Facts About Sickle Cell Anemia." *Journal of the American Medical Association* 281 (May 12, 1999): 1768.

Schecter, Alan, and G. P. Rodgers. "Sickle Cell Anemia: Basic Research Reaches the Clinic." *The New England Journal of Medicine* 332 (May 18, 1995): 1372-1374.

Serjeant, Graham R. *Sickle Cell Disease*. New York: Oxford University Press, 1985.

Tapper, Melbourne. *In the Blood: Sickle Cell Anemia and the Politics of Race*. Philadelphia: University of Pennsylvania Press, 1999.

Silverstein, Shel (1932, Chicago, Illinois—May 10, 1999, Key West, Florida): Writer, cartoonist, and songwriter. Shelby "Shel" Silverstein is well known for his best-selling collections of illustrated poems, including *Where the Sidewalk Ends: The Poems and Drawings of Shel Silverstein* (1974), *The Missing Piece* (1976), and *A Light in the Attic* (1981), and for the prose book *The Giving Tree* (1964). His best-known musical work is a country crossover song, "A Boy Named Sue," which was one of Johnny Cash's biggest hits. His poetry and songs displayed an enchanting, if occasionally somewhat macabre, sense of humor and whimsy.

Silverstein began writing for and contributing cartoons to *Playboy* magazine in 1956. In 1963 *Playboy's Teevee Jeebies* appeared; a second collection was released in 1965. By then, Silverstein had released several "Uncle Shelby" titles, including *Uncle Shelby's Story of Lafcadio, the Lion Who Shot Back* (1963) and *Uncle Shelby's A Giraffe and a Half* (1964), that appealed especially to the juvenile market but also caught the attention of adults. Initially, publishers worried that his simple, moralistic tales would not appeal to either children or adults; his popularity, however, steadily increased. In 1981 *A Light in the Attic*—placed in bookstores' children's sections—occupied the number-one spot on the adult nonfiction best-seller list for several weeks.

Silverstein also composed the scores for several films, including *Ned Kelly* (1970), which starred Mick Jagger, and *Who Is Harry Kellerman and Why Is He Saying Those Terrible Things About Me?* (1971), which featured Silverstein himself. In 1980 he released a satirical album, *The Great Conch Train Robbery*, and in 1981, his one-act play "The Lady or the Tiger" was produced, starring Richard Dreyfuss. By the time of his death in 1999, Silverstein's books had sold more than 14 million copies.

Shel Silverstein's diverse writings are popular among both children and adults. *(AP/Wide World Photos)*

Simmons, Paul A. (b. August 31, 1921, Monangahela, Pennsylvania): Federal JUDGE. Simmons graduated with high honors from the University of Pittsburgh with a bachelor's degree in 1946. To help pay for his schooling, Simmons worked in construction and worked for the Pennsylvania Railroad from 1941 to 1946. He received his law degree from Harvard Law School in 1949. After graduation from Harvard, Simmons served as a professor on the faculty of South Carolina College Law School from 1949 to 1952. In that year, he joined the faculty of North Carolina College Law School. He taught law until 1956.

Simmons left teaching in 1956 to enter the private practice of law in PENNSYLVANIA. He worked with Clyde G. Tempest from 1958 to 1970 and then became a partner in the law firm of Hormell, Tempest, Simmons, Bigi, and Melenyzer from 1970 to 1973. Simmons's judicial career began when he was appointed judge of the Court of Common Pleas of Washington County, PENNSYLVANIA, in 1973. Simmons became active in local affairs and served on the Pennsylvania Human Relations Commission, the Pennsylvania Minor Judiciary Education Board, and the Washington County Redevelopment Authority. He had the unusual distinction of receiving nominations from both the REPUBLICAN and the DEMOCRATIC parties when he was elected to a full ten-year term on that court in 1975. Simmons's term was cut short in 1978, when President Jimmy Carter appointed him to serve as U.S. district judge for the Western District of Pennsylvania. Simmons served on the federal bench until 1981, when he retired.

Simone, Nina (Eunice Kathleen Waymon; b. February 21, 1933, Tryon, North Carolina): Singer, composer, and pianist. In addition to her emotional singing, Simone is known for her deep commitment to fighting racism and her pioneering efforts to support the CIVIL

Nina Simone, the "High Priestess of Soul." *(Archive Photos)*

RIGHTS movement through her music.

Born Eunice Kathleen Waymon, Simone attended New York's prestigious Juilliard School of Music. She changed her name to Nina Simone in the 1960's. Her recording career began in 1959 with her hit "I Loves You, Porgy," a song from the musical *Porgy and Bess*. She went on to have a successful career in the United States and England in the 1960's.

Between 1960 and the late 1990's Simone composed more than fifty songs and instrumental pieces, including several protest songs that describe directly and bitterly the racial situation in the United States. Among the best known of these are "Mississippi Goddam" (1963), mourning the death of civil rights activist Medgar Evers, and "Four Women" (1966). Simone recorded a number of best-selling albums, including *Wild in the Wind* and *Pastel Blue*. Her piano skills play a prominent role in many of her interpretations

Simone left the music business and lived in Europe and Africa for a few years in the 1970's, then returned with *Baltimore* in 1978. Her recording of "My Baby Just Cares for Me" was used in a television commercial in 1987, bringing her to the attention of a new generation, and she published a well-received autobiography, *I Put a Spell on You*, in 1991. In 1993 her music was featured in the film *Point of No Return*, and she released the album *A Single Woman* that same year.

—*Alvin K. Benson*

See also: Blues; Gospel music and spirituals; Jazz; Rhythm and blues.

Simpson, Carole (b. December 7, 1940, Chicago, Illinois): Broadcast journalist. Carole Simpson attended the University of Michigan and did graduate work at the University of Iowa. Her first professional job in journalism, in 1965, was as a news reporter for Chicago radio station WCFL.

In 1970 she became CHICAGO's first black female television reporter. She also taught journalism at Northwestern University's Medill School of Journalism from 1971 to 1974. In 1974 she and her husband moved to WASHINGTON, D.C., where she began working for the news department of the National Broadcasting Company (NBC). She moved to the American Broadcasting Company (ABC) in 1982. Simpson served as president of the Radio-Television Correspondents Association from 1982 to 1983.

Simpson was promoted to the position of anchor of ABC's *World News Saturday* in 1988. Her 1988 report on children with ACQUIRED IMMUNODEFICIENCY SYNDROME (AIDS) for ABC News's *American Agenda* earned her an Emmy nomination. In August, 1989, she filled in for *World News Tonight* anchor Peter Jennings for two nights, becoming the first black woman to anchor a major national weekday newscast.

In 1992 Simpson was moderator of the U.S. presidential debate held in Richmond, Virginia. That year the National Association of

Black Journalists named Simpson the journalist of the year. After 1999 she no longer hosted *World News Saturday* but remained with ABC as a correspondent for *World News Tonight*.

Simpson, O. J. (b. July 9, 1947, San Francisco, California): Professional FOOTBALL player, FILM actor, television sports broadcaster, and accused murderer. Orenthal James "O. J." Simpson, nicknamed "the Juice," was one of pro football's most thrilling performers and one of the game's leading career ground gainers.

As a youngster, Simpson fell in with neighborhood troublemakers, but his interest in sports deterred him from juvenile delinquency. He wore leg braces as a child because of lack of strength in his legs, but by the time he reached McClymonds High School in Oakland, California, he was among the area's best high school athletes, excelling in both football and track.

After high school graduation, Simpson attended City College in San Francisco for two years. His performances in football and track at City College earned Simpson a scholarship offer from the University of Southern California (USC), and he enrolled there in September, 1967. Simpson immediately won the job as the Trojans' starting tailback, and he became one of the best runners in USC's history. In two varsity seasons, he rushed for 3,295 yards, much of that yardage coming on long open-field gallops. He was awarded the Heisman Trophy as college football's best player in 1968, and he was drafted by the Buffalo Bills of the American Football League the following year.

Pro Football Career

Simpson was used sparingly by the Bills during his first three seasons, but in 1972 he received the ball more often and responded by gaining a league-leading 1,251 yards. It was the first of four league rushing titles for

Simpson. At six feet, one inch and 212 pounds, Simpson was bigger than most of the league's halfbacks, but he retained his track-star speed. At USC, he had been part of a world-record 440-yard relay team. The combination of size and speed gave him the power to run through the center of the line as well as the ability to break loose on end sweeps.

Simpson's best season came in 1973, when he gained 2,003 yards, breaking the single-season record that Jim BROWN had set a decade earlier. The record-breaking yardage came during the season's last game, when Simpson gained two hundred yards on thirty-four carries against the New York Jets on the snow-covered Shea Stadium turf. For his performance in 1973, Simpson received the league's player of the year award, which he also won in 1972 and 1975.

Media Personality

After nine seasons with the Bills, Simpson was traded to his hometown San Francisco 49ers. He played two seasons with San Francisco and retired in 1979 with 11,236 career rushing yards. In 1985 he was inducted into the Pro Football Hall of Fame.

In the mid-1980's Simpson became a sideline reporter for football telecasts on the NBC network. His commentary focused on the performance of running backs and other nuances of each team's offensive line. In his first major sportscasting job, Simpson had worked as a color analyst for ABC's *Monday Night Football* shows, but he was dropped after the 1983-1984 NFL season. His performance on camera had not been well received by some critics who found him to be smug and often inarticulate in his commentary. As a sideline reporter, however, he showed remarkable poise and a confidence that attracted viewers, and he was among the most popular NBC sports broadcasters during his tenure there.

Having launched a Hollywood career by capitalizing on his football celebrity, Simpson had begun to show promise as a comic actor by the 1990's. He played the role of Detective Norberg in the comedic police department spoof *The Naked Gun: From the Files of Police Squad!* (1988) and returned for two sequels, *The Naked Gun 2½: The Smell of Fear* (1991) and *The Naked Gun 33⅓: The Final Insult* (1994). He also had a starring role on the HBO cable network's *First and Ten*, a football-themed series that aired from 1989 through 1993. Simpson had also become a popular spokesperson for Hertz Rent-a-Car and owned a number of food franchises throughout the Los Angeles area.

After divorcing his first wife, Marguerite, Simpson married Nicole Brown in 1985, shortly before his induction into the Football Hall of Fame. Simpson's second marriage drew criticism from many in the black community who saw his decision to marry a white woman as a betrayal of his African American heritage. While the couple had two children together, rumors began to circulate about O. J. and Nicole's lavish lifestyle, sexual proclivities, and drug use. A series of battery complaints filed by Nicole Brown Simpson against her husband resulted in his agreement to plead no contest to charges of spousal abuse. The couple divorced in 1992.

On Trial for Murder

During the early morning hours of June 13, 1994, the bodies of Nicole Brown Simpson and her friend Ronald Goldman were found. They had been the victims of a grisly double murder. Their bodies were discovered outside Nicole Brown Simpson's condominium in Brentwood, an affluent neighborhood on the west side of Los Angeles.

Although Simpson had been en route to Chicago around the time of the murders, there were discrepancies in his alibi and his account of his whereabouts during the time leading up to the murders. Simpson was placed in the Los Angeles County central jail five days after the murder. He was arrested after the conclusion of a bizarre low-speed chase on several Southern California freeways during Friday rush-hour traffic on June 17—a chase that was broadcast on national television. Police investigators uncovered evidence that seemed to link him to the crime. They also collected police records documenting a volatile history of domestic arguments and physical fights between Simpson and his wife during their marriage and after their divorce. A grand jury was convened shortly after Simpson's arrest, and he was ordered to stand trial for the murders.

The trial, which began in October of 1994, became one of the most bizarre displays in American popular culture. Simpson assembled a powerful and expensive legal team, which included Johnnie L. COCHRAN, to defend him against a prosecution team led by Marcia Clark and Christopher DARDEN. A television camera was allowed to monitor and record the court proceedings. Local Los Angeles radio and television stations broadcast the trial live, and the daily courtroom proceedings were updated regularly on both local and national news and sports broadcasts. Tabloid magazines seized every opportunity to run stories about any individual connected with the murder trial.

Simpson was acquitted on both murder charges; the verdicts were announced on October 3, 1995. After a nearly year-long trial, the jury deliberated for only about half a day. Many observers were stunned by the swiftness of the jury's decision. (The jury comprised ten women and two men; there were nine blacks, two whites, and one Latino on the jury.) With its racial overtones, the trial polarized the opinions of blacks and whites concerning Simpson's guilt or innocence and the conduct of the trial itself. African Americans were more likely to believe that members of the Los Angeles police department had conspired to frame Simpson, whereas many white Americans were convinced that the physical

O. J. Simpson (left) reacts to the not-guilty verdict in his murder trial, as attorney Johnnie L. Cochran looks on. (AP/Wide World Photos)

evidence left little doubt of Simpson's guilt.

Simpson's troubles were by no means over. The murder charges had cost him his lucrative product endorsements and likely future roles in films and sports broadcasting, although he vehemently maintained his innocence throughout the trial proceedings. Simpson published his own account of his marriage, the divorce, and the abuse allegations, along with a denial of his involvement in the murders, in a book entitled *I Want to Tell You: My Response to Your Letters, Messages, and Your Questions* (1995). Simpson was also interviewed by journalist Ed Gordon in a controversial one-hour program broadcast live on the BLACK ENTERTAINMENT TELEVISION (BET) cable network in February of 1996.

The families of Nicole Brown Simpson and Ronald Goldman filed a civil suit—a wrongful death lawsuit—against Simpson in 1995. In

February, 1997, Simpson was found liable for their deaths and ordered to pay a substantial settlement. He appealed the verdict in July, 1998. Simpson's financial troubles led him to sell his house in July, 1997, for just under $4 million. (The new owners tore it down a year later.) Meanwhile, a custody battle continued between Simpson and the Brown family over Justin and Sydney, the two children he had with Nicole. In 1996 a judge awarded full custody to Simpson, but in 1998 an appeals court overturned the decision and ordered a new trial. In mid-2000 the matter remained unresolved.

—*Updated by Joel N. Rosen*

Selected Readings:

Clark, Marcia, with Teresa Carpenter. *Without a Doubt*. New York: Viking, 1997.

Cochran, Johnnie L., with Tim Rutten. *Journey to Justice*. New York: Ballantine, 1996.

Darden, Christopher A., with Jess Walter. *In Contempt*. New York: Regan Books, 1996.

Shapiro, Robert L., with Larkin Warren. *The Search for Justice*. New York: Warner Books, 1996.

Sims, Naomi (b. March 30, 1949, Oxford, Mississippi): FASHION model. Named model of the year in 1969, Sims was the first African American to reach the top of the fashion industry. Sims was the most prominent African American model from 1967 until her retirement in 1973. She developed her own line of beauty products and wrote several books on beauty and success.

Single-parent households: One of the most significant changes that has occurred in the composition of American families since 1960 has been the steady increase in the number of single-parent households headed by women. By the 1990's more than one-fourth of all U.S. families with children were headed by single mothers. A disproportionately large number of these families are African American. In 1970, for example, slightly more than 10 percent of all white families with children were headed by a single parent; by 1990 the figure had reached 21 percent. For African American families, the figures were 35 percent in 1970 and 60 percent in 1990.

Historical Background

Before the 1960's, most African American families were headed by two parents, even during SLAVERY. After slavery, most African Americans lived in rural areas of the South, subsisting primarily as sharecroppers or independent farmers. Family ties were based on extended family formations, strong marital bonds, and important roles played by the elderly. Children received considerable guidance and discipline from this sort of stable family environment. Consequently, they were reared to meet the challenges and demands of that agrarian way of life successfully, despite the hardships imposed on them by RACIAL DISCRIMINATION and POVERTY. Moreover, this agrarian way of life was characterized by self-sufficiency. The community, through its churches and mutual-aid societies, took responsibility for satisfying the needs of its members. In fact, when it came to shaping the moral climate and social norms, the church was second only to the family.

Throughout much of the first half of the twentieth century, African Americans migrated in large numbers from the rural South to the urban centers of the South, North, and West of the United States. Family members became separated, and consequently family life became somewhat destabilized. Several interrelated factors contributed to this destabilization. First, this migration was rapid and extensive, quickly eliminating the roots of the African American extended family, which was based on a rural environment. In 1910 approximately three-fourths of all African Americans lived in rural areas, with nine out of ten living in the former slave states of the South. By 1960, however, three-fourths of African Americans were city dwellers, with slightly more than one-half living outside the South.

Second, a significant number of elderly African Americans either were unable to, or chose not to, migrate to the city. Moreover, for those who did, the relatively small size of most affordable urban residential units made it difficult for African Americans to find housing that could accommodate both themselves and their aging parents, and they began to develop new family arrangements. As a result, the importance of the role that older family members had played in African American family life declined considerably. This role included fostering pride in family and racial heritage; encouraging a sense of group belonging and family loyalty; teaching ways of surviving in a racially hostile environment; mediating in family conflicts; passing down family stories, remedies, and recipes; and in general personifying African American cultural patterns.

Third, poverty, unemployment, and economic deprivation limited the ability of a significant portion of this growing urban population to maintain stable family units. Without

the opportunity to grow their own food that they had in the rural South, many African American families were forced to depend on government assistance to make ends meet. This assistance—in the form of a widely used government program called AID TO FAMILIES WITH DEPENDENT CHILDREN (AFDC), among others—served to undermine one of the most important functions of the family unit: its self-reliance. Until the 1980's, when the law changed, one of the most destabilizing aspects of this government assistance was the requirement that a father had to be absent in order for a family in poverty to be eligible for AFDC support.

Finally, because city life required parents to find work away from the home, they were unable to provide their children with the same sort of guidance and discipline that they had been able to provide as home-employed rural farmers. Consequently, a growing number of children began to be heavily influenced by values and norms found in the streets and/or promoted by the mass media; these values and norms were often inconsistent with those of traditional African American families.

As a result of these and related factors, by 1960 many African American families were having considerable difficulty meeting the challenges and demands of modern, urban America. One manifestation of this problem was the drastic increase in the number of single-parent households, moving from 22 percent of all African American families being headed by a female single parent in 1960 to slightly more than 60 percent of all African American families with children being headed by a single parent—nearly always the mother—in 1990.

Black Female Heads of Households

Characteristic	1980	1990	1997
Marital status:			
Percent never married (single)	27	39	46
Percent married, spouse absent	29	21	19
Percent widowed	22	17	13
Percent divorced	22	23	22
Presence of children under age 18:			
Percent with one child	26	30	30
Percent with two children	23	22	21
Percent with three children	11	9	10
Percent with four or more children	11	7	6

Source: U.S. Bureau of the Census
Note: Numbers of black female-headed households: 2.5 million in 1980, 3.3 million in 1990, 3.9 million in 1997.

Causes

Perhaps the most significant cause of single-parent families among African Americans is economic hardship. Poverty has contributed significantly to the very high divorce and separation rates in the African American community. Statistics clearly show that poorer families are far more vulnerable to family break-ups than are wealthier ones. Therefore, since the African American median family income was only slightly greater than one-half of the white median family income in the 1990's, it is not surprising that the divorce rate in the African American community was approximately twice that of the white community.

The disproportionate number of African American men who are in prison also accounts for a large segment of single-parent households. Another, smaller, segment is created by the high rate of HOMICIDE among black men. Both these problems break up families, but they also decrease the number of young men available for marriage. The traffic in illegal drugs in the United States has made the problems of homicide and BLACK-ON-BLACK VIOLENCE in general considerably worse: In an effort to gain control of the financially lucrative trade in illegal drugs, numerous GANGS have engaged in turf battles, resulting in countless killings of gang members as well as innocent victims.

Some family sociologists note another possible factor in the high number of single-parent households headed by women: African American men being unwilling to take on the responsibility of being husbands and fathers. Having grown up in families in which the father was absent, many men have not been socialized into pursuing marriage or fulfilling the role of father. Instead, they have learned that they can maintain emotional ties and satisfy their sexual needs with women without ever having to take on the responsibility of being a husband or father. This situation, in part, has contributed to the drastic increase in TEEN-AGE PREGNANCY within the African American community. In the 1990's the fastest growing family type in the African American community was the single-parent family headed by a

A single mother in New Jersey who found a job and got off welfare in 1987. (AP/Wide World Photos)

woman who had never married, often a woman who began having children in her teenage years.

Consequences

The consequences of this dilemma are varied, interrelated, and complicated. The most important consequence identified by social scientists is that the absence of the father, especially in cases of divorce and separation, frequently results in the loss of a significant amount of income and often results in impoverishment. In fact, 65 percent of all single-parent African American families live below the "poverty level" (a household income level defined, and periodically adjusted, by the government); this figure increases to 85 percent when the single parent is twenty-five years of age or younger. Such poverty makes it difficult to perform many of the basic functions that are an integral part of family life.

For example, a poor single mother often cannot rear her children to perform well in school and, in general, to meet the demands and challenges of an economic environment that is becoming increasingly automated and technologically sophisticated. As a result of financial constraints and, usually, their own educational limitations, low-income single parents have a difficult time providing for their children the type of academic environment at home that is necessary to ensure academic success in school. Their ability to supervise their children's homework, provide specialized tutoring when necessary, and encourage intellectual pursuits by setting an example is severely limited. Consequently, the offspring of these families are disproportionately represented in the unemployment lines and among those most susceptible to being involved in the crime and violence that characterize the American urban scene.

The problems of single-parent households are by no means confined to the African American community. They affect nearly all segments of the American population. As a result of the degree of racial discrimination and economic hardship that the African American community faces, however, the problems are felt particularly acutely by that community.

—*Michael W. Williams*

See also: Black matriarchy myth; Extended family; Kerner Report; Parenting.

Suggested Readings:

Battle, Juan J. "What Beats Having Two Parents?: Educational Outcomes for African American Students in Single- versus Dual-parent Families." *Journal of Black Studies* 28 (July, 1998): 783-801.

Cheatham, Harold E., and James B. Stewart, eds. *Black Families: Interdisciplinary Perspectives.* New Brunswick, N.J.: Transaction, 1990.

Gutman, Herbert. *The Black Family in Slavery and Freedom, 1750-1925.* New York: Pantheon Books, 1976.

Jewell, K. Sue. *Survival of the Black Family: The Institutional Impact of U.S. Social Policy.* New York: Praeger, 1988.

Jones, Jacqueline. *Labor of Love, Labor of Sorrow: Black Women, Work, and the Family from Slavery to the Present.* New York: Basic Books, 1985.

McAdoo, Harriette P., ed. *Black Families.* Newbury Park, Calif.: Sage Publications, 1988.

Sisters of the Holy Family: ROMAN CATHOLIC religious order for African American women. The original members were Creoles, who often were rejected by both the white and the African American communities. The organization was founded in NEW ORLEANS, LOUISIANA, in 1842 to serve abandoned slaves. The sisters have always worked with the poor. In the 1990's, they numbered more than two hundred members, mostly in Louisiana and Texas. They also direct the training and development of Nigerian sisterhoods and serve in the Central American country of Belize.

Sister Souljah (Lisa Williamson; b. 1964, Bronx, New York): RAP singer and social activist. During the early 1990's, Sister Souljah was a powerful speaker and frequent lecturer on college campuses. She became active on the rap music scene through her guest vocals with the group PUBLIC ENEMY and her cameo appearances on their videos. Sister Souljah's debut rap album, *360 Degrees of Power*, was released by Sony Records on its Epic Records label in 1992. She made national headlines in June of 1992, when presidential candidate Bill Clinton, speaking to the National RAINBOW COALITION Convention, criticized this quote by Souljah, published in an article in *The Washington Post*: "If black people kill black people every day, why not have a week and kill white people?" Souljah later said she meant "if a person would kill their own brother . . . what would make white people think that (he) wouldn't kill them?"

Between 1981 and 1987, Sister Souljah attended Rutgers University, where she majored in history and African studies, but she left before completing her final semester. She was also enrolled in Cornell University's advanced placement program and participated in an exchange program at the University of Salamanca in Spain. She initiated, funded, and ran a two-month program for children of homeless families in North Carolina, worked in a Zimbabwe hospital, and toured refugee camps in Mozambique.

In addition to lecturing at American colleges and universities, Sister Souljah lectured in the former Soviet Union and in Western Europe. Her book *No Disrespect* was published by Times Books in 1994.

Sit-ins: Form of political action in which a group of people would occupy an area until their demands were met or until they were removed physically. On February 1, 1960, in Greensboro, NORTH CAROLINA, four African American college students sat down at a segregated lunch counter and initially refused to leave until served. Having been refused service, they left, but returned the following day, accompanied by dozens of fellow students. Over the next few days, the number of participants in the sit-ins grew, as did the number of targeted lunch counters. Finally, restaurant owners closed all the available lunch counters rather than serve African Americans. The sit-in strategy eventually proved effective, because it used and displayed the economic power of African American consumers. Lunch counter managers realized the need to remain open on an integrated basis rather than closed on a segregated one. This sit-in followed some earlier examples set by protesters from the CONGRESS OF RACIAL EQUALITY (CORE), who sat in at a Chicago lunch counter in 1942.

Sit-ins spread from Greensboro into surrounding cities, such as Durham, Fayetteville, Raleigh, and Winston-Salem, all cities with African American colleges. By the third week in February, 1960, sit-ins were occurring in the bordering states of VIRGINIA and SOUTH CAROLINA. Eventually they occurred in every state in the South. The support for sit-ins moved outside racial boundaries when scores of white students joined the movement.

Sit-in demonstrators followed a nonviolent strategy, as advocated by leaders such as Martin Luther KING, Jr., and Bayard RUSTIN. They refused to retaliate, even if they were spat upon, jeered at, or dragged from counter seats.

White residents of Jackson, Mississippi, pour condiments on the heads of students sitting in at a lunch counter in 1963. *(AP/Wide World Photos)*

This strategy gained the support of traditional CIVIL RIGHTS groups, which offered to assist in organizing the strategy. Martin Luther King, Jr., addressed a group in Durham on February 16 and urged it to form a coordinating group. Hesitant to merge with the traditional civil rights groups, students met from April 15 to April 17 and formed the STUDENT NONVIOLENT COORDINATING COMMITTEE.

Sit-ins continued through the firt half of the 1960's. By the end of the sit-in campaign, most of the lunch counters in large southern cities were integrated. Sit-ins inspired other successful strategies such as stand-ins at segregated film theaters, wade-ins at segregated municipal swimming pools, and read-ins at local segregated libraries.
See also: Segregation and integration.

Skiffle: Musical genre taking its name from a term for "hodge-podge." Skiffle was an essentially African American genre that, through an unlikely route, influenced English pop music in the 1950's. The term was probably first used in the 1920's in NEW ORLEANS or CHICAGO,

In 1994 a bronze plaque was embedded in the sidewalk in front of the Greensboro, N.C., Woolworth store where four students had participated in the famous February, 1960, lunch-counter sit-in; the plaque bears the names and footprints of the four students. *(AP/Wide World Photos)*

and it referred to groups of musicians playing early JAZZ on instruments that ranged from accepted instruments such as piano, cornet, and banjo to makeshift items such as washboards, kazoos, jugs, and single-string washtub basses.

Ken Colyer, a cornetist in the British navy, jumped ship in New Orleans and spent three months performing with the surviving members of the late cornetist Bunk JOHNSON's band. After his subsequent deportation and return to England, Colyer formed the Ken Colyer Band, a skiffle group steeped in the New Orleans tradition that made use of a plethora of homemade instruments. It rejected the sounds of electric guitars and other modern styles.

Following an internal dispute, Colyer left the band to saxophonist Chris Barber and banjoist Lonnie Donegan, whose 1955 recording of LEADBELLY's "Rock Island Line" made Donegan the king of British skiffle. Skiffle marked a radical shift away from typical pop music by a group of English musicians. Although it was a short-lived phenomenon, it served as the foundation for England's blues and folk scenes of the late 1950's and 1960's.

Skinner, Elliott P. (b. June 20, 1924, Port of Spain, Trinidad): Anthropologist. Skinner received his bachelor's degree from New York University in 1951, his master's degree from Columbia University in 1952, and his Ph.D. from Columbia University in 1955. He began teaching at Columbia in 1957, then moved to New York University in 1963. He returned to Columbia in 1963. He became an internationally known anthropologist.

In 1966 President Lyndon B. Johnson appointed Skinner as ambassador to Upper Volta (later Burkina Faso) in West Africa. The appointment was considered impressive and appropriate, because Skinner had focused his scholarly research on the Mossi people of that nation. He served as ambassador until 1969, then returned to Columbia University, where he held the position of Franz Boas Professor of Anthropology, one of the most prestigious chairs in the United States. Beginning in the 1960's, he was an outstanding teacher and mentor for students at Columbia, and he served as department chairman for a time. His teaching specialties became ethnological and cultural history, cultural change and political anthropology in AFRICA, and urbanization in Africa, particularly in Burkina Faso.

As a cultural anthropologist and scholar of African peoples, Skinner was prolific in his lectures and writings. He lectured on African affairs at the Foreign Service Institute of the Department of State and was the author, coauthor, or editor of numerous books, including *Peoples and Cultures of Africa* (1973), *Strangers in African Societies* (1979, with William Shack), *Transformation and Resiliency in Africa: As Seen by Afro-American Scholars* (1983, with Pearl T. Robinson), *The Mossi of the Upper Volta: The Political Development of a Sudanese People* (1964), and *Beyond Constructive Engagement: U.S. Foreign Policy Toward Africa* (1986).

See also: African heritage; Herskovitz, Melville J.

Elliott P. Skinner (left) presents a gift to a representative of Operation Crossroads Africa while he was U.S. ambassador to Upper Volta in 1968. *(AP/Wide World Photos)*

Slang and street language: Form of speech that is used within the African American community. This language speaks to the underlying drive of the community and the hardships and triumphs that its members have experienced. The roots of slang can be traced back to the tribal customs and memories that Africans held onto when they were brought to the United States as slaves. The desire to maintain ties with their ancestral culture persists within the African American community.

As years passed, African Americans began to create a slang vocabulary with words that were specific to certain regions and segments of black culture. Slang terms commonly used in the rural South differed from those used in the Midwest or in the urban North. Some slang terms grew out of elements common to black folk culture, including the traditions of playing THE DOZENS, engaging in lying contests, and telling riddles. Many terms developed within close-knit communities of JAZZ and BLUES musicians, who popularized these terms and phrases within the black community as well as among white musicians. Other slang terms were derived from the highly coded street language developed by those who engaged in various criminal activities, including prostitution and illegal drug sales. Other street vocabulary developed out of the urban GANG milieu and among African Americans serving time in prison.

Slang is a language that lives on the pulse of the community. Slang and street language embody the force, the power, and the natural rhythms of African American speech patterns. There are aspects of slang and street language that have grown out of the grammatical differences between speech patterns common within the black community and those found in Standard American English. Slang includes black dialect, but black slang and idiom cannot be equated with black dialect per se. BLACK ENGLISH vernacular has its own structure, grammar, and syntax that are not directly

related to slang. Some examples of grammar and usage within Black English include using double negatives ("ain't no"), switching of verb tenses (for example, "we be" instead of "we are"), dropping the s in third-person singular, present tense constructions ("he come").

There are many slang terms that reflect certain divisions within the black community, particularly the secular language of black street culture as compared to the sacred language of the black church. Because slang cuts across all socioeconomic and educational backgrounds, it has become pervasive in the African American community. Slang terms common in the period from the 1920's through the early 1940's had specific regional usage and meanings, but the advent of radio and television began to break down these regional differences. The pervasiveness of rock and roll and rap music, particularly as broadcast on cable video channels in the 1980's and 1990's, further homogenized black slang and street language. Many black ministers and preachers use certain terms derived from slang and street language in their sermons on Sunday mornings as they guide and instruct their congregations. Neighborhood barber shops and beauty salons often serve as a hub for community news and gossip that incorporates slang.

Slang and Racial Stereotypes
Historically, the use of slang and black dialect has divided the African American community. During the HARLEM RENAISSANCE, for example, many black writers deliberately chose not to include slang or dialect in their writings. These writers were committed to conveying a positive image in their works in the hopes of eliminating painful and derisive stereotypes of African Americans as lazy, backward, and uneducated. The writers believed they could best demonstrate this by portraying African Americans who spoke and wrote clearly, using Standard English.

Other black writers of the same period, however, did include slang and dialect in their writings. Writer and anthropologist Zora Neale HURSTON, for example, made a special point of incorporating and preserving the slang and dialect of African Americans in her writing. She studied the people of HARLEM and of communities in the South, recording elements of their folk culture such as their vocabulary and speech patterns. Hurston developed a "Dictionary of Harlem Slang" that was included in the posthumously published collection *Spunk: The Selected Short Stories of Zora Neale Hurston* (1985).

Slang and Oral Traditions
Slang is part of a long oral tradition within the African American community. Words or phrases that had double meanings were often used in spirituals sung by black slaves; such traditions continued in the lyrics of music performed and enjoyed by African Americans in the 1990's. The lyrics to the spiritual "Wade in the Water," for example, appear to be quite innocuous in a literal sense. On another level, however, the song secretly directed slaves who were planning to flee from the plantation to follow water routes during the course of their escape. Walking in stream beds or traveling by boat made tracking and capturing these runaways more difficult because dogs were unable to pick up their scent.

Some slang terms have come into use as part of the changes brought about by the GREAT MIGRATION of African Americans from the rural South to the urban North. The term "Russian," which was frequently used in Harlem during the 1940's, did not refer to a Russian immigrant, but to blacks from the South who "rushed" to come up North—"rushing" was transformed into "Russian."

Call and response is another device that has been inherited from the black oral tradition. Drawing on the call and response tradition of the black church, soul singer James

BROWN called on the black community of the 1960's to "Say It Loud," and his audiences yelled back "I'm Black and I'm Proud." RAP artists of the 1990's continued the call and response tradition while incorporating street phrases and code words derived from urban gang culture into their lyrics. Performing their song "O.P.P.," the rap group Naughty by Nature asked "You down with 'O.P.P?'" and their listeners responded, "Yeah, you know me."

BLUES music has incorporated and popularized certain slang terms. Both blues and slang use everyday events that occur in human lives—ordinary, uncelebrated events—to tell their stories. Both forms of expression talk about taboo subjects. For example, the titles of many early blues songs contained deliberate sexual puns, and their lyrics were sometimes coy and sometimes explicit when speaking about sex.

Many slang words have crossed over and have been incorporated into mainstream society, including terms such as "cool" and "dig." Musical terms, such as "jam session," have given rise to such popular phrases as "jamming." Other terms have grown out of black slang's tendency to create a sort of verbal shorthand—"dis" for "disrespect," "'hood" for "neighborhood," "bro" for "brother." Once a slang term has crossed over into popular culture, the original meaning of the word shifts; use of the word often diminishes in the community, and it is replaced by a new term. Although slang is continually changing, certain words and their meanings have remained the same over many decades. In the 1980's and 1990's, the word "cool" continued to have the same meaning as it did in the 1940's and 1950's.

The Heritage of Black Slang
As author Clarence Major has pointed out, black slang "serves as a device for articulating every conceivable thing imaginable." Phrases derived from the SLAVERY experience, such as

"jump the broom," can be found alongside more recent rhyming jargon such as Muhammad ALI's "rope-a-dope." African Americans who create and use slang are participating in a long tradition of maintaining the cultural roots of the black community. The words that they use reflect their desire to assert their individuality rather than be assimilated into white society. The persistence of black slang and street language also reveals the black community's determination to keep African American culture, social behaviors, and institutions alive.

—*Sheila V. Baldwin*
See also: African heritage; Oral and family history.

A New Jersey couple wed in a Presbyterian church in 1999 perform the traditional "jumping of the broom" ceremony. *(AP/Wide World Photos)*

Suggested Readings:

Baugh, John. *Black Street Speech: Its History, Structure, and Survival.* Austin: University of Texas Press, 1983.

_____. *Out of the Mouths of Slaves: African American Language and Educational Malpractice.* Austin: University of Texas Press, 1999.

Dillard, J. L. *Black English: Its History and Usage in the United States.* New York: Random House, 1972.

_____. *Lexicon of Black English.* New York: Seabury Press, 1977.

Holloway, Joseph E., and Winifred K. Vass. *The African Heritage of American English.* Bloomington: Indiana University Press, 1993.

Major, Clarence, ed. *From Juba to Jive: A Dictionary of African-American Slang.* New York: Penguin Books, 1994.

McWhorter, John H. *The Word on the Street: Fact and Fable About American English.* New York: Plenum Trade, 1998.

Mufwene, Salikoko S., ed. *African-American English: Structure, History, and Use.* New York: Routledge, 1998.

Rickford, John R. *African American Vernacular English: Features, Evolution, Educational Implications.* Malden, Mass.: Blackwell, 1999.

Smitherman, Geneva. *Black Talk: Words and Phrases from the Hood to the Amen Corner.* Boston: Houghton Mifflin, 1994.

Williams, Robert L. "The Ebonics Controversy." *Journal of Black Psychology* 23 (August, 1997): 208-212.

Slaughter, John Brooks (b. March 16, 1934, Topeka, Kansas): Physicist and electrical engineer. Slaughter was named as scientist of the year in 1965. He earned an M.S. in engineering (1961) and a Ph.D. in engineering science (1971) at the University of California. He was an administrator with the U.S. government naval electronics laboratory center (1960-1975) and the director of the applied physics laboratory at the University of Washington (1957-1977) before becoming the assistant director of the National Science Foundation (1977). He was the first African American to be a director of the National Science Foundation (1980-1982). Following that service, he became chancellor of the University of Maryland at College Park.

See also: Engineers; Physicists.

Slave codes: Laws enacted at the very beginning of American SLAVERY, in both the Northern and Southern hemispheres. Initially, there were no legal statutes that established the terms under which people could be forced into labor and deprived of their freedom, so slaveholders quickly instituted a range of laws to do this.

In the early seventeenth century, British colonial slavery in Barbados, Jamaica, and Virginia evolved according to slave codes developed within each colony to meet the desires of local slaveholders. These early slave codes legally declared the status of slaves to be property, prohibited marriage among slaves, made legitimate the use of force to coerce labor, and reassured slaveholders that the conversion of their slaves to Christianity would not alter the slaves' status as property. Slave codes also were insti-

tuted by the Spanish government in the Spanish colonies to the same effect. These laws denied the humanity, legally speaking, of millions of North and South American slaves. Codes varied from area to area but had these provisions in common. Other common provisions forbade slaves from gathering in other than very small groups, from testifying in court in litigation involving white people, from leaving their plantation without first getting permission, from owning firearms, and from learning to read.

Slave codes later were fully institutionalized in what became the United States, where slaves legally were prohibited from learning to read, were not allowed to testify in court against whites, had no legal protection from violence on the part of their owners, and were maintained as "property" as late as 1865. Even a legislative action such as the 1850 FUGITIVE SLAVE LAW can be considered a slave code, legalizing as it did the capture of escaped

Slave codes defined slaves as property that owners could force to work or move as they saw fit. *(Library of Congress)*

slaves in what previously had been the relatively safe North.

In the years following the CIVIL WAR, "BLACK CODES" were enacted in both the North and the South that essentially reproduced some of the segregation and legal barriers of slavery. Slave codes thus persisted, in effect if not in name, into RECONSTRUCTION and well beyond.

Slave narratives: Autobiographical stories about life in SLAVERY, recounted orally or in writing. Slave narrative, as a literary genre, is extremely diverse and complex, ranging from the earliest recorded narratives of the 1600's to the thousands of oral histories collected from elderly former slaves in the 1930's by the U.S. Works Progress Administration.

Slave narratives are rooted in oral traditions of story telling. Many narratives of the eighteenth and nineteenth centuries were developed as speeches on the antislavery lecture

Olaudah Equiano wrote one of the most famous slave narratives. *(Associated Publishers, Inc.)*

circuit and then later were written down for publication and distribution by the abolitionist presses. In this regard, slave narrative has been an explicitly political tradition, combining both autobiography and social criticism. Famous American slave narratives include *The Interesting Narrative of the Life of Olaudah Equiano, or Gustavas Vassa, the African* (1789), *Narrative of the Life of Frederick Douglass, an American Slave* (1845), and *Incidents in the Life of a Slave Girl* (1861, by Harriet Jacobs).

Many themes commonly occur in slave narratives: human suffering under the bondage of slavery, physical and spiritual abuse, longing for freedom, the struggle to acquire literacy and its association with power and freedom, the importance of family and the difficulty of maintaining family bonds when enslaved, a growing determination to escape, stories of actual escape, and a new self-definition after freedom. Many narratives use extensive religious references and draw parallels between the escape from slavery and the Hebrew exodus from Egypt.

Literary critics and historians have examined the issue of authenticity in regard to slave narratives. Do these stories represent the authentic voice of African Americans, speaking their experience in their own terms, or are the narratives sometimes distorted by transcribers and abolitionists with their own political agendas? Despite disagreement on this issue, most scholars agree that slave narratives represent the beginning of an African American literary tradition and must be studied both in relation to the literary and oral forms that preceded them and as a source or influence for later African American fiction and autobiography.

See also: Literature; Oral and family history.

Slave religions: Religious beliefs are complex and dynamic within any culture. In the case of slave religions in the Americas, this complexity is even more challenging because of the unique history of American SLAVERY. African peoples—an estimated eight to twelve million—were forcibly brought to North America, South America, and the Caribbean via the SLAVE TRADE. These Africans had been captured from expansive regions of AFRICA, especially the sub-Saharan regions of West Africa, Central Africa, and South-Central Africa. Languages, religious beliefs, and ritual practices in these broad areas were highly varied. Newly arrived slaves in America, often cut off from other Africans who spoke their language or shared their cultural background, were then confronted with a variety of European religious traditions, ranging from Anglican, Congregationalist, BAPTIST, and METHODIST forms of Protestant Christianity in North America to the ROMAN CATHOLICISM of Spanish and Portuguese colonists in South America. This cross-cultural confrontation provided the backdrop for evolving slave religions.

Religions create and reflect unique worldviews—unique understandings of the relationships between human beings, the natural world, and the sacred. Both oral tradition and written sources exist to help chart the extraordinary diversity of slave religions. Some early scholars of the subject claimed that the trauma of the forced removal from Africa and the subsequent trauma of enslavement were so great that American slaves remembered or retained little of African worldviews. Yet over time a consensus has emerged that African religious and cultural traditions did, in fact, persist in the experience of American slaves. These persistent Africanisms were expressed in complex relation to, and synthesis with, the religious worldviews of white slaveholding culture.

Africa: The Source

It is difficult to generalize about African religions because regional and clan variations are so significant. Most African slaves came to the Americas from West Africa. Major West African religious cultures include the Yoruba, Ashanti, Nuer, Ibo, Akan, Fon, Dogon, and Mawu. Despite the risks of broad generalizations, these cultures can provide a useful backdrop for understanding the religious worldviews brought by Africans to the Americas. It is important to remember, though, that these broad generalizations are largely based on language and categories originating in European intellectual traditions, and so cannot be presumed to account fully for the complexity of African religious culture.

West African religions emphasize the social and communal nature of religious life. Individual encounters with the sacred are understood as part of community experience, with repercussions for not only the person involved but also the entire group. In most West African religions, there is a high, or supreme, god, the creator, ultimate power, and source of all life. Although present as spirit, this high god is simultaneously distant, removed from the daily realm of human activity. People instead encounter and interact with a range of lesser divinities (who sometimes mediate between humans and the high god) and the ever present spirits of the ancestors. These interactions are profoundly important. Many of the rituals of West African religious traditions express, in intricate detail, human relationships with these spirits. In turn, the spirits affect community life for better or worse depending on the success of these rituals. In this cosmology, spirit is pervasively present in all natural and material things, in all human actions, and in the form of living spirits of the dead. All nature and all human experience are thus infused with the sacred. Consequently, every rainstorm and every crop is imbued with sacred significance; the rituals and interactions between people and spirits have a profound effect on the natural world.

West African religions thus involve an intimate sacred relationship between the high god, the spirits and lesser gods, the human community, and the environment. Although this might seem to suggest that African traditions would not survive the geographic dislocation caused by the slave trade, strong evidence suggests the survival of African religious heritage into slavery, despite the cultural ruptures in language, ritual, and social structure that occurred when Africans were forced out of the communal sacred space of their homelands.

North American Slave Religions

The religion that newly arrived Africans (and later generations of African Americans) most frequently encountered in North America was Protestant Christianity, although Catholicism was also present in parts of the American South. More specifically, American slaves were presented with varieties of slaveholding Christianity that were finely tuned to sanctify and perpetuate slavery. Although some white Christians were troubled by slaveholding from its earliest days in North America, a majority of Christian slaveholders (and non-slaveholding whites) accepted religious doctrines that asserted black racial inferiority and denied the full spiritual status of Africans and African Americans. Simultaneously, these same doctrines claimed the sanctity of slaveholding as a broad cultural institution. Slaves were confronted with this deeply destructive theology as they struggled toward individual psychological survival and social cohesion in newly forming slave communities. Religion played a critical role in the evolving nature of slave experience.

In these early decades of slavery, how did African and African American slaves respond to a theology from outside that denied their humanity and constrained their freedom? Responses varied dramatically depending on individual experience, the size and nature of the emerging slave community, and many other factors. Some slaves ignored or ridiculed

Christianity; the religious hypocrisy of slaveholders who preached love on Sundays and whipped slaves all week was readily apparent. Other slaves participated in Christian worship services and conversion ceremonies as a means of publicly accommodating the demands of the white community and avoiding the conflict that could result if they refused to "go along."

Many slaves responded by more fully and genuinely embracing aspects of Christianity. Of these, some adapted the practices of Christianity but also maintained African traditions in private, or fused elements of both traditions in their public and private religious practice. Some slaves more fully maintained their African beliefs and practices without attempting to integrate Christian forms or precepts. It is interesting to note that early SLAVE CODES made such African religious practice by slaves illegal. Slaveholders were threatened by the autonomy implied in the practice of these Africa-based traditions. Slave laws did not stop such expressions of African religious worldviews but, more often, drove them underground and rendered them invisible to white slaveholders.

Fusion of Religious Beliefs

As the percentage of American-born slaves increased, the relationship between African tradition and Christianity became more complex; neither tradition stayed discrete and unchanged by the other. Many scholars point to the emergence of a dynamic African Christianity that fused elements of African religious worldviews with various forms of Christianity. The nature of this fusion is intricate and highly varied.

In some cases, Christianity became the dominant, or more visible, form, while African ritual and language patterns created a unique expression of Christianity within slave churches and communities. In addition, slaves sometimes rejected the theological claims of slaveholding Christians and created a unique African American Christian liberation theology, which looked back to the Hebrew liberation from slavery in Egypt as a guiding story and which embraced Jesus as the liberating messiah for enslaved African Americans. In other cases, such as that of Louisiana VOODOO, African or Caribbean-based "neo-African" traditions were primary, but Christian language or ritual patterns were also visible. One important illustration of the complex nature of slave religions is the case of "conjure," the working of spirits and nature by conjurers, people of special power. In many slave communities, conjure—with its clear antecedents in African religious tradition—was practiced alongside Christianity with no apparent conflict felt by those who believed in these two very different religious worldviews.

South American and Caribbean Slave Religions
The African slave trade in South America and the Caribbean differed in significant ways from its counterpart in North America, with important consequences for the development of slave religions. First, the death rate of slaves in these southern regions was comparatively very high. Slaves were worked to disability or death on huge sugar PLANTATIONS, then replaced. As a result of the high turnover in slave populations, there was more direct continuity with, and exposure to, African religious traditions. Newly arriving African slaves renewed slave exposure to African languages, customs, and religious rituals. Second, Roman Catholicism was the dominant Christian force in the Caribbean and South America. Catholicism generally offered a richer tradition of elaborate ritual and a more fluid attitude toward the forms of the sacred than did the Protestant traditions in North America. Catholicism's ritual traditions facilitated its synthesis with African tradition, at least on the level of visible ritual practice, if not on the harder to measure level of internal religious experience. Slave religions in South America and the Caribbean were locally varied and included much more diverse and developed forms of Africa-based religious practice, including voodoo, conjure, spirit possession, ritual interaction with spirits, and other intricate fusions between Africanisms and Catholic belief.

Because religion plays such a complicated social role, it is necessarily part of larger social and political patterns. The various religious worldviews held by American slaves were not without profound social consequence. For slaves, these worldviews sometimes allowed, or promoted, a religion-based accommodation to slavery. Sometimes religion provided the means for resistance to slavery; sometimes slave religion expressed both accommodation and resistance. Many scholars argue that, despite pressures to conform to white precepts, religious life in many slave communities was significantly free from white control. While slaves were often compelled to attend white-led church services and were prohibited by law from learning to read (including learning to read the Bible) and from holding religious gatherings without white supervision, in fact, both practices were widespread. Slaves shared spirituals, folk sermons, oral recitations of Bible stories, conjure rituals, and prayer meetings. In bringing slaves together for such purposes, slave religions provided an important cornerstone in the development of African American slave communities in particular and, more broadly, in the development of African American history.

—*Sharon Carson*

See also: Presbyterians; Religion; Roman Catholics.

Suggested Readings:
Goatley, David E. *Were You There? God-forsakenness in Slave Religion.* Maryknoll, N.Y.: Orbis Books, 1996.
Harding, Vincent. *There Is a River: The Black*

Struggle for Freedom in America. New York: Vintage Books, 1983.

Levine, Lawrence W. *Black Culture and Black Consciousness.* New York: Oxford University Press, 1977.

Mbiti, John S. *African Religions and Philosophy.* London: Heinemann, 1969.

Raboteau, Albert J. *Slave Religion.* New York: Oxford University Press, 1978.

Sobel, Mechal. *Trabelin' On: The Slave Journey to an Afro-Baptist Faith.* Princeton, N.J.: Princeton University Press, 1979.

Wilmore, Gayraud S. *Black Religion and Black Radicalism: An Interpretation of the Religious History of African Americans.* 3d ed. Maryknoll, N.Y.: Orbis Books, 1998.

_____, ed. *African American Religious Studies: An Interdisciplinary Anthology.* Durham, N.C.: Duke University Press, 1989.

Slave resistance: The rebellions of CATO, GABRIEL, Denmark VESEY, and Nat TURNER indicated the extremes of resistance by blacks to the institution of SLAVERY. Armed insurrection and killings clearly marked the lengths to which slavery pushed its victims. Despite the examples of the insurrectionists, though, stereotypes of the docile, happy, stupid, indolent, and childlike slave persisted, as slaveholders wanted to believe that most blacks were not "Nat." As late as 1959, some historians—most prominently, Stanley Elkins—continued to argue for the childlike black even in the face of scholarship that revealed "Sambo" behavior as a mask by which slaves hid their true selves from white society. Modern reinterpreters of slavery have shown that blacks were discontented with their enslavement and that their day-to-day resistance to bondage took myriad forms.

Aware of their masters' economic exploitation of their labor, individual slaves, small groups, and communities took daily action to maintain as much control as possible over their lives. In *The Slave Community: Plantation Life in the Antebellum South* (1979), John BLASSINGAME described the relationship between slave and master as "one continual tug of war." In *Roll, Jordan, Roll: The World the Slaves Made* (1972), Eugene Genovese called "accommodation and resistance . . . two forms of a single process by which the slaves accepted what could not be avoided and simultaneously fought individually and as a people for moral as well as physical survival." The precise forms resistance took depended upon such factors as the size of the slave community, the temerity of the individual, the harshness of the master, the particular situation, and precedent. Because slaves adapted responses based upon specific conditions, masters were often frustrated by what they saw as unpredictable, baffling behavior. While whites ascribed clumsy, destructive actions to "Sambo" and worried over monetary losses that came from the disruption of order, blacks kept their self-respect through their renitency.

Resistance to Work

Perhaps the most common resistance involved the work slowdowns that occurred in the fields. Slaves realized that they were involved in a system of rewards and punishments that revolved around whether or not their plantation was financially secure. They thus had to balance resistance against cutbacks in food or clothing or the dissolution of families by masters who were not making enough money. As far as possible, slaves set their own pace, protested against any attempt to increase their labors or to work them longer than the established routine, withheld their labor, and conserved their energy by feigning listlessness. Slaves persistently tried to "lay in" by pretending to be sick. Many women faked pregnancies to avoid work. Never certain if illnesses were real or contrived, worried over their investments, and knowing of instances in which owners had mistakenly stood by while epidemics decimated entire gangs of slaves, planters bitterly complained, used the lash as a corrective, or threw up their hands and ministered to those "abed." In addition to feigning illnesses, slaves broke tools, sabotaged equipment, set fire to fields or buildings, pleaded ignorance about new tasks, acted clumsy, mistreated animals, and malingered in novel and infinite ways.

If slowdowns failed to improve conditions, some slaves protested effectively by hiding out in the fields and woods as runaways. Generally, runaways stayed near their PLANTATIONS and survived by returning to slave quarters at night and disappearing again before dawn. Most foiled the attempts by owners and slave patrols to recapture them and usually returned after a few days. Those slaves who hid out for long periods of time and attempted to maintain isolated independence in groups were called "MAROONS."

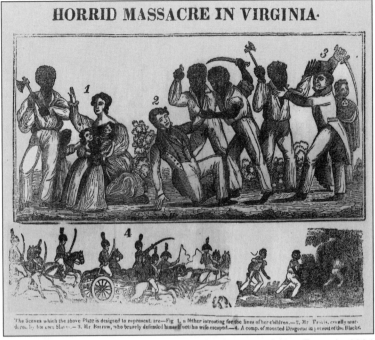

Contemporary illustration recounting the horrors of Nat Turner's 1831 rebellion in Virginia. *(Library of Congress)*

Physical Resistance

Some runaways became outlaws who wreaked vengeance through raids, vandalism, arson, assault, or murder. Outlaws could only return to their plantations at risk of severe punishment or execution. While a slave might escape conviction if he killed a white man in defense of his life or his family, most understood that the death penalty would generally be applied to any black who killed a white. While the number of cases of resistance involving assaults and murders is unknown, probably hundreds of slaves resisted in this way and paid the price.

Evidence that slaves refused to be whipped is widespread, if underanalyzed. Many blacks would not submit to the whip. The most publicized account of a slave resisting a whipping is the story told by Frederick DOUGLASS in his autobiographies. Douglass recalled that, after a series of floggings from a slavebreaker

> I had made up my mind that if Mr. Covey tried to beat me in spite of my best efforts to please him, I would defend and protect myself to the best of my ability. . . . I was no longer afraid to die.

When Covey tried to whip him, Douglass fought him to a draw. "This battle with Mr. Covey was the turning point in my life as a slave. I was a changed being after the fight." Certainly, other slaves understood that physical resistance to physical attacks helped them maintain their sense of self. Yet many masters increased beatings or even killed slaves who resisted violently, because of the danger they posed to the entire system.

Resistance and Slave Ethics

More common resistance involved acts of stealing and lying. Slaves realized that the system and their owners did both. Masters purloined the fruits of slave labor, robbed slaves of freedom, sold their children from them, and lied about the "positive good" and "civilizing" influences of slavery upon slaves. Slaves believed that stealing from their masters and lying to avoid punishment was a reasonable—indeed, an obligatory—response to an iniquitous system. It was an altogether different thing to pilfer from another slave, which was something the slave community would not tolerate. Thieving, lying, assaults, and other forms of resistance that were admired when perpetrated against masters were condemned when carried out against other slaves.

From sundown to sunup, slaves interacted in a well-defined society beyond the eyes of their masters. The slave quarters provided a place where slaves participated in group solidarity against deprivations and exploitations. Close-knit families provided the support group slaves needed to maintain senses of self, obligation, and self-respect. The family and community provided a safety net and acted as mechanisms for survival during the hardships of slavery. Much of the world the slaves made existed at night in community meetings, one-on-one encounters, and prayer sessions.

Resistance Through Religion

Slave religion became the center of organized resistance to slavery. Slaves relied on their religious beliefs to carry them into a better world in the future. Still, they hoped for salvation in this world and prayed for the appearance of a

Twentieth-century painter Jacob Lawrence's depiction of a cruel master driving his slaves to revolt. *(National Archives)*

savior to lead the people to the promised land.

Spirituals and work songs demonstrated the resistance to slavery, the survival of African culture, the creativity of bondsmen, and the strength of the slave community. Folk songs and tales depicted the weak as triumphant over the strong or, as in the Brer Rabbit stories, as victorious tricksters. Several revisionist historians have argued that songs and tales provided the religiosity of the church service and added a means of secret communication. Whites believed the singing, shouting, and storytelling showed slaves content and happy. Blacks understood that the spirituals held double meanings that emphasized freedom and deliverance and announced community meetings and other news. In music and dance, slaves kept their traditions alive, resisted the loss of Africanisms, and affirmed their humanity in the face of chattel slavery.

Survival Tactics

The extent to which slaves resisted the indecent institution took indecent forms. Mutilations relieved the work load; slaves sometimes disfigured themselves or chopped off fingers or toes. Occasionally, mothers smothered their babies to keep them out of slavery. Others committed SUICIDE rather than submit to the loss of liberty. Many poisoned their masters or themselves. Some rose up in insurrection and killed all whites who happened in their way.

Thousands walked out of slavery via the UNDERGROUND RAILROAD. During the CIVIL WAR, untold numbers fled plantations and followed northern armies. Thousands more showed their resolve to fight for freedom by joining the Union army.

As far as possible, slaves used their wits to resist slavery, developed family and community life in the slave quarters, tugged with masters over conditions, acted the "Sambo" or became the "Nat," and gave deference to or sought revenge against their exploiters. Physical and psychological resistance took an infinite variety of forms, from the wayward smile to the spiritual to the slave insurrection to the black man in a blue uniform. Steady resistance was a survival tactic that became fact and fabric of the peculiar institution.

—*Russell Duncan*

See also: Slave runaways.

Suggested Readings:

Aptheker, Herbert. *American Negro Slave Revolts.* New York: International Publishers, 1963.

Blassingame, John W. *The Slave Community: Plantation Life in the Antebellum South.* Rev. ed. New York: Oxford University Press, 1979.

Bly, Antonio T. "Crossing the Lake of Fire: Slave Resistance During the Middle Passage, 1720-1842." *Journal of Negro History* 83 (Summer, 1998): 178-186.

Forbes, Ella. "African Resistance to Enslavement: The Nature and Evidentiary Record." *Journal of Black Studies* 23 (September, 1992): 39-59.

Franklin, John Hope, and Loren Schweninger. *Runaway Slaves: Rebels on the Plantation.* New York: Oxford University Press, 1999.

Genovese, Eugene D. *Roll, Jordan, Roll: The World the Slaves Made.* New York: Pantheon Books, 1974.

Levine, Lawrence W. *Black Culture and Black Consciousness: Afro-American Folk Thought from Slavery to Freedom.* New York: Oxford University Press, 1977.

Wepman, Dennis. *The Struggle for Freedom: African-American Slave Resistance.* New York: Facts on File, 1996.

Wyatt-Brown, Bertram. "The Mask of Obedience: Male Slave Psychology in the Old South." *American Historical Review* 93 (1988): 1228-1252.

Slave runaways: Slaves who managed to escape from their owners faced three options. They could flee to areas of less restrictive bondage or areas where SLAVERY was not practiced, could live in communities of escaped slaves known as Maroon societies, or could be returned to bondage. Runaways often were tracked down by mercenaries hired by their former owners. Some states required, by law, that runaway slaves be returned. Examples often were made of returned runaways through varying degrees of physical punishment.

See also: Maroons; Slave resistance.

Typical reward poster distributed to capture a runaway slave. *(Library of Congress)*

Slavery: Few subjects in American history have been as deeply controversial as slavery. American slavery has been analyzed and explored from a wide range of perspectives, including historical, political, sociological, theological, psychological, and economic. Historians and other analysts from varied races and social backgrounds have, over time, offered often radically conflicting views as to the causes of slavery, its day-to-day realities, and its continued legacy in American culture. Debates have focused on issues including the continuity between African heritage and African American experience; the role of racism, perhaps as cause or effect, in American slavery; the economics of slavery; the political and social ramifications of slavery in early American history; the nature (or existence) of slavery's lingering effects; and the political and moral implications of slavery for an American culture allegedly built on principles of equality and freedom.

From its North American inception in 1619 to its legal end in the United States in 1865, slavery involved the systematic denial of freedom to millions of Africans and African Americans. The brutal conditions of slavery

Slaves picking cotton on a southern plantation. *(National Archives)*

provided a backdrop for early African American history, and debates continue within diverse African American communities as to slavery's significance in the evolution of African American culture. Black historians, social critics, activists, and community members have come to sometimes differing conclusions about what slavery means in the overall context of the African American experience. These debates will continue to inspire stimulating social criticism and historical analysis. What follows is a brief historical overview of slavery, a look at life under slavery, and a critical examination of ongoing issues in the interpretation of American slavery.

Historical Overview
The African SLAVE TRADE continued over the course of almost four centuries, from the middle 1400's to the late 1800's. Millions of Africans were removed forcibly from large areas of AFRICA and enslaved in North America, South America, and the Caribbean. Historians estimate that between eight and twelve million Africans lost their freedom to the slave trade. Many subsequent generations of African Americans were born into slavery in the New World.

African peoples who were swept up in the slave trade came from diverse regions of sub-Saharan West Africa, Central Africa, and South Central Africa. African cultures in these areas were developed and highly varied. Most American slaves were taken from West Africa, particularly from the Niger River delta regions and along the coasts. Yoruba, Ibo, Ashanti, and Benin peoples were among those taken during the long period of the African slave trade.

Slavery was not new to Africa: It had existed among African peoples for centuries, and early Muslim invaders of Africa had seized slaves for transport to Muslim states in the Near East. The European trade in human beings for the emerging colonies in the Americas was significantly different in character and severity from earlier forms of slavery in Africa or during Mediterranean antiquity. Never before had slavery so systematically brutalized such huge numbers of people in a slave trade developed exclusively for a mass market. Europeans who embarked on the slave trade possessed a notion of human freedom that makes their denial of freedom to millions of other people morally reprehensible. Europeans also marshaled the force and resources of a rapidly developing commercial economy to enslave Africans on a scale unimaginable in the servant-oriented slave cultures of Africa.

Early slave routes supplied the emerging Spanish and Portuguese colonies in South America and the Caribbean. Some of the earliest North American slaves were brought up from large PLANTATIONS in the WEST INDIES, where sugar was the dominant crop. Once in North America, slaves often were sold to smaller-scale plantations and farms, where other crops such as tobacco and cotton provided the local economic base.

Conditions varied for slaves depending on whether they lived in the Northern or Southern Hemisphere. In South America and the Caribbean, environmental and labor conditions were extremely harsh; the mortality rate was very high for slaves and the birth rate was extremely low. As a result, the large majority of slaves coming from Africa were shipped into these areas to replenish the constantly diminishing slave population. This provided a constant influx of newly arriving Africans and a renewal of African language, religion, and cultural practice in slave communities. In contrast, while North American slaveholders could be brutal with their slaves, working conditions on smaller plantations were somewhat less harsh because the physical environment was often less severe. Slaves generally lived longer in North America, and the birth rate was much higher. As a result, although the majority of the slave trade went to South America and the Caribbean, the total number of slaves was higher, over time, in North America. Because such a large proportion of slaves in North America were born in America, there was less immediate continuity with African language, religion, and culture.

American Roots

Historians generally agree that the first African slaves arrived in North America in 1619, at the British colony of Jamestown, although this is impossible to know with certainty given the inevitable loss of parts of the historical record. Slavery, as a legal institution, did not exist formally in the colonies at this time. It was only in the ensuing decades that white American colonists enacted laws and "SLAVE CODES" that legalized slavery and formally established the "property" status of African and African American slaves. Slavery expanded to all regions of the colonies, including those in the North, and slave labor provided a critical underpinning for the economies of the emerging colonies. The numbers of slaves in the American colonies grew relatively slowly through the 1600's but increased rapidly in the 1700's.

As the eighteenth century drew to a close and the creation of the Constitution of the United States followed the American Revolution, slavery was an issue of debate among white colonists seeking to unify the new nation. Despite a growing opposition to slavery among the colonists, slavery was implicitly acknowledged in the Constitution by the early leaders of the nation, many of whom were themselves slaveowners. Slaves (implied by the phrase "all other Persons," after "free Persons" and "Indians not taxed" were named) were counted as three-fifths of a person for purposes of the legislative census, and the abolition of the African slave trade was postponed.

Africans and African Americans had resisted slavery from its earliest days. Explicitly political forms of protest against slavery began to increase during the late 1700's and early 1800's. Free blacks in the North petitioned Congress for legal rights and the end of slavery. Black abolitionists and fugitive slaves formed antislavery societies and began the first autonomous black churches and newspapers. These would provide a bedrock for African American ABOLITIONIST MOVEMENT organizing. Slaves continued to resist slavery by revolting, running away, or sabotaging plantation operations. White Americans also began to form abolitionist groups, carrying on the tradition of early Quaker protests against slavery and mobilizing into an increasingly vocal and adamant political movement. These abolitionists, black and white, worked hard to pressure the nation into a confrontation over slavery. Slaves, in the meantime, continued to suffer.

Conditions

By 1730 there were nearly 750,000 African Americans in North America. Only a tiny percentage of them were free. Slavery was on the decline in the northern states during this period, but it flourished in the South Atlantic states, where hundreds of thousands of African Americans were forced into unpaid labor, denied legal protection and CIVIL RIGHTS, and subjected to dehumanizing psychological and physical abuse. By the 1860's, nearly four million slaves labored in the American South. It is important to note that the nature of slave experience varied considerably, depending on locality, size of farm or plantation, number of slaves, nature of the slave community, and temperament of the slaveowners. Even on plantations or small farms where overtly bru-

tal treatment was relatively rare, however, slaveowners maintained their authority by depending on an undercurrent of fear. Slaves knew that escape was difficult at best and the consequences horrendous—even fatal—should the escape fail. Regardless of their specific situation, all slaves labored in a society that had politically, legally, and religiously institutionalized deep racial inequity and coercion.

Although several northern states outlawed slavery in the late 1700's, it was not until late in 1807 that Congress outlawed the Atlantic slave trade. This did not outlaw slavery within the United States, but it made the shipping of new slaves into the country illegal. England also outlawed the slave trade at about the same time. Despite the end of the Atlantic slave trade, slavery flourished in the slave and border states in the early decades of the nineteenth century. The slave population increased steadily. At the same time, abolitionist efforts intensified. African American political and literary writings from this time provide important primary sources for understanding this growing demand for freedom from the perspective of black activists. In 1850 the notorious FUGITIVE SLAVE LAW mandated that northerners return escaped slaves to their former owners in the South. In response, antislavery fervor increased. Accounts by fugitive slaves such as Frederick DOUGLASS and others helped further document the inhumanity of slavery.

The Civil War

Although the issue of slavery was central to the American CIVIL WAR as a moral and political issue in its own right, slavery was also a representative issue in the ongoing debate over states' rights. The complex history of the Civil War defies attempts to give a brief account, especially where politics is concerned. One clear result of the Union victory was the abolition of slavery in the United States in

Many slaves took advantage of the disorder brought to the South by the Civil War to escape to freedom in the North. *(Associated Publishers, Inc.)*

1865. At the end of the war, four million African Americans in the South were freed from bondage by the Thirteenth Amendment to the Constitution. In the late 1880's, slavery was ended in South America and the Caribbean as well.

The formal end of slavery was not the end of the story. Slavery's racial and economic inequity was so fully woven into the fabric of American culture that disentangling it would prove to be a long and difficult project. As the official period of Reconstruction demonstrated, social tensions wrought by slavery often escalated, rather than declined, in the aftermath of America's "peculiar institution" of slavery. Millions of African Americans struggled to define their own place in American culture. Millions of white Americans remained unable to recognize and respect the humanity and full equality of black Americans. Freedom from slavery was just the beginning of the search for a more encompassing freedom for African Americans and for all Americans.

Daily Life Under Slavery
Research on slave life has increased greatly since the 1950's. Although historical sources and documents are often difficult to evaluate, they provide important information about the day-to-day slave experience. Unfortunately, many records kept by slave traders and slaveholders provide insight into their views of slavery but give no access to the experience of slavery from the perspectives of slaves themselves. Fortunately, more African American sources are being uncovered all the time. As these sources are studied, scholars are able to balance the historical record.

For Africans who were taken by force from Africa, enslavement began with violence and trauma. Often captured after bitter resistance,

One of the greatest sources of satisfaction that African American troops fighting for the Union had was helping to liberate slaves in the southern territories they conquered. *(Associated Publishers, Inc.)*

African people were separated from family and community, forced to march long distances to the coast, then loaded onto impossibly overcrowded SLAVE SHIPS. In many cases, these captives were unable to speak to other Africans on board because they had been taken from different African communities with different languages, religions, and customs. For individuals, the psychological and cultural dislocation caused by this traumatic experience cannot be overstated. Slave traders themselves documented the frequent occurrence of depression, mental illness, and SUICIDE among Africans forced into the notorious Middle Passage, the ocean journey from coastal West Africa to the Americas. For African cultures, the trauma of such a massive loss of populace cannot be overstated. The continent lost millions of people, often removed at the prime of life, from cultures in which the relationships between community and geographic location were intimate and long-lasting.

Once on the slave ships, Africans were confined in cramped spaces. To maximize profits, the ships often carried human "cargo" in numbers far exceeding the ships' official capacity. Historians estimate a mortality rate of up to 16 percent from disease and malnourishment during the ocean crossing itself. When the opportunity arose, some slaves jumped overboard to certain death rather than continue life as human chattel. Those who survived the ocean crossing were exhausted and often were physically injured as well.

Upon arrival in the American colonies, people of diverse African heritage came to share a dramatically new identity, one imposed upon them by white colonists: that of "American slave." Newly arrived slaves were marketed and sold to farmers and city dwellers from all over the colonies. Often separated from shipboard companions, slaves struggled to cope with a foreign language (English), an unfamiliar culture, the inability to speak fluently to other Africans who did not share a common language, the profound loss of freedom and control over daily life, and the often brutal imposition of a new life of forced labor.

For the first generation of slaves, those born in Africa, slave experience demanded an adjustment to the New World and a denial—at least in public—of basic elements of African culture. Slaveholders outlawed African language and religious practice, and they demanded conformity to the rules and customs of the white slaveholding community. The intricate persistence, even in altered forms, of African language, language patterns, music patterns, and religious practice is testimony to the power of African culture and identity. As it evolved, the confrontation between African tradition and European slave culture was very complex. Although the nature of this cultural exchange still is widely debated among scholars, most would agree that many slaves maintained important aspects of African identity even through the trauma of enslavement. The influence of this African heritage on subsequent generations of American-born slaves is an area of intense historical interest.

The conditions of daily life for slaves varied greatly, depending on location, time period, size of farm or plantation, personality of slaveholder, and personality of slave. Slave narratives provide important autobiographical accounts of daily life from the perspective of slaves themselves. In addition, historians study the archives of early churches, government records, the diaries of slaveholders, and the writings of people who traveled through slaveholding regions. Less is known about the early years of slavery than about conditions in the late 1700's and early 1800's.

Peter Parish, in *Slavery: History and Historians* (1989), has summarized conditions of slave work life on which most historians agree, although they may disagree in interpreting the cultural implications of these patterns. Especially in the Deep South, a significantly large percentage of white families eventually owned slaves, up to 35 percent or more in some states. The extent to which the overall economy of the emerging nation depended on the unpaid labor of slaves has been debated, but slave labor clearly provided a significant base for local and regional economies and later for the national economy. Most slaves worked in agriculture, but some were used in trades and a smaller number of slaves labored in urban areas.

The nature of daily work life depended on the crop and the size of the farm. On large plantations, with many slaves and relatively little direct contact between owner and slave, laborers were subject to the temperaments of overseers and plantation managers. During long work days, slaves usually were under close supervision, although again this varied from place to place. On small farms, where there were sometimes only a handful of slaves, the owner would often work alongside them. Some slaves were well fed, and some were not. Some were beaten often and arbitrarily, but some rarely faced overt physical violence. Some were allowed significant "off hours" autonomy in slave quarters, and others were allowed very little time away from the close scrutiny of owners. Sexual harassment of female slaves similarly varied. It is fair to say that slaveholders had a vested self-interest in maintaining the relative good health of their "investment," but it is also fair to say that the system of slavery, even in its less overtly violent forms, rested on the constant possibility of the use of force.

Families

The conditions of slave FAMILIES also varied greatly. Although legal marriage usually was forbidden, many slaves did form longlasting monogamous unions. Children born to these couples often knew both parents as they grew up, even if the parents lived on separate farms or plantations. Slave families often were

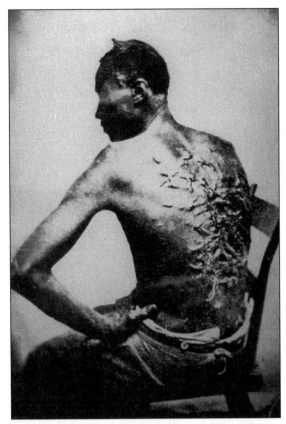

The overseer who severely whipped this Louisiana man, named Peter, was discharged from his position by Peter's owner, who would not have liked to see his "property" damaged. *(National Archives)*

large. Family members who resided on the same plantation often were forced to watch their loved ones whipped or otherwise abused without having any power to intervene or protect them. Slave families also were faced with the threat of a forced sale of loved ones on the always-active slave markets. In some cases, small children were sold away from mothers and fathers, couples were separated, and siblings were lost to each other by sale. Cases of slaveowners fathering children with female slaves were commonplace, and sometimes these children were sold to avoid social embarrassment. Other times, these children grew up side by side with white sisters and brothers who legally owned them. In some cases, slaves were offered few or no opportunities for long-term bonds, so had shorter sexual relationships. Serial monogamy was not unusual. Ironically, the topic of "promiscuous" slaves was much discussed among white clergy, who condemned behavior that was fostered by the same slavery that their sermons supported.

Many details of slave family life have been debated rigorously by historians. Family and friendships obviously were of central importance to individual slaves and slave communities. A key point shared by contending historians is that slave family life, friendship, child rearing, and sexual behavior cannot be understood except in relation to the constrictions placed on slaves by the patterns of institutionalized slavery.

Religion

Religion played an important role in slave life as well. Here, the question of persisting African influence is central, especially in the early years of slavery but also in the later decades. Like any topic related to slavery, religion inspires heated debate by virtue of its inherent complexity. Evidence suggests that significant aspects of African religious tradition persisted into slavery and came into a synthesis with New World forms of Christianity. Slaves often retained African religious practices despite laws against them in many areas, but some slaves also genuinely embraced aspects of Christianity. What emerged over time was a dynamic African Christianity that fused elements of both traditions into a unique whole.

Slaves who kept closer to African beliefs and practices often had to do so secretly, by gathering late at night in the woods or by hiding their religious life in the relative privacy of slave quarters. Even Christian worship was hidden at times, since in many areas it was illegal for slaves to learn to read, and independent religious gatherings among African Americans often were prohibited. Thus, slaves who managed to learn to read the Bible were forced to gather secretly when they wished to meet with other slaves. In many of these meetings, slaves applied their own interpretations to biblical stories, often rejecting the slaveholding theology that they heard preached in white churches, often by slaveholding preachers. Slaves were, in fact, often compelled to attend church services in which the clergy offered an interpretation of Christianity meant to justify the practice of slavery. This attempt at convincing slaves of the sacredness of slavery sometimes succeeded but just as often failed. Some slaves developed an African American Christianity to challenge slaveholding theology, and other slaves rejected Christianity out of hand.

Accommodation and Resistance

A related question concerns the dynamics of accommodation and resistance as responses to slave experience. Daily life under slavery presented individual slaves with a wide range of pressures to conform to the demands of slaveholders. This conformity demanded conceding not only to specific rules and requirements but also to white definitions regarding the nature of African and African American identity. In other words, slaves constantly were challenged to maintain their self-defined humanity in the face of those who labeled them as property.

Some slaves responded to these pressures by conforming, accommodating, and accepting their status. Accommodation took different forms for newly arrived African slaves compared with African Americans who were born into slavery. Some African slaves were so mentally and physically exhausted once they arrived in the colonies that they fell into apparent obedience very quickly. African Americans who were born into slavery grew up in a system that taught them their status as slaves from birth. Slave children grew up being constantly reminded that in the eyes of white society, they were property, not free people. Thus, slaves would sometimes adopt the role of slave with little overt questioning or resistance. Some also embraced a Christianity that sanctified slavery and religiously reinforced their status as slaves. The psychology of these types of accommodation obviously is very complex. Some slaves took on an identification with their owners, at times going as far as betraying other slaves and working as slave drivers themselves. When the Civil War broke out, some slaves refused to abandon these same owners when the opportunity for escape presented itself.

Along with these instances of accommodation, there existed a long-standing tradition of resistance to slavery. Beginning on the shores of Africa, newly captured slaves revolted, escaped, and sometimes committed suicide rather than board slave ships. Once en route, there were instances where slaves mutinied against ship crews, jumped overboard to death rather than endure enslavement, or simply stopped eating and starved to death rather than face slavery. Once in the colonies, slaves escaped and joined Maroon bands of fugitive slaves or led organized revolts against specific plantations. In an important act of cultural resistance, some slaves rejected the slaveholding theology of white Christians and formed a vigorous liberation theology out of African, Hebrew, Christian, and sometimes Islamic traditions.

Fugitive slaves escaped to the northern free states and joined abolitionist groups. They traveled to speak on the antislavery lecture circuits, published firsthand accounts of slavery (slave narratives), worked for the autonomous black press, and risked their own safety to aid other escaped slaves. On plantations and farms, some slaves employed conjure, poison, and sabotage against owners. At great risk to their own safety, slaves secretly learned to read, claiming the valuable link between literacy and mental freedom. Slaves protected one another from physical abuse when they could and held families and friendships together under even the harshest circumstances. These efforts to create a slave community separate from the mandate of white slaveholders constitute an important form of resistance.

Patterns of accommodation and resistance are crucial in illustrating the complexity of African American slave experience. It is important to note that survival under slavery often required a blend of accommodation and resistance: These two responses did not always exist separately from one another. The psychological, spiritual, and political complexity here suggests a reason slavery has remained a controversial subject for historians and other social analysts. Different interpreters offer different observations on the implications of slavery for the people directly involved and for generations of Americans who followed.

Issues in Interpretation
There are many questions related to American slavery that inspire animated and interesting debate among historians: What were the causes of slavery? What were its underpinnings as a social institution? How does racism figure into the picture? What were slave communities actually like? How do we know? To what extent did (and does) African culture persist in African American experience? How did slaves respond to slavery, and what do those responses tell us? What is slavery's legacy in American culture? There are no definitive answers to these sorts of questions; instead there is an ongoing dialogue among writers and researchers that often reflects the concerns and priorities of the present as well as the past.

Debate about the causes of slavery has tended to center on two broad issues: economics and race. Although almost all historians concede the importance of both issues, they differ in how they emphasize the role of one in relation to the other. Some historians, such as Eugene D. Genovese (*Roll, Jordan, Roll: The*

World the Slaves Made, 1976), analyze slavery primarily in economic terms. Genovese and others argue that slavery was a "system of class rule," in which one group of people controlled and appropriated the labor of another group of people. Thus, the root cause of slavery was this economic impulse on the part of European colonists of the Americas. Genovese concedes that slavery involved a racial subordination that led to a pervasive legacy of racism in American culture, but he also argues that because slavery as a system existed in other cultures without a racial component, American slavery presents a specifically racial instance of a more basic class structure. From his perspective, the primary emphasis for analyzing slavery is on economic patterns and implications. For historians concerned with the economic causes and effects of slavery, key areas of inquiry include the relationships between economic and social history, the efficiency (in economic terms) of slavery, the relationships between agricultural slavery and the evolving industrial and capitalistic economies of Europe and North America, and the relationship of slavery to American and world economic history as a whole.

Other historians, while conceding the important role of economics, have argued that race and racism provided the basic underpinning and root cause of American slavery. From this perspective, European colonists looked to Africa as a source for slave labor primarily because of deeply racist attitudes toward black peoples. Also from this perspective, racism opened the door to a massive project of enslavement that never would have been attempted on a white population. Although slavery had an extensive history in other parts of the world, the unique aspect of American slavery was that it was deeply grounded in racial subordination. Slaveholders were white, and slaves were black. Proponents of race as the primary category for analysis argue that racism set the course of American slavery, and

the persistence of racism beyond the economic structures of slavery shows that racism can be analyzed as a primary, and enduring, factor.

Racism, as a social force in American society, is a topic of concern in other ways to scholars of American slavery. How did the "color line" affect the formation of colonial and antebellum American culture? What were the psychological and political effects of racism in early African American history? How did slavery's racial division of people set the stage for American race relations after the official end of slavery? These are complex and difficult questions that continue to attract the attention of historians and social critics.

One debate central to the study of slavery is the debate over whether, and to what extent, African tradition persisted in African American culture. Some scholars have maintained that the experience of enslavement was so traumatic for African people that little of African tradition and culture survived into American slavery. Advocates of this view claim that profound psychological and social disruption shattered any significant continuity with African cultures based so strongly on ties of community, language, and local tradition. Other scholars argue that African tradition, or Africanisms, did persist into the Americas. Many argue that Africanisms had profound and long-lasting effects on the evolution of black culture. These historians point to black dialect, slave music, slave religions, and slave resistance as areas in which African traditions flourished and were expressed. Although scholarly consensus points to the presence of Africanisms in American culture, the extent and form of these cultural traces are still the subject of debate. Additionally, scholars ponder the effects of these Africanisms not only on African American culture but also on the rest of American society in the slave period and beyond.

Another topic of debate among historians is the nature of African American life under slavery. Early scholarly accounts of slavery were written by white historians, some of whom maintained various theories that slavery was paternalistic and benevolent. These early histories usually focused on slavery as a subtopic in white southern history and offered almost no insight into the experience and perceptions of slavery from the viewpoint of slaves themselves. Later historians, both black and white, began to focus on slavery from the perspective of slaves. Within this body of research, opinions vary as to the nature of slave life. Some argue that slavery traumatized slaves to an extent comparable with the Nazi concentration camps of World War II. Slaves and slave culture were controlled fundamentally by whites and showed the psychological and social effects of abuse: submissive behavior, depression, passivity, and fragmented identity.

Other historians have argued that this is not the case. They claim that slave communities, in varied forms, provided a place for the development of a resilient and autonomous African American identity. While conceding the real physical and psychological pressures of enslavement, these researchers outline the emergence of slave communities where much of daily life was controlled by slaves rather than by slaveholders, where family and community life offered individual slaves a source of positive identity, and where African American culture provided a haven from some of the worst abuses of slavery. Proponents of all these views recognize the complexity of slave experience and the risks of making claims about slavery that overgeneralize, but these differing interpretations add a rigor to historical inquiry that continues to prove very productive.

Perhaps one of the most demanding areas in the study of African American experience under slavery centers on the complex phenomena of accommodation and resistance. This topic, introduced earlier, merits further

analysis since these two responses to slavery are important to almost all aspects of slave history and especially to the study of slavery's legacy in African American experience. The key issue is that of response: To what degree can, or should, early African American culture be analyzed as a response to white slaveholding culture? To what extent was early African American experience conditioned by the slave experience? To what degree was it conditioned by other things? To what extent did black culture develop autonomously from the direct influences of slavery? What were the psychological and political costs and gains of accommodating to the demands of white slaveholding culture? What were the gains and costs of resistance? How did individual slaves and larger slave communities express accommodation and resistance? How might both responses coexist, sometimes in the same act?

Answers to these questions help define the nature of African American identity under slavery, and beyond. Perhaps more than with other issues, interpretation varies according to the cultural perspective and political sympathies of the interpreter. Is accommodation classified as weakness or as a necessary step for individual and political survival? Is resistance (including the use of force) seen as the only moral or healthy response to slavery or as a destructive tactic? Historians, offered the advantages and limitations of hindsight, take very different approaches to these sorts of questions and often come to dramatically different conclusions.

One example that illustrates the challenge of analyzing dynamics of accommodation and resistance is the topic of abolitionism. Black Americans, some of whom were former slaves and some of whom were not, devoted lifetimes to the abolition of slavery, as did some white antislavery activists. Beginning in the late 1700's and continuing through the first half of the nineteenth century, abolitionists organized antislavery societies, abolitionist newspapers, lecture circuits, assistance groups for fugitive slaves, and political campaigns aimed at pressuring Congress to abolish slavery. It would seem that abolition encompassed a clear act of resistance for both black activists and white. It was not that simple, however. From the outset, abolitionists of both races debated whether to push for gradual reform rather than radical confrontation. Some activists, especially in African American communities, charged that gradualism and reformism were luxuries of accommodation that only people free from slavery could afford.

Some African American abolitionists worked in coalition with whites, grappling with frequent efforts on the part of white abolitionists to control the extent of black participation in activist organizations. African Americans critical of such coalition work charged that it represented an accommodation to white values and political priorities. Some of these critics became early proponents of BLACK NATIONALISM, arguing that separation and PAN-AFRICANISM were the only valid grounds for genuine resistance. African American opponents of this view argued that true resistance involved breaking through racial boundaries and joining forces with abolitionist allies wherever they could be found. From this perspective, a multiracial coalition was itself a radical confrontation with racism and slavery. As just this brief description illustrates, dynamics of accommodation and resistance are complicated, but they are central to the analysis of African American responses to slavery.

The Legacy of Slavery

Finally, a key issue of interpretation in the study of slavery is that of slavery's enduring legacy in American history. Within various African American communities, people have debated the legacy of slavery since the first days of Reconstruction. Did slave experience set persisting social and psychological patterns for African American life? If so, what were those patterns and how have they appeared in subsequent generations? If not, how should slavery be understood in the overall context of African American social and political history? To what extent have African Americans gained political strength from both slave experience and early resistance to slavery? To what extent might the experience of slavery have had a negative impact on the development of African American political culture?

In addition to these questions, historians also ask how slavery, as a pervasive early American institution, influenced the evolution of American culture as a whole. To what extent are continued racial, social, and economic problems in the United States rooted in the dynamics of slavery? Is it politically constructive or destructive to open the question of slavery's possible continued legacy in American society? The important issues here are the nature of African American identity and community and the nature of American identity, more broadly defined. Historians, social critics, community leaders, and thinking people from all walks of life have offered a range of answers to these questions.

Whatever conclusions are drawn in response to the many questions regarding slavery, the subject remains a cornerstone issue in American history. One thing that most scholars will agree on is that slavery cannot be studied as a subtopic in history; instead, it must be studied as a fundamental part of the evolution of American society. As a far-reaching social, political, and economic institution, slavery touched all Americans, either directly or indirectly. Slavery's broad impact on American culture challenges any serious student of American and African American history.

—*Sharon Carson*

See also: American Anti-Slavery Society; Archaeology of slavery; Fugitive Slave Act; Quakers and slavery; New England Anti-

Slavery Society; Race, racism, and race relations; Slave religions; Slave resistance; Slave runaways.

Suggested Readings:

Berlin, Ira. *Many Thousands Gone: The First Two Centuries of Slavery in North America.* Cambridge, Mass.: The Belknap Press of Harvard University Press, 1998.

Blassingame, John W. *The Slave Community: Plantation Life in the Antebellum South.* Rev. ed. New York: Oxford University Press, 1979.

Fogel, Robert W. *Without Consent or Contract: The Rise and Fall of American Slavery.* New York: W. W. Norton, 1989.

Genovese, Eugene D. *Roll, Jordan, Roll: The World the Slaves Made.* New York: Pantheon Books, 1974.

Harding, Vincent. *There Is a River: The Black Struggle for Freedom in America.* New York: Vintage Books, 1983.

Johnson, Charles, and Patricia Smith. *Africans in America: America's Journey Through Slavery.* New York: Harcourt Brace & Company, 1998.

Miller, Randall M., and John D. Smith, eds. *Dictionary of Afro-American Slavery.* Westport, Conn.: Praeger, 1997.

Morris, Thomas D. *Southern Slavery and the Law, 1619-1860.* Chapel Hill: University of North Carolina Press, 1996.

Parish, Peter J. *Slavery: History and Historians.* New York: Harper & Row, 1989.

Patterson, Orlando. *Rituals of Blood: Consequences of Slavery in Two American Centuries.* Washington, D.C.: Civitas/Counterpoint, 1999.

Potts, Howard E. *A Comprehensive Name Index for the American Slave.* Westport, Conn.: Greenwood Press, 1997.

Rose, Willie L. *Slavery and Freedom.* New York: Oxford University Press, 1982.

Smith, John D. *Slavery, Race, and American History: Historical Conflict, Trends, and Method, 1866-1953.* Armonk, N.Y.: M. E. Sharpe, 1999.

Tise, Larry E. *Proslavery: A History of the Defense of Slavery in America, 1701-1840.* Athens: University of Georgia Press, 1987.

Von Frank, Albert J. *The Trials of Anthony Burns: Freedom and Slavery in Emerson's Boston.* Cambridge, Mass.: Harvard University Press, 1998.

White, Deborah G. *Ar'n't I a Woman? Female Slaves in the Plantation South.* New York: W. W. Norton, 1985.

Slave ships: Slave ships were sea vessels used to transport newly enslaved people from AFRICA to the Americas. Ships used in the SLAVE TRADE varied in size and configuration, but all such ships had the bulk of their cargo capacity in the hull below decks. There, slaves were chained for the infamous Middle Passage, the voyage to the New World and a life of SLAVERY.

Loading

Slave ships were typically outfitted with canoes, which were used to transport slaves from the African coast to slave ships anchored offshore. Once on board, the cargo of slaves would usually be arranged according to one of two methods. The "loose packing" method was the more humane of the techniques, but was not employed for humanitarian reasons; loosely packed slaves were given a relative abundance of space below decks, but solely because slave traders believed such conditions would keep the slaves healthy and allow them to fetch high prices at New World auction blocks.

The more common method of stowing slaves was "tight packing," an arrangement in which as many slaves as possible were squeezed into a ship's hull. Tightly packed slaves were given just enough space to lie on their backs for the duration of the voyage, which usually lasted between two and three

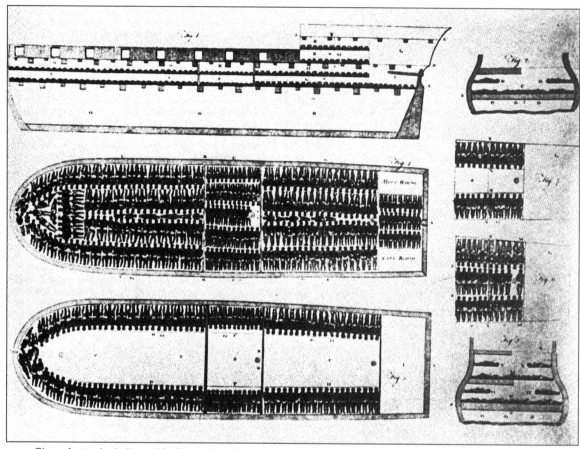

Plan of a typical slave ship illustrating "tight packing" of human cargo. *(Associated Publishers, Inc.)*

months. Favorable winds and currents could shorten the trip, but usually not enough to prevent extreme physical discomfort and many deaths among slaves so packed.

Slave ships were usually constructed out of unfinished timbers. Slaves were typically transported with little clothing; thus, there was no buffer to protect prostrate slaves' bodies from contact with the rough wood of the hull. The constant rocking motion of the ships rubbed sores onto slaves' buttocks and backs and often gave them splinters. Often, such untreated wounds contracted gangrene.

Sanitary Conditions

To add to the misery of the human cargo, most slave ships lacked even simple toilet facilities for slaves. Ships' hulls became foul-smelling cesspools of urine and feces; it was said that when the wind was right, a slave ship could be smelled five miles away.

In addition to being unpleasant, such conditions made a perfect environment for the spread of diseases. Such scourges as smallpox ran rampant aboard slave ships. The presence of huge quantities of human waste proved particularly conducive to a malady known as "the flux," a disease that caused nausea and head pains and that was usually fatal.

Slave ships' hulls were cleaned only when the weather was favorable. Rough seas and overcast skies prevented any attempts at cleaning; in good weather, slaves would be brought on deck while crew members cleaned the filth from the ship's interior. While on deck, slaves were closely watched, and guns were trained on them at all times. While on deck, too, slaves were often forced to exercise. Slaves developed leg sores from the constant wearing of shackles, and it was an arduous chore to exercise in such a condition. The penalty for not participating was often a whipping.

Traders and Profits

Slave ships were expected to generate a profit at all ports of call. Thus, an empty ship on the high seas simply was not allowed, especially in the colonial period. As a result, the Middle Passage came to constitute only one-third of the typical slave ship's circuit. After disposing of their human cargo in North America, South America, or the Caribbean, slave ships would be loaded with raw materials from the Western Hemisphere such as tobacco, sugarcane, and cotton. These commodities were carried to Europe, where they would be processed into finished products. In Europe, ships would take on wares to be traded to Africans in exchange for slaves, and the Middle Passage would begin again for a new load of human beings bound for a life of slavery.

Despite the profits slave trading generated, because of the wretched conditions in which such work was conducted, a stigma was attached to it. Slave traders were viewed as wretched, and even slaveowners came to think of themselves as superior to those who supplied their human chattel.

Resistance

Despite the ever-present physical intimidation, many slaves on slave ships rebelled. The most frequent form of protest was SUICIDE. While on deck, slaves often jumped overboard; it was said that so many slaves jumped ship that a school of sharks would follow a slave ship all the way from the African coast to the Americas.

In other cases, slaves turned their protests upon their captors. Successful takeovers of

slave ships, however, were rare. Traders had possession of all the weapons, and slaves were usually chained together at the wrists and ankles; effective movement was thus nearly impossible. Resistance was further hampered by precautions taken in loading a ship. Various stops were made along the African coast in order to mix up the cargo. From a trader's perspective, it was desirable, for example, to have an Ashanti chained next to a Yoruba, who on the other side might have an Ibo. Such a mixture of ethnic groups and their languages hindered communication, and hampered schemes for mutinies.

Occasionally, though, slaves succeeded in taking over a vessel. The most celebrated of these maritime revolutions was the AMISTAD SLAVE REVOLT, which occurred off the coast of Cuba in 1839. The slaves who took over the ship spared the lives of two crewmen, who were commanded to pilot the ship back to Africa. The navigators, though, guided the *Amistad* to the New York coast, where it was seized by a U.S. Navy ship. The Africans were promptly arrested and incarcerated; the legal proceedings surrounding them eventually reached the U.S. SUPREME COURT, where former President John Quincy Adams argued on the Africans' behalf. The Court ruled that the Africans had been unjustly enslaved and ordered them returned to their homeland.

Few slave mutinies, however, had similar happy endings. In some cases, mutinies resulted in shipboard battles that ended in the deaths of all those aboard. There were some instances, although rare, in which entire ships, along with their cargoes and crews, sank as a result of slave rebellion on the high seas.

Death

Death was thus a constant companion to the slave ship. It has been estimated that no more than half of a typical ship's cargo ever arrived in the Americas to become laborers. Those who did not die often were disabled or diseased from the effects of the trip.

Deaths were thus anticipated and treated as routine aboard slave ships. Callous slave traders saw the Africans only as commodities from which a profit could be gained. As a result, decisions involving life and death on the high seas were sometimes made solely with regard to their economic implications. There were documented instances in which slaves who were considered too troublesome or too sick to fetch a desirable price were drowned. The *Hannibal* in 1694 and the *Zong* in 1781 were examples of ships that buried living slaves at sea. In most instances, such vicious acts were performed because traders could collect insurance on their lost cargo. In much the same way as more modern criminals often use arson to rid themselves of undesirable property, such slave traders would use murder to beat an anticipated loss on the auction block.

—*Randolph Meade Walker*

See also: Colonization movement; Slave codes; Slave resistance; Slave runaways.

Suggested Readings:

Cable, Mary. *Black Odyssey: The Case of the Slave Ship Amistad.* New York: Viking Press, 1971.

Cottman, Michael H. *The Wreck of the Henrietta Marie: An African American's Journey to Uncover a Sunken Slave Ship's Past.* New York: Harmony Books, 1999.

Franklin, John Hope, and Alfred A. Moss, Jr. *From Slavery to Freedom: A History of Negro Americans.* 6th ed. New York: Alfred A. Knopf, 1988.

Jones, Howard. *Mutiny on the Amistad: The Saga of a Slave Revolt and Its Impact on American Abolition, Law, and Diplomacy.* New York: Oxford University Press, 1987.

Quarles, Benjamin. *The Negro in the Making of America.* 2d rev. ed. New York: Collier Books, 1987.

Slave trade: The slave trade was a commercial activity that brought human beings to a lifetime of servitude on PLANTATIONS and other places of toil in the Western Hemisphere. Most slaves came from AFRICA; there were some, however, who were brought from Australia and New Guinea. The slaves from outside Africa were relatively few in number and were generally obtained only when a ship was in the area and needed more wares to complete its load.

Background

The overwhelming majority of the slaves held in the Americas came from the west coast of Africa. European enslavement of Africans began on a sustained basis even before Christopher Columbus's voyage in 1492. In 1444 the Com-

The Middle Passage Monument dedicated in Harrisburg, Pennsylvania, in July, 1999, commemorates the countless Africans who died en route to the New World on slave ships. *(AP/Wide World Photos)*

pany of Lagos was founded by the Portuguese to engage in commerce between Europe and Africa. Among the cargo the company's ships brought from Africa were slaves.

After Columbus's voyage, slave trading became big business. Of the needs of the European colonists in the Western Hemisphere, labor was among the most pressing. At first, Native American labor was used; however, the Indians did not prove suitable as slaves, mainly because they lacked immunity to the Old World diseases carried by the Europeans, a condition that resulted in their wholesale deaths. Furthermore, the Native Americans were in their own territory and knew the terrain; apprehension of an escaped slave was thus difficult, if not impossible, for the Europeans.

Once Native American SLAVERY proved inadequate to their purposes, colonists attempted to meet their labor needs with Europeans contracted through the INDENTURED SERVITUDE system. The limited tenure of such service and the legal restrictions placed upon the abuses of the arrangement, however, contributed to the demise of the system.

The enslavement of Africans in the Western Hemisphere by Europeans was almost contemporaneous with Columbus's voyage. In 1501 the Spanish government authorized the use of African slaves in its American colonies. Because of the danger of rebellion that growing numbers of slaves presented, however, African slavery in the Americas was all but abolished from 1506 to 1517. It was in the latter year that a Spanish priest in Hispaniola, acting, ironically, out of humanitarian concern for Native Americans, suggested that Africans should be used as Spain's labor force in the

Slavers marching their captives to the coast in nineteenth century East Africa. *(Associated Publishers, Inc.)*

new colonies of the Western Hemisphere. Bartolomé de Las Casas lived to regret his suggestion. Despite his remorse, African slavery became big business, and the black race came to be viewed as the answer to the need for labor in the Americas.

African Slave Trade

To meet the demand for slaves, Europeans established trading posts along the African coasts. These posts were staffed by traders whose job it was to maintain friendly relations with the natives. Before a transaction could take place, the tribal chief who controlled the territory had to give his consent, which was usually obtained through gifts (essentially bribes). Once his personal whims were satisfied, the chief would not only grant his permission for the trade but also dispatch members of his tribe to round up slaves to be sold.

The persons who were enslaved were primarily prisoners of war. They most often were from societies other than those who sold them and therefore were viewed as outsiders— indeed, even as enemies—by the tribes that traded them. Africans, in this regard, were no different from Europeans; just as the Irish and the English often viewed each other with hostility, so did the Yoruba and the Ibo. Thus, if an

African sold another African into slavery, it was not viewed as a betrayal; the sellers did not see themselves as selling their own but instead as punishing an enemy.

Expansion

Because of the enormous profitability of the slave trade, the enterprise grew throughout the sixteenth century. During that era, the trade's principal customers were Spain's American colonies. The Spanish government, however, in compliance with a papal ruling, did not allow Spaniards to venture into Africa for the purpose of obtaining slaves. Instead, Spain granted permission to non-Spanish traders to supply Spanish colonies with slaves.

The seventeenth, eighteenth, and nineteenth centuries saw other European powers compete for places in the lucrative slave trade. Eventually, England supplanted the others as the dominant slave-trading nation, even though it was late, by comparison, in entering the business.

The slave trade brought Africans to all areas of the Americas. This diaspora saw the greatest numbers of slaves exported to the Caribbean islands, while the fewest were sent to Canada.

In the Western Hemisphere, the United States and Latin America, including Brazil, also imported African bondmen. The United States became the major market for slaves once West Indian slavery became unprofitable. It was in 1619 that the first African slaves were brought to the North American colonies. In that year, a Dutch ship traded twenty Africans to settlers in the Jamestown colony in exchange for food.

From this beginning, all the colonies in what would become the United States came to rely upon a slave economy. Southern colonies became dependent upon Africans to labor in agricultural production, and many colonial New Englanders became noted slave traders.

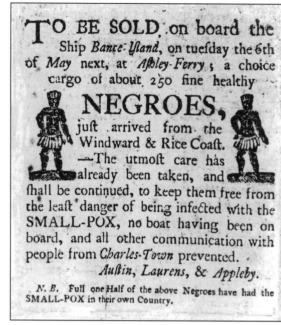

Typical advertisement for a slave auction during the colonial era. *(Library of Congress)*

Such ports as Boston and Newport saw many SLAVE SHIPS unload their human cargoes, which were then sold to southern plantations. Thus, in the first two centuries of the slave trade's existence, both northerners and southerners profited from the trade in African flesh.

End of the African Slave Trade

An antislavery sentiment began to spread in the United States following the AMERICAN REVOLUTION. MANUMISSION became so common that many southern states passed laws requiring the removal of any freed slaves from their domains.

Still, proslavery sentiment was so strong during the American Revolution that Thomas Jefferson had to delete from the original draft of the Declaration of Independence a paragraph accusing George III of England of perpetuating the slave trade. The indictment of the English monarch was struck from the document's final draft because it might have put American traders in an awkward predicament once independence came to the United States.

Nevertheless, there were some humanitarians who began to press for the end of the slave trade. Particularly important in the early abolition movement was the Society of Friends, or QUAKERS. Repeatedly, Quakers sponsored bills and petitions before Congress calling for the abolition of the slave trade. These humanitarian efforts, however, did not get serious support until the growing threat of insurrection was realized. Freshly imported African slaves presented a much more dangerous threat than did domestic slaves who had grown up under the rigorous rules of slavery. Moreover, home-grown slaves did not have to be broken in or seasoned as did newly arrived Africans.

In response to this combination of humanitarian concern and the threat of insurrection, under a clause of the U.S. CONSTITUTION, the United States outlawed the African slave trade on January 1, 1808. Despite the illegal status of the African slave trade after 1808, however, black people continued to be smuggled into the United States. The practice was known to have lasted until the CIVIL WAR rendered the commerce obsolete.

Domestic Slave Trade

The invention of the cotton gin just prior to the termination of the African slave trade breathed new life into the "peculiar institution." Thus, there arose in the border states and the older settled areas of the East a domestic system for the express purpose of trading slaves to the deep South, where cotton was becoming king. Male bondmen were assigned the role of professional studs; it was their job in the slave-trading states to produce offspring who could be sold to the cotton culture of the lower South.

Although slave family life had always been unstable, it became even more so as a result of the domestic commercial activity in human beings. Children were callously begotten to be marketed as slaves. When the youngsters reached weaning age, they were torn from their homes and shipped elsewhere in the nation. Likewise, the "buck" never had the opportunity to act as a husband or father; he was simply a baby-making machine. This was his only connection to the slave family.

With the outlawing of the African slave trade, prices for slaves in the United States skyrocketed. By the eve of the Civil War, a young, healthy male slave could easily fetch $2,000. As a result of such exorbitant prices, the stealing of slaves became common. A notable example of this was the theft of George Washington CARVER and his mother.

Slave pen used in Alexandria, Virginia, during the mid-nineteenth century. *(National Archives)*

As a result of such behavior, slave traders came to be viewed as an unsavory element. Ironically, this was the perspective even of many slaveowners, who, though they did business with the trader, did not socialize with him.

Exactly how many slaves were taken from Africa or transported to the deep South from the border states is unknown. Scholars have put forth estimates on the number of Africans that were transplanted to the Americas ranging from fewer than 10 million to a high of 100 million. Regardless of the actual total, though, the cost of the slave trade in lives and human misery was unquestionably enormous.

—*Randolph Meade Walker*

See also: Black slaveowners; Diaspora, African; Slave resistance.

Suggested Readings:

Bancroft, Frederic. *Slave Trading in the Old South.* Columbia: University of South Carolina Press, 1995.

Bennett, Lerone, Jr. *Before the Mayflower: A History of Black America.* 6th ed. Chicago: Johnson, 1987.

Burnside, Madeleine, and Rosemarie Robotham. *Spirits of the Passage: The Transatlantic Slave Trade in the Seventeenth Century.* New York: Simon & Schuster Editions, 1997.

Davidson, Basil. *The African Slave Trade.* Boston: Little, Brown, 1961.

Elbl, Ivana. "The Volume of the Early Atlantic Slave Trade, 1450-1521." *Journal of African History* 38 (January, 1997): 31-75.

Harding, Vincent. *There Is a River: The Black Struggle for Freedom in America.* New York: Vintage Books, 1983.

Northrup, David, ed. *The Atlantic Slave Trade.* Lexington, Mass.: D. C. Heath, 1994.

Palmer, Colin "The Cruelest Commerce." *National Geographic* (September, 1992): 62-91.

Redding, Sanders. *They Came in Chains: Americans from Africa.* Philadelphia: J. B. Lippincott, 1950.

Tadman, Michael. *Speculators and Slaves: Masters, Traders, and Slaves in the Old South.* Madison: University of Wisconsin Press, 1996.

Thomas, Hugh. *The Slave Trade: The Story of the Atlantic Slave Trade, 1440-1870.* New York: Simon & Schuster, 1997.

Sleet, Moneta, Jr. (February 14, 1926, Owensboro, Kentucky—September 30, 1996, New York, New York): Photographer. Sleet was the first black man to earn a Pulitzer Prize, winning in 1969 for feature photography. The award was given for his photographs of Coretta Scott King and her daughter, taken at the funeral of Martin

Moneta Sleet, Jr., the first African American photographer to win a Pulitzer Prize. *(AP/Wide World Photos)*

Luther King, Jr. Sleet had been employed by Johnson Publications since 1955. Numerous exhibitions of his photography have been held. *See also:* Johnson Publishing Company; Photographers.

Sly and the Family Stone: Rock, SOUL MUSIC, and FUNK group. The inspirational and driving force of this influential group was Sly Stone (born Sylvester Stewart on March 15, 1944). He was born in Dallas, Texas, and at the age of four was singing in the family GOSPEL MUSIC group, the Stewart Four. The Stewart family moved to Vallejo, CALIFORNIA, when Stone was nine years old. He continued to develop his musical talent and became highly skilled on a number of instruments, including guitar and drums. When he was sixteen, he recorded "Long Time Away," which became a successful single locally, for the G&P label. Stone and his brother, Freddie, formed a number of groups, including the Stewart Brothers and the Viscanes.

Stone decided that he would like to study music theory and composition, so he enrolled at Vallejo Junior College. In 1964 he met San Francisco radio personality Tom Donahue, who owned the record label Autumn. Stone was given the opportunity to produce records for Autumn. Some of the more noteworthy names that he produced were the Beau Brummels and Bobby Freeman. He also produced the original version of "Somebody to Love" when Grace Slick was the featured singer for the group the Great Society. Stone also tried his hand at being a disc jockey for local African American radio stations KSOL and KDIA.

In 1966 Stone decided to form his own musical group, which was named the Stoners. This group eventually was disbanded because Stone was frustrated with its musical sound. Out of the breakup, Stone brought together his brother Freddie on guitar, his sister Rose on keyboards, Greg Errico on drums, Jerry Martini on reeds and keyboards, Cynthia Robinson on trumpet, and Larry Graham on bass, to form Sly and the Family Stone.

With Stone sharing the vocals as well as playing guitar and keyboards, this new group became a mixture of rock instrumentation, funk rhythms, and gospel harmonies. Sly and the Family Stone showed freshness and vitality in its approach to musical performance. In 1967 the group signed with Epic Records, releasing its first album, *A Whole New Thing*, in the fall. The album was not a hit, but its "psychedelic soul" sound was not to be denied. The title song of the group's second album, *Dance to the Music* (1968), became a hit on both the pop and rhythm-and-blues charts. Sly and the Family Stone was catching on with an ever-widening listening audience. During 1969 and 1970, the group reached its stride with the album *Stand!* (1969) and with such classic songs as "Hot Fun in the Summertime," "Everyday People," "Sing a Simple Song," "Thank You Falettinme Be Mice Elf Agin," "Everybody Is a Star," and "I Want to Take You Higher." Sly and the Family Stone struck a responsive chord with political messages driven by an infectious dance beat. In 1969 the group made a powerful appearance at Woodstock with its fiery rendition of "Dance to the Music" and "I Want to Take You Higher."

Stone began to be considered unreliable after failing to appear at a number of concerts in 1970. In 1971 the group released its most militant and dark album to date, *There's a Riot Goin' On*; it contained a number-one single, the subdued "Family Affair." Stone's personal problems, though, were breaking the group apart. The group continued to release albums throughout the 1970's, but Stone's drug problems sabotaged the inspiration that had sparked the group in its early years. Nonetheless, although Stone squandered much of his musical genius, through his group, he greatly influenced popular music with his fusion of rock, soul, and funk. Group bassist Larry Graham, it should be noted, was also an influential musician who pioneered the "popping" style of bass playing; he formed Graham Central Station after leaving Sly and the Family Stone in the 1970's. In 1993 Sly and the Family Stone was inducted into the Rock-and-Roll Hall of Fame.

See also: Parliament/Funkadelic.

Smalls, Robert (April 5, 1839, Beaufort, South Carolina—February 23, 1915, Beaufort, South Carolina): Sailor. Smalls became a naval hero for the Union during the CIVIL WAR, even though he had been impressed into the Confederate Navy. On May 13, 1862, Smalls and a small group of other African Americans commandeered the Confederate ship *Planter* and turned it over to the Union. Smalls continued to serve on the *Planter* for the duration of the war, becoming ship's captain in 1863. He later served in the U.S. House of Representatives.

See also: Congress members; Politics and government.

During World War II the Navy named a training camp for African American sailors after Robert Smalls; pianist Dorothy Donegan is seen here entertaining sailors at the camp in 1943. *(National Archives)*

Smalls' Paradise: Nightclub in HARLEM, New York. Ed Smalls opened the club in 1925, and it throve for more than sixty years. It was especially popular with JAZZ audiences in the 1930's, partly because such superior musicians as trumpeter Oran "Hot Lips" PAGE led bands there.

See also: Apollo Theater; Cotton Club.

Smith, Anna Deavere (b. September 18, 1950, Baltimore, Maryland): Stage actor, director, and writer. Smith made her stage debut in *Horatio* (1974) at the American Conservatory Theatre in San Francisco, California. She was with that company from 1974 to 1976. She also became a teacher of theater and acting and is the author of the plays *On the Road* (1983) and *Aye, Aye, Aye, I'm Integrated* (1984), among other books. Her one-woman shows include *A Birthday Card and Aunt Julia's Shoes* and *Fires in the Mirror: Crown Heights, Brooklyn, and Other Identities*, which won on Obie Award.

In 1992 and 1993 Smith wrote and performed the highly acclaimed *Twilight: Los Angeles, 1992*, written in response to the LOS ANGELES RIOTS. In 1995 she wrote the libretto for, and performed in, *A Hymn for Alvin Ailey*; choreography for the work was by Judith Jamison. She wrote *House Arrest: An Intorgression*, another one-woman performance, in 1999.

Smith, Barbara (b. November 16, 1946, Cleveland, Ohio): Feminist editor and essayist. Smith questioned the omission of black women writers from feminist and black literary studies. When she published "Toward a Black Feminist Criticism" in 1977, she declared that by writing about not only the black woman writer but also the black lesbian writer, she was pursuing "something dangerous."

According to Smith, no one else had addressed this topic—not any male critics (black or white) or any feminists. Smith believed that this lack of representation negated the black woman's experience. What was required, she believed, was to uncover writers who give voice to the unique culture of these women's existence, who speak of the oppression that they face daily as women and as people of color. Although such writers exist, they had long been omitted from traditional literary studies. By including them, Smith hoped to show the "connections between the politics of black women's lives, what we write about, and our situation as artists."

Smith shocked many in the literary community by identifying several black women characters in late twentieth-century novels as lesbians, not because of their sexual preference, but because in the stories "they are the central figures, are positively portrayed and have pivotal relationships with one another." She believed that the close bonds which exist between black women in many of these novels were born out of necessity—these women created close relationships to survive in a world that did not welcome them.

Smith became sharply critical of white feminists, asserting that many of them fail to understand the nature and extent of the difficulties faced by black women. She also leveled criticism at those black men who continue to ignore the sexism that confronts black women inside and outside their own neighborhoods. It is Smith's commitment to portraying black women's realities and society's stereotyping of their lives that underlies her literary works. Smith is the coeditor of *Conditions V: The Black Women's Issue* (with Lorraine Bethel, 1979) and *All the Women Are White, All the Blacks Are Men, but Some of Us Are Brave: Black Women's Studies* (with Gloria T. Hull and Patricia Bell Scott, 1982); the editor of *Home Girls: A Black Feminist Anthology* (1983); and the coauthor of *Yours in Struggle: Three Feminist Perspectives on Anti-Semitism and Racism* (with Elly Bulkin and Minnie Brue Patt, 1984). She also published numerous essays on topics such as the Anita Hill/Clarence THOMAS hearings, the black feminist movement, and the unique relationship between black and Jewish women. Smith published a collection of her essays, *The Truth That Never Hurts: Writings on Race, Gender, and Freedom*, in 1998.

An active organizer of black feminist causes beginning in 1973, Smith was a founding member of the Combahee River Collective (a black feminist group in Boston) and was a cofounder of the publishing company Kitchen Table: Women of Color Press. She also became a member of the board of directors for the National Coalition of Black Lesbians and Gays and a member of the NATIONAL ASSOCIATION FOR THE ADVANCEMENT OF COLORED PEOPLE (NAACP). Smith taught at numerous colleges and was an artist-in-residence at Hambidge Center from the Arts and Sciences, Millay Colony for the Arts, Yaddo, and Blue Mountain Center. In 1982 she won the Outstanding Woman of Color Award and, in 1983, was presented with the Women Educators' Curriculum Award.

See also: Black feminism; Homosexuality.

Smith, Bessie (April 15, 1894, Chattanooga, Tennessee—September 26, 1937, Clarksdale, Mississippi): BLUES singer. Billed as the "Empress of the Blues," Bessie Smith is widely recognized as the greatest of all female blues singers. One of seven children of William and Laura Smith, she was orphaned at the age of seven and was often forced to sing on the streets of Chattanooga for pennies.

Smith's professional career began in 1912, when she was hired to work with blues great "Ma" RAINEY in the Moses Stokes Show at the Ivory Theater in Chattanooga. Over the next few years, Smith earned her living by touring constantly as a singer and dancer in traveling minstrel shows. In 1918 she sang, danced, and acted as a male impersonator in her own

Singer Bessie Smith in 1936. *(Library of Congress)*

VAUDEVILLE show, called the Liberty Belles Revue, which played a long stint at Atlanta's 81 Theater.

In the early 1920's, Smith moved to Philadelphia and continued to work the vaudeville circuit, sometimes with a review and sometimes with her own band. She married Earl Love in 1920, but he soon died. Three years later, Smith remarried, to Jack Gee, a night watchman. Also in 1923, Smith began an eight-year recording stint for the Columbia label and had her first hit record, "Downhearted Blues," which sold nearly eight hundred thousand copies in seven months.

By the mid-1920's Smith frequently was headlining at the Lafayette Theater in NEW YORK CITY. She also toured the South with a new revue of her own called the *Harlem Frolics.* In 1926 Smith and Gee adopted a son, whom they named Jack Gee, Jr., but their troubled marriage ended in 1930.

Smith lost a major source of income when her recording contract with Columbia was terminated in 1931. Club engagements also be-

came more scarce. Smith persevered, recording with Benny Goodman and others for the OKeh label and touring theaters the length of the East Coast with a seemingly endless succession of musical revues.

On September 26, 1937, while on tour with the Broadway Rastus Revue in Mississippi, Smith was in an automobile accident. She was treated for shock and had an arm amputated but nevertheless died of her injuries. According to legend, her condition was aggravated because she was turned away from a segregated hospital, but such was evidently not the case.

Smith, James McCune (April 18, 1813, New York, New York—November 17, 1865, Williamsburg, New York): Medical doctor. Smith was the first African American to receive a medical degree. He received his early education at the New York AFRICAN FREE SCHOOL. After failing to gain admission to an American

James McCune Smith. *(Associated Publishers, Inc.)*

medical college, he received a medical degree from the University of Glasgow (Scotland) in 1837. Smith later became a practitioner in New York City, as well as operating two drugstores. He embraced the ABOLITIONIST MOVEMENT and edited *The Colored American*, in which he published his antislavery views. Some of his work focused on dispelling such myths as the beliefs that black people have higher rates of lunacy and smaller brains than white people. *See also:* Medicine.

Smith, Mamie (1883-1946): Singer. Smith's 1920 recording of "Crazy Blues" is considered to be the first BLUES number ever recorded. Smith worked with many of the period's legendary artists, including bandleader Perry BRADFORD and his Jazz Hounds, which featured saxophonist Coleman HAWKINS and trumpeter Bubber Miley. She also appeared in a number of films from the late 1930's through the early 1940's, adding to her reputation as a well-rounded and versatile entertainer.

Smith, Tommie C. (b. June 5, 1944, Clarksville, Texas): TRACK AND FIELD sprinter. During the 1968 Olympics in Mexico City, 200-meter gold medalist Smith and bronze medalist John Carlos protested the treatment of African Americans by refusing to acknowledge the American flag and by raising their fists in a black power salute. They were expelled from the Olympic village.

Smith's time in the Olympics, 19.83 seconds, set an Olympic and world record. He had been named as *Sun Reporter* athlete of the year in 1966, when he made his debut as a record breaker with a time of 19.5 seconds for the 220-yard and 200-meter dashes on a straight track, reducing previous world records by a half second, the single biggest advance in the history of the events. That year, he also set a world record for 220 yards and 200 meters on a

One of the most enduring images to emerge from any Olympics is that of American 200-meter medalists Tommie Smith (center) and John Carlos (right) bowing their heads and raising their fists in protest as the American anthem was played during the victory ceremony. *(Library of Congress)*

turn in 20.0 seconds. He set the world record for 400 meters, at 44.5 seconds, in 1967. He was the top ranked 200-meter and 220-yard runner in the world in 1967 and 1968, according to *Track and Field News*.

At various times, Smith held eleven world records, both indoors and outdoors, at distances up to 440 yards. Considered to be one of the world's best all-time sprinters, Smith gained world rankings in the 100-, 200-, and 400-meter races, as well as in the long jump. His best time in the 100-yard dash is 9.35 seconds, and it is 10.1 seconds in the 100 meters. In 1968 Smith became a physical education professor and coach at Santa Monica College near Los Angeles.

See also: Olympic gold medal winners.

Smith, Will (b. September 25, 1968, Wynnefield, Pennsylvania): Television and FILM actor and RAP vocalist. Originally known by his rap nickname of "Fresh Prince," Smith won success in television and film as well as popular music.

While still in high school, Smith turned down a scholarship to the Massachusetts Institute of Technology in order to pursue a promising career in rap music. Rapping since the age of twelve, Smith (as the Fresh Prince) in 1986 teamed up with Jeffrey Townes (as DJ Jazzy Jeff) to perform as DJ Jazzy Jeff and the Fresh Prince (later shortened to Jazzy Jeff and Fresh Prince). In 1988 the duo's double album *He's the DJ, I'm the Rapper* became one of the first rap albums to achieve platinum status, selling more than one million copies—it eventually went triple platinum. The hit single "Parents Just Don't Understand" from the album won the first-ever Grammy Award in the category of rap music in 1989.

Drawing on their experience growing up in middle-class homes, the duo created much less confrontational music and lyrics than creators of ghetto-based gangsta rap. While such accessibility won them a wide audience, it also cost them critical acceptance and credibility in the rap community.

A video of "Parents Just Don't Understand" led to an offer for Smith to star in his own television series. Premiering in the fall of 1990 and running until 1996, *The Fresh Prince of Bel-Air* showcased Smith's rap persona transplanted to the upscale Bel-Air section of Los Angeles. A ratings winner, the program consistently placed in the Nielsen Top Twenty during its first two seasons. In 1992 it received the IMAGE AWARD for best situation comedy from the NATIONAL ASSOCIATION FOR THE ADVANCEMENT OF COLORED PEOPLE (NAACP). That same year, Smith won a Golden Globe nomination for best performance by an actor in a television series.

Applauded as a "naturally engaging comic

Will Smith holds the World Music Awards trophy he won in 1999 for being the world's best-selling male pop artist of the year. *(AP/Wide World Photos)*

talent," Smith sought a dramatic challenge in his film debut, *Where the Day Takes You* (1992). For his next film he chose another dramatic role, playing a gay con man pretending to be actor Sidney POITIER's illegitimate son in the 1993 film adaptation of John Guare's Tony Award-winning play *Six Degrees of Separation*. In 1993 he also appeared in *Made in America*, in a comedic role that traded on his Fresh Prince persona.

Smith next appeared in *Bad Boys* (1995), an action film. He chose the project partly because it involved the chance to costar with Martin Lawrence, significant because Hollywood had yet to produce a big-budget action film with two African American leads. Smith's film career continued to be varied and remarkably successful throughout the 1990's. He costarred in the science fiction thriller *Indepen-*

dence Day (1996) and in the more lighthearted science fiction film *Men in Black* (1997). In 1999 he starred in *The Wild, Wild West*.

While working in film and television, Smith also continued with his music career. In 1991 he and Towne won a second Grammy for "Summertime," from the 1991 *Homebase* album, and in 1992 they garnered an Image Award for outstanding rap artists. *Code Red* (1993), with a somewhat harder edge than the previous releases, was the duo's last album. In 1997 Smith put out his first solo record, *Big Willie Style*, which contained the rap song "Men in Black," the title song from the film; the song earned Smith his third Grammy Award. He released *Willenium* in 1999.

Smith, Willie Mae Ford (b. 1906, Rolling Fork, Mississippi): GOSPEL MUSIC singer and evangelist. Smith was one of fourteen children. Her father was a railroad worker and Baptist deacon, and her mother was a restaurant operator. The family moved to MEMPHIS, TENNESSEE, when she was a young girl. She dropped out of school in the eighth grade to help her mother in the family restaurant. In the early 1920's, she sang the lead in the Ford family quartet, made up of herself and three sisters. They appeared at the National Baptist Convention in 1922, singing "Ezekiel Saw the Wheel" and "I'm in His Care."

In 1926 Ford was inspired to become a gospel singer after hearing Artelia Hutchins. In 1932 she met Thomas DORSEY and Sallie MARTIN, who were spreading the newer style of gospel music around the country. In 1936 Dorsey appointed her as the director of the Soloists Bureau of the National Convention of Gospel Choirs and Choruses. In that position, she demonstrated the proper style and delivery of gospel songs to younger singers. She also frequently gave solo gospel recitals, with Roberta Martin as the accompanist. In 1937 she received a major ovation at the National

Baptist Convention when she performed her composition "If You Just Keep Still."

Because the BAPTIST Church did not allow women to preach, Smith left it in 1939 to join the Holiness Church of God Apostolic. She became an ordained evangelist and limited her singing to religious revivals and similar appearances. As an evangelist, Smith frequently interspersed her songs into a brief sermon. This practice became known as the "sermonette and song." Although Smith devoted herself to evangelizing instead of pursuing a professional gospel singing career, she made appearances in New York City at Radio City Music Hall and at the Newport Jazz Festival. She also made occasional recordings. In 1982 she was the subject of a gospel documentary, *Say Amen, Somebody*, which featured her own performances as well as those of many of her protégés, including Mahalia JACKSON, the O'Neal twins, and Delois Barrett Campbell. *See also:* Gospel music and spirituals.

Smith, Willie "the Lion" (William Henry Joseph Bonaparte Bertholoff; November 25, 1897, Goshen, New York—April 18, 1973, New York, New York): JAZZ pianist. A legend of the New York stride piano school, Smith's signature was the bowler hat and cigar. Reared in NEWARK, NEW JERSEY, Smith, a product of Jewish and African American ancestry, reportedly was a cantor during the 1940's. The influence of his mother, a church pianist, was evident in his early interest in the instrument. Smith's introduction to the piano at the age of six led to an equally precocious beginning as a professional musician during his teenage years.

A veteran of WORLD WAR I, Smith was dubbed "the Lion" as a result of his heroism during that conflict. On returning from Europe, Smith became known in the San Juan Hill or "The Jungle" section of NEW YORK CITY as well as in Harlem for his prodigious abilities in stride piano performance, a skill which earned him the friendship and admiration of fellow stride artists James P. JOHNSON and Fats WALLER, both of whom he competed with at cutting sections in nightclubs. Duke EL- LINGTON was also an admirer of "the Lion."

Smith toured with BLUES artist Mamie SMITH and participated in the recording of "Crazy Blues" (1920). He could be heard in performance at the Rhythm Club in Harlem and at uptown rent parties, where he displayed his bravura style. In 1935 Smith was brought to greater public attention as a result of his recordings for Decca. He also recorded solo pieces for Commodore in 1939. Smith, who appeared in the 1954 film *Jazz Dance*, toured Europe in the late 1940's and mid-1960's and composed works which were used by white jazz artists Tommy Dorsey and Artie Shaw.

Smith's solo recordings include "Echoes of Spring/Fading Star" (1939), "Rippling Waters/Finger Buster" (1939), "Morning Air/Passionatte" (1939), and "Concentrating/Sneak Away" (1939). He also can be heard on *Reminiscing the Piano Greats* (1950). One of his celebrated works as a leader contained a tribute to Duke Ellington, "Portrait of Duke," which can be heard on *The Lion Roars* (1957). In addition, Smith's *Music on My Mind: The Memoirs of an American Pianist* (1964), written with George Hoefer and containing a foreword by Duke Ellington, expresses Smith's recollections of his own life and the musical eras he spanned.

Smith v. Allwright: U.S. SUPREME COURT case in 1944 involving voting rights. The Court overturned GROVEY V. TOWNSEND (1935) by ruling that a state's delegation to political parties, of the right to determine voting qualifications, was a state action and thus governed by the Constitution. Previously, political parties in Texas had banned black voters from participating in primary elections. This decision banned that practice.
See also: Voters; Voting Rights Act of 1965.

Smythe, Hugh H. (August 19, 1913, Pittsburgh, Pennsylvania—1977): Government official and educator. Smythe received his B.A. from Virginia State College, an M.A. from AT- LANTA UNIVERSITY, and a Ph.D. from Northwestern University in CHICAGO, ILLINOIS. As an anthropologist, he taught at Brooklyn College in New York and at the Foreign Service Institute of the State Department. He was also a trainer of Peace Corps volunteers. He was appointed as ambassador to Syria by President Lyndon B. Johnson in 1965, during a critical phase of Middle Eastern conflict. He served as ambassador until 1967. He was also special counsel to the Senate Foreign Relations Committee, a research consultant to the State Department, and a member of the U.S. delegation to the United Nations General Assembly.
See also: Diplomats; Politics and government.

Snoop Dogg (Calvin Broadus; b. October 20, 1971, Long Beach, California): RAP vocalist and lyricist. Snoop Dogg was known as Snoop Doggy Dogg until the release of *Da Game Is to Be Sold, Not to Be Told* in 1998, around which time he dropped the "Doggy" from his stage name. A West Coast rapper known for his relaxed, low-pitched delivery of hard-edged lyrics, Snoop Dogg grew up in the Southern California community of Long Beach, playing piano and singing in the choir at the Baptist Church. As a teenager he began rapping on the streets, gathering spontaneous audiences for his performances with his original rhymes influenced by hardcore rap artists such as N.W.A. and Eric B & Rakim. At eighteen, Snoop served a year in county jail for drug possession. During this time, he turned his experiences as a prisoner into rap lyrics and decided to commit himself to music upon his release.

In 1990 Snoop began to collaborate with DR. DRE, the producer and composer for the gangsta rap group N.W.A. As a lyricist and featured guest artist on Dr. Dre's solo album *The Chronic* (1990), Snoop quickly established an audience for his leisurely gangsta raps that paved the way for his own success as a solo artist. Snoop wrote the number-one single "Nuthin' but a 'G' Thang" on *The Chronic*, and he cowrote and performed another successful single, "Dre Day." Before even releasing a solo album, Snoop was featured on the covers of the music magazines *Rolling Stone, Vibe,* and *The Source*.

Snoop's solo debut, *Snoop Doggy Dogg* (1993), attested rap's widespread appeal by becoming the first album by a new artist to enter *Billboard* magazine's pop album chart at number one. Produced by Dr. Dre, the album incorporated Dre's characteristic musical arrangements suggestive of 1970's funk styles, and Snoop's explicit lyrics. His conversational vocal style belied the graphic images he described—lyrics criticized by some as needlessly violent, sexist, and homophobic, but which the artist defended as honest portrayals of life as he knew it. Among songs evincing casual attitudes toward violence and sex, such as "Gin and Juice," was the contrasting piece "Murder Was the Case (Death After Visualizing Eternity)"—the story of the singer's own murder in which he is offered a second chance at life as a lesson about the bleak and final consequences of violence. The album also contained Snoop's cover version of rapper Slick Rick's "La-Di-Da-Di." His "Lodi Dodi" follows a time-honored tradition in which JAZZ, BLUES, and RHYTHM-AND-BLUES musicians cover other artists' works as an expression of both camaraderie and competition.

Snoop Dogg spoke openly of growing up in the GHETTO and about GANG life. In 1993 he was charged as an accomplice in a murder—the shooting death of Phillip Woldermarian—allegedly committed by his bodyguard. The publicity undoubtedly boosted sales of *Snoop Doggy Dogg*. Nonetheless, following his initial success as a musician, Snoop asserted that he

no longer engaged in gang activities and that his descriptions of gang life were intended to depict reality, not to endorse the lifestyle. Snoop Dogg stated that he chose not to preach but viewed his successful musical career as a visible lesson to his fans in overcoming prejudice and pursuing alternatives to gang life.

Snoop Dogg in 1993. *(Death Row/Interscope Records, Inc.)*

Snoop Dogg at pretrial hearings in his murder trial in 1995. *(AP/Wide World Photos)*

In February of 1996, Snoop Dogg was found not guilty of murder and conspiracy and was acquitted on charges of being an accessory after the fact to the 1993 shooting death of Woldermarian. Snoop and his bodyguard were tried on charges of manslaughter as well, but the jury deadlocked and a mistrial was declared. The time and energy Snoop had to spend preparing for his trial slowed his career.

Snoop Dogg released *Tha Doggfather* in 1996—it sold about two million copies, creditable but not in the same league as his first album. Snoop began to revamp his image somewhat, moving away from gansta rap, which was declining in popularity. In 1997 he had a song on the sound track album of the film *Men in Black*. He released *Da Game Is to Be Sold, Not to Be Told* in 1998 and *Topp Dogg* in 1999.

Soledad Brothers: Symbols of black revolutionary consciousness in the late 1960's and early 1970's. The Soledad Brothers included John Cluchette and Fleeta Drumgo, prisoners at the Soledad correctional facility at Soledad, CALIFORNIA, who were accused of murdering a prison guard. Cluchette and Drumgo were associates of the third Soledad Brother, George JACKSON, a radical black prison leader and writer, and of the BLACK PANTHER PARTY. Through Jackson and the Black Panthers, they were acquainted with Angela DAVIS, a noted black radical professor and member of the Communist Party.

In August, 1970, while an unrelated trial of four African Americans was taking place in Marin County, California, Jonathan Jackson, George Jackson's brother, commandeered the courtroom, freed the black prisoners, and took the prisoners and the trial judge, whom he held hostage, out of the courthouse. The alleged goal of the raid was to exchange the judge and the prisoners for the Soledad Brothers. In the ensuing shoot-out with police, Jonathan Jackson, the judge, and two of the prisoners were killed.

The guns that Jonathan Jackson had used in the shoot-out were registered to Angela Davis, who was charged with conspiring with Jackson. She immediately went into hiding and was for a time placed on the Federal Bureau of Investigation's Ten Most Wanted list. Apprehended in October, 1970, Davis was tried and acquitted on conspiracy and murder charges in June, 1972. Cluchette and Drumgo were acquitted of murder charges in March, 1972. George Jackson later died under suspicious circumstances in an abortive prison escape.

Songwriters and composers: Composers in the African American musical tradition include anonymous creators of spirituals and BLUES; JAZZ arrangers and improvisers from the conservatory-trained to the self-taught; composers working in the strictly notated style of concert music; songwriters crafting popular songs for scenarios from the minstrel stage to the modern recording studio; and RAP artists making new music partially from existing recordings. The composers of African American music have created their work in formats as diverse as their art is expressive.

The Antebellum Period

Slaves in the United States drew upon and adapted traditions they brought with them from Africa to create work songs and shouts, spirituals, satirical songs, dance music, and marches. With neither training nor access to materials to write their music down, they played by ear and memory, creating compositions by the process of repeated performance. After the CIVIL WAR, slave songs were collected and published in *Slave Songs of the United States* (1867), a volume which, though not attributing individual composers, preserves some of the earliest African American musical creations.

FREE BLACKS were active as composers in the North during the antebellum period, writing popular music such as dances, marches, and ballads. Frank Johnson (1792-1844) of Philadelphia toured with his military band and dance orchestra performing his original material. His audiences often included prominent white artists, and his extensive touring included a command performance for Queen Victoria of England. Modern editions of his work were published in 1977 and 1983.

Music was also an important element of the antislavery movement. The protest songs of William Wells BROWN and Sojourner TRUTH were featured at many emancipation rallies.

Art Music

Emancipation and then the beginning of the twentieth century brought to the fore a generation of black "nationalist" concert composers. Following similar creative trends in Europe, these composers drew on black work songs, spirituals, and dance music in their work as emblems of national creative power.

Harry Thacker Burleigh, one of the first nationalist composers, studied with Antonin Dvorák at the National Conservatory of Music. Burleigh composed ballads, art songs—such as "Lovely Dark and Lonely One," a 1935 setting of a Langston HUGHES poem—choral pieces, spiritual arrangements, and instrumental pieces. Much of his work was popularized by white concert singers of the time.

William DAWSON trained in composition at the TUSKEGEE INSTITUTE of Alabama and the American Conservatory of Music. His *Negro Folk Symphony* was premiered by Leopold Stokowski in Philadelphia in 1934 to critical acclaim.

The most famous black nationalist composer was William Grant STILL. After training at the Oberlin Conservatory, with the French avant-garde composer Edgard Varèse, and with blues composer and publisher W. C. HANDY, Still achieved fame with his *Afro-American Symphony* (1931), which incorporated elements of jazz and BLUES. With its 1935 performance by the New York Philharmonic at Carnegie Hall, the work became the first symphony by an African American to be performed by a major orchestra. Still's work was notable for breaking racial barriers in both content and performance contexts, and he left a repertoire of more than one hundred concert works, as well as popular jazz songs, film scores, and television music.

Concert composers work in a wide variety of styles. Ulysses Kay, despite being the nephew of famous jazz trumpeter Joe "King" OLIVER, wrote in an abstract, dissonant style. Hale Smith used serial composition techniques mixed with jazz influences and composed scores for jazz musicians Dizzy GILLESPIE, Ahmad Jamal, and Eric DOLPHY. Olly Wilson was a pioneer in electronic music. Anthony Davis (b. 1951) composed formally notated pieces with an improvisational sound. His opera *X: The Life and Times of Malcolm X*, debuted in 1985.

Religious Music

Christianity has been a formative influence on much black American composition. The first black hymnal was published by Richard ALLEN, a minister of the AFRICAN METHODIST EPISCOPAL (AME) CHURCH and former slave who purchased his own freedom. Allen's *A Collection of Spiritual Songs and Hymns Selected from Various Authors* was published in 1801, probably with his own alterations, embellishments, and compositions.

Black hymns eventually became known as spirituals. John Wesley Work, Sr. (1873-1925) brought spirituals to international attention as director, arranger, and composer for the Fisk Jubilee Singers. Work toured the world with his choir from 1900 to 1916, presenting European-style choral arrangements that created a new standard for spiritual performance.

The founder of modern gospel was Thomas A. DORSEY, a blues pianist from Georgia who moved to Gary, Indiana, to work in the steel mills and play in local dance bands. After touring with blues singer Gertrude "Ma" RAINEY and writing "Tight Like That," Dorsey founded the Thomas A. Dorsey Gospel Songs Music Publishing Company in 1931 and devoted himself to sacred composition. Dorsey composed more than four hundred gospel songs, updating spirituals by infusing them with the sounds of jazz and blues. Many were made famous in recordings by singer Mahalia JACKSON, including the classic "Take My Hand, Precious Lord" (1932).

One of the most active composers of religious music in the late twentieth century was Andrae CROUCH, a San Francisco-based vocalist and songwriter who created a mix of pop and rock songwriting techniques, African and Caribbean sounds, and traditional gospel music to create an eclectic crossover style.

Minstrelsy and Musical Theater

Emancipation brought an international craze for black minstrel music. Minstrel composers wrote ballads, comic songs, and specialty numbers for theatrical performance by traveling troupes. Singers sometimes commissioned their own songs from composers, which they would buy outright.

James Bland was known as "The World's Greatest Minstrel Man." The Long Island native was educated at HOWARD UNIVERSITY, where he listened to the songs of local former slaves and taught himself the banjo. Bland left college to join a minstrel troupe and became immensely popular as a performer throughout America, England, and Germany; he was perhaps the first internationally known African American musical idol. Bland composed some seven hundred songs for the minstrel stage. His most famous, "Carry Me Back to Old Virginny" (1878), was adopted as Virginia's official state song in 1940.

On Broadway, Will Marion Cook composed and directed the first successful all-black musical comedy— *Clorindy: Or, the Origin of the Cakewalk* (1898); his 1902 show *In Dahomey* (1902) was the first black theatrical work to open in Times Square. Cook also wrote ragtime songs, led his own touring dance orchestra, and was one of six black founding members (among 164 whites) of the American Society of Composers, Authors, and Publishers (ASCAP).

Ragtime

Texan pianist Scott JOPLIN ushered in the ragtime era with his 1899 publication of "Maple Leaf Rag," a lively, syncopated piano piece that earned instant popular acclaim. Joplin wrote many more rags in a precise style mixing the cross-accents and blue notes of black music tradition with formal European structure, as well as a rag ballet (*The Ragtime Dance*, 1899), two rag operas (*A Guest of Honor*, 1903, and *Treemonisha*, 1911). Joplin's work was revived in the 1973 film *The Sting*.

Other important ragtime composers included Eubie BLAKE of Baltimore and Thomas "Fats" WALLER of New York. Blake, a child of former slaves, composed his first rag at age sixteen ("Charleston Rag," 1899), and went on to a long career writing and performing ragtime, theater, popular, and art music. Waller grew up playing organ and piano in Harlem and wrote many popular songs, including "Honeysuckle Rose" (1929), "Ain't Misbehavin'" (1929), and "I'm Gonna Sit Right Down and Write Myself a Letter" (1935).

Blues

The blues began as an oral tradition, created on the spot or learned by ear; they entered the written world when W. C. Handy, a minstrel musician from Alabama, published "Memphis Blues" in 1912 and ushered in a new era of popularity for the blues ballad. Called "The Father of the Blues," Handy composed and published many more songs, including the famous "St. Louis Blues" (1914), spiritual arrangements, marches, hymns, and rags.

Blues guitarist and singer Robert JOHNSON never published his works, but he recorded twenty-nine songs in his short life. His classics such as "Crossroads Blues," "Sweet Home Chicago," and "Hellhound on My Trail" later influenced rock musicians including Eric Clapton and the Rolling Stones. Other important blues writers of the early twentieth century included LEADBELLY (Huddie Ledbetter), "Blind" Lemon JEFFERSON, Big Bill BROONZY, Eddie "Son" House, and Sam "Lightnin'" Hopkins.

B. B. KING's "Three O'Clock Blues" (1950) was one of the first up-tempo blues hits performed on the electric guitar. King earned worldwide fame and became a Grammy Award-winning artist; his guitar-oriented compositional style has been continued by younger songwriters such as Robert Cray.

Jazz

The first published arrangement in jazz history was "Jelly Roll Blues" (1905) by Ferdinand "Jelly Roll" MORTON. A New Or-

leans bordello pianist by age twelve, Morton pioneered the swinging rhythms and complex textures that became characteristic of jazz. Several of his compositions, such as "King Porter Stomp" (1906), are jazz classics.

Trumpet player Louis ARMSTRONG was known as the first great jazz improviser. Armstrong composed on the spot every time he performed, and his improvisations on recordings of "Struttin' with Some Barbeque" (1927) and "West End Blues" (1928) have been studied and copied note for note by later jazz players.

The great jazz composer Duke ELLINGTON had little formal music training other than piano lessons, but he was a visionary who created complex jazz without losing its essential swing. Renowned for balancing formal arrangements with improvisational passages, orchestra with soloist, Ellington embodied both the collective spirit and the individual creativity of the African American musical tra-

Composer Duke Ellington performing at a dinner given by the White House Correspondents' Association in 1955. *(AP/Wide World Photos)*

dition. His works include classic songs such as "Mood Indigo" (1930); several symphonic jazz compositions including *Black, Brown, and Beige*, which debuted in Carnegie Hall in 1943; and two *Sacred Concerts* (1965 and 1968). He collaborated closely with pianist-composer Billy STRAYHORN throughout his career.

The next jazz innovators were bebop players such as Charlie PARKER, Miles DAVIS, Dizzy Gillespie, Thelonious MONK, and John COLTRANE, all of whom contributed to a new style emphasizing improvisation, harmonic and melodic complexity, quick tempo, and the element of surprise. One of the few bebop composers to notate his work was Charles MINGUS, who mixed improvisation with composition in works such as "Pork Pie Hat" (1957).

Herbie HANCOCK, once a child virtuoso on the piano, created his own jazz style drawing on electronic sounds, the styles of funk and rock, and collaboration with musicians from many different traditions. His songs such as "Maiden Voyage" and "Watermelon Man" (1963) have been re-recorded by many musicians, and his film compositions include the score for the film *Death Wish* (1974). He won an Academy Award for his score to the film *'Round Midnight* (1986).

Rhythm and Blues, Soul, Rock, Funk, and Popular Music

RHYTHM AND BLUES composer Louis Jordan (1908-1975) turned jazz and blues in a new direction in the 1940's with up-tempo "party" songs such as "Five Guys Named Moe" and "Boogie Woogie Blue Plate." Ray CHARLES followed in Jordan's footsteps with hit songs such as "I've Got a Woman" (1955) and "Hallelujah, I Love Her So" (1956), which was based on a gospel song and caused considerable controversy in the church. Songs such as these laid the groundwork for rock and roll, which began in the work of musicians such as Missouri-born guitar player Chuck BERRY. A jazz guitar player who learned music in church, Berry be-

came famous in 1955 with "Maybellene"—an inaugural rock and roll song and one of the first to appear on both the rhythm-and-blues and popular music charts.

Berry's contemporary, James BROWN, has been called the "Godfather of Soul" for his funky, shouting style. Brown's first soul hit was "Please, Please, Please" (1956). He was an active voice during the struggle for civil rights with songs such as "Say It Loud, I'm Black and I'm Proud."

Other important soul songwriters were Eddie Holland, Lamont Dozier, and Brian Holland of Motown Records. Smoothing out soul with rich orchestral arrangements, hand-clapping rhythm tracks, and romantic love themes, the team wrote many hits for MOTOWN artists including "Where Did Our Love Go?" (1964) for the SUPREMES and "I Can't Help Myself" (1965) for the FOUR TOPS.

Funk songwriters moved away from the sweet positivity of Motown soul to embrace the counterculture of the 1960's. George Clinton (b. 1940) incorporated aspects of psychedelia and science fiction into his music and lyrics, and employed heavy, looping rhythms that laid the basis for rap and HIP-HOP beats. His songs include "Dr. Funkenstein" (1976) and "Atomic Dog" (1982).

In the 1980's Michael JACKSON became one of the most widely known popular songwriters. He began his career as a solo songwriter with his 1979 album *Off the Wall*, which blended soul and rock into a new style with broad appeal. His 1982 album *Thriller* sold thirty million copies. Other works include *Bad* (1987) and *Dangerous* (1991) as well as "We Are the World," written with Lionel Richie in 1985 to benefit famine victims in Africa. Jackson's innovative rhythms, arrangements, and lyrics opened new directions in popular songwriting.

Quincy JONES became widely recognized as one of the most versatile and accomplished black composers. A jazz pianist and trumpet player who composed and arranged for Count

BASIE and performed with Lionel HAMPTON, Dizzy Gillespie, and his own touring band, Jones went on to form his own production company and record label. He wrote and produced music for top pop performance talent, including Michael Jackson, and created collaborative projects such as his 1978 album *Sounds—And Stuff Like That* with performances by Herbie Hancock, Chaka Khan, Patti Austin, and ASHFORD AND SIMPSON. Jones also composed concert pieces such as *Soundpiece for String Quartet and Contralto* and numerous film scores, including the score for *The Color Purple* (1985).

Rap and Hip-Hop
Rap style began in the late 1970's with the work of "rapping DJs" such as the Sugarhill Gang and GRANDMASTER FLASH AND THE FURIOUS FIVE. Kurtis Blow interjected the note of political protest that was to guide rap's future with his 1980 song "The Breaks." L.L. COOL J brought rap to a broad popular audience with "I Can't Live Without My Radio" (1985); his "I Need Love" (1987) may have been the first rap love ballad.

The group PUBLIC ENEMY combined the intensely political lyrics of rapper Chuck D. with dense musical textures to create the hard-hitting sound represented on their 1988 work *It Takes a Nation of Millions to Hold Us Back*. The political stance of Public Enemy is echoed in work by West Coast gangsta rap writers such as ICE CUBE and Ice-T.

Los Angeles rap writer and producer DR. DRE draws on the sounds and rhythms of 1970's funk in his work. His 1993 album *The Chronic* spawned a new, more musical style of rap embraced by artists such as SNOOP DOGG and Warren G.

African American songwriters and composers have a long history of innovating, renovating, creating and re-creating tradition to serve diverse expressive and social ends. Their voices have responded to and created community in America; their work has wielded cultural and economic force around the world.

—*Elizabeth J. Miles*

See also: Music.

Suggested Readings:
Abdul, Raoul. *Blacks in Classical Music: A Personal History.* New York: Dodd, Mead, 1977.
Baker, David N., Lida M. Belt, and Herman C. Hudson, eds. *The Black Composer Speaks.* Metuchen, N.J.: Scarecrow Press, 1978.
Baraka, Amiri. *Blues People: Negro Music in White America.* New York: William Morrow, 1963.
Caldwell, Hansonia L. *African American Music: A Chronology: 1619-1995.* Los Angeles: Ikoro Communications, 1995.
Redd, Lawrence N. *Rock Is Rhythm and Blues: The Impact of Mass Media.* East Lansing: Michigan State University Press, 1974.
Shaw, Arnold. *Black Popular Music in America: From the Spirituals, Minstrels, and Ragtime to Soul, Disco, and Hip-Hop.* New York: Schirmer Books, 1986.
Southern, Eileen. *The Music of Black Americans: A History.* New York: W. W. Norton, 1971.
_____, ed. *Readings in Black American Music.* 2d ed. New York: W. W. Norton, 1983.

Soul City, North Carolina: Town founded in 1968 by CIVIL RIGHTS advocate Floyd B. McKISSICK. McKissick, who was named director of the CONGRESS OF RACIAL EQUALITY in 1966, left that organization to launch Floyd B. McKissick Enterprises, a corporation involved in organizing and financing businesses in the African American community. An arm of that corporation, Warren Regional Planning Corporation, was formed for the specific purpose of developing Soul City.

Soul food: Certain food items typically cooked and eaten by African Americans. Modern soul food originated in traditional slave and southern food. Most soul food is related to pork products, but the term also encompasses collard, turnip, and mustard greens, black-eyed peas, sweet potatoes or yams (taken from the African word *nyami*, meaning "to eat"), okra, cornbread, chicken, and fried fish. Although these dishes are cooked in traditional ways related to slave or African culture, many of them were not eaten regularly by slaves. The basic slave diet consisted of meat (often sow belly), meal, and molasses.

The diet of slaves was determined in large part by which foods were abundant, cheap to produce or purchase, or unwanted by slaveowners. Sweet potatoes, for example, grew particularly well in the South and gave a high yield, often two hundred to four hundred bushels per acre. Pork products became part of soul food because they were unappealing to white people. These products include chitterlings, or chitlins, made from the small intestine of a pig, pigs' ears, pig knuckles and feet, hog maws, neck bones and tails of pigs, fatback, and pork chops.

The food given to slaves often had little taste. Soul food cooking reflects that in its use of hot spices and peppers and in a tendency to use large amounts of fat or grease to give flavor to food. Deep fat frying is a practice that comes from Africa, and the pit barbecue was probably invented by black people.

Moses W. Vaughn of the University of Maryland, Eastern Shore, found that soul food had been given little scholarly attention. Even a Department of Agriculture handbook failed to mention soul food pork products. In 1975 Vaughn received a $175,000 grant to study the nutritive value of soul food.

See also: Foodways.

Soul music: Although some music critics and scholars apply the term "soul music" broadly to virtually all African American popular music produced in the 1960's and early 1970's, most use the term more narrowly to refer to a particular genre of African American music that combined RHYTHM AND BLUES with gospel. The most striking characteristic of this music was its use of gospel shouting, a technique in which the singer shouts a song's lyrics over the sound of the band. These vocals, described by critics as grainy, gritty, or rasping, led many to view soul music as an authentically "black" music form.

Among the primary names associated with soul music at its peak in the 1960's are James BROWN ("soul brother number one"), Otis REDDING, and Aretha FRANKLIN ("the queen of soul"). Other noted soul performers range from Sam COOKE and Solomon Burke to Sam and Dave, Wilson Pickett, Carla Thomas, Percy Sledge, Al GREEN, and Ann Peebles.

Soul music was important both for its commercial success and for its association with the black nationalism that grew out of the CIVIL RIGHTS movement in the mid-1960's. Black nationalists urged African Americans to take pride in their culture and their heritage. Soul music, because it was perceived as being authentically black, became a powerful symbol of the new emphasis on "black pride."

In the United States, soul music gained an audience not only among African Americans but also among young whites, particularly in the South. Soul enjoyed international popularity as well, especially in Europe, Africa, and the Caribbean.

Sources

Following WORLD WAR II, small African American dance bands replaced the big swing bands that had been popular since the 1930's. These new dance bands consisted of a rhythm section (typically featuring keyboards, drums, guitar, and bass) and a small horn section. Musicians in these bands drew on the blues, added elements of JAZZ and swing, and increased the rhythm to make the blues into dance music. This new music was rhythm and blues.

Soul music bands were basically rhythm-and-blues bands that added elements of gospel to their music. Most soul singers had gospel backgrounds (in contrast to rhythm-and-blues vocalists, most of whom began as street-corner singers). Sam Moore and Dave Prater (of Sam and Dave) and Otis Redding, for example, had all begun singing in church in their youth. Wilson Pickett and Eddie Floyd had been members of the Falcons, a Detroit gospel group that crossed over to become pop recording artists. Aretha Franklin had a career as a gospel recording star before becoming a soul singer.

These singers brought with them not only gospel shouting but other gospel techniques as well. Soul singers would talk on their recordings, as if they were ministers preaching to their congregations, or they would engage in call-and-response with their backup singers, imitating a preacher calling out to the congregation and the congregation responding. The influence of gospel was not confined to vocals. The piano on soul recordings might take on gospel overtones. The use of the organ gave soul music a churchlike feel.

Country music was also an influence. Soul singers were African American, but many soul musicians and songwriters were white and had backgrounds in country music. Many African Americans involved in soul music had also been influenced by country music, since they had grown up in the South and had listened to country music on the radio. Aaron Neville, for example, developed his distinctive falsetto by imitating the yodeling he heard as a child while listening to country music radio stations. Some critics have noted the country-flavored bass playing on soul recordings. Others have pointed out the similarity in lyrics between soul and country—both often tell love stories or hard-luck stories. The clearest indication of country's influence on soul is the fact that a number of soul singers recorded country songs. Both Percy Sledge and Solomon Burke recorded "Just Out of Reach," and Burke recorded "I Really Don't Want to Know." Ray CHARLES recorded two country-and-western albums.

The lyrics of soul music are rooted in the blues. Soul lyrics are about emotions—self-pity, pain, loneliness, love, joy, sexual ecstasy. Most songs deal with relations between men and women. They tell stories of love and loss or of sexual infidelity, and they feature male boasting about sexual prowess, all major blues themes.

Minstrel shows provided another source for soul music. After the Civil War, African American entertainers had joined the minstrel shows that traveled throughout the United States. These shows continued to tour the rural South until the 1950's. One feature of the minstrel show was the comic dance. Soul star Rufus Thomas, who began his career as a minstrel comedian and dancer, brought this element into soul music with recordings that concerned comic dances such as "Walking the Dog" and "The Funky Chicken."

Soul music combined the sacred and the secular, not only in its merger of gospel with rhythm and blues but in its lyrics as well (for example, Otis Redding's "Lover's Prayer," in which the singer literally prays to his lover). This combination of the sacred and the secular follows an African pattern. Africans did not distinguish between sacred and secular realms; for Africans, religion was part of everyday life. This same pattern may be found in nineteenth-century African American spirituals. These religious songs could be used for secular purposes (as work songs or marching songs) or could have secular content (descriptions of food and clothing). Seen in this context, soul music may be understood as belonging to an African American tradition that had its origins ultimately in Africa.

(continued on page 2341)

Notable Soul and Funk Musicians

Bass, Fontella (b. July 3, 1940, St. Louis, Mo.). Bass's vocal recording of "Rescue Me," a soulful RHYTHM-AND-BLUES single, soared to the top of the popular music charts in both the United States and England in 1965. She also recorded memorable jazz with the Art Ensemble of Chicago. Proud of her roots in GOSPEL MUSIC, Bass released *No Ways Tired* in 1995.

Brown, James. *See main text entry.*

Clinton, George. *See* PARLIAMENT/FUNKADELIC.

Franklin, Aretha. *See main text entry.*

Hayes, Isaac (b. Aug. 20, 1942, Covington, Tenn.). Musician, songwriter, and singer. Hayes helped to create the "Memphis sound" of soul music and wrote a number of hit songs, including "Soul Man," before releasing *Hot Buttered Soul* in 1969. The album set the direction for soul music in the 1970's and was a forerunner of disco. Hayes also produced the hit sound track for the movie *Shaft*, in 1971. In the 1990's he began supplying the voice of "Chef" on the animated television series *South Park*.

AP/Wide World Photos

Houston, Cissy (Emily Drinkard; b. 1932, Newark, N.J.). From 1960 to the mid-1970's, Houston was much in demand as a soul and pop music backup singer. Her own group, the Sweet Inspirations, produced a number of hits. Notable among her many recordings is *Herbie Mann Surprise Featuring Cissy Houston* (1975).

Jackson, Millie (b. July 15, 1944, Thompson, Ga.). Jackson's single, "A Child of God," reached number twenty-two on the rhythm-and-blues chart in 1972. Her follow-up singles, "Ask Me What You Want" and "It Hurts So Good," reached number fourteen and number three, respectively. Her album *Caught Up* (1974) produced the hit single "(If Loving You Is Wrong) I Don't Want to Be Right," which went gold. In 1979 Jackson recorded duets with Isaac Hayes on her album *Royal Rappin's*.

James, Rick (James Johnson; b. Feb. 1, 1952, Buffalo, N.Y.). An instrumentalist, producer, and writer, as well as a singer, James became known in the 1980's as the "father of punk funk," a combination of dance-party funk grooves and streetwise sexual posturing. In the early 1970's, James accepted a staff position as songwriter and producer with Motown. In 1978 he released *Come Get It*, which went platinum. Its single, "You and I," reached number thirteen on the pop charts and number one on the rhythm-and-blues charts. James recorded two 1979 disco-based albums, *Bustin' Out of L Seven*, with its hit single "Bustin' Out," and *Fire It Up*, which remained on the soul charts through 1980. The 1980 release *Garden of Love* spawned four more soul chart singles. James began producing sessions for other artists, including singer Teena Marie, with whom he enjoyed a long and productive association. Much of *Street Songs* (1981) focused on societal ills; its singles "Give It to Me Baby" and "Super Freak" solidified James's position as a major artist.

AP/Wide World Photos

Mayfield, Curtis. *See main text entry.*

Pickett, Wilson (b. Mar. 18, 1941, Prattville, Ala.). Pickett began his career as a gospel singer but crossed over to popular music as a member of the Falcons, singing lead on that group's 1962 hit "I Found a Love." As a soul artist, Pickett recorded such classics as "In the Midnight Hour" (1965), "Mustang Sally" (1966), and "Funky Broadway" (1967).

Preston, Billy (b. Sept. 9, 1946, Houston, Tex.). Soul and gospel vocalist and organist. Although he received his greatest public attention through his work with the Beatles (notably on *Let It Be*, 1970) and the Rolling Stones, he had already developed a solid and committed audience through his tours with Sam COOKE, LITTLE RICHARD, and Andrae CROUCH. He had pop hits in 1973 with "Will It Go Round in Circles" and in 1974 with "Nothing from Nothing," and he was featured in the film *Sergeant Pepper's Lonely Hearts Club Band* (1978).

Rawls, Lou (b. Dec. 1, 1935, Chicago, Ill.). In 1966 Rawls achieved popular music success with "Love Is a Hurtin' Thing," a hit record on both the pop and rhythm-and-blues charts. He had his first gold album with *Lou Rawls Live.* In 1971 he won a Grammy Award for "A Natural Man." In the mid-1970's, he made disco-flavored, lushly orchestrated recordings such as "You'll Never Find Another Love Like Mine" and "Sit Down and Talk to Me."

AP/Wide World Photos

Redding, Otis. *See main text entry.*

Sledge, Percy (b. 1941, Leighton, Ala.). Sledge's 1966 recording of "When a Man Loves a Woman" was the first soul recording to reach the number-one position on the popular music charts. He never matched that success again, but other hits included "Warm and Tender Love," "It Tears Me Up," "Out of Left Field," "Any Day Now," and "Take Time to Know Her."

Starr, Edwin (Charles Hatcher; b. Jan. 21, 1942, Nashville, Tenn.). Starr made several hit vocal records in the late 1960's and 1970's, including "Stop Her on Sight" and "Headline News" in 1966, and "Twenty-five Miles" in 1969. He is best known for his antiwar song "War" (1970).

Taylor, Johnnie (b. May 5, 1938, Crawfordsville, Ark.). In 1957 Taylor replaced Sam Cooke in the Soul Stirrers, recording extensively with that group as it rose to the status of the nation's best-selling gospel group. As a solo artist, he released his 1968 smash single "Who's Making Love," which reached number one on the rhythm-and-blues charts and number five in pop. In 1976 Taylor had a number-one hit with "Disco Lady," one of the first certified platinum singles.

Thomas, Carla (b. 1942, Memphis, Tenn.). Thomas was the most prominent female soul artist of the 1960's before the emergence of Aretha FRANKLIN. Her first record, "Cause I Love You," a 1960 duet with her father, Rufus Thomas, was the first Memphis soul hit and helped to establish Memphis's Stax Records as the dominant soul music record company. Her hits include "Gee Whiz" (1961), "B-A-B-Y" (1966), and "Tramp" (1967), a duet with Otis REDDING.

White, Barry (b. Sept. 12, 1944, Galveston, Tex.). Singer, songwriter, and record producer. In 1963 White wrote "The Harlem Shuffle," a rhythm-and-blues hit recorded by Bob and Earl that same year. White began a solo recording career in 1973, becoming known for his deep, husky voice and lush orchestral arrangements on such songs as his 1974 hit "Can't Get Enough of Your Love, Baby." "Love's Theme" (1973), written for the Love Unlimited Orchestra, reached the top position on the pop music charts. White was also a pioneering disco record producer and songwriter.

White, Maurice (b. Dec. 19, 1941, Memphis, Tenn.). Singer, percussionist, songwriter. In 1969 White formed the first edition of Earth, Wind, and Fire with the aid of his brother Verdine on bass, vocals, and percussion. *Last Days and Time* (1972) was the band's first charted release. Its first certified gold record, 1973's *Head to the Sky*, was followed by another gold in 1974, *Open Our Eyes.* In 1975 the group released the sound track to *That's the Way of the World* and became a unique and memorable live act with a flair for space-age lighting and effects.

Womack, Bobby (b. Mar. 4, 1944, Cleveland, Ohio). Singer, guitarist, and songwriter. While still a teen, Womack began singing with the Soul Stirrers. In 1964 he embarked upon a solo career; he moved to Memphis and became a much-heralded songwriter and session musician. Never a major commercial success on his own—1974's "Lookin' for a Love" was his highest-charting single—he maintained a loyal fan base. In 1984 he released *The Poet II* and in 1985, *Someday We'll All Be Free.*

AP/Wide World Photos

Notable Soul and Funk Groups

Atlantic Starr (Clifford Archer, Sharon Bryant, Porter Carroll, Jr., Joseph Phillips, David Lewis, Jonathan Lewis, Wayne Lewis, Damon Rente, and William Sudderth; later, Barbara Weathers). Atlantic Starr's self-titled debut album was released in

1978. The group had a string of hit singles on the RHYTHM-AND-BLUES chart, including "When Love Calls" (1981), "Circles" (1982), and "Touch a Four Leaf Clover" (1983). Barbara Weathers joined the group, and *All in the Name of Love*, which went platinum in 1988, generated the hit single "Roses Are Red."

Bar-Kays (James Alexander, Ben Cauley, Jimmy King, Ron Caldwell, Phalin Jones, and Carl Cunningham; later, Larry Dodson, Harvey Henderson, Winston Stewart, Charles Allen, Vernon Burch, and Donnelle Hagan). Vocal and instrumental group. Officially formed in MEMPHIS in 1966, the Bar-Kays had come together at the Stax/Volt recording studio in the early 1960's. They worked closely with Otis REDDING and were accompanying Redding on tour in 1967 when their plane crashed. Alexander was not on the plane, and only Cauley survived the crash. Cauley reorganized the group with Alexander in 1968. The band achieved prominence partly because of its work with Isaac Hayes, producing such hit albums as *Hot Buttered Soul*, *Isaac Hayes Movement*, and *To Be Continued*. Its biggest hit single was the theme from *Shaft* (1971), recorded with Hayes.

Booker T. and the Mgs. Musical group that helped create the "Memphis sound" in soul music. The group was the rhythm section of the house band at Stax Records and played on most of the soul recordings from that Memphis studio in the 1960's. Members included Booker T. Jones, keyboards; Donald "Duck" Dunn, bass; and Steve Cropper, guitar. The group turned out instrumental hits of its own, including "Green Onions" (1962) and "Hip Hug-Her" (1967). The group split up in the early 1970's. Jones later recorded under his own name.

Chi-Lites (Marshall Thompson, Robert Lester, and Creadel Jones; later, Eugene Record). Vocal group. The Chi-Lites' falsetto voices and close harmonies added a new dimension to the RHYTHM AND BLUES of the early 1970's. Between 1969 and 1974, the Chi-Lites had eleven songs that hit the top twenty on the rhythm-and-blues charts. "Have You Seen Her" (1971) was a number-one soul and number-three pop hit. In 1972 "Oh Girl" was number one on the soul and pop charts.

Commodores. Pop and FUNK group. The Commodores emerged in 1974 as an immensely successful funk band. Their most successful albums, *Machine Gun* (1974), *Caught in the Act* (1975), and *Movin' On* (1975), present solid content in a funk package. Lead singer Lionel

Richie's "Three Times a Lady" (1978), a number-one hit for the Commodores, was nevertheless outside the straightforward funk formulas the Commodores had followed.

DeBarge (Eldra "El" James, Randy and Bunny DeBarge). Soul, rhythm-and-blues, and dance music act. A family group, DeBarge was conceived as a replacement for the Jackson 5 at MOTOWN Records. Its 1982 debut album, *All This Love*, went gold, and *In a Special Way* and *Rhythm of the Night* were also successful. The group peaked with the title-track single "Rhythm of the Night" (1985), the best example of its experiments with a Latin beat and sound. The group performed that song and others in the Motown film *The Last Dragon* (1985).

Dells. The Dells scored big with "Oh What a Night" in 1956, but an automobile accident forced the group to disband in 1958. In the 1960's it regrouped and recorded a number of best-selling records, including the 1968 hits "There Is," "Always Together," and "Stay in My Corner," its biggest hit. In the early 1970's, the Dells recorded the hits "Give Your Baby a Standing Ovation" and "The Love We Had Stays on

My Mind." Robert Townsend's 1991 film *The Five Heartbeats* was based on the Dells.

Dramatics (Ron Banks, J. Reynolds, Lenny Mayes, Willie Ford, and Larry Demps; later, Craig Jones). The group began performing in the early 1960's, when each of the members was approximately thirteen years old. It signed with Stax Records in 1969 and had a successful and critically acclaimed album in 1972, *Whatcha See Is Whatcha Get*. The group was instrumental in helping to define the direction of post-Motown African American popular music.

Earth, Wind, and Fire (Maurice and Verdine White, Philip Bailey, Larry Dunn, Johnny Graham, Al McKay, Ralph Johnson, and Andrew Woolfolk). Pop and funk music group. With its first seven albums selling between one-half million and three million copies each, the group spread its message of universal love and oneness with the universe throughout the 1970's and into the mid-1980's. Among its biggest hits were "Shining Star" (1975), "Sing a Song" (1975), and "After the Love Has Gone" (1979).

Warner Records

Emotions (Wanda, Sheila, and Jeanette Hutchinson, and Teresa Davis; later, Pamela Hutchinson). Music group composed of female backup singers from the popular group Earth, Wind, and Fire. The Emotions recorded two moderately successful albums, *Flowers* (1976) and *Rejoice* (1977), and the number-one 1977 hit "Best of My Love" in addition to several less popular records.

First Choice. Female vocal trio. The members of First Choice grew up in PHILADELPHIA and were influenced by Gamble and Huff's Philly sound. Their 1973 albums *Armed and Extremely Dangerous* and *Smarty Pants* were released on Philly Groove Records with title singles that were hits on the *Cash Box* chart. The group's highest chart single was 1974's "The Player," which peaked at number seven.

Junior Walker and the All-Stars (Vic Thomas, Willie Woods, James Graves, and Autry DeWalt Walker,

Jr.). In 1965 the group put four singles on the charts, including "Shotgun," which made it to number one on the soul charts. Similar success came the following year, with "How Sweet It Is (to be Loved by You)" and a cover of Bo Diddley's "(I'm a) Road Runner," in addition to the *Soul Session* and *Road Runner* albums. Other hit singles included "Pucker Up, Buttercup" (1967), "What Does It Take," and "These Eyes." In the 1970's pop hits included "Do You See My Love (for You Growing)," "Take Me Girl, I'm Ready," "Way Back Home," and "Holly Holy"; soul hits included "Walk in the Night" and "Gimme That Beat."

Kool and the Gang. The group was the brainchild of Robert "Kool" Bell, a fourteen-year-old bass player and jazz fan from Jersey City. After experiencing moderate chart success, the group finally managed to reach the top five in 1973 with "Funky Stuff" on the soul charts, followed by "Jungle Boogie" on both soul and pop charts. "Hollywood Swingin'" reached number one on the soul charts in 1974. Adapting to disco resulted in the platinum album *Ladies Night* (1979), with its top-ten singles "Ladies Night" and "Too Hot," and the 1980 smash release *Celebrate*, whose track "Celebration" not only achieved a rare platinum designation as a single but has become a staple for special events worldwide.

O'Jays (Eddie Levert, pictured; Walter Williams; William Powell, Bill Isles; and Bobby Massey). Vocal and dance group. The O'Jays charted three singles in 1963 and released their debut album, *Comin' Through*, in 1965. After the departures of Isles and Massey, the group had their first major hit, "Back Stabbers" (1972), which sold more than a million copies in the first year. The *Back Stabbers* album, which featured another hit single, "992 Arguments," met similar success, as did the 1973 *In Philadelphia*, which featured "Time to Get Down" and the number-one crossover single "Love Train."

AP/Wide World Photos

Parliament/Funkadelic. *See main text entry.*

(continued)

Raeletts. Originally called the Cookies, the vocal group was formed by singer, bandleader, and pianist Ray CHARLES. The Raeletts, whose roster changed frequently, also released five of their own singles and at least one album. Minnie RIPERTON was a member of the group from 1967 through 1969.

Rufus (Chaka Khan, Kevin Murphy, and Andre Fisher). Rufus released six gold and platinum albums before Khan left to pursue a solo career in 1978. The band took their name from Ask Rufus, the title of a column in *Mechanics Illustrated*, later shortening it to Rufus. Their debut album produced their first major crossover hit, "Tell Me Something Good," a gold record that also won a Grammy Award for best vocal performance in 1974. *Rags to Rufus* (1974) followed.

Sam and Dave (Sam Moore and Dave Prater). Vocal duo. One of the most successful soul acts of the 1960's, Sam and Dave's hits included their first single, "You Don't Know Like I Know" (1966), "Hold on, I'm Comin'" (1966), "When Something Is Wrong with My Baby" (1967), and "Soul Man" (1967).

Sister Sledge (Kathy, Joni, Kim, and Debbie Sledge). The group released its first single, "Time Will Tell," in 1971. The 1979 hit album *We Are Family* featured three smash singles, "He's the Greatest Dancer," "Lost in Music," and "We Are Family," which reached number one on the charts.

Sly and the Family Stone. *See main text entry.*

Spinners (Robert Smith; Pervis Jackson; Henry Fambrough, pictured; Billy Henderson; and George W. Dixon; later, Philippe Wynn(e), John Edwards, Edgar Edwards, and G. C. Cameron). Vocal group. The group's first hit single was "That's What Girls Are Made Of" (1961), and "I'll Always Love You" followed in 1965. Among the group's most popular record-

AP/Wide World Photos

ings are "I'll Be Around" (1972), "Could It Be I'm Falling in Love" (1972), "The Rubberband Man" (1976). The Spinners teamed with Dionne Warwick in 1974 to record "Then Came You," a number-one single that marked the first appearance at the top of the charts for both Warwick and the Spinners.

Staple Singers (Roebuck "Pops" Staples, Mavis, Cleo, Yvonne, and Pervis Staples). Also known as the Staples, the group began as a family GOSPEL MUSIC act in the mid-1950's. In the early 1970's, the group switched from gospel to soul; they achieved success with million-selling hits such as "Respect Yourself" (1971), "I'll Take You There" (1972), "If You're Ready (Come Go with Me)" (1973), and "Let's Do It Again" (1974), the biggest hit of the group's career.

Stylistics (Russell Thompkins, Jr., Airrion Love, James Smith, Herbie Murrell, and James Dunn). Vocal group. The Stylistics were famous during the early 1970's for their smooth, harmonious love songs. They achieved national fame in 1971 with "You Are Everything." Among their million-selling records are "People Make the World Go Round" (1972), "Betcha By Golly, Wow" (1972), and "You Make Me Feel Brand New" (1974).

Sweet Honey in the Rock. Female vocal group. Formed in 1973 by Bernice Johnson Reagon, the group performed gospel and other black music unaccompanied. Its songs protested social evils and addressed humanitarian issues. The group's concerts were signed for those with impaired hearing.

Sylvers. Vocal group. Part of the 1970's craze for family singing groups, the Sylvers were a nine-member collection of brothers and sisters. They released several albums containing some disco hits. By the early 1980's, the group had slimmed down to five members. The Sylvers released the lively album *Concept* in 1981.

Troop. Rhythm-and-blues vocal group. The group signed a recording contract with Atlantic records, which released the debut album *Troop* as well as *Attitude* (1989) and *Deepa* (1992). Troop performed with QUEEN LATIFAH and Levert on the "For the Money/Living for the City" single on the sound track for *New Jack City* (1991).

War (Thomas Sylvester "Papa Dee" Allen, Harold Ray Brown, Morris Dewayne "B.B." Dickerson, Lonnie Lee Jordan, Charles William Miller, and Howard E. Scott). Funk music group. War's 1973 album, *Deliver the World*, contained the hit single "The

Cisco Kid," which reached number two on the pop chart and number five on the rhythm-and-blues chart. The title cut from their album *Why Can't We Be Friends?* (1975) reached number six on the pop chart and number seven on the rhythm-and-blues chart. The follow-up single, "Low Rider," was even more successful, reaching number one on the pop chart. *Galaxy* (1977) produced a disco hit with the title single.

Whispers (Wallace ["Scotty"] and Walter Scott, Nicholas Caldwell, Gordy Harmon, and Marcus Hutson). Vocal group. The group's first successful release was the 1978 album *Headlights*. *Whisper in Your Ear* (1979) went platinum and featured several gold singles. Another 1979 release, *Happy Holidays to You*, was followed by *Imagination* (1980), *This Kind of Lovin'* (1981), and *Best of the Whispers* (1982). All produced hit singles. *Love Is Where You Find It* came out in late 1981 and went gold, producing two 1982 hit singles, "In the Raw" and "Emergency." *Love for Love* (1983) and *So Good* (1985) added to the group's list of hit albums. *Just Gets Better with Time* was released in 1987.

Historical Development

It is difficult to say exactly when rhythm and blues evolved into soul music. In the 1950's Sam Cooke, the lead singer for the Soul Stirrers, a gospel group, crossed over to become a successful pop singer, providing a role model for other gospel singers who wanted to seek popular success. At about the same time, rhythm-and-blues singers Ray Charles and James Brown were using gospel techniques in their music. Solomon Burke, a minister turned singer, also helped to create soul music.

By the early 1960's, singers, musicians, and producers at Stax Records in MEMPHIS, TENNESSEE, had developed a distinctive soul style, the "Memphis sound," which would be the most influential soul style of the decade. Recording artists associated with Stax included Rufus Thomas and his daughter Carla, Otis Redding, Sam and Dave, Eddie Floyd, Wilson Pickett, William Bell, and Booker T. and the MGs.

Fame Studios in Muscle Shoals, Alabama, also became a center for recording soul music. Artists who recorded at Muscle Shoals included Jimmy Hughes, Clarence Carter, Joe Tex, and Percy Sledge. Sledge's "When a Man Loves a Woman," released in 1966, was the first soul song to reach the number-one position on the pop charts and was largely responsible for bringing soul into the pop mainstream.

At the end of the 1960's, there emerged a soul artist whose popularity eclipsed that of the rest—Aretha Franklin. Franklin had begun her career in gospel and had tried to cross over to popular music, but had failed. Given a new recording contract with Atlantic Records (which distributed Stax nationally), she got

Singer Sam Cooke played a leading role in the development of the soul music sound during the late 1950's. *(AP/Wide World Photos)*

another chance. Jerry Wexler, a producer at Atlantic, encouraged her to sing and play piano in the style made popular by the Memphis sound. Beginning with her recording of "I Never Loved a Man (the Way I Love You)" in 1967, she produced a series of hit records that included a number-one pop single, "Respect" (written by Otis Redding), and that made her the most popular soul singer of all. Aretha Franklin—and soul music—achieved the height of public recognition in 1968, when Franklin was featured on the cover of *Time* magazine and was invited to sing a soul version of the national anthem at the Democratic National Convention.

Decline and Legacy

Record companies continued to produce soul music in the early 1970's (Al Green emerged from Memphis as a soul star in 1970), but the genre was clearly in decline. Perhaps the history of Stax Records, the most important pro-

The death of singer Otis Redding was a blow to soul music in general and to Stax Records in particular. *(Frank Driggs/Archive Photos)*

ducer of soul music, best illustrates the problems soul music encountered in the 1970's. Trouble for Stax began in 1967 when its most important star, Otis Redding, was killed in a plane crash. Redding had just achieved considerable recognition after his standout performance at the Monterey Pop Festival in the spring of 1967 and was poised to become a major crossover star; his song "Dock of the Bay," recorded shortly before his death, was a number-one hit in 1968.

The company never fully recovered from the blow of Redding's death. In 1968 Stax's record distribution deal with Atlantic ended, and a new distribution deal with Gulf and Western did not bring the profits that Stax's owners had anticipated. By the early 1970's, too, Stax's audience was declining; young whites had deserted soul music for rock. By 1976, beset with financial difficulties, Stax was forced to cease operations.

As soul, with its up-front emotional and sexual craving, was overtaken by other musical forms on the pop charts, its greatest male star, Al Green, abandoned it for gospel. Funk bands adopted a new rhythm, and disco dominated the dance floor. Rap germinated in the inner cities, addressing issues that disco could not and funk generally did not. Nevertheless, soul's appeal endured, particularly among middle-aged African Americans who still enjoyed melodic, song-oriented music rooted in the blues. Throughout the 1980's and 1990's, soul artists who did not adapt to new genres flocked to the small but distinguished Malaco record label.

Green returned to soul in the late 1990's. Gospel and soul music were always differentiated chiefly by the object of the singer's devotion. With Green no line was ever that clearly drawn, with sexual and religious ecstasy often seeming to share the same lyric. Green's success on the concert circuit and at festivals attested the simmering vitality of soul, as did the international following and critical acclaim of

Ted Hawkins, who before his death in 1995 gained his reputation as one of the great soulsters with a handful of recordings and, near the end of his life, a notorious stint singing for tips on the boardwalk in Venice, California.

Soul is also important for its place in the continuum of American popular music. As it represented an evolution of rhythm and blues and gospel, so it led the way for FUNK, disco, and RAP.

—*Donald M. Whaley*
—*Updated by Janet Long*

See also: Gospel music and spirituals; Minstrels.

Suggested Readings:

George, Nelson. *The Death of Rhythm and Blues.* New York: Pantheon Books, 1988.

Guralnick, Peter. *Sweet Soul Music: Rhythm and Blues and the Southern Dream of Freedom.* New York: Harper & Row, 1986.

Hirshey, Gerri. *Nowhere to Run: The Story of Soul Music.* New York: Da Capo Press, 1994.

Miller, Jim, ed. *The Rolling Stone Illustrated History of Rock and Roll.* Rev. ed. New York: Random House/Rolling Stone Press, 1980.

Pruter, Robert. *Chicago Soul.* Urbana: University of Illinois Press, 1991.

_____, ed. *The Blackwell Guide to Soul Recordings.* Cambridge, Mass.: Blackwell, 1993.

Shaw, Arnold. "Soul Is . . ." In *The Popular Arts in America,* edited by William M. Hammel. 2d ed. New York: Harcourt Brace Jovanovich, 1977.

Tee, Ralph. *Soul Music: Who's Who.* Rocklin, Calif.: Prima, 1992.

Whaley, Donald M. "'Memphis Soul Stew': Minstrelsy, Black Nationalism, and the Memphis Sound of Soul Music." In *Tennessee in American History,* edited by Larry H. Whiteaker and W. Calvin Dickinson. 2d ed. Needham Heights, Mass.: Ginn, 1991.

Whitall, Susan. *Women of Motown: An Oral History.* New York: Avon Books, 1998.

South African boycott: The arrival of black majority rule in South Africa in 1994 came about, to an extent, because of American-inspired worldwide political and economic sanctions. Pressures by people of the United States were extremely effective, particularly political pressure by the African American community. In the United States, a leader in the call for sanctions and boycotts was TRANSAFRICA, a nonprofit lobbying organization concerned with issues affecting people of African descent globally.

The participation of African Americans in the sanction movement illustrates the importance of ethnic politics as traditionally practiced in the United States. The arrival of African Americans on the international policy-making scene can be ascribed to a change in attitude and political rationale of the group. There was a change in attitude regarding the role of African Americans in foreign policy formulation. The idea that African Americans should have no interest in blacks outside the United States was challenged and changed drastically during the 1960's.

Internally, African Americans became aware that the black majority situation in South Africa should not be considered only a South African domestic matter. The radicalization of black politics during the 1960's changed the path of African American interest in foreign affairs. The problems of discrimination and state-sanctioned racism were elevated to an international platform, and the possibility that African Americans might influence international policy toward South Africa seemed more promising. This was not the first time that African Americans had fought against racism in an international context. After the founding of the United Nations in 1945, black politicians fought for the United Nations charter to include the protection of minority rights. Between the 1940's and the 1960's, African Americans clearly understood the connections between politics, race, and

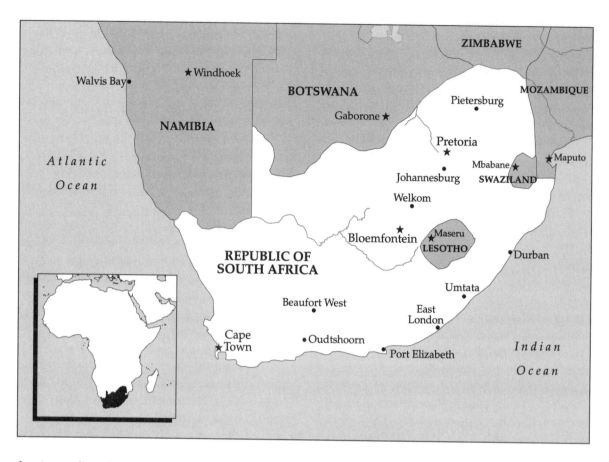

foreign policy. As a result, much of the burden of delivering South Africa fell on the African American population.

By the late 1980's, the United States had imposed trade and other economic sanctions against South Africa. State and local governments instituted laws prohibiting investment in South Africa. South Africa's ability to lure capital and other investment resources was extremely curtailed. By the early 1990's, the South African economy started showing signs of the effect of the worldwide sanctions for which the African American community had lobbied so successfully. Genuine political changes in South Africa brought about the relaxation and eventual elimination of many of the sanctions against South Africa. The ending of trade sanctions had African American businesses eyeing new trade and economic opportunities in Africa's most resource-rich country, South Africa.

Taking a Giant Step

The arrival of independence brought increased interest in South Africa once again. U.S. companies capitalized on business opportunities in Africa's most prosperous country. Some of the American companies that entered South Africa were owned by African Americans. Several African American business groups appeared in the country in the early 1990's. South Africa was particularly interested in the development of small businesses and black-owned companies. The government initiated rules directed at encouraging black-share ownership. African American businesses showed an interest in growth areas such as consumer products and service-related businesses. They envisioned relationships and dealings with black and white South Africans. Although most of the African American businesses interested in South Africa are small-entrepreneur companies, generally

African Americans can meet capital requirements.

Post-apartheid South Africa presented a business challenge for African American entrepreneurs. The end of sanctions brought a heightened awareness among African American businesspeople that there was a challenge and that something had to be done in terms of developing South Africa. Apart from the moral stake that African Americans had regarding South Africa, there was an added economic incentive. Building economic bridges that would connect producers and consumers, importers and exporters, goods and services between South Africans and African American businesses was a solid reason for African American involvement.

African American businesspeople realized that if black businesses in the United States were to expand, they had to discover new market opportunities, and South Africa appeared to the biggest and most profitable market in Africa. As a result, African American businesspeople concluded that postapartheid South Africa deserved special attention. Once again, TransAfrica worked with African American businesspeople to increase their presence in South Africa. The varied nature of America's top black-owned businesses demonstrated just how much African American entrepreneurs had to offer.

The end of apartheid and the onset of artistic liberty also brought African American performers to South Africa. In 1994 Whitney HOUSTON was one the first popular African American musicians to perform in and tour South Africa. As part of her commitment to a new South Africa, the musician announced a sizeable donation to various South African children's charities.

The ties between African American leaders and their South African counterparts fostered a surge in investment and cultural enrichment from the United States to South Africa. For some African Americans, doing business or performing in South Africa involved a sense of coming home.

—*Abdul Karim Bangura*

Suggested Readings:

"The Color of Money Is Starting to Change: Savvy South African Blacks Are Buying Pieces of White-Owned Companies." *Business Week* (March 14, 1994): 42.

"Justin F. Beckett: Taking a Giant Step into New Africa." *Minority Business Journal* 9, no. 1 (January/February, 1994).

Khan, Haider. *The Political Economy of Sanctions Against Apartheid*. Boulder: L. Rienner, 1989.

Sithole, Masipula. "Black Americans and United States Policy Toward Africa." *African Affairs* 85 (April, 1986): 175-180.

Skinner, Elliott P. "Afro-Americans and Africa: The Continuing Dialectic." *Minority Report*. New York: Urban Center, Columbia University, 1986.

"USA/South Africa: Why Reagan Sanctions Apartheid." *Africa* 175 (March, 1986): 52-53.

South Carolina: In 1997, according to estimates of the U.S. CENSUS, South Carolina had a population of just under 3.8 million. Just over 1.1 million of the state's residents, or 30 percent of the total, were African American. African Americans represented a higher percentage of the population in only two states, MISSISSIPPI and LOUISIANA. South Carolina has always had a large black population. By 1860, the year before the CIVIL WAR began, about 60 percent of the state's residents were of African descent. South Carolina was one of the original thirteen states, ratifying the U.S. Constitution in 1788.

The slave trade began to thrive in South Carolina with the rice boom of the early 1700's. As far as white farm and plantation owners were concerned, Africans seemed well suited to working the rice paddies along the low-country and coastal regions. Unlike whites and Native Americans, Africans adapted readily to the semitropical climate and were relatively immune to the diseases that plagued the area. Many were also skilled botanists and yeomen of cattle, facts which made them invaluable to the white landowners.

From the outset, however, the young black male population did not easily submit to bondage. Many ran away; others feigned ignorance or instigated work stoppages. Plantation owners had to quell many slave insurrections. One of the earliest and perhaps most notorious of these happened in 1739, 20 miles west of Charleston at Sono. Blacks led by CATO secured arms and ammunition and headed for FLORIDA, killing anyone who tried to stop them. At least twenty-five whites and thirty blacks were killed. Twelve blacks escaped.

Another slave conspiracy was led by Denmark VESEY in Charleston in 1822. Vesey, a former slave who had been free since 1800, had plotted the uprising for several years. He conspired with several whites and more than five thousand blacks to carry out an insurrection in July, 1822, but their plans were thwarted when a spy infiltrated their ranks. Thirty-seven blacks were executed, and forty-three were deported. The aftermath resulted in vigorously enforced SLAVE CODES that restricted blacks' movements in South Carolina even more than before.

Hostilities in the Civil War broke out in 1861 when South Carolina troops attacked Fort Sumter, near Charleston. During the war, in 1862, Robert SMALLS, an African American sea pilot, sailed a Confederate steamer out of Charleston's harbor; he turned it over to the Union as spoils of war. Smalls was later elected for five terms to serve in the U.S. House of Representatives during the RECONSTRUCTION era.

In 1868, three years after the Civil War ended, the new South Carolina legislature met in the state capital, Columbia. More than half the lawmakers were black. This was the only state legislature in American history to have a black majority. There were also two black lieutenant governors of the state during Reconstruction, Alonzo J. RANSIER in 1870 and Richard H. Gleaves in 1872. Moreover, two African Americans, Samuel J. Lee and Robert B. ELLIOTT, were speakers of the House between 1872 and 1874. One of the most accomplished officeholders was Francis CARDOZO, who served as secretary of state from 1868 to 1872 and as state treasurer from 1872 to 1876.

Soon after 1876, blacks began to lose their stronghold in government, partly because of pressures from white supremacist organizations such as the KU KLUX KLAN. Several legislators were murdered, and most blacks were afraid to vote. JIM CROW LAWS were passed that required blacks to pay poll taxes or to take literacy tests in order to vote.

Contemporary engraving of black Union soldiers fighting in South Carolina during the Civil War. (Associated Publishers, Inc.)

By the early 1940's, fewer than 1 percent of blacks in South Carolina were registered to vote.

In the GREAT MIGRATION of the early twentieth century, almost 275,000 blacks left South Carolina, hoping for a better life in the North. The state saw another exodus between 1940 and 1960, when about 333,000 left. In the last part of the twentieth century, however, the population remained much more stable.

Blacks began to make social and legal progress in the 1940's and 1950's. In 1940 the NATIONAL ASSOCIATION FOR THE ADVANCEMENT OF COLORED PEOPLE (NAACP) successfully brought court cases to equalize black and white teachers' salaries and to fight school segregation in the state. The school-segregation case BRIGGS V. ELLIOTT, in litigation in the state beginning in 1951, was heard by the U.S. SUPREME COURT when the Court combined it with the landmark case BROWN V. BOARD OF EDUCATION (1954). The actual integration of South Carolina's schools took many years, but most of the school systems in the state were integrated by 1970.

By the early 1960's, 37 percent of blacks in South Carolina were registered voters. In 1966 African American candidate Ernest Hollings won a state senate seat, and by 1970 three African Americans had been elected at the county level. In 1992 James CLYBURN was elected to the U.S. Congress.

Through the hardships blacks suffered in South Carolina, they managed to carry on a rich tradition of culture and history. Some African Americans living in the low country still practice many of the same traditions as their forefathers who were forced from their African homelands many years ago. The people on the SEA ISLANDS off South Carolina speak a language called GULLAH, which is a language of African, English, and Spanish combined. It is a secret language developed by the slaves to be able to communicate with one another in a language that the white landowners could not understand. Many sea islanders became skilled artisans in basketweaving and working with precious and semiprecious metals and stones.

—L. Norrine Simpson

1997 Population: 3,760,000
African American Population: 1,130,000
African American Percentage of Total: 30.05

South Dakota: In 1889 South Dakota became the fortieth state to enter the union. According to 1997 estimates of the CENSUS OF THE UNITED STATES, the state's population of about 738,000 ranked it the forty-fifth most populous state. The state's approximately 5,000 African Americans represented 0.7 percent of the total.

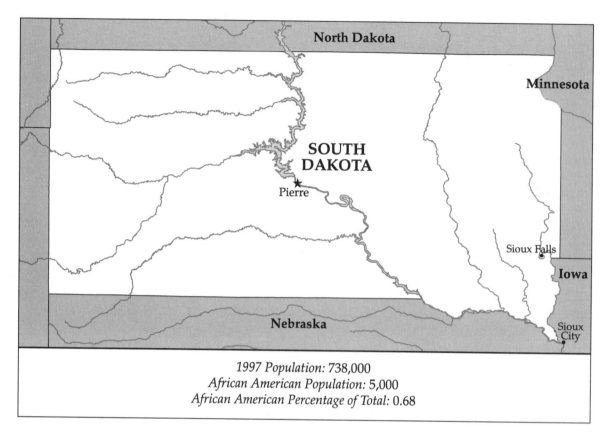

North Dakota

Minnesota

SOUTH
DAKOTA

★
Pierre

Sioux Falls

Iowa

Nebraska

Sioux
City

1997 Population: 738,000
African American Population: 5,000
African American Percentage of Total: 0.68

In 1854 the KANSAS-NEBRASKA ACT provided that issues of SLAVERY in newly organized U.S. territories were to be decided by the vote of territorial settlers rather than by the U.S. Congress. Unlike NEBRASKA to the south, the region then known as the Dakotas was not geographically close enough to any slave state to become involved in the pre-Civil War conflicts over slavery.

The Northern and Southern Dakotas officially became the Dakota Territory in 1861. The Ninth Regiment Cavalry, U.S. Colored Troops, served in the Dakota Territory after the end of the CIVIL WAR in 1865, with the primary mission of preventing raids by Plains Indian nations and keeping the Indians confined to reservations. Isaiah Dorman served as a scout for George Armstrong Custer at the 1876 Battle of the Little Bighorn, where he died in battle. Dorman was not scalped, because the Sioux considered him one of their people.

In 1867 the Dakota Territory granted suffrage to black men. The 1870 U.S. Census reported ninety-four African Americans living in South Dakota. The 1879 exodus of blacks from the South did not bring many African Americans to South Dakota, and neither did the GREAT MIGRATION of the early twentieth century. As an agricultural region, South Dakota did not offer many opportunities for southern blacks seeking employment.

One of the most well-known African Americans associated with South Dakota in the early twentieth century was Oscar MICHEAUX. He migrated from Chicago to South Dakota in 1904 to homestead, and he obtained a claim for 500 acres of land on the Sioux Rosebud Indian Reservation. Micheaux farmed, wrote books, and founded a film company with his brother. For the Micheaux Film and Book Company, he directed more than thirty low-budget "race films"—films featuring black performers and made for African American audiences—between 1919 and the late 1940's.

—*Ione Y. DeOllos*

See also: Buffalo soldiers; Frontier marshals and sheriffs; Frontier wars; Ninth Cavalry and Tenth Cavalry; Frontier Society.

Southern Christian Leadership Conference: Organization formed in 1957 to assist in directing the growing CIVIL RIGHTS MOVEMENT. After a year-long struggle for civil rights and desegregation of the buses in MONTGOMERY, ALABAMA, Martin Luther KING, Jr., and more than sixty other ministers met on January 9, 1957, in Atlanta, Georgia, to form an organization able to assist in coordinating a movement intended to blanket the South. From its inception until King's death in 1968, the Southern Christian Leadership Conference (SCLC) was one of the most effective civil rights groups.

Initially, the SCLC consisted of local affiliates, each of which sent five voting delegates to SCLC conventions. The delegates returned to their local churches or other groups to coordinate local civil rights activities. The SCLC intended to be an organizing body for groups, rather than an activist group with individuals as members. The goal of the SCLC was to stimulate nonviolent, direct mass action to remove segregationist and discriminatory laws existing throughout the South.

The SCLC's VOTER EDUCATION PROJECT trained volunteers to launch voter registration campaigns in their hometowns. Its ef-forts were important both before and after the VOTING RIGHTS ACT OF 1965 was passed.

Several national leaders in the Civil Rights movement were members of the Southern Christian Leadership Conference, including Andrew YOUNG, Fred L. SHUTTLESWORTH, Ralph ABERNATHY, Jesse JACKSON, and Hosea WILLIAMS. Abernathy succeeded King as leader of the SCLC and attempted to carry out the programs initiated under King, such as the POOR PEOPLE'S CAMPAIGN in Washington, D.C. Abernathy's efforts met with little success, however, and the SCLC's importance declined. Joseph LOWERY, president of the SCLC beginning in 1977, concentrated civil rights activities on issues surrounding the African American family and voter registration in the South. One of the SCLC's major projects in the decades following King's death was OPERATION BREADBASKET, a program designed to improve economic opportunities for African Americans.

Although the group did not regain the importance it had held in the 1960's, it remained

The last SCLC campaign planned by Martin Luther King, Jr., the Poor People's Campaign attracted many fewer people to Washington than he had hoped for and was generally considered a failure. *(AP/Wide World Photos)*

active, sponsoring protests and calling for boycotts of companies in attempts to get them to open opportunities to blacks. In the 1990's the SCLC was a multiracial organization with support from people of many denominations. It maintained headquarters in ATLANTA, GEORGIA, and its affiliates were active in seventeen southern states and the District of Columbia. The SCLC's structure was still one of membership consisting of groups, with individuals holding membership in local affiliates rather than in the main body. Affiliated organizations included churches, civic bodies, and fraternal orders. Lowery remained president until 1998, when Martin Luther King III was sworn in as president. The transition marked the passing of leadership to a new generation.

Southern Poverty Law Center: CIVIL RIGHTS organization established in MONTGOMERY, ALABAMA, in 1971. The organization gained a reputation as a leader in bringing lawsuits against and monitoring hate groups.

The Southern Poverty Law Center (SPLC) was founded by Morris Dees and Joe Levin as a small civil rights law firm. After winning several high-profile landmark lawsuits against prominent hate groups, the center emerged as an internationally recognized leader in monitoring hate groups and in fighting against discrimination in court.

The center was established as a nonprofit organization, financed through donations from thousands of individuals. The SPLC located its headquarters in MONTGOMERY, ALABAMA, arguably the birthplace of the Civil Rights movement. Its mission was stated as combating "hate, intolerance, and discrimination through education and litigation." Since its founding, the SPLC has represented African Americans and other victims of hate. Undertaking controversial and newsworthy cases, the SPLC has shut down several racist organizations, argued cases before the U.S. Su-

PREME COURT, and helped numerous victims of hate crimes.

The center's Teaching Tolerance project was initiated in 1991 to provide resources for teachers, including curriculum aides such as teaching kits, posters, and videos promoting respect for diversity. The SPLC began to offer research fellowships to educators and to publish a biannual educational magazine.

The center's Intelligence Project incorporated the organization's Klanwatch and Militia Task Force programs. Klanwatch was created in 1981 to monitor the activities of neo-Nazi and racist groups. The Militia Task Force was developed in 1994, in response to public concern over militias, to track extremist anti-government and "patriot" groups. The Intelligence Project sought to provide information to the public, the media, and law enforcement agencies on hate groups through its quarterly publication, the *Intelligence Report*. The SPLC also became a sponsor of the Civil Rights Memorial, dedicated to those who lost their lives during the Civil Rights movement.

—*Robert P. Watson*

Southern Tenant Farmers' Union: Interracial protest movement of agricultural workers and tenant farmers in the southern United States. Founded in July, 1934, in the ARKANSAS delta, the STFU represented economically displaced southern blacks and poor whites in the GREAT DEPRESSION-era South.

The STFU was initially organized to protest the price stabilization policies of the Agricultural Adjustment Administration (AAA), one of the U.S. government's New Deal programs. The AAA provided economic incentives for landowners to scale back farming, which often prevented tenants from growing and harvesting crops. In the mid-1930's, movement leaders organized several high-profile strikes by cotton choppers and pickers, which were met with hostility and violence by white southerners. White violence and intimidation along with friction between black members and the organization's white leadership weakened the STFU in the late 1930's and early 1940's. The movement continued under various names and with limited effectiveness until 1960.

The STFU represents an early example of interracial cooperation in the twentieth-century South. From its inception, the organization attempted to unite black and white tenants and laborers in protest against inequities in the southern agricultural economy. The organization had between twenty-five thousand and thirty-five thousand members at its height, and about half its membership was African American. A broad-based movement that addressed various economic and CIVIL RIGHTS issues, the STFU was largely ineffective in altering public policy. Yet the publicity that surrounded it called attention to the abuses of SHARECROPPING as well as the POVERTY, illiteracy, and ill health common among sharecropping families. The hostility and violence that the movement provoked in the South highlighted the vulnerability and desperation of southern blacks and poor whites.

—*Michael H. Burchett*

Home of an Oklahoma tenant farmer whose out-of-state landlady had no interest in maintaining her property during the late 1930's. *(Library of Congress)*

Sowell, Thomas (b. June 30, 1930, Gastonia, North Carolina): Economist, author, and educator. Sowell received his Ph.D. from the University of Chicago in 1968. He served as an economist at the U.S. Department of Labor and taught at Rutgers, Howard, Cornell, Brandeis, and Louisiana. Sowell is the author of *Civil Rights: Rhetoric or Reality?* (1984), *Edu-* *cation: Assumptions Versus History, Collected Papers* (1986), and *Compassion Versus Guilt, and Other Essays* (1987), among other books. Much of his work focuses on the economics of discrimination. Sowell published *The Vision of the Anointed* in 1995 and *Migrations and Cultures: A World View* in 1996.

Spanish-American War: In the nineteenth century, Spain faced more than one revolution in its colony of CUBA, but on each occasion, the mother country's military crushed the rebellions. In 1895 revolt flared anew, as Cuban leaders once again demanded independence.

By 1898, as a result of economic, strategic, and humanitarian concerns, U.S. public opinion favored the rebel cause, and President William McKinley was pressed to intervene on behalf of the Cubans. The president resisted until February 15, when the USS *Maine* blew up while docked in Havana harbor (the ship was there to provide safe transportation for Americans in Cuba who wanted to leave). Although the cause for the sinking of the *Maine* remains widely disputed, the American public and its leaders blamed the Spaniards. More than 250 American sailors, at least twenty-two of them African Americans, died as the ship went down. When Spain was slow to respond to McKinley's ultimatum that Cuba should be freed, the United States went to war.

Black Units in the War

Americans fought on two fronts, invading both Cuba and the Philippines. African American servicemen became immediately involved in the conflict when the War

Black troops preparing to be sent into action during the Spanish-American War. *(National Archives)*

Department transferred the four regular regiments of the famed BUFFALO SOLDIERS from frontier duty in the American West and sent them to Cuba. The buffalo soldiers left their frontier posts and streaked toward the East for their embarkation points. Several soldiers remembered that through all towns along their railroad route, crowds, black and white, lined the tracks and cheered.

In addition to the regulars—the NINTH Cavalry and Tenth Cavalry and the Twenty-fourth Infantry and Twenty-fifth Infantry—four more black regiments recruited by the government joined the fray. At the state level, other African American volunteer units were organized, including such forces as the Ninth Ohio Infantry, the Eighth Illinois Infantry, the Third Alabama Infantry, the Third North Carolina Infantry, and units from Virginia, Kansas, and Massachusetts, among others.

Wartime Segregation

The African Americans fought in segregated units and usually received shoddy, used equipment and material that whites had cast off. In the cavalry, that trend even extended to the horses given to black soldiers. Further, the

War Department refused to commission African American officers in staff and line positions. Whites commanded all the regular forces, while approximately one hundred blacks served as junior officers—second lieutenants—in the four new volunteer units. Even before experiencing the fighting in Cuba, African American soldiers faced shoddy treatment; they were segregated on the transports that took them to the front. White troops took the upper decks; blacks went into the hold (as in the slaving days), where they faced stale air and much heat and where they had to burn candles even in the daytime to see.

One black unit embarking from Tampa, Florida, was not allowed shore leave, although white units came and went as they pleased. For a week, the African Americans remained virtual prisoners on their vessel, except when a white officer took the men ashore and supervised them while they exercised and bathed. Once the ship pulled out of the harbor, the white commanding officer ordered that there be no mixing between the races; he drew an imaginary line through the ship and ordered blacks to stay to their side of the assigned space, despite the fact that the black soldiers were on good terms with the white units with whom they had served in the West.

Opportunities in Volunteer Units

More opportunity for blacks existed in the volunteer forces raised from state to state. For example, the Third North Carolina Infantry had an all-black officer roll; the Ninth Ohio Infantry had an African American, Major Charles Young (a graduate of West Point), as its commander; and the Massachusetts troops, among a few others, had some black officers. Some African Americans secured noncombat staff positions as paymasters, chaplains, physicians, and assistant physicians.

A few white officers volunteered to lead the black soldiers, the promise of fast promotion possibly luring them on. Another factor may have influenced junior men such as Lieutenant John J. Pershing (later General "Black" Jack Pershing, hero of World War I) to join the veteran buffalo units—they had a better chance of coming out of the war alive fighting with the black veterans than with untested units.

The men of the Ninth and Tenth Colored Cavalry units distinguished themselves at the Battle of Las Guásimas, near Santiago, where they enabled Theodore Roosevelt to rout the Spanish defenders. *(Library of Congress)*

Black Units in Action

Of all the African American units mustered, the buffalo soldiers saw the most action during the short war. The first significant fighting was at the Battle of Las Guásimas. On June 24, Theodore Roosevelt's Rough Riders (the First Volunteer Cavalry) were moving along the Santiago Road trying to reach Las Guásimas when two of Roosevelt's battalions met a strong, entrenched enemy force, the entrenchments including an improvised fort surrounded by barbed wire. When the Spaniards had pinned down the Rough Riders, experienced black cavalrymen from the Ninth and Tenth Cavalry came up, cut the barbed wire, and knocked down the improvised fort, all the while loudly singing "There'll be a hot time in the old town tonight." They thus allowed the Rough Riders to advance on the Spaniards, routing them. One white southern officer said that, if not for the action of the African Americans, the Rough Riders would have all perished. "I am not a Negro lover," he said, but he staunchly maintained that the black troopers deserved credit for the victory. Even white newspapers in the United States commented that the buffalo soldiers did not know the meaning of fear.

Six days later, at El Caney, the Rough Riders again found trouble, and this time the Twenty-fifth Infantry came to their rescue. In three days of bitter action, the African Americans again protected the Rough Riders, enough to earn praise from their white commanders. Even the Spanish had praise for their black enemies, whom they called the "smoked Yankees."

Later, at the Battle of San

Juan Hill, the black soldiers again came to the aid of Roosevelt's troops, who were taking massive fire from the Spaniards on the hilltop. The buffalo soldiers advanced, allowing the Rough Riders to follow behind in the attack; the enemy was swept away by the combined assault of Americans both black and white. Afterward, one of the whites said that the black troops were "all right" and that he would gladly share his canteen with any of them.

Service in the Pacific

Some of the volunteer units also served with distinction in Cuba, while the Third North Carolina Infantry served in the Pacific with Admiral George Dewey, whose fleet had steamed northwestward from Hawaii. Dewey found the pickings easy in the Pacific. When his fleet approached the Spanish island of Guam, the Spanish defenders had not learned that war had been declared, and when Dewey's guns first fired on defensive placements, the Spaniards thought that they were being honored with a salute—until the shells exploded around them. Approximately the same thing happened in Manila Bay. In the Philippines, moreover, the Americans met a folk hero, Emilio Aguinaldo, whose forces were already fighting a war of liberation against the Spaniards.

When the war ended with the Treaty of Paris in 1898 without a grant of Filipino independence, Aguinaldo continued his insurgency, this time attacking United States forces of occupation, which included the Third North Carolina. By mid-July of 1899, the Twenty-fourth and Twenty-fifth Infantry had arrived in Manila. Later in 1899, the War Department recruited two more all-black regiments—the Forty-eighth and Forty-ninth Infantry—to fight Aguinaldo. Not until 1902 did Aguinaldo's rebellion finally run its course; the revolt ended only after Aguinaldo was captured.

The Filipino defeat, however, pointed up a sad historical fact. Patriotic African Americans, trying to prove their worth to American society, had helped their country win an imperialistic war over "darker" peoples. It followed that white racism reached high tide, as white Americans embraced what Rudyard Kipling had called the "white man's burden." Indeed, only two years before the war, the U.S. SUPREME COURT had issued the *Plessy v. Ferguson* decision, which gave federal sanction to racial segregation. Moreover, between 1890 and 1910, the old Confederate states followed the "Mississippi Plan," which stripped most African Americans of their right to vote, a right not regained until the 1960's. Perhaps the "smoked Yankees" fought the wrong war at the wrong time.

—*James Smallwood*

Suggested Readings:

David, Jay, and Elaine Crane, eds. *The Black Soldier from the American Revolution to Vietnam*. New York: William Morrow, 1971.

Foner, Jack D. *Blacks and the Military in American History*. New York: Praeger, 1974.

Gatewood, Willard B., Jr. *Black Americans and the White Man's Burden, 1898-1903*. Urbana: University of Illinois Press, 1975.

_____. *"Smoked Yankees" and the Struggle for Empire*. Urbana: University of Illinois Press, 1971.

Lanning, Michael L. *The African American Soldier from Crispus Attucks to Colin Powell*. Secaucus, N.J.: Birch Lane Press, 1997.

Spaulding, Asa (b. July 22, 1902, Columbus County, North Carolina): Business executive Spaulding was president of North Carolina Mutual Life Insurance, the largest insurance company in the world owned by African Americans. He also ran a chain of advisory and consulting services for corporations in the United States. He was awarded several honorary doctorates, and some of his writings on insurance and history were published in the *Congressional Record*.

Spaulding, Charles C. (August 1, 1874, Clarkton, North Carolina—August 1, 1952, Durham, North Carolina): Business leader. Benjamin M. Spaulding was a successful farmer, artisan, and blacksmith who tended horses, made farm equipment, and manufactured furniture. He was also a county sheriff during the RECONSTRUCTION period after the Civil War. His son Charles was a confident and ambitious young man who entered the business world as a grocer in Durham, NORTH CAROLINA. Like many African American entrepreneurs of this era, Spaulding had been influenced by Booker T. WASHINGTON. Washington, the premier black spokesman, had gained a reputation for his conciliatory tone in race relations. Spaulding shared this outlook.

Charles Spaulding later joined the management team of the North Carolina Mutual Life Insurance Company. Spaulding was not a founder of the company, but he is recognized as building it from a tiny operation to a firm with millions of dollars in policies. The Mutual, created in 1898, was founded by former slaves who had educated themselves while working in occupations such as barbering. These entrepreneurs saved their money and used their white patrons as a resource when creating and running the organization. According to a contemporary of Spaulding, wealthy whites such as the Duke family of Durham provided financial support to the Mutual during its infancy.

John Merrick, one of its founders, called on Spaulding to manage the Mutual in 1900. Spaulding achieved immediate success, and the board of the company elevated him to the vice presidency in 1908. Spaulding was a pioneer in saturation advertising and made sure that local businesses had their share of matchbooks, calendars, and pens advertising his company. In 1923 the board promoted him again to lead the North Carolina Mutual Insurance Company. Under his direction, the or-

Insurance executive Charles C. Spaulding. *(Associated Publishers, Inc.)*

ganization became one of the most successful black-owned businesses in American history, with more than two hundred million dollars in assets in 1992 and $8.2 billion worth of policies in force.

See also: Black capitalism; Frontier marshals and sheriffs.

Spearman, Leonard (b. July 8, 1929, Tallahassee, Florida): Political appointee and educator. Leonard Hall O'Connell Spearman attended Florida A&M University and graduated with his bachelor of science degree in 1947. He headed north for graduate school and graduated with his M.A. degree from the University of Michigan in 1950. He completed his Ph.D. work at the university in 1960. While working on his master's degree, Spearman taught high school biology from 1949 to 1950. He joined the faculty of Florida A&M as an associate professor of psychology in 1950 and served in that post for ten years. He left in 1960 to accept a post as professor of psychology and dean at Southern University. During the next ten years, Spearman also taught as a visiting professor at Queens College of New York and was a Martin Luther King Scholar at Rutgers University.

Spearman's first political appointment came in 1970, when he was selected to serve as director of the division of student special services at the U.S. Office of Education. In 1972 he became director of the division of student assistance. He was promoted to associate commissioner for student assistance in 1975. In that year, he received the Superior Service Award for his work in the Office of Education. Spearman became associate deputy commissioner for higher and continuing education in 1978 and received the Distinguished Service Award for his work from the Department of Health, Education, and Welfare. In 1980 he was promoted to associate deputy secretary for higher and continuing education, but he left public service later in the year to return to academia. Spearman accepted an appointment to serve as president of Texas Southern University and became active in various community organizations in Houston.

Spelman College: Private BAPTIST liberal arts school in ATLANTA, GEORGIA. Established in 1881, Spelman College is the oldest HISTORICALLY BLACK COLLEGE in the United States for women. It maintained an enrollment of almost two thousand students in the late 1990's.

Located in an urban environment, Spelman College is a nonprofit, independent institution that offers programs leading to the bachelor's degree. Sophia B. Packard and Harriet E. Giles founded the college in 1881 with the primary goal of providing an education for African American women. Spelman College, ATLANTA UNIVERSITY, Morehouse College, Morris Brown College, and the Interdenominational Theological Center form the Atlanta University Center.

Of the nation's top one hundred colleges awarding degrees to minorities in the 1990's, Spelman ranked first in conferring English degrees and second in conferring both physical science and life science degrees. During that decade more than 35 percent of Spelman students majored in mathematics, the sciences, and engineering, and more than 45 percent engaged in some form of community service. Upon graduation, approximately 38 percent of Spelman women went on to graduate studies.

The Women's Research and Resource Center of Spelman places its main emphasis on curriculum development in women's studies, community service, and research. Another unique part of Spelman College is the Dow Jones-Spelman Col-

From 1987 through 1993 the campus of Spelman College was used for the fictional Hillman College of television's *A Different World* series. *(Jean Higgins/Unicorn Stock Photos)*

lege Entrepreneurial Center, which offers consultation and technical assistance to develop new and expanding businesses. In 1999 Spelman College was ranked first on the Day Star list of the top fifty colleges for African Americans.

—*Alvin K. Benson*

Spencer, James Wilson: Politician. Spencer worked as a special assistant to the MISSOURI state attorney general before being elected to serve in the Missouri House of Representatives from the state's Thirteenth District from 1967 to 1968. After leaving the state house, he worked as an assistant prosecuting attorney for Jackson County, Missouri, and later became a partner in the law firm of Sheskin, Adelman, Flemington, Wurdack, and Spencer in Kansas City, Missouri.

Spingarn Medal: Award given annually by the NATIONAL ASSOCIATION FOR THE ADVANCEMENT OF COLORED PEOPLE (NAACP) to an African American for an outstanding achievement. Started in 1914 by Joel E. Spingarn, then the chairman of the board of directors of the NAACP and later president of the organization (1930-1939), the award acknowledges the "highest or noblest achievement by an American Negro."

Spingarn donated a gold medal each year until his death in 1939; thereafter the award was provided from the resources of a fund that Spingarn bequeathed in his will. The purposes of the award are both to honor the accomplishments of the recipient and to serve as a incentive to young African Americans.

The medal is awarded by a nine-member committee selected by the NAACP board of directors. Any American citizen can nominate a person for the medal. The committee is free to choose a person from any field of endeavor when making its selection; however, the nominee must be of African ancestry and an American citizen. Although the medal is intended to recognize a notable achievement from the previous year, the committee may choose to award it for a commendable achievement in prior years. The award is traditionally presented to the recipient at the annual NAACP convention.

Recipients of the Spingarn Medal have come from various disciplines, such as the arts, athletics, commerce, education, law, literature, politics, science, and the military. The first medal was awarded in 1915 to Ernest E. JUST, head of the physiology department at the HOWARD UNIVERSITY MEDICAL SCHOOL. He was acknowledged for his research in biology. In 1922 Mary B. Talbert became the first woman awarded a Spingarn Medal. Her distinguished achievement was her work as president of the National Association of Colored Women.

Other notable winners of the award have included a founding member of the NAACP, W. E. B. DU BOIS, botanist George Washington CARVER, singer Marian ANDERSON, author Richard WRIGHT, U.S. SUPREME COURT Justice

Spingarn Medal awarded to singer Roland Hayes. *(Library of Congress)*

Spingarn Medal Recipients

1915 Ernest E. JUST	1944 Charles DREW	1974 Damon Keith
1916 Charles Young	1945 Paul ROBESON	1975 Hank AARON
1917 Harry T. Burleigh	1946 Thurgood MARSHALL	1976 Alvin AILEY
1918 William Stanley BRAITHWAITE	1947 Percy JULIAN	1977 Alex HALEY
1919 Archibald H. Grimké	1948 Channing H. Tobias	1978 Andrew YOUNG
1920 W. E. B. Du BOIS	1949 Ralph J. BUNCHE	1979 Rosa L. PARKS
1921 Charles S. Gilpin	1950 Charles Hamilton HOUSTON	1980 Rayford W. LOGAN
1922 Mary B. Talbert	1951 Mabel Keaton Staupers	1981 Coleman YOUNG
1923 George Washington CARVER	1952 Harry T. Moore	1982 Benjamin E. MAYS
1924 Roland HAYES	1953 Paul R. Williams	1983 Lena HORNE
1925 James Weldon JOHNSON	1954 Theodore K. LAWLESS	1984 Tom BRADLEY
1926 Carter G. WOODSON	1955 Carl Murphy	1985 Bill COSBY
1927 Anthony Overton	1956 Jackie ROBINSON	1986 Benjamin L. HOOKS
1928 Charles Waddell CHESNUTT	1957 Martin Luther KING., Jr.	1987 Percy Ellis SUTTON
1929 Mordecai Wyatt JOHNSON	1958 Daisy BATES and the Little Rock Nine	1988 Frederick Douglass Patterson
1930 Henry A. Hunt	1959 Duke ELLINGTON	1989 Jesse JACKSON
1931 Richard B. HARRISON	1960 Langston HUGHES	1990 L. Douglas WILDER
1932 Robert MOTON	1961 Kenneth B. CLARK	1991 Colin T. POWELL
1933 Max Yergan	1962 Robert C. WEAVER	1992 Barbara JORDAN
1934 William T. B. Williams	1963 Medgar EVERS	1993 Dorothy Irene HEIGHT
1935 Mary McLeod BETHUNE	1964 Roy WILKINS	1994 Maya ANGELOU
1936 John HOPE	1965 Leontyne PRICE	1995 John Hope FRANKLIN
1937 Walter Francis WHITE	1966 John H. JOHNSON	1996 A. Leon HIGGINBOTHAM, Jr.
1938 *No award*	1967 Edward W. BROOKE	1997 Carl ROWAN
1939 Marian ANDERSON	1968 Sammy DAVIS, Jr.	1998 Myrlie EVERS-WILLIAMS
1940 Louis Tompkins WRIGHT	1969 Clarence M. MITCHELL, Jr.	1999 Earl G. GRAVES, Sr.
1941 Richard WRIGHT	1970 Jacob LAWRENCE	
1942 A. Philip RANDOLPH	1971 Leon Howard SULLIVAN	Names in SMALL CAPS are
1943 William Henry HASTIE	1972 Gordon PARKS, Sr.	subjects of encyclopedia essays.
	1973 Wilson C. RILES	

Thurgood MARSHALL, baseball player Jackie ROBINSON, civil rights activist Martin Luther KING, Jr., musician Duke ELLINGTON, poet Langston HUGHES, opera singer Leontyne PRICE, entertainers Lena HORNE and Bill COSBY, politician L. Douglas WILDER, military hero Colin L. POWELL, and author Maya ANGELOU.

The medal was not awarded in 1938 because the person named as the recipient, William A. Hinton (a bacteriologist at Harvard University) declined it. He did not want his work to be recognized on the basis of his race.

Since its inception, 1938 was the only year the Spingarn Medal was not awarded.

—*Andrea E. Miller*

Spiritual Israel Church and Its Army: Church founded by Derks Field and W. D. Dickson sometime between the mid-1920's and the late 1930's. The association was headquartered in DETROIT, MICHIGAN, in the 1990's and had about thirty congregations and several missions in the Midwest, Southeast, and NEW YORK CITY. Spiritual Israelites refer to the head of their association as the King of All Israel. The group blends elements from the African American spiritual movement and black Judaism.

See also: Jewish Americans and African Americans.

Sports: Among early African tribes, athletic feats were used during manhood rituals and were part of special celebrations held during the year, particularly at harvest time. Team competition in wrestling was commonplace, and wrestlers generally were accorded great honors within their villages.

Athletics also was an important aspect of the American slave's life. Slaves were not permitted much recreational time, although some slaves were allowed Saturday afternoon to do their personal chores, and Sunday was considered a day of rest by even the harshest masters. In addition, most slaves were given brief holidays from toil after harvest time and during the Christmas holidays; slaves owned by devout masters also enjoyed other religious holidays.

Slaves often engaged in physical contests with other slaves. During the festival seasons such as harvest and Christmas, athletic competitions, including races and wrestling matches, were organized. On occasion, white masters would amuse themselves by arranging to have their slaves fight one another. These matches, which seldom were fought with rules or referees, sometimes ended in death.

Slaves continued to fight at their masters' bidding until the Civil War ended the institution of slavery. Since that time, African American men and women have attempted to prove their worth in all areas of American life, including the battlefield and the sports arena, sometimes under the most dire circumstances.

Boxing

The first competitive sport in which African Americans were able to achieve success was

BOXING. It was the custom in the old South for wealthy plantation owners to send their sons to England to be educated; at the time, boxing was considered a gentleman's sport in England. As a result, many of these young southerners learned boxing skills, mainly for use in self-defense. When those young men returned to their homes in the South, however, it was often almost impossible for them to find sparring partners.

Many young masters thus began to train their personal male slaves in the art of boxing. Slave boxers soon became so proficient at the sport that competitions were held between the champions of various plantations. Victorious African American boxers earned considerable money for their masters, who often wagered large sums of money on these matches, and earned special privileges for themselves. A number of slaves were even able to gain their freedom in this way, and some earned a living by boxing as freedmen in the North and in England.

The first known African American boxing champion was Joe Lashley, who had recorded fights in 1792 and 1796. Of his match against Tom Treadway on June 13, 1796, it was written that Lashley "showed great agility, excellent bottom and a thorough knowledge of the art not to be exceeded by the most skillful among boxers." Bill Richmond became the first celebrated African American boxer. Brought to the attention of a British military commander in 1777, Richmond was taken back to England, where he became a hero to the English working classes. Richmond fought—and won—his last fight in 1818, at the age of fifty-six.

Richmond's achievements inspired another African American, Tom Molyneux. Said to have been the son or grandson of famous boxing slaves from VIRGINIA, Molyneux was born in 1784 in SOUTH CAROLINA. He earned his freedom and eventually made his way to England, where he gained such fame that many black boxers used his name to give themselves credibility. One such fighter was Jim Wharton, who made a great amount of money fighting as "Molyneux."

George Godfrey was the first heavyweight champion among African Americans. Godfrey was scheduled to fight John L. Sullivan, the white heavyweight champion of the 1880's, but Sullivan refused to box against Godfrey, or Charles Hadley, or any other good boxer of African heritage. Significantly, the first black boxing champion in any division recognized by the United States was a Canadian, George Dixon.

In 1908 Jack JOHNSON became the first African American to win the world heavyweight boxing championship when he knocked out Tommy Burns in the fourteenth round of a bout held in Sydney, Australia. The boxing world tried to find a "great white hope" to top-

ple Johnson, but Johnson proceeded to defeat a succession of white challengers. Johnson flouted the racial mores of his times, and he was hated by many whites, particularly for his involvement with white women. In 1912 Johnson was convicted on largely trumped-up charges of violating the Mann Act, and he fled to Europe, where he spent the next few years putting on exhibitions and fighting a few matches. On April 5, 1915, in Cuba, Johnson lost to white fighter Jess Willard; some observers believed that Johnson threw the fight.

After the breaking of boxing's color line, African American men achieved success in all weight divisions. Scores of black boxers have won championships, and many, such as Henry Armstrong, Joe LOUIS, Sugar Ray ROBINSON, Muhammad ALI, Joe Frazier, George FOREMAN, Larry Holmes, and Mike TYSON,

Boxer Joe Louis (right) dominated the heavyweight division from the late 1930's through the 1940's. *(AP/Wide World Photos)*

rank among the sport's all-time greats. African American boxers have been especially dominant in the heaviest weight divisions. From around 1960 to the year 2000, they held almost every world heavyweight and light heavyweight title.

Baseball

A peculiarly American adaptation of primitive stick-and-ball games, baseball evolved into its modern form during the nineteenth century. During the Civil War, baseball spread throughout the North and the South and was encouraged by the military leaders of both the Union and Confederate armies as an excellent recreational outlet for soldiers and prisoners alike. It was also during the North-South conflict that baseball became widely played by African American slaves and freedmen.

After the Civil War, African American men continued to play baseball, and many became expert at the sport. In the northern states, there was a higher level of organization, because African American athletes were not hindered by the hostility generated by Reconstruction or the intrusion of the black codes. In the North, as a result, African American baseball players formed their own leagues and played "colored" championship series that determined the best teams. As far back as 1867, some of these teams were playing all-white teams in exhibition games. In the South, however, African American players were forced to mask their serious interest and skill in the game by performing minstrel shows on the baseball diamond.

The racial chaos following the Civil War took its toll in a number of ways. In baseball, race was injected into the charter of the National Association of Baseball Players. When that group became the National Association of Professional Baseball Players in 1871, the ban against African American ballplayers was omitted, but the exclusionary policy continued as an unwritten "gentlemen's agreement."

Despite this, African Americans did play in the white leagues. John W. "Bud" Fowler was the first known African American to earn a salary in organized baseball. Fowler was born in Cooperstown, New York. Fowler—who could play any position, including pitcher—spent the years from 1872 to 1897 playing all over the country, primarily with white teams. He began his career with the Newcastle, Pennsylvania, team, but by 1885, he was playing with the Keokuk, Iowa, team in the Western League.

At least thirty other African American men played in the white leagues before 1900. Among them were Moses Fleetwood Walker, an Oberlin College graduate, who became the first African American major league player in 1884, when he was signed to catch for the Toledo Blue Stockings of the American Association. Five weeks later, his brother, Welday Walker, signed to play the outfield with the same team. Robert Higgins pitched for the Syracuse, New York, team in 1887 in the International League.

These early African American players were met with all forms of racism. Further, there was a concerted effort, led by Adrian "Cap" Anson, the manager and star first baseman for the Chicago White Stockings, to purge black ballplayers from the major leagues. Within nine years, African Americans were out of organized baseball, as racism—bolstered by the "separate but equal" doctrine set down in the U.S. SUPREME COURT decision in PLESSY V. FERGUSON—took its toll.

There were, however, a few whites who attempted to circumvent the ban on African Americans in baseball. While managing the Baltimore Orioles, John McGraw tried unsuccessfully to pass off second baseman Charlie Grant as a Cherokee Indian with the name of Charlie Tokohamo. When McGraw joined the New York Giants in 1902, he brought with him an African American trainer, Ed Mackall, and before World War I, he hired Andrew "Rube" Foster as a pitching coach.

For most of the first half of the twentieth century, however, African Americans in professional baseball were limited to playing in NEGRO LEAGUE BASEBALL, the name given to a loose collection of leagues and teams that flourished before 1949. Playing before largely black crowds in the East, Midwest, and South, Negro League teams featured such stars as Josh Gibson and Buck Leonard, who were widely regarded as comparable to the best white players.

Major-league baseball remained white until after 1945, when Jackie Robinson was signed by Branch Rickey to play for the Brooklyn Dodgers' Triple A farm team, the Montreal Royals. On April 15, 1947, Robinson made his debut in a Dodger uniform. By the end of the season, he had compiled an impressive record, and in the process had proven that African American men could be as good as their white counterparts in baseball.

Despite Robinson's quick success, some major-league teams were slow to integrate their rosters. It was more than another decade before all major-league teams had African American ballplayers. Many black stars, including Roy Campanella, Don Newcombe, Monte Irvin, Willie Mays, Hank Aaron, Ernie Banks, Larry Doby, and Satchel PAIGE, were recruited out of the Negro Leagues. Faced with the loss of their best players and, after the breaking of baseball's color line, deprived of their reason for existing, the Negro Leagues quickly disappeared.

By 1980 more than one-fourth of all major-league players were African Americans. As black players attained equality on the field, a push began to integrate the front offices and managerial staffs of major-league teams, but the effort met with minimal success. By the 1990's, only a handful of African Americans

In 1999 ESPN polled sports authorities to determine who were the greatest one hundred athletes of the twentieth century. Willie Mays was ranked sixth. Among baseball players, only Babe Ruth ranked higher. *(National Baseball Library, Cooperstown, New York)*

held major-league managerial and front-office positions. Meanwhile, the proportion of African American players in the major leagues began to decline, reflecting a diminishing interest in baseball among blacks at various levels of the sport. By the late 1990's, only 17 percent of major league players were African Americans.

Horse Racing
Like boxing, horse racing was first introduced to African Americans during slavery. When the sport of horse racing spread throughout the South, plantation owners began to import and breed thoroughbreds, turning over the chores of grooming, feeding, breaking, exercising, and training the horses to their slaves.

It was also the slaves who rode the horses to victory or defeat. Unfortunately, although official records were kept of the winning horses and their owners, the names of the jockeys and trainers were not included, so the feats of those early African American sportsmen are lost to history.

Following the Civil War, African American men continued to excel at horse racing. At the first Jerome Handicap at Belmont Park in 1866, a rider known simply as Abe won, riding a horse called Watson. Abe also rode a horse named Merrill to victory at the third Travers Stakes, at Saratoga Springs in 1866. Fourteen of the fifteen jockeys in the first KENTUCKY DERBY—held at Churchill Downs in Louisville in May, 1875—were African Americans, including the winning rider, Oliver Lewis, who rode a horse called Aristides.

The most celebrated African American jockey was Isaac Burns MURPHY, who was born in 1861. Murphy won his first race at the age of fourteen, and by his early twenties, he was on a $10,000 retainer so that a particular horse owner could have first call on his services. Murphy rode three winners in the Kentucky Derby—Buchanan in 1884, Riley in 1890, and Kingman in 1891—a record that stood unmatched for forty years.

In 1896, the year Murphy died, Willie Simms won the Kentucky Derby on a horse named Ben Branch, and two years later, he won again on Plaudit. Simms went to England and became the first American jockey to win on an English course with an American horse, owner, trainer, and equipment. Jimmy Winkfield was the jockey with the best winning record in the Kentucky Derby, with two victories, one second, and one third in four starts. His victory on Alan-a-Dale in 1902 was the last by an African American jockey for more than ninety years.

During the early twentieth century, there were many noted African American jockeys, including Alonzo "Lonnie" Clayton, James "Soup" Perkins, John H. Jackson, Robert "Tiny" Williams, Anthony Hamilton, Henry J. Harris, and William Porter. Several jockeys, including George B. "Spider" Anderson and Bud Haggins, went on to become excellent steeplechase riders. Jockey Jimmy Lee rode six winners in one day at Latonia in 1909, and he twice rode five winners in one week. In 1911 Jesse Conley was the last African American of his era to ride in the Kentucky Derby, finishing third on a mount named Colston. After that, African Americans were systematically excluded from horse racing. Jim Crow laws and practices had brought an end to the illustrious history of the African American jockey.

Jackie ROBINSON's success with BASEBALL's Brooklyn Dodgers in 1947 helped prompt the reintegration of African Americans into horse racing. Nevertheless, black jockeys made no particular impact on the sport through the rest of the century.

Football
The first intercollegiate football game was played four years after the end of the Civil War, between Princeton and Rutgers. Shortly thereafter, Harvard, Yale, Cornell, and the University of Michigan also established football teams. Although black colleges did not organize football teams until the 1890's, African American athletes were probably playing intramural football before then. In 1892 Biddle University and Livingston College became the first black colleges to play each other; they were soon followed by Howard, Lincoln, Tuskegee, Atlanta, and Shaw.

Football began as a college sport, and even today the vast majority of professional football players are drafted from college teams. Consequently, football, more than any other sport, created the first real opportunities for African American men as coaches and assistant coaches, at more than one hundred private and land-grant institutions. Black college football also gave southern African American athletes the chance to exhibit their skills on the gridiron.

Great rivalries quickly developed between schools, such as that between Howard and Lincoln (Pennsylvania) or between Tuskegee and Wilberforce. Kentucky State, Morris Brown, Florida A&M, Southern, Langston, and Xavier were other football powerhouses that drew large followings. Football scholarships to black colleges and universities also provided the entry for many young African American men into the fields of medicine, law, dentistry, business, teaching, and social work.

Before the exploits of the gridiron heroes from black institutions were chronicled, African Americans were starring on football teams at predominantly white schools in the North and Northeast. Among the first to be recognized was William Henry Lewis, a center on the Amherst team who was chosen for Walter Camp's All-American team in both 1892 and 1893. Because athletic eligibility rules were not rigid in those days, Lewis was also the captain of the football team at Harvard while he was in law school. Lewis went on to become the first African American to be admitted to the American Bar Association.

Numerous African American football players came out of college to play in the early years of professional football. Among them was Frederick Douglass "Fritz" Pollard of Brown University, who played for the undefeated Akron Pros in the American Professional Football Association (APFA) in 1920. Pollard became the first African American professional football coach in 1923, after the APFA evolved into the National Football League (NFL). The renowned singer and actor Paul ROBESON was an All-American player at Rutgers; Robeson went on to play professionally with the Hammond Pros, the Akron Pros, and the Milwaukee Badgers, a team that had three African American players.

Other outstanding early black professional players included John Shelbourne from Dartmouth, who played with the Hammond Pros; Edward "Sol" Butler from Dubuque, Iowa, who first joined the Rock Island Independents before playing with the Hammond Pros in 1924 and again in 1926; James Turner, who followed Robeson to the Milwaukee Badgers in 1923; Jay Mayo "Inky" Williams, a teammate of Pollard at Brown who joined the Hammond team from 1923 to 1924; Fred "Duke" Slater, from the University of Iowa, who played with the Rock Island team, the Milwaukee Badgers, and the Chicago Cardinals; the University of Oregon's Joe Lillard, who played with the Cardinals in 1932 and 1933; and Ray Kemp, who played with the 1933 Pittsburgh Pirates.

The professional African American football player disappeared after 1933, when George Preston Marshall, the owner of the Washington Redskins, George Halas, the owner of the Chicago Bears, and Art Rooney, the owner of the Pittsburgh Pirates, entered into an agreement to exclude them from professional teams. The nation was four years into the GREAT DEPRESSION, and the team owners rationalized that black men should not be able to earn more money than white men. Twelve years later, in 1946, the National Football League had to compete with the fledgling All-America Football Conference, which had signed a number of African American athletes; in response, the NFL once again included African American players on its rosters.

Racism in football—both collegiate and professional—persisted, although blacks came to account for more than half of the NFL's players. African Americans make up a large majority of the league's linebackers, defensive backs, and running backs, but the so-called thinking positions—quarterback, center, kicker, and punter—have remained basically white, despite the fact that dozens of African American players have starred at those positions for college teams. By the late 1990's, however, there were signs of change. During the 1999 season, ten different African American players started games as quarterbacks at least once, and two of the four teams that made it to the conference finals were led by black quarterbacks.

By the 1999 season, there were only three African American head coaches in professional football, and scarcely one in ten NFL assistant coaches was black, despite the fact that two-thirds of the players in the league were black. On the college level, fewer than 2 percent of the head coaches at predominantly white institutions were African American. Black employment in the front offices of NFL teams was equally sparse.

Track and Field

It was more difficult for racist practices to keep African Americans out of track-and-field events, which are based more on individual than team effort. Although track-and-field contests—especially foot races—had gone on for centuries, the start of the modern Olympic Games in Athens, Greece, in 1896 was the primary impetus for modern organization of the sport.

No African Americans competed in the modern Games until the 1904 Olympics in St. Louis, Missouri, where George Poage of the University of Wisconsin won a bronze medal in the 400-meter hurdles. On the national scene, African American athletes began to excel in track-and-field events. In 1912 Howard P. Drew won national titles in the 100-yard dash and the 220-yard dash. Sol Butler, from Dubuque, Iowa, won the Amateur Athletic Union (AAU) title in the long jump in 1920, beginning a domination of the event by African American men that would extend to 1996, when Carl Lewis won his fourth consecutive gold medal in the Olympic long jump. In one early thirty-six-year span, African Americans won twenty-six AAU championships in the long jump, with DeHart Hubbard of Cincin-

nati winning six consecutive AAU titles from 1922 to 1927.

A steady stream of exceptional African American track-and-field athletes followed Poage. Jesse Owens's performance at the May, 1935, Big Ten meet in Ann Arbor, Michigan, may have been the greatest one-day accomplishment in track history. Although Owens fell down a flight of stairs and injured his back shortly before the meet, he jumped 26 feet, 8¼ inches, a world record; ran the 100-yard dash in 9.4 seconds, tying his own world record; ran the 200-yard dash in 20.3 seconds, another world record; and ran the 220-yard low hurdles in 22.6 seconds, also a world record—and he performed these feats in less than one hour. Owens went on to star at the 1936 Olympics in Germany, where he became the first athlete to win four gold medals in a single Olympics, set two world records, and tied an Olympic record in a another event in the process.

At the 1960 Olympic Games in Rome, Italy, another African American, Wilma Rudolph, became the first American woman to win three gold medals. Rudolph won the 100-meter and 200-meter dashes and came from behind as the anchor leg of the 400-meter relay team to win her third gold.

At the 1984 Los Angeles Olympics, Carl Lewis duplicated Jesse Owens's feat of winning four gold medals. Lewis won the 100-meter dash, won the 200-meter dash in an Olympic-record 19.8 seconds, took first place in the long jump, and won a fourth gold as part of the men's 400-meter relay team in a world record time of 37.83 seconds.

International competition in the sprint races, inclusive of the hurdles, came to be dominated by African American men and women, as did the long jump and the triple jump. For many years, it was held that black runners could win races only at short distances, but John Woodruff destroyed part of that myth when he won a gold medal in the 800-meter run at the 1936 Olympics. When John Borican, a student at Virginia State College, beat the legendary white runner Glenn Cunningham twice in the 1,000-yard run, and Frank Dixon of New York University won the prestigious Millrose Mile, the myth was shattered. By the late 1960's, many Africans had emerged as among the world's best runners at the longer distances. By the late 1990's, East Africans—particularly from Kenya—dominated the men's running events from 800 through 1,500 meters; North Africans dominated the longer races; and Africans from North and Eastern Africa ruled the marathon. Meanwhile, North American blacks—including Canadians—dominated the men's and women's sprints.

Basketball

Basketball was invented by James A. Naismith in 1891, and the game grew rapidly in popularity in the United States. As in other sports, however, there was an early unwritten rule that blacks and whites should not play on the same teams, or against one another. African Americans did sometimes play on predominantly white college teams, although they were often banned from competing when their teams played southern schools. Some excellent early black collegiate basketball players were Wilbur Woods of Nebraska, John Johnson of Columbia, Paul Robeson of Rutgers, Maynard Garner of Hamilton College, John and Samuel Barnes of Oberlin, and Ralph J. BUNCHE of the University of California at Los Angeles (UCLA).

At black colleges, basketball flourished, even though competition was limited primarily to games against other black schools. Despite their exclusion from mainstream college basketball, superb black players developed, particularly at Xavier University in New Orleans, where the starting five players during the mid-1930's were all from Wendell Phillips High School in Chicago. The team won sixty-seven games and lost only two in four years, a remarkable achievement.

In the early years, professional basketball for African Americans was limited to traveling teams. There were many African American teams, but only two became well known. Organized in 1922 by Bob Douglas, the Renaissance Big Five (also known as the HARLEM RENS, short for "Renaissance") won their first professional game on November 11, 1923; until the team disbanded after the 1948 season, the Rens, in the words of Douglas, "treated the fans to the classiest basketball in the world."

The other well-known black professional team was the HARLEM GLOBETROTTERS, organized in 1926 in Chicago by a white man named Abe Saperstein as the Savoy Big Five. Saperstein renamed the team the Harlem Globetrotters and took it on the road. The team proved to be so good that it had difficulty finding teams to play against. Saperstein devised a strategy whereby the team would play seriously for the first part of each game, then slow the game down and switch to clowning around—tactics similar to the skilled yet minstrel-like antics African American baseball players were sometimes forced to employ when playing white teams.

At the end of WORLD WAR II, the Renaissance Big Five and the Harlem Globetrotters were still in business. The Globetrotters were primarily entertainers, while the Harlem Rens were still playing competitive basketball against all comers. The Rens became a memory, however, when they joined the white National Basketball League as the Dayton (Ohio) Rens in mid-December, 1948, and finished the season with a 14-26 record. Dayton fans refused to accept an all-black team, and the league's refusal to allow the team to move to another city led to the team's demise.

After World War II, thousands of African American veterans took advantage of the G.I. Bill to attend white colleges and universities outside the South, and many played collegiate basketball. Soon, blacks were playing on previously all-white professional teams, beginning with the drafting of Charles "Chuck" Cooper, an All-American forward from Marquette University, on April 25, 1950, by the Boston Celtics, a National Basketball Association (NBA) team.

While Cooper was the first African American drafted to play pro basketball, Earl Lloyd, a center-forward from all-black West Virginia State College, was the first actually to play in the NBA when he suited up for the Washington Capitols, one day before Cooper took the floor with the Celtics. That same year, the New York Knickerbockers purchased Nat "Sweetwater" Clifton's contract from the Globetrotters.

During the 1950's, many NBA teams began to sign African American players. The Globetrotters' Saperstein responded by refusing to allow his team to play in some NBA cities, because he thought his control over his ballplayers was being challenged. The NBA owners persevered and signed more Globetrotter players, including the legendary Wilt CHAMBERLAIN.

African American men have been extremely successful in basketball, financially and otherwise. Blacks make up about half of the players in college ball and more than three-fourths of the players in the NBA. Blacks have found far greater opportunities in coaching and management in basketball than in baseball or football, and African American businessmen and former basketball stars have made serious bids to purchase NBA teams.

Basketball has also become a popular sport among women. Title IX of the Civil Rights Act of 1964 has forced colleges and universities to treat women's sports the same as men's. This has meant vastly improved facilities, more experienced coaches, and more generous scholarships. At the college level, women's basketball has benefitted most visibly from these changes. By the late 1990's, the women's game was catching up with the men's game in popularity. The improving standards of play and growing fan interest led to the creation of two women's professional leagues in 1996. By 1999 only the Women's National Basketball League (WNBA) survived—thanks in part to its support by the NBA—but it was flourishing in a dozen cities, with plans for expansion. African American players dominated the rosters of all the clubs, but not to the same extent as in the men's league.

Tennis

In tennis, the road was very rocky for African Americans. African American colleges began organized tennis competition in the late 1800's, and by 1916, they had formed the American Tennis Association (ATA). The ATA held its first na-

During the 1960's Bill Russell became the first African American head coach in the National Basketball Association and led the Boston Celtics to two championships. *(National Archives)*

tional tournament at Druid Hill Park in Baltimore, Maryland, in 1917. Individual African American tennis players performed very well in the years prior to World War II at schools including the City College of New York, the University of Chicago, and the University of Illinois.

Yet it took the outstanding play of Althea Gibson to begin to erase the color barrier in tennis. Gibson, the ATA women's champion, in 1950 became the first African American invited to play at the U.S. National Championship at Forest Hills, New York. Gibson went on to win both the U.S. championship and the Wimbledon championship in 1957 and again in 1958, and she won the French Open in 1956. In 1975 Arthur Ashe became the first African American man to win at Wimbledon. The most successful African American tennis player in the 1980's and 1990's was Zina Garrison, who defeated Steffi Graf to advance to the 1990 Wimbledon final match and was herself defeated by Martina Navratilova.

During the late 1990's, sisters Venus and Serena Williams injected a new kind of energy into the women's pro tennis tour, with their strong and aggressive style of play and their striking appearance on the court. Venus made a strong run for the title at the 1997 U.S. Open, establishing her presence on the tour. She and her sister each won several Grand Slam titles in mixed doubles in 1998. In early 1999 Serena won two tournaments in singles. Later that year Serena became the first African American woman since Althea Gibson to win a Grand Slam title by taking the singles title at the U.S. Open.

Golf

Golf, like tennis, was considered a sport for the elite, although John Shippen, the first professional African American golf professional, entered the third U.S. Open in 1896 at the age of eighteen. Many African American men were hired as caddies for white players, and some became very proficient at the game. There were enough black golfers to form the black United Golfers' Association (UGA) in the 1920's, and an African American tournament was established in 1926.

For much of the twentieth century, African American golfers either played on inferior black private courses or waited for "caddy day" at white courses and clubs in order to play on good eighteen-hole courses. In 1948 John F. Law sued for the right to use the municipal golf courses in BALTIMORE. He won his case, and within the next decade, most of the public courses in the United States were integrated.

Professional golf remained a largely white sport throughout the twentieth century, although black professionals such as Charlie Sifford, Lee Elder, Calvin Peete, and Tiger WOODS achieved notable successes. One of the reasons for the relatively low representation of blacks in professional golf is the fact that many Professional Golfers' Association (PGA) tournaments are played at private clubs, and many of those clubs, particularly in the South, have always had race-restricted memberships. By 1990 pressure had been put on many PGA clubs to integrate their memberships; some clubs withdrew their facilities from the PGA tour rather than integrate.

Competitors in Other Sports

African Americans have performed well in many other sports. Stock-car racer Wendell Scott is well known in the field of auto racing, and Cheryl Glass was the first African American female professional race-car driver in the nation. In 1986 George Branham III became the first African American to win a Professional Bowling Association (PBA) tournament. In the 1984 Olympics, Nelson Vails parlayed the skills he honed as a bicycle messenger to win a silver medal in the cycling sprints.

(continued on page 2371)

Notable Figures in Various Sports

See also tables in articles on Baseball, Basketball, Boxing, Football, Golf, Jockeys, Tennis, and Track and Field.

Campbell, Chris (b. Sept. 21, 1954, Westfield, N.J.). A member of the 1980 Olympic wrestling team, Campbell won national championships in 1983, 1990, and 1991. In 1981 he won the world championship in the 180.5-pound weight division, and in 1990 he won a silver medal in the world championship 198-pound division. He was also world-team-trials champion in 1990 and 1991. He retired from Olympic competition in 1984 after being injured before the Olympic trials but attempted a comeback in 1992.

Coage, Allen James (b. Oct. 22, 1943, New York, N.Y.). The first African American to win a medal in judo at the Olympics, Coage took the bronze in the heavyweight division in 1976. He also won gold medals in the 1967 and 1975 Pan-American Games. He was named New York Athlete of the Year in 1968 and won a *Sports Illustrated* Special Achievement Award in 1968. After being captain of the U.S. Olympic judo team in 1976, he entered professional wrestling in Tokyo.

Davenport, Willie. Bobsledder. *See Track and Field table entry.*

Davis, John Henry, Jr. (Jan. 21, 1921, Smithtown, N.Y.—July 13, 1984, Albuquerque, N.Mex.). Weight lifter. Never defeated in competition between 1938 and 1953, Davis won Olympic gold medals in 1948 and 1952.

Dawes, Dominique (b. Nov. 20, 1976, Silver Spring, Md.). After launching her competitive gymnastics career in 1988, Dawes came to the attention of fans when she tied Kim Zmeskal for first place in the floor exercise at the national championships in 1991. She finished first on the uneven bars at the 1992 championships. In 1992 she joined Betty Okino as the first Afri-  can American women to qualify for spots on the U.S. Olympic gymnastics team. The team won a bronze medal in team competition at the 1992 Olympics. In the 1993 world championships held in England, Dawes won a silver medal on the uneven parallel bars and a silver in the balance beam competition. She also placed first in the vault and the balance beam at the 1993 U.S. national championships.

DeFrantz, Anita (b. Oct. 4, 1952, Philadelphia, Pa.). The first African American woman to compete for the United States in Olympic rowing, DeFrantz won a bronze medal in the eight-oar event at the 1976 Games. During her career, she also won six different national titles and shared a silver medal in the coxed fours at the 1979 world championships. After retiring from competition, she worked to support the Olympic movement and became a member of the President's Council on Physical Fitness and of the Executive Board of the U.S. Olympic Committee (USOC). She also served as assistant vice president for the Los Angeles Olympic Organizing Committee and played a major role in persuading African nations not to boycott the 1984 Games. In 1986 she became the first female African American member of the International Olympic Committee.

Flack, Rory (b. Apr. 28, 1969, Belleville, Ill.). Flack began winning ice skating competitions at the age of six. As an amateur, she trained with Olympic coach John Nicks and was a Pacific Coast champion in 1986 and 1987. She placed twelfth at the national competition for the 1987 season and won a gold medal at the Olympic Festival competition and in several international competitions. After turning professional in 1990, she won the first annual Golden Blade Award at the United States Open Professional Championships the following year.

Francis, Herbert (b. May 26, 1940, Miami, Fla.). Francis was the first black man to compete in Olympic bicycling. He raced in the 1960 1,000-meter match sprints for the United States team but did not place.

Fuhr, Grant (b. Sept. 28, 1962, Edmonton, Alberta, Canada). Hockey player. After turning down an opportunity to play baseball with a Pittsburgh Pirates BASEBALL farm team in 1979, Fuhr dropped out of school to play ice hockey full-time for the Victoria

(continued)

Cougars of Canada's Western Hockey League. He was the Edmonton Oilers' first draft choice in 1981. As a goalie for the Oilers, he helped the team win five Stanley Cup championships between 1984 and 1990 and played as an All-Star five times. In 1988 he won the Vezina Trophy as the outstanding goaltender in the National Hockey League. Substance abuse threatened to end his career in 1990. However, after a one-year suspension, he was reinstated as a player. After ten seasons with Edmonton during the 1980's, he played for five different teams during the 1990's: Toronto, Buffalo, Los Angeles, St. Louis, and Calgary, with whom he started the 1999-2000 season.

Galimore, Ron (b. Tallahassee, Fla.). Gymnast. The son of Chicago Bears football player Willie Galimore, Ron Galimore became interested in gymnastics in 1969, at a time when no African Americans were active in the sport. After attending Louisiana State University for two years, he transferred to Iowa State University for the 1979-1981 seasons. He became the first gymnast to win National Collegiate Athletic Association (NCAA) titles in four different years, and he received the only perfect score during the championships. He was a member of the 1980 Olympic team that boycotted the Games.

Hyman, Flo (July 29, 1954, Los Angeles, Calif.—Jan. 24, 1986, Matsue, Japan). The top women's player of her era and a powerful spiker, Hyman led the U.S. women's volleyball team to a silver medal in the 1984 Olympics. The six-foot-five-inch, hitter did not take up volleyball until she had almost reached her full height as a teenager but made up for lost  time through hard work and the influence of coach Arie Selinger. With no professional indoor volleyball in the United States open to her after the Olympics, she briefly did public relations for the national team and pursued an acting career. Later, she and three teammates joined the Japanese league. In 1986 she suddenly collapsed while playing the third set of a match; she later died of heart failure attributed to Marfan's Syndrome, which tends to attack tall, slender people.

Keaser, Lloyd (b. Feb. 9, 1950, Pumphrey, Md.). Keaser won both the national Greco-Roman title and the Pan-American Games freestyle wrestling championship in 1975. He took a silver medal in the 1976 Olympics as a lightweight. He and his coaches thought that he could afford to lose his final match, and that he would win the gold medal based on  previous performances if he simply could avoid being pinned. They miscalculated, however. When Soviet Pavel Pinigan won that final match, he also won the gold medal.

McKegney, Tony (b. Feb., 1958, Montreal, Quebec, Canada). One of the few African Americans to play hockey in the National Hockey League (NHL). Raised in Canada by adoptive parents, McKegney was drafted by a World Hockey Association team in the mid-1970's but he decided to remain an amateur. In 1978 he was drafted by the NHL's Buffalo Sabres. In 1984 he was traded to the Quebec Nordiques, with whom he remained for about eighteen months before being sent to the Minnesota North Stars. In 1986 he was traded to the New York Rangers, for whom he became a productive goal scorer. Nevertheless, he was traded to the St. Louis Blues in 1987. After being moved around the league in frequent trades between 1989 and 1991, he decided to play in Europe.

Okino, Betty (b. June 4, 1975, Entebbe, Uganda). A member of the bronze medal-winning 1992 U.S. Olympic team, Okino also helped the 1991 U.S. World Championship team win a silver medal. She won the all-around, vaulting, and uneven bars competitions at the 1991 McDonald's America Cup. Her original move on the balance beam, involving a triple turn or pirouette, has been named the "Okino" in her honor.

O'Ree, Willie (b. Oct. 5, 1935, Fredericton, New Brunswick, Canada). O'Ree became the first black player in the NHL when he joined the Boston Bruins for a two-game trial in 1957. In the 1960-1961 season, he played in 43 games, scoring four goals and ten assists. He then played in the minor leagues for nineteen years, including a seven-year stint with the Los Angeles Blades.

Scott, Wendell (1921?—Dec. 22, 1990, Detroit, Mich.). Stock car racer. Stock car racing's first important black driver, Scott was an integral part of Winston Cup Grand National racing from 1961 to 1973, despite frequent harassment from spectators and promoters. Although he rarely drove the best machinery, he finished sixth in National Association for Stock Car Auto Racing (NASCAR) points in 1966, tenth in 1967, and ninth in 1968. In 495 Winston Cup races, Scott won once, finished in the top five 20 times, and in the top ten 147 times. His only NASCAR win was in 1963, in Jacksonville, Fla. Scott aspired to pave the way for other black drivers, but that did not happen within his lifetime. Only two other African Americans, Willy T. Ribbs and George Wiltshire, started Winston Cup races before 1990.

Scott retired from racing in 1973 after he broke his pelvis in a crash during the Winston 500. In 1977, Richard Pryor portrayed Scott in the film *Greased Lightning*.

Taylor, Major. Bicyclist. *See main text entry.*

Thomas, Debi. Ice skater. *See main text entry.*

Walker, Hershel. Bobsledder. *See entry in Football table.*

White, Ruth (b. 1951 or 1952). At seventeen years of age, White became the youngest national fencing champion and the first African American to win a major American fencing title, in 1969. She was also one of the first black Americans to compete on an Olympic fencing team, and took part in the 1972 Olympics.

Ron Galimore became the first African American gymnast to win a National Collegiate Athletic Association (NCAA) championship. Debi THOMAS became the number-one figure skater in the United States in the mid-1980's and won a bronze medal in the 1988 Olympics. John Davis was among the greatest weightlifting champions of all time; from the late 1930's until 1953, Davis won numerous national and world championship competitions, including gold medals in the 1948 and 1952 Olympics. African American Odis Wilson, Jr., and his younger sister Alicia won numerous professional water-skiing tournaments.

In late 1999, Fred Whitfield became the first African American all-around champion in the Professional Rodeo Cowboys Association's national finals, held in Las Vegas, Nevada. Whitfield was one of only twelve African Americans even to qualify for the event since it began four decades earlier.

—*Philip G. Smith*

Suggested Readings:

Ashe, Arthur, Jr. *A Hard Road to Glory: A History of the African American Athlete Since 1946*. New York: Warner Books, 1988.

_____. *Pioneers of Black Sport: The Early Days of the Black Professional Athlete in Baseball, Basketball, Boxing, and Football*. New York: Dodd, Mead, 1975.

Edwards, Harry. "Black Athletes: Minority Access to Sports Programs." *Current* (June, 1999): 15-18.

Gilmore, Al-Tony. "Black Athletes in an Historical Context: The Issue of Race." *Negro History Bulletin* 58 (October-December, 1995): 7-14.

Hoberman, John M. *Darwin's Athletes: How Sport Has Damaged Black America and Preserved the Myth of Race*. Boston: Houghton Mifflin, 1997.

Leavy, Walter. "Fifty Years of Blacks in Sports." *Ebony* (October, 1995): 131-139.

Porter, David L., ed. *African-American Sports Greats: A Biographical Dictionary*. Westport, Conn.: Greenwood Press, 1995.

Rashad, Ahmad. "Fifty Years of Blacks in Sports." *Ebony* (November, 1995): 156-159.

Sailes, Gary A., ed. *African Americans in Sport: Contemporary Themes*. New Brunswick N.J.: Transaction, 1998.

Shropshire, Kenneth L. *In Black and White: Race and Sports in America*. New York: New York University Press, 1996.

Simons, John, and David Butow. "Improbable Dreams: African Americans Are a Dominant Presence in Professional Sports—Do Blacks Suffer as a Result?" *U.S. News and World Report*, March 24, 1997, 46-51.

Sinnette, Calvin H. *Forbidden Fairways: African Americans and the Game of Golf*. Chelsea, Mich.: Sleeping Bear Press, 1998.

Wiggins, David K. *Glory Bound: Black Athletes in a White America*. Syracuse, N.Y.: Syracuse University Press, 1997.

Spottswood, Stephen Gil (July 18, 1897, Boston, Massachusetts—December 1, 1974, Washington, D.C.): Clergyman. Spottswood was pastor of churches in several states before he was elected as a bishop of the African Methodist Episcopal Zion Church in 1952. He served as chairman of the board of the National Association for the Advancement of Colored People from 1961 until his death.

Stallings, George Augustus, Jr. (b. March 17, 1948, New Bern, North Carolina): Religious leader. Stallings founded the Imani Temple African American Catholic Congregation in 1989 in response to alleged insensitivity of the Roman Catholic Church to the spiritual and cultural needs of African Americans. By 1992 the organization had churches in Philadelphia, Pennsylvania; Washington, D.C.; and

Stephen G. Spottswood (right) with Roy Wilkins and Attorney General Robert F. Kennedy in 1964. *(AP/Wide World Photos)*

Bishop George Augustus Stallings, Jr. (center) during a Baton Rouge protest against Louisiana governor Mike Foster's stance on affirmative action in February, 1996. *(AP/Wide World Photos)*

Norfolk, Virginia; and had approximately fifteen hundred members.

Staples, Brent A. (b. September 13, 1951, Chester, Pennsylvania): Journalist and author. After graduating from college and earning a doctorate in psychology from the University of Chicago, Staples entered journalism, soon becoming an editorial writer at *The New York Times*. In 1994 he published a memoir entitled *Parallel Time: Growing Up in Black and White*. It recounts Staples's POVERTY-ridden youth and adolescence in Chester and his extraordinary escape from that world into success in college

and graduate school. It also describes the brutal fate of many of the friends he left behind, including the murder of his younger brother, a cocaine dealer.

Steele, Shelby (b. January 1, 1946, Chicago, Illinois): Writer and educator. A professor of English at San Jose State University, Steele stirred controversy by writing about the concept of "racism within." Steele argued that it is not always racism in a community that creates difficulties for African Americans, but rather their own attitudes and sense of identity. He contended that sometimes racism has been used by African Americans as an excuse for not taking the initiative to succeed.

Steele's first book, *The Content of Our Character: A New Vision of Race in America* (1990), received the 1990 National Book Critics Circle Award. A collection of Steele's essays, the work focuses on his personal journey toward understanding the issue of race.

Born to a black father who never completed grade school and a white mother who was a social worker, Steele never lacked for loving relatives of either color. One of his essays describes the horrible surprise he received when he encountered a white person who was truly unpleasant: his sixth-grade teacher. This teacher, a former marine, chose Steele as a target, ridiculing him in front of other students and inflicting severe punishments. Steele's parents sought community support in mounting a successful boycott of the school—a boycott that resulted in the firing of the former Marine and several other teachers.

With his parents' support, Steele was able to regain his self-confidence as well as his desire to succeed in school. He became student council president during his senior year in high school and went on to be involved in civil rights activities in college. It was not until Steele married a white woman and became a father himself that he began a serious examination of the conflict he felt inside. He was torn between the civil rights teachings of Martin Luther KING, Jr., and the BLACK POWER teachings of MALCOLM X. Steele's frustration came to a head in 1986, when he was listening to a radio broadcast on the anniversary of King's birthday. His disagreement with the speakers led Steele to write an article detailing his views. The piece was published, leading to Steele's successful career as a writer for several well-known magazines.

Steele's essays came to the attention of filmmaker Thomas Lennon, who wanted to make a documentary about race in the United States. While the two men were planning their approach to this subject, a sixteen-year-old black man named Yusuf K. Hawkins was killed. Hawkins was murdered by a gang of white teenagers in Bensonhurst, an Italian American neighborhood in Brooklyn, New York. Two youths were arrested for the killing, African American leaders led a protest march on the area, and racial tensions increased throughout the nation.

Lennon and Steele used the incident as the focus of their filming. Their documentary, *Seven Days in Bensonhurst*, aired on television on May 15, 1990. Steele served as anchor of the documentary. He expressed his anger over the killing, but he also stated that racial hatred had increased because of the behavior of the activists, politicians, and media personalities who became involved in the aftermath of the incident. Steele's comments brought him much attention. While his proposed solutions to race problems were bluntly stated for shock value, Steele's concern for and empathy with the black community are clearly apparent in his work. He published *A Dream Deferred: The Second Betrayal of Black Freedom in America* in 1998. *See also:* Biracial and mixed-raced children; Hate crime.

Steward, Susan McKinney (1847, Brooklyn, New York—March 7, 1918, Wilberforce, Ohio): Physician and activist. Born the seventh of ten children of prosperous farmer Sylvanus Smith and the former Ann Springsteel, Susan Maria Smith was a brilliant student and a trained musician. She enrolled in New York Medical College for Women in 1867, emerging as the class valedictorian three years later. Smith became the first African American woman in New York State, and only the third nationally, to graduate from a medical school.

Susan Maria Smith had a lucrative private practice in Brooklyn and cofounded the Brooklyn Woman's Homeopathic Hospital and Dispensary in 1881. A strong advocate of civil liberties and women's rights, she was invited to address local, national, and international audiences on social and medical issues. She was active as a member of the Homeopathic Medical Society of the State of New York, the Kings County Homeopathic Medical Society, Women's Loyal Union Society of New York and Brooklyn, and the Women's Christian Temperance Union, and she served as the organist and choir director of the Siloam Presbyterian Church and later the Bridge Street AME Church.

Susan Maria Smith married the Reverend William G. McKinney in 1871; after his death in 1894, she married the Reverend Teophilus Steward in 1896. In 1898 the Stewards gained faculty positions at Wilberforce University in Ohio. Susan Maria Smith McKinney Steward taught at the school until her death on March 7, 1918. Eulogized by W. E. B. Du Bois, she was buried at Greenwood Cemetery in Brooklyn three days later.

Suggested Readings:

Alexander, Leslie L. "Susan Smith McKinney, M.D., 1847-1918." *Journal of the National Medical Association* 67 (March, 1975): 173-175.

Seraile, William. "Susan McKinney Steward: New York State's First African-American Woman Physician." *Afro-Americans in New York Life and History* 9, no. 2 (1985): 27-44.

Stewart, Bennett McVey (August 6, 1914, Huntsville, Alabama—April 26, 1988, Chicago, Illinois): U.S. representative from ILLINOIS. Stewart was raised in ALABAMA and graduated from high school in BIRMINGHAM. He remained in Birmingham for college, graduating with a B.A. degree in 1936 from Miles College. After graduation, Stewart took a position as assistant principal at Irondale High School in Birmingham. In 1938 he returned to Miles College to serve on the faculty as an as-

sociate professor of sociology. He left teaching in 1940 to join Atlanta Life Insurance Company. He became an executive with the company and moved to Chicago in 1950, when he was promoted to be the company's director for the state of Illinois. Stewart retired from the company in 1968.

Upon retirement, Stewart became a building inspector for the city of CHICAGO from 1968 to 1970 and served in the city's department of urban renewal as a rehabilitation specialist. He was elected to the Chicago city council in 1971 as an alderman from the city's Twenty-first Ward. Stewart later was elected as Democratic committeeman from that ward in 1976 and served until 1978.

After U.S. congressman Ralph Metcalfe died in October of 1978, the DEMOCRATIC PARTY committeemen from Illinois's First Congressional District were authorized to select the party's candidate to fill the remainder of Metcalfe's term. Stewart was selected to run, and he defeated former alderman A. A. Rayner in the November election. Stewart took his seat in Congress on January 3, 1979, and was appointed to serve as a member of the House Committee on Appropriations. During his term in Congress, Stewart advocated emergency appropriations to provide low-income housing residents with financial assistance in paying their home heating bills and supported loan guarantees to stave off bankruptcy for Chrysler Corporation, a major employer providing fifteen hundred jobs in Stewart's district. He reintroduced Ralph Metcalfe's resolution to designate February as Black History Month, a measure which eventually was approved.

Stewart ran for reelection in 1980 but was defeated in the March Democratic primary by Harold WASHINGTON, who went on to win the election in November. Stewart completed his term in Congress and returned to Chicago, where he served as interim director of the city's Department of Intergovernmental Affairs from 1981 to 1983. He then retired from public office and remained a resident of Chicago until his death.

Stewart, Maria Miller (1803, Hartford, Connecticut—December 17, 1879, Washington, D.C.): ABOLITIONIST MOVEMENT leader. Orphaned when she was five years old, Stewart was bound out as a servant and began her struggle to educate herself. After moving to BOSTON, MASSACHUSETTS, in the early 1820's, she met James Stewart, whom she married in 1826. Widowed three years later, she overcame her grief only after an intense religious conversion which transformed the balance of her life. Stewart became an outspoken proponent for William Lloyd Garrison in 1831 and for the moral and intellectual uplift of African Americans. She was among the first women in the United States to challenge conventional thinking on women's role in society, speaking before audiences and arguing for the right of women to be religious teachers and active combatants in the struggle for racial and political justice. In 1834 she moved to New York City, where she continued teaching, writing, and working for abolition. In 1863 she moved to WASHINGTON, D.C., and began working for the Freedmen's Hospital, becoming its matron by the early 1870's. Despite declining health, she remained an active teacher and Episcopalian apostle and published her antislavery, religious, and autobiographical writings.

Still, William (October 7, 1821, Medford, New Jersey—July 14, 1902, Philadelphia, Pennsylvania): ABOLITIONIST, historian, and philanthropist.

William Still was born the youngest of eighteen children to Levin and Charity Still. William's father purchased his freedom, and Charity later escaped with most of their children and joined him. As a young man, William

Abolitionist William Still. *(Associated Publishers, Inc.)*

moved to Philadelphia and worked for local abolitionist groups. He was elected secretary for the Philadelphia Society for the Abolition of Slavery and chairman of its Vigilance Committee. He became a conductor on the UNDERGROUND RAILROAD, a secretive network of people who helped runaway slaves to freedom. Hundreds of runaway slaves passed through the Philadelphia Vigilance Committee's hands and were safely commuted northward.

One of the runaways William Still assisted turned out to be his own brother, who had been left behind in slavery. In hopes of assisting other former slaves to find their lost relatives when slavery ended, William Still began saving correspondence and interviewing runaway slaves. In 1872 he published his collection in *The Underground Railroad*. It detailed the lives of dozens of slaves and recounted how and why they escaped. This anthology is one of the earliest historical records of slave life, making William Still one of the first African American historians.

After the CIVIL WAR, Still opened a successful coal yard, and he and his wife, Letitia, had four children. He continued to fight for civil rights and was instrumental in establishing hospitals, orphanages, and schools for African Americans. William Still died in Philadelphia at the age of eighty-one.

—*Leslie A. Stricker*

Still, William Grant (May 11, 1895, Woodville, Mississippi—December 3, 1978, Los Angeles, California): Composer. Still is considered one of the most prominent African American composers. He was the first African American to conduct an orchestra, the New Orleans Philharmonic Symphony, in the Deep South, and became the first African American to conduct a major U.S. orchestra, the Los Angeles Philharmonic, in 1936. His *Afro-American Symphony*, written in 1931, was the first symphony of full length written by an African American to be recorded by a major record company.

Stitt, Sonny (February 2, 1924, Boston, Massachusetts—July 22, 1982, Washington, D.C.): Saxophonist. A consistently important JAZZ musician, Edward "Sonny" Stitt often has been linked with Charlie Parker and bebop music. He began his career in the 1940's, playing

with legendary trumpeter Dizzy GILLESPIE and his group. He also performed in the 1950's with Norman Granz's Jazz at the Philharmonic. He led his own combos in the 1950's and 1960's, traveling throughout the United States as well as in Europe. For the last thirty years of his performance career, however, he most often was a solo act.

Stitt's association with the early BEBOP music and its progenitors brought him a steady and devoted following. His performances reminded listeners of his claim to fame within the crowded pantheon of jazz. As the jazz that originated in the 1940's and was developed in

Saxophonist Sonny Stitt in 1963. *(AP/Wide World Photos)*

the 1950's and 1960's grew subservient to the rock and roll of the 1960's and beyond, important jazz figures such as Stitt tended to fade from the public consciousness. Stitt was conscious of his musical identity. He switched from the alto saxophone to the tenor, in fact, to avoid comparisons between his music and that of Charlie PARKER. Stitt proved to be equally talented on the tenor, alto, and baritone saxophones.

Stokes, Carl Burton (June 21, 1927, Cleveland, Ohio—April 3, 1996, Cleveland, Ohio): OHIO politician and broadcast journalist. Carl Burton Stokes became the first African American elected MAYOR of a major American city when he won Cleveland's 1967 mayoral race. In office, Stokes was charismatic and articulate, and he knew the issues that concerned Cleveland residents. He believed that he could achieve positive reform in Cleveland politics and that he could create a better city for all Cleveland residents. Stokes also was the first African American to hold high offices in all three branches of government—legislative, executive, and judicial.

Youth and Early Adulthood
Stokes's father died when Carl was two years old, leaving Carl's mother and grandmother to rear Carl and his brother, Louis. Stokes's mother worked as a domestic, and the family eked out a living. The Stokes brothers were greatly influenced by their mother's encouragement to get an education and to make something of their lives (Louis later became a member of the U.S. House of Representatives). Carl's education, however, was interrupted when he dropped out of Cleveland East Technical High School at the age of seventeen. Street life was so enticing that he became a pool hustler.

Street life soon paled for Stokes, and in July, 1945, dissatisfied with his circumstances and realizing that he was going nowhere, he joined the Army. At the completion of his military service, which included a tour of duty in Germany, he quickly realized that, as his mother had said, an education was indispensable if he was to achieve success. He therefore returned to high school, earned his diploma, and enrolled in college. While attending college, he worked as a state liquor enforcement agent and was responsible for closing down illegal establishments in African American neighborhoods. He soon transferred to the University of Minnesota and graduated with a B.S. degree in 1954. Stokes later attended law school at night while serving as a probation officer during the day. He graduated in 1956 and set up a law practice, but he soon turned toward politics.

Political Life
Stokes began his political career in 1962, when he became the first African American Democrat elected to the Ohio legislature. Elected to two terms in the state legislature, he began to set his sights on the mayoral seat in Cleveland. The decades preceding Stokes's quest for the mayoral job had seen the city's population change; many whites had left the city, while the black population had increased. By 1965 Cleveland was one-third black, and the growing black community meant a greater pool of potential voters that Stokes could mobilize behind him. He entered the 1965 mayoral election as an independent candidate, since the local DEMOCRATIC PARTY organization backed incumbent Ralph Locher. He nearly won an upset victory, losing by slightly more than twenty-two hundred votes, less than 1 percent of the total. The election was of great value in providing experience for Stokes and his supporters, and it enabled him to assess his chances in a second attempt at the mayor's seat in 1967.

Stokes entered the 1967 mayoral election knowing that he needed a solid turnout from the African American community and that he had to make greater inroads among white voters. Many voters were attracted to Stokes by his personal charm and his knowledge, command, and articulation of the issues. His strategy for attracting white voters was to neutralize their fear of an African American becoming the leader of the city. Stokes downplayed the race issue, and he ventured to Cleveland's west side, which was virtually all white, in order to curry support. He argued that voters should base their support of him on his ability and should not let race interfere in their choice. In the black community, efforts were made to increase registration of voters and to see that residents actually cast their votes.

As Stokes was the first African American to campaign seriously for mayor in Cleveland, many residents were concerned about his ability to prevent racial disorders. Racial tension in Cleveland and throughout the country had risen during the previous years, and racial disturbances had erupted across the nation between 1964 and 1966. Cleveland's Hough community had been the scene of one of these racial disorders in 1966, and voters wondered if Stokes would be able to defuse Cleveland's racial tension.

In the 1967 primary election, Stokes defeated incumbent Locher. He then faced Republican Seth Taft in the general election. Taft was a descendant of a former president, while

Carl Stokes, the first African American elected mayor of a major city. *(Library of Congress)*

Stokes was a descendant of slaves. The most controversial moment of the campaign came during a debate between the two candidates. The issue of race was present throughout the campaign; everyone in the city knew that a black candidate and a white candidate were running against each other for mayor, but both candidates were reluctant to talk about racial issues. At the debate, though, Stokes decided to bring the issue before the people. He remarked that political experts claimed that Taft would win the election because he was white. The audience loudly booed Stokes, and staff members of both candidates believed that the campaign had shifted in favor of Taft. Despite this political gaffe, Stokes recovered and defeated Taft, becoming the first African American elected mayor of a major American city.

Mayor

The new mayor saw his election as a victory for egalitarianism; he viewed himself as a poor boy who had risen from poverty to occupy the highest office in the city. Cleveland's African American community was ecstatic that one of their own had become mayor; Stokes's election seemed to demonstrate that, like other ethnic groups in the past, African Americans were gaining their place in the political world.

Stokes's early months in office went well and were highlighted by the introduction of his Cleveland: NOW! program, which involved citizens in housing projects, youth programs, city planning, and urban renewal. Also noteworthy was Stokes's assistance in preventing the city from exploding into riots in the aftermath of the assassination of Martin Luther King, Jr., as many other large American cities did.

The honeymoon period for the mayor ended in July, 1968, with an outbreak of violence in Cleveland's Glenville community. Although black nationalism was not an especially strong force in Cleveland, a black nationalist group led by Fred Ahmed Evans fired on policemen in the Glenville neighborhood, and for several days, the area was plagued by looting.

The Ohio National Guard was called out, and by the time peace had been restored, seven people were dead, fifteen had been wounded, and two million dollars in damage had been done. Stokes, in a controversial decision during the riot, kept all white officers and the National Guard out of the Glenville area while he led several African American leaders

into the riot district in order to reduce tension and to prevent additional deaths. He was bitterly criticized for this decision by many on the police force and by some members of the white community at large. His popularity in the white community suffered, and Stokes himself admitted that the incident haunted the rest of his administration. Not only did funds for his projects dry up, but also the city's resolve to make strides in race relations was stymied. Many African Americans recognized the violence as an unfortunate incident but also realized that resentment had existed in the black community for some time over perceived harassment by members of the police force.

Achievements

The Glenville incident notwithstanding, Stokes won reelection in 1969. His achievements during his two terms as mayor were impressive. While he served as mayor, more public-housing units were constructed than during any other period in recent Cleveland history. Funds were made available for small entrepreneurs and for minority businesses, and Cleveland adopted an equal employment opportunity ordinance in 1969 to guarantee fair employment practices by firms contracting business with the city. Stokes was the first Cleveland mayor to appoint blacks to high-level public offices, and he increased the number of blacks working for the city.

The mayor was instrumental in getting the federal Department of Housing and Urban Development to release more than $11 million in federal funds earmarked for Cleveland but held up during Locher's administration. The most extensive program in Stokes's administration, however, was Cleveland: NOW! This was a multimillion-dollar project in which citizens were asked to participate in various programs, ranging from raising funds to establishing day care centers, with the objective of building up and rejuvenating the city. Stokes also was responsible for the formation of the Twenty-first Congressional District Caucus, an organization of political leaders that could be used to continue an African American presence in Cleveland politics.

Life After Politics

Stokes left Cleveland politics after refusing to seek a third term in office, and he turned his sights on a journalism career. In 1972 he became the first African American newscaster to appear on a daily basis in New York City (on WNBC), and in 1978 he won an Emmy Award from the New York chapter of the National Academy of Television Arts and Sciences.

Stokes's autobiography, *Promises of Power: A Political Autobiography*, was first published in 1973; it was reprinted with a new prologue, illustrations, and other material in 1989.

In 1983 Stokes, who had returned to Cleveland in 1980 to practice law, successfully ran for election as a municipal court judge. With his election to the bench, Stokes had served in all three branches of government—legislative, executive, and judicial. He served as a judge until 1994, when President Bill Clinton appointed him to serve as ambassador to the Republic of Seychelles, an island nation off the east coast of Africa north of Madagascar in the Indian Ocean. Stokes took a medical leave from his diplomatic post in June of 1995 after learning that he had CANCER of the esophagus. Returning to Cleveland, he had surgery to remove a tumor and underwent chemotherapy and radiation treatment. He remarried his second wife, Raija Kostadinov, in December of 1995. In April of 1996, he lost his battle with cancer and died in a Cleveland medical clinic at the age of sixty-eight.

—*Lester S. Brooks*
—*Updated by Wendy Sacket*

Suggested Readings:
"Carl B. Stokes, Sixty-eight, First Black Mayor of a Major U.S. City, Dies." *Jet* (April 22, 1996): 58-60.

Elliot, Jeffrey M., ed. *Black Voices*. San Diego, Calif.: Harcourt Brace Jovanovich, 1986.

Masotti, Louis, et al. *Shoot-Out in Cleveland*. New York: Bantam Books, 1969.

Nelson, William E., and Philip J. Meranto. *Electing Black Mayors*. Columbus: Ohio State University Press, 1977.

Stokes, Carl B. *Promises of Power, Then and Now*. Cleveland: Friends of Carl B. Stokes, 1989.

Weinberg, Kenneth G. *Black Victory: Carl Stokes and the Winning of Cleveland*. Chicago: Quadrangle Books, 1968.

Stokes, Louis (b. February 23, 1925, Cleveland, Ohio): OHIO politician. After service in the Army in World War II, Stokes attended Case Western Reserve University and Marshall College of Law in Cleveland. He subsequently became one of Cleveland's most successful black lawyers.

In 1967 Carl STOKES, Louis's brother, gained national attention when he was elected mayor of Cleveland. In the same year, Louis Stokes's legal career led him into politics. He represented Charles P. Lucas, a black Republican, in a suit against the Ohio legislature charging that it had GERRYMANDERED the state's congressional district boundaries to divide black voting strength and prevent the election of minority candidates. The case eventually reached the U.S. SUPREME COURT, where Stokes won a court order requiring the redrawing of the state's congressional districts. In 1968 Stokes bested a crowded field to win the Democratic nomination for Ohio's new Twenty-first District on Cleveland's east side. He then went on to win the general election, against Lucas. Stokes was the first African American to be elected to Congress from Ohio. He won subsequent reelections by large margins.

In Congress, Stokes enjoyed a long career that saw him become one of the House's most influential members. He rose to be one of the

Louis Stokes announcing his retirement from Congress in January, 1998. After twenty-nine years of continuous service, he ranked eleventh in the House in seniority. *(AP/Wide World Photos)*

senior majority members on the powerful House Appropriations Committee. A liberal Democrat, Stokes was chairman of the CONGRESSIONAL BLACK CAUCUS and a consistent and effective spokesman on minority affairs. He stressed the need to broaden educational and employment opportunities. Stokes was also a member of the House Permanent Select Committee on Intelligence, in which capacity he played a prominent role in the House investigation of the Iran-Contra scandal in 1987. The House's trust in Stokes was evidenced by the fact that he twice served as chairman of the House Ethics Committee. In 1992 this position thrust him into the spotlight when it was revealed that many members of the House, including Stokes himself, had written checks against insufficient funds in their accounts in the House bank. Stokes retired in 1998.

Stono rebellion: The largest slave uprising in colonial North America occurred southwest of Charleston, SOUTH CAROLINA, in September, 1739. The Stono Rebellion (named for the river where it began) was eventually quelled after the loss of some sixty lives and the destruction of several plantations. Although unsuccessful, the episode illustrated the tenuousness of white control and led to permanent adjustments in the attitudes and behavior of white South Carolinians. It marked a turning point in the history of the colony's black population.

Background

Colonial South Carolina was a slaveholding society with a substantial black majority. As a result of the development of rice cultivation—a labor-intensive enterprise—in the 1690's, white planters had become increasingly dependent upon black workers. By 1739 blacks outnumbered whites nearly two to one among the colony's fifty-six thousand inhabitants. Most were slaves, and a sizable proportion had recently been imported from Africa. Moreover, most slaves worked on large plantations owned by absentee masters, who spent much of their time away in Charleston. There was increasing tension between the races and a spreading anxiety on the part of whites, who had a very real fear of slave revolt.

The possibility of slave escape was equally real. Only coastal GEORGIA, some two hundred miles of largely unsettled terrain, lay between South Carolina and Spanish FLORIDA. Throughout the early months of 1739, a rising number of slaves had managed to flee the colony and find their way to the Spanish fort at St. Augustine. Such defections were encouraged by the Spanish, who one year earlier had offered asylum to runaway blacks from the British colonies rather than return them as officials demanded. White South Carolinians feared that their slaves were conspiring to rise up and leave the colony by force.

Rebellion

The Stono Rebellion began in the early morning hours of Sunday, September 9, 1739, when some twenty slaves gathered near the western branch of the Stono River in St. Paul's parish, twenty miles from Charleston. The conspirators, many of whom were from the African region that is now Angola, hoped to make their way to St. Augustine. Led by a slave named Jemmy, they proceeded to the Stono Bridge and sacked a general store. After seizing gunpowder and several guns, they executed the two storekeepers and left their victims' heads upon the front steps. Once armed, the rebels moved on to a nearby house, plundering and burning it and killing the owner and his two children.

The band of slaves then turned southward along the main road to Georgia and St. Augustine. Proceeding along this route, they came to

a tavern before dawn; because of the tavernkeeper's reputation for kind treatment of his slaves, his life was spared. Moving on several miles, the rebels burned at least five plantation houses, killing every white they captured. A man named Bullock eluded their grasp. One white planter, Thomas Rose, was hidden by his slaves. Not all bondmen flocked to the rebel band; some were forced to join to keep the alarm from being spread. Many, though, were voluntarily recruited. As the numbers increased, confidence rose. Before long, two drums were found, a banner was raised, and shouts of "Liberty!" were heard. The company may have numbered fifty or more by this time.

About 11:00 A.M., Lieutenant Governor William Bull and four companions came within view of the rebels while returning to Charleston on horseback for the opening of the legislative session. Bull and company immediately wheeled about and, although several blacks pursued them, managed to escape unharmed. By then, the alarm had been sounded. Had the slaves been able to capture Bull or to evade pursuit for a few days while their numbers increased, the rebellion might have seriously threatened or even overthrown slavery in South Carolina, changing the course of American history. The rebels' failure to do either soon brought defeat.

Turning Point of the Rebellion

Late on Sunday afternoon, after pursuing but failing to apprehend Bull and his companions, the rebels halted in a field not far from the Edisto River. Their number now approached one hundred. They may have stopped for a variety of reasons—overconfidence, exhaustion, intoxication from stolen liquor, or a desire to allow other slaves time to join their band. This proved to be a fatal mistake. Alerted to the insurrection, a contingent of armed and mounted white planters located the rebels about 4:00 P.M. and opened fire. The slaves were caught off guard. Some hesitated, a few fired back, many fled. At least fourteen blacks were killed or wounded in the confusion. Others were quickly seized and shot while attempting to return to their plantations. Victorious whites severed the heads of some of the rebels and set them on mileposts along the main road as a warning to other recalcitrant slaves.

At least thirty of the rebellious slaves escaped. The entire colony was quickly armed, guards were posted at key ferry points, and militia companies conducted intensive man-hunts. Most of the fugitives were captured and executed within a week. After several days of pursuit, one militia company caught up with the largest rebel band some thirty miles closer to the Georgia border. A few of the rebels remained at large for months or even years, but the main body had been effectively dispersed. The unsuccessful insurrection had resulted in localized property damage, the deaths of twenty-five whites and thirty-five blacks, and a surge of white terror.

Consequences

The Stono Rebellion confirmed the worst fears of South Carolina's white minority. In the wake of the uprising, colonial officials moved quickly to reassert white control and to lessen the likelihood that slaves would flee to Florida or rise in revolt. This effort entailed three distinct changes in the system of slave supervision within the colony.

First, the colonial assembly approved and rigorously enforced a comprehensive new SLAVE CODE, one of the most stringent in the hemisphere. The Negro Act of 1740, as it was known, became the basis of South Carolina's system of slave control for more than a century. The law curtailed many of the personal liberties that slaves had enjoyed in the colony for several generations, including the freedom to assemble, to move about, to grow their own food, to earn money in their leisure time, and to learn to read. It mandated careful surveillance of black activity and established stiff fines for masters who failed to keep their slaves in line. It also removed jurisdiction over slave manumissions from individual planters and placed it in the hands of the assembly.

Second, the assembly sought to alter the ratio of blacks to whites by imposing a prohibitive duty on new slaves carried into the colony from Africa and the WEST INDIES. This action brought quick results. Although slavers had unloaded more than one thousand blacks a year in South Carolina during the 1730's, slave importations slowed to about a tenth of that number in the decade that followed. The duties collected were used to encourage white immigration from Europe. The slave trade into the colony would resume its prerebellion dimensions by 1750, but as a result of the limited importation of the intervening decade, newly arrived slaves would never again constitute such an overwhelming proportion of the colony's total population.

Finally, South Carolina authorities attempted to eliminate the escape routes that slaves used to reach Spanish Florida. They waged war on the Spanish, hoping to punish them for their meddling and, if possible, to drive them from the region, where their proximity to the British colonies proved a perpetual incitement to slave escapes. They persuaded Georgia officials to rigorously police the most convenient passages through that colony. South Carolina strengthened its own slave patrol system, making service in the patrols a required part of militia duty and dividing the colony into well-organized beats. This permanently changed the nature of slave resistance in South Carolina. After the Stono Rebellion, seditious slaves could no longer simply flee across the frontier to Florida. They were left with but two options—feigned submission or armed struggle.

—*Roy E. Finkenbine*

Suggested Readings:

Littlefield, Daniel C. *Rice and Slaves: Ethnicity and the Slave Trade in Colonial South Carolina.*

Baton Rouge: Louisiana State University Press, 1981.

Sirmans, M. Eugene. "The Legal Status of the Slave in South Carolina, 1670-1740." *Journal of Southern History* 28 (November, 1962): 462-473.

TePaske, John T. "The Fugitive Slave: Intercolonial Rivalry and Spanish Slave Policy, 1689-1764." In *Eighteenth-Century Florida and Its Borderlands*. Edited by Samuel Proctor. Gainesville: University Presses of Florida, 1975.

Thornton, John K. "African Dimensions of the Stono Rebellion." *American Historical Review* 96 (October, 1991): 1101-13.

Weir, Robert M. *Colonial South Carolina: A History*. Millwood, N.Y.: KTO, 1983.

Wood, Peter H. *Black Majority: Negroes in Colonial South Carolina from 1670 Through the Stono Rebellion*. New York: W. W. Norton, 1975.

Strauder v. West Virginia: U.S. SUPREME COURT decision in a JURY SELECTION case in 1880. The case involved a claim by an African American that he had been denied a fair trial when he was found guilty of murder.

On October 20, 1874, Taylor Strauder was indicted for the murder of his wife. When the case came to trial, a jury in the Ohio Circuit Court in West Virginia found Strauder guilty. Appealing the verdict, Strauder maintained that he had been denied a fair trial because West Virginia law did not allow African Americans to serve on juries. Since he was denied having any people of his own race on the jury, he was not given rights equal to those of a white man.

The U.S. Supreme Court ruled in favor of Strauder, indicating that the FOURTEENTH AMENDMENT made it illegal for states to pass laws that supported RACIAL DISCRIMINATION. West Virginia's law, which stated that jurors had to be white men, was deemed discrimina-

tory. The Court ruled that Strauder had been denied the right to a jury of his peers. The decision in *Strauder v. West Virginia* confirmed that black men should be accorded the right to serve on juries. This decision was the first instance of racial protection under the equal protection clause of the Fourteenth Amendment.

—*Annita Marie Ward*

See also: Jury selection.

Strayhorn, Billy (November 29, 1915, Dayton, Ohio—May 31, 1967, New York, New York): Pianist, arranger, and composer. Strayhorn's career is tied to the band and music of Duke ELLINGTON. From the time that he joined the band in 1939 as a pianist, arranger, and lyricist until his departure in 1965 (because of serious illness), he wrote arrangements and collaborated with Ellington in practically every phase of the band's life.

Ellington was one of the most influential musicians in the development of big bands and their music, a process beginning in the 1930's and not exhausting itself until the 1960's. One cannot underestimate the influence of the Ellington group, from the ensembles to the individual artists. Throughout the most fruitful and exciting years of the group's development, Strayhorn was a guiding force. Strayhorn's progressive inclinations probably moved the band in directions Ellington would not have taken without Strayhorn's influence.

In addition to his collaboration with Ellington on arrangements and compositions, Strayhorn composed on his own the lyrics and melodies of superb works. "Lush Life" (1938), a ballad recorded by countless popular singers in the United States and abroad, is but one of his beautiful pieces. He wrote "Take the A Train" (1941), the theme song of the Ellington band, familiar to audiences worldwide as a signature piece of American swing music, Ellington style. Approximately two hundred compositions have been attributed to Strayhorn, either alone or in collaboration with Ellington. Listeners sometimes could not tell whether Ellington or Strayhorn had written a particular song.

Strikes and labor law: One of the most powerful tools available to labor unions has been the ability to strike in order to settle disputes with management. When unions initiate a strike by forming picket lines and refusing to work, they attempt to impose measurable costs on employers in order to gain concessions, usually in the form of improved wages and working conditions for union workers. In addition to reducing the production of salable goods or services, strikes force targeted companies to lose income from consumers and from other companies who refuse to conduct business with a company whose employees are on strike. In many cases, substantial public sympathy and private support for their cause has allowed unions simply to threaten a strike in order to win concessions from employers.

The right to strike was won by the labor movement over an extended period of time in the United States. Before the 1900's, most conflicts between American workers and employers involved spontaneous boycotts, strikes, and other work actions. The early labor law cases growing out of these incidents established precedents that affected employees regardless of race. Later, affirmative action concerns produced labor law cases that specifically affected the employment opportunities available to African American workers. In addition, many court rulings concerning direct action by labor unions in the form of picket lines and strikes provided legal precedents that protected the nonviolent protests launched by African Americans as part of the Civil Rights movement of the 1950's and 1960's.

Labor Law Background
One of the earliest labor law cases was *Commonwealth v. Pullis* (1806), a case heard in the Philadelphia Mayor's Court. In this case, the court held that the employees would not go to jail for union activities, but they could be fined. In the Massachusetts case of *Commonwealth v. Hunt* (1842), the state court established a precedent of imposing civil liabilities, or monetary fines with no jail sentences, on employees who participated in boycotts, strikes, or other labor actions.

During the early decades of the twentieth century, federal courts controlled union growth by using the provisions of the Sherman Antitrust Act (1890), which prohibited corporations or individuals from entering into contracts or conspiring to restrain interstate trade or commerce. In *Loewe v. Lawlor* (1908), the U.S. SUPREME COURT held that worker boycotts amounted to a conspiracy to restrain trade. In this case, popularly known as the Danbury Hatters' Case, the employees of the hatmaker had refused to work unless they were paid a specified rate; furthermore, they tried to get other workers to join them. Eventually, the workers were convicted of criminal conspiracy.

In a nation that prized the idea of protecting individual rights, however, criminal sentencing of activists who fought for their rights became relatively unpopular. Congress stepped in and tried to diminish the liability of union organizers by passing the Clayton Antitrust Act (1914), which was intended to bar federal courts from interfering with or prohibiting peaceful picketing and other activities associated with strikes or boycotts. When applying the Clayton Act to the case of *Duplex Printing Press Co. v. Deering* (1921), the Supreme Court interpreted the statute quite narrowly. This narrow reading did not give the unions as much protection as Congress had intended; as a result of public pressure, Congress passed the Norris-La Guardia Act in 1932. This act specifically withdrew the court's power to prevent peaceful union organizers from picketing and refusing to work.

The Norris-La Guardia Act also specifically prohibited federal courts from involving themselves in labor policy.

In 1935 Congress passed the National Labor Relations Act, also known as the Wagner Act. The act included a declaration of employee rights, defined unfair labor practices, prohibited discrimination based on union membership, and forced employers to bargain with employees collectively through their appointed union representatives. Through this act, Congress also established the National Labor Relations Board (NLRB), a federal administrative agency that served as the basic judicial system for settling disputes between labor unions and employers. The NLRB established special administrative law judges who were responsible for settling labor disputes. After the Wagner Act was signed into law, union organizing flourished. The growth in membership brought substantial power to the unions.

Congress amended part of the Wagner Act by passing the Taft-Hartley Act (formally known as the Labor Management Relations Act) in 1947. These amendments prohibited unions from using secondary boycotts and from using strikes to force an employer to fire an employee based on union or nonunion affiliation. The Taft-Hartley Act also made collective bargaining agreements enforceable in federal district court. Congress later passed the Landrum-Griffin Act (formally known as the Labor Management Reporting and Disclosure Act) in 1959. The act served as a basic bill of rights for union members, outlining policies and procedures for unions to follow when electing officers and making financial disclosures to the membership. It also imposed criminal penalties on union officers who misused membership money.

Soliciting, Picketing, and Striking
In *National Labor Relations Board v. Babcock & Wilcox Co.* (1956), the Supreme Court allowed nonemployees access to employees for the purpose of organizing unions, despite protests from employers. The Court upheld the employees' right to hear about the union and specifically granted access to labor organizers and other nonemployees because the company's location did not allow access from adjacent public property. In a 1971 NLRB case involving Monogram Models, Inc., however, unions were not granted the right to enter an employer's property when the adjacent property was merely impractical to access. Eventually, in a 1972 case involving Dexter Thread Mills, Inc., the NLRB made it clear that nonemployee access for union organizing would not be permitted unless the employees lived on the company property.

For unions, the high point of court protection for picketing came with *Thornhill v. Alabama* (1940), in which the Supreme Court held that peaceful congregation and picketing fell within the constitutionally guaranteed right to free speech. Later, in *American Federation of Labor v. Swing* (1941), the federal court held that a broad state law prohibiting picketing was unconstitutional. Eventually, however, the Supreme Court made it clear in *Teamsters, Local 695 v. Vogt* (1957) that a state could enforce specific injunctions against picketing, depending on the circumstances.

By the 1970's, legal cases began to address concerns specific to African American employees. In *United Steelworkers of America v. Weber* (1979) the Supreme Court specifically addressed the issue of affirmative action in employment, upholding the right of employers to establish hiring goals and other voluntary affirmative action programs in order to eliminate conspicuous racial imbalance in job categories that had a history of segregation.

Organizing Among African American Workers
In the nineteenth and early twentieth centuries, African Americans were excluded from most organized labor unions. Although some

all-black local union chapters received charters from the American Federation of Labor (AFL) in the early 1900's, this segregation prevented black workers from participating fully in the collective bargaining gains achieved by white union members. In 1925 A. Philip RANDOLPH was hired as a labor organizer by African Americans employed as sleeping car porters by the Pullman Company. Randolph's efforts brought recognition to the Brotherhood of Sleeping Car Porters as a negotiating agent for black employees, and the organization received a contract from the Pullman Company by 1937. Eventually, the union became affiliated with the AFL, and Randolph was appointed to the AFL's board of directors in 1955.

In the late 1940's, labor organizers launched Operation Dixie, a campaign to organize industries in the South. The Congress of Industrial Organizations (CIO) and other labor unions began organizing efforts among tobacco workers, textile workers, iron miners, lumber mill workers, and dockworkers and river boatmen in the South, many of whom were African Americans. Some of the labor organizers faced the same threats and types of intimidation that were later confronted by civil rights activists in the 1960's. In BIRMINGHAM, ALABAMA, racial tensions came to a head when white members of the United Steel Workers fought against a local chapter of the Mine, Mill, and Smelter Workers' Union that represented the area's black mine workers. Anticommunist feelings combined with racism to destroy the Mine, Mill, and Smelter local, an important fixture of Birmingham's black community.

Civil Rights and the Labor Movement

After the 1964 Civil Rights Act made employment discrimination on the basis of race or gender illegal, the federal government began developing affirmative action guidelines that required public agencies, large corporations, and craft and labor unions to compensate for historic patterns of discrimination. Many important corporate employers, including U.S. Steel, were encouraged to recruit and promote African American workers out of the occupational ghettos to which they had been consigned.

In LOS ANGELES, African American janitors who had organized their own union began to agitate successfully for better pay, better hours, and the kinds of fringe benefits that had already been extended to other unionized blue-collar workers. During the late 1960's, union organizers began lobbying for support among black textile workers in the South to provide the impetus for unionization in the textile industry.

Other unions began forging direct links to the Civil Rights movement by sending members to participate in civil rights marches and creating slogans that articulated their solidarity with civil rights activists. MALCOLM X and trade union leader A. Philip Randolph were among those attending rallies in support of Local 1199 of New York's Drug and Hospital Employees' Union. In 1965 hospital workers who were waging a strike in Bronxville, New York, carried signs that proclaimed "Lincoln Freed the Slaves, but Bronxville Hasn't" and "Freedom Now!" By the late 1960's, the membership of Local 1199, largely composed of black, Puerto Rican, and female workers, had begun to secure important improvements in labor conditions for hospital workers and had created a network of cooperative links with hospital workers in other states.

Martin Luther KING, Jr., also had important links to the labor movement. In the wake of his shocking assassination in 1968, many people forgot that King's purpose for being in Memphis, Tennessee, was to rally support for striking city garbage workers, many of whom were African Americans seeking economic justice in the form of better wages and a fair labor contract with the city.

Black Representation in Industrial Unions

At the height of the Civil Rights movement, disagreements existed within the AFL-CIO on the issue of civil rights. Although the labor federation's new constitution included language forbidding discrimination and its members worked hard for the passage of civil rights laws, the federation seemed unable to eliminate lingering racial discrimination within its union affiliates. Although local chapters of large industrial unions were forced to integrate their seniority lists and their meeting halls, many construction trades continued to exclude black workers by awarding union cards primarily to relatives and friends and limiting competition for apprenticeships and for contracts on construction projects.

In 1969 the federal government endorsed affirmative action goals for six building trades under a plan known as the Philadelphia Plan. Unfortunately, these efforts to provide a level playing field for black construction workers failed because of the combined effects of a growing economic recession and continued resistance within the unions. In 1970 the Nixon administration agreed to back down on its enforcement of the plan in exchange for a union guarantee of support for the president's policies on the Vietnam War.

Other more progressive unions, such as the International Ladies' Garment Workers Union (ILGWU), also came under fire for failing to provide opportunities for African American workers. Older skilled garment workers, many of whom were Jewish and Italian immigrants, opposed the creation of federal job training programs within union shops and refused to grant more than token representation of the ILGWU's growing black membership in union leadership positions. Civil rights organizations such as the NATIONAL ASSOCIATION FOR THE ADVANCEMENT OF COLORED PEOPLE (NAACP) and the CONGRESS OF RACIAL EQUALITY (CORE) attacked the ILGWU for its unwillingness to recruit and promote more African American laborers.

During the 1960's, the United Auto Workers (UAW) also came into conflict with its African American membership. By 1960 black auto workers made up more than 25 percent of the union's total membership, but few were given the opportunity to advance beyond the most dangerous and physically demanding assembly line positions. In protest, African American members of the union staff formed the Trade Union Leadership Conference as a forum for their civil rights concerns. As more than seven thousand union workers joined the conference, it succeeded in its goal of placing African Americans on the UAW executive board, but it failed to make significant improvements in conditions faced by black workers in DETROIT's auto plants.

In the wake of the 1967 DETROIT RIOT, militant black workers organized wildcat strikes against the main Dodge automobile plant near Detroit and formed the DODGE REVOLUTIONARY UNION MOVEMENT (DRUM). Similar caucuses were formed at other Detroit-area automobile plants: CADRUM at General Motor's Cadillac plant, FRUM at the Ford plant, and GRUM among the other General Motors affiliates. Through their support of more than a dozen wildcat strikes, these militant workers gained attention for their claims that grievance procedures and seniority systems within the union hierarchy were inherently racist and grossly inadequate. As a result of the activities of these militant caucuses, the UAW hired and promoted more black staff members, Chrysler and other automobile manufacturers hired and promoted more African Americans to positions as foremen, and many African American union members became heads of inner-city locals of the UAW.

The 1980's

The economic recession of the 1980's and influx of foreign imports cut deeply into the profits of many American industrial manufacturers, prompting a wave of mass layoffs and plant shutdowns. In the steel industry alone, some 150,000 jobs were eliminated between 1979 and 1982, and the United Steelworkers of America lost nearly half of its members. The UAW lost 500,000 members when the automobile industry was forced to implement drastic changes after 1978 in order to compete against Japanese imports. Union workers in various industries who tried to protest the transfer of their jobs to overseas plants or antiunion cities in the American Sunbelt and the reduction of their wages and benefits were often unable to summon public support for their efforts and lacked the union strike funds to wage indefinite campaigns. Many of their jobs were filled by nonunion laborers or were eliminated and replaced by lower-paying jobs in the service sector.

Activism in the 1990's

Despite these changes, black labor leaders continued to push for greater recognition of their concerns by AFL-CIO leadership during the 1990's. As a result of declining union membership among white workers, the representation of African Americans within unions rose from 14 percent in 1986 to 15.6 percent in 1994. During the 1995 battle for leadership of the AFL-CIO, the Coalition of Black Trade Unionists drew up a list of eleven demands that were placed before competing candidates John J. Sweeney and Thomas R. Donahue. Formed in 1972 to encourage support among African American laborers for Democratic presidential candidate George McGovern, the coalition withheld any official endorsement of a new labor federation president in order to place pressure on the union hierarchy to pay more attention to minority hiring, minority promotion to union staff positions, and minority concerns about important national labor policy debates, including the impact of the North American Free Trade Agreement (NAFTA) on black unemployment.

Building on the tradition of A. Philip Randolph, black labor interests have continued to play an important role in the struggle against racism and discrimination. The concerns of the African American working class formed a key component of Jesse JACKSON's political agenda as expressed in his RAINBOW COALITION. Aspiring to achieve greater recognition for their concerns, black labor leaders and union workers have made it clear that they are willing to use the courts and the picket line to seek more than token representation in the workplace and in labor unions themselves.

—*Sybil P. DioNe*

Suggested Readings:

Bracey, John H., ed. *Black Workers and Organized Labor*. Belmont, Calif.: Wadsworth, 1971.

Freedman, Russell. *Kids at Work: Lewis Hine and the Crusade Against Child Labor*. New York: Clarion Books, 1994.

Griffler, Keith P. *What Price Alliance? Black Radicals Confront White Labor, 1918-1938*. New York: Garland, 1995.

Jones, Jacqueline. *American Work: Four Centuries of Black and White Labor*. New York: W. W. Norton, 1998.

Kent, Ronald C., ed. *Culture, Gender, Race, and U.S. Labor History*. Westport, Conn.: Greenwood Press, 1993.

Kirkley, A. Roy. *Labor Unions and the Black Experience: A Selected Bibliography*. New Brunswick, N.J.: Labor Education Center and Library, Rutgers University, 1972.

Leader, Sheldon. *Freedom of Association: A Study in Labor Law and Political Theory*. New Haven, Conn.: Yale University Press, 1992.

Stuckey, P. Sterling (b. 1932, Chicago, Illinois): Historian. Stuckey was one of the significant scholars to examine the rich culture created by slaves in the southern United States and to provide substantive analysis of cultural continuances among African Americans and West African peoples.

Stuckey began his career as an elementary and high school teacher in Chicago after completing undergraduate work at Northwestern University. In 1972 he earned a doctorate degree in history, also from Northwestern University, and he was invited to join the university's History Department in 1971 at the rank of associate professor. In 1977 he was appointed full professor. He remained on the Northwestern faculty until 1989, when he accepted a professorship at the University of California, Riverside.

Stuckey's scholarly worked filled a void in the field of black cultural history, beginning with his often-reprinted essay "Through the Prism of Folklore: The Black Ethos in Slavery." First published in 1968 in the *Massachusetts Review*, the essay examines the role of slave folklore as essential to understanding slave thought and culture. In 1972 Stuckey edited *The Ideological Origins of Black Nationalism*, which illustrates his early interest in black nationalist thought. His seminal work *Slave Culture: Nationalist Theory and the Foundations of Black America*, published in 1987, combines his early interest in slave FOLKLORE with his research on nationalism. *Going Through the Storm: The Influence of African American Art in History*, published in 1994, is a compilation of previously published essays that explore African American art and intellectual and cultural history. Stuckey received numerous prestigious fellowships and awards to support his research.

—*Paulette Brown-Hinds*

See also: Intellectuals and scholars.

Student Nonviolent Coordinating Committee: Organization founded in April, 1960, to coordinate the activities of students involved in protest activities, such as SIT-INS, and voter registration. Student leaders who were hesitant to join with traditional CIVIL RIGHTS groups formed the Student Nonviolent Coordinating Committee (SNCC) after an organizing conference in April, 1960, on the Shaw University campus in Raleigh, North Carolina. Initially, SNCC was dedicated to practicing nonviolent protests. The contrast between well-groomed, peaceful sit-in demonstrators and hate-filled attackers proved successful in drawing national support to the movement. The group urged a "jail, no bail" campaign beginning in February, 1961, in which arrested protesters would stay in jail rather than paying fines or getting out on bail. In the early years, SNCC was a democratically operated, multiracial organization. A wave of young white people flowed to the South to work with SNCC, in an atmosphere in which everyone's contribution to the decision-making process was considered.

By 1964 some members of SNCC were losing patience with the nonviolent strategy. These individuals, exemplified by Stokely CARMICHAEL, felt more aggressiveness in response to southern white reactionaries and southern institutions. Eventually, Carmichael's more militant position came to dominate SNCC. Tensions began to rise between African American and white members, and white members began to leave the organization. In addition, SNCC male leadership began to take on beliefs and positions that diminished the female leadership roles.

After 1963 SNCC's most important work was in the area of voter registration. Facing intense resistance, it succeeded in registering African American voters throughout the South. SNCC also founded the MISSISSIPPI FREEDOM DEMOCRATIC PARTY and attempted to gain seats at the 1964 Democratic National Convention.

Carmichael was named head of SNCC on May 19, 1966, succeeding John LEWIS, who then resigned from the group in July. Under Carmichael's leadership, SNCC came to the

SNCC leader Stokely Carmichael addressing students on black power from the hood of an automobile at Florida A&M University in 1967. *(AP/Wide World Photos)*

forefront of the BLACK POWER MOVEMENT, which served to alienate SNCC from middle-class African Americans and erode its base of support among northern white liberals. SNCC began to focus activities on northern cities following the breakdown of segregation throughout most of the South and the passing of the VOTING RIGHTS ACT OF 1965. Its effective leadership, including Carmichael, left to pursue other interests. H. Rap BROWN, who continued to call for confrontation with the American system, took over leadership on May 12, 1967, and in the summer of 1969 changed SNCC's name to the Student National Coordinating Committee. Brown indicated that the group would retaliate violently if required to do so. Shortly thereafter, SNCC became all but defunct, as Brown's legal problems left him little time to work with the group.

Substance abuse: Studies have shown that the African American population displays different patterns of substance abuse than other ethnic groups show. Depending on how the data are collected, these patterns can be interpreted in various ways.

One important factor in studying rates of substance abuse seems to be the age of the individuals being studied. According to the National Household Survey conducted by the U.S. Substance Abuse and Mental Health Services Administration in 1993, African American men and boys between the ages of twelve and thirty-five were more likely to use illegal drugs than were white men and boys of the same age. Over the age of thirty-five, African American men were seven times as likely to use cocaine as white men. However, rates of substance abuse were no different between the ages of twelve and seventeen. In fact, the National High School Senior Survey, conducted by the U.S. National Institute on Drug Abuse beginning in the 1970's, consistently indicates that African American teenagers are less likely to abuse alcohol, drugs, and tobacco than are white teenagers.

Most experts agree that perceived differences among ethnic groups in patterns of substance abuse are largely attributable to factors other than race. Such factors include the educational and employment history of the substance abuser as well as the person's social and economic environment. In one study published in 1993, researchers who considered such factors found no significant difference in rates of cocaine use between similar groups of African Americans and whites.

The apparent shift in the rate of substance abuse among African Americans from relatively low in adolescence to relatively high in adulthood may also be explained by similar factors. Surveys of high school students, for example, fail to measure substance abuse among dropouts, which is known to be higher. The high school dropout rate has been shown to be higher for African American teenagers than for white teenagers. Therefore, the actual rate of substance abuse among all African American teenagers is likely to be at least as high as the rate among white teenagers.

For adults, higher rates of unemployment and POVERTY among African Americans than among whites are likely to be responsible for higher rates of substance abuse. Such factors

are also likely to bring African American substance abusers in contact with police and government agencies more frequently than white substance abusers, who are more likely to have access to private treatment programs. According to the U.S. Justice Department, African Americans are at least three times as likely as whites to be arrested for drug violations. African Americans are also about three times as likely to be in public treatment programs for substance abuse as whites.

Historical Background

Until the twentieth century, the incidence of substance abuse was relatively low among African Americans. During the nineteenth century, opium derivatives, in the form of legal medications, tended to be abused mostly by whites; whites were simply more likely to see physicians. Cocaine use began to appear among African Americans in NEW ORLEANS by 1900. Although whites still used the drug at a higher rate, exaggerated reports of violence by African American cocaine users led to four days of RACE RIOTS in Atlanta in 1906.

After WORLD WAR I, African Americans began to move from the largely rural southern states to large cities in the North. This GREAT MIGRATION brought them into contact with sources of opium, marijuana, and cocaine. Although most African Americans still avoided such substances, a small number began to develop a new subculture associated with JAZZ music and drug abuse. By 1940 African Americans were two and one-half times as likely as whites to be arrested for drug violations. However, this statistic more likely reflects the fact that African Americans were more likely to come into contact with police officers than an actual significant difference in rates of drug abuse.

After WORLD WAR II, heroin (an opium derivative) began to appear in economically depressed areas of large American cities, where many lower-class African Americans lived. The extremely addictive nature of this drug led to an increase in substance abuse among African Americans in the inner city. By 1950 African Americans were five times as likely as whites to be arrested for drug violations.

Heroin continued to be the most serious drug abuse problem among urban African Americans until the 1980's, when a new form of cocaine began to appear. Known as crack, this form of cocaine is relatively inexpensive but extremely addictive. Crack also has a very short period of action, so addicts often used the drug several times each day. The fact that crack is smoked rather than injected with a needle led to a large increase in the number of female African American substance abusers, who are less likely to use injectable drugs than men are. The rapid onset of addiction in crack users, combined with the need to use large amounts of the drug, led to a rise in violent crime associated with drug abuse. Although the obvious dangers of crack led to a decrease in the use of the drug in the 1990's, it remained the most serious substance abuse problem among lower-class African Americans.

Consequences

Surveys published in 1995 indicated that more than three million African Americans had used illegal drugs within the past year, with nearly two million using them within the past

Among African American adults, high rates of unemployment and poverty tend to account for greater levels of substance abuse than among white adults. *(Martin A. Hutner)*

month. The negative effects of substance abuse are often more serious among African Americans than among other ethnic groups, for a variety of social and economic reasons. However, as with much social science research, it is difficult to determine causality: In other words, it is often difficult to determine whether unemployment, unstable family structures, elevated school dropout rates, and other adverse situations are the cause of substance abuse, the consequences of it, or a complex combination of the two.

African Americans, about 13 percent of the U.S. population, accounted for about 30 percent of all drug-related deaths in the United States in the 1990's. The majority of these were adult men. Cocaine, particularly crack, was the most frequently involved drug, followed by heroin and morphine. African American drug abusers have also been shown to have increased rates of gonorrhea, hepatitis, pneumonia, anemia, and other diseases. In addition, ALCOHOLISM is more likely to lead to liver disease in African Americans than in whites, probably because of socioeconomic factors such as poor nutrition and limited access to health care.

One of the most serious consequences of the abuse of injectable drugs is ACQUIRED IM-MUNODEFICIENCY SYNDROME (AIDS). A report published in 1995 showed that more than one-third of all newly reported AIDS cases in the United States were in African Americans. Injectable drug abuse was the primary source of AIDS infection in adult heterosexual African Americans. African Americans made up about half of all AIDS cases associated with abuse of injectable drugs. The frequent practice of needle sharing among injectable drug users contributed heavily to this situation.

African Americans also made up about half of all AIDS cases in those who were heterosexual sex partners of injectable drug users. The fact that many female users of injectable drugs turn to prostitution to support their addiction increased the rate of AIDS infection. Of children with AIDS, the majority of which were born to women who used injectable drugs or who had sexual contact with injectable drug users, more than half were African American.

A serious consequence of the large increase in the number of female African American substance abusers after the introduction of crack was health problems among infants born to these women. If the infant survives, expensive long-term hospitalization is often required. The inability of crack addicts to care for these children created an economic and social problem.

Prevention

Efforts to prevent substance abuse in the African American population usually focus on young people. Techniques used to reduce substance abuse among young middle-class whites are often ineffective for lower-class African American youths. To be effective, many experts believe, reduction programs designed for young, lower-class African Americans must address issues such as racism and lack of economic opportunity. Such programs often include efforts to educate young people about vocational and parenting skills.

A study published in 1989 indicated that African American high school students were more likely to be influenced by substance abuse education than were white high school students. In the National High School Senior Survey, about three-quarters of African American students stated that education about substance abuse made them less likely to use drugs, tobacco, and alcohol. Fewer than one-half of white students made the same statement. However, fewer African American students than white students actually received such education. A weakness with school-based programs is that young African Americans who attend school are less likely to abuse drugs than dropouts are. Therefore, these educational programs fail to reach those most at risk for substance abuse.

Many substance abuse education programs have gone beyond schools in attempts to reach entire communities. Such programs do not focus on substance abuse alone but include education designed to improve life skills for individuals, families, and communities. Individuals are aided in developing respect for self and others. Families are encouraged to provide emotional support and healthy role models for children. The community as a whole is also educated about health care.

Various studies have evaluated the results of these programs. Some projects, which emphasize planning for the future, appear to be effective for young African American men. Other projects, which emphasize social skills and emotional maturity, appear to be more effective in young African American women. In general, educational programs seem to be most effective in reducing the rate of tobacco abuse among African American youths and least effective in reducing the rate of alcohol abuse.

Treatment

Many researchers are uncertain whether traditional substance abuse treatment programs, most of which were developed to treat middle-class whites, are as effective for lower-class African Americans. Some studies have shown that African Americans, although much more likely to be in formal treatment programs than whites, receive less benefit from the programs. Other studies, however, have indicated that availability of employment, community support, and other socioeconomic factors is more important than race in determining the effect of treatment programs.

A substance abuse treatment program designed for African Americans with limited economic resources is provided by the Center for Family Health in Washington, D.C. This program provides medical and psychological treatment, provides shelter and employment counseling, and allows children to remain with their parents. In the 1990's the program cost about $20,000 per year for each family—compared with the $100,000 per year that it cost to provide hospitalization for an abandoned infant born to a substance-addicted mother.

A treatment program designed to make use of cultural norms within African American families was developed in San Francisco as the African American Extended Family Program. This project adapts the traditional twelve-step recovery program, first developed by Alcoholics Anonymous, to African American neighborhoods. The spiritual aspect of the twelve-step program is connected to a local church, an important part of the community. The program uses historical aspects of the African American experience by comparing substance abuse to SLAVERY. Another part of the program draws upon the important role of the grandmother as a positive role model in many African American families.

—*Rose Secrest*

See also: Black-on-black violence; Crime and the criminal justice system; Gangs.

Suggested Readings:

Bell, Peter. *Chemical Dependency and the African American: Counseling Strategies and Community Issues.* Center City, Minn.: Hazelden, 1990.

Drew, Humphries. *Crack Mothers: Pregnancy, Drugs, and the Media.* Columbus: Ohio State University Press, 1999.

Gray, Muriel. "African Americans." In *Cultural Competence in Substance Abuse Prevention.* Edited by Joanne Philleo and Frances Larry Brisbane. Washington, D.C.: National Association of Social Workers, 1997.

James, William H., and Stephen I. Johnson. *Doin' Drugs: Patterns of African American Ad-*

diction. Austin: University of Texas Press, 1996.

John, Stanley, Lawrence S. Brown, Jr., and Beny J. Primm. "African Americans: Epidemiologic, Prevention, and Treatment Issues." In *Substance Abuse: A Comprehensive Textbook.* Edited by Joyce H. Lowinson et al. Baltimore: Williams and Wilkins, 1997.

Jonnes, Jill. *Hep-Cats, Narcs, and Pipe Dreams: A History of America's Romance with Illegal Drugs.* New York: Scribner, 1996.

Lusane, Clarence. *Pipe Dream Blues: Racism and the War on Drugs.* Boston: South End Press, 1991.

Suburbanization: The movement of African Americans from central city locations to suburban neighborhoods became a significant demographic trend throughout the United States in the 1970's and 1980's. Suburban relocation implies a new social and economic status; city residents often move to the suburbs as their financial situation improves and they enter the lower-middle and middle classes. The growth of the African American population in the suburbs does not always indicate integration, however. Sometimes a predominantly white suburb becomes predominantly black, and sometimes even in mixed neighborhoods there is little contact between blacks and whites.

African American relocation from central cities to suburbs is not a consistent trend or pattern. The movement has been more apparent in cities with large concentrations of black residents, such as WASHINGTON, D.C., and ATLANTA, GEORGIA, than in smaller cities, and it has not persisted at the same level in all years. African Americans tend to relocate when the nation's economy is strong and when there is a relatively high rate of employment among African Americans. In the 1990's in some metropolitan areas, such as FLORIDA's Miami-Hialeah region, many blacks who live in pre-

dominantly white suburbs are not American-born residents but West Indian immigrants from middle-class families in JAMAICA and the BAHAMAS.

Although significant, the movement to the suburbs is nowhere near as dramatic as were the mass migrations of African Americans from the South to the northern and western United States during and following World Wars I and II. During those eras of the GREAT MIGRATION, metropolitan areas such as NEW YORK, CHICAGO, DETROIT, and (especially in the 1940's and 1950's) LOS ANGELES were transformed culturally and socially by the influx of millions of black migrants from the South.

Urbanization

The migration of poor rural blacks (and of some other minorities) to inner-city neighborhoods was most noticeable in the prosperous decades following WORLD WAR I and WORLD WAR II. Particularly in the 1950's and 1960's, a related phenomenon was the movement of largely white middle-class residents from downtown neighborhoods to the suburbs, a type of migration sometimes referred to as "WHITE FLIGHT."

The inducement for blacks to relocate to cities was the same as that which led to the influx of immigrants to America during the previous century: economic opportunity. However, URBANIZATION was not sufficient to resolve the challenges faced by African Americans with regard to employment and economic well-being. Most did not have job skills that applied to urban employment. In addition, they faced widespread discrimination in housing, education opportunities, and employment. In 1940 black unemployment was only 20 percent higher than that of whites nationally, but by 1963 black unemployment nationally was more than double the rate for whites.

Two types of inner-city neighborhoods became established. The first type included a

The historical shift of African Americans from inner cities to suburbs has accelerated the deterioration of inner city neighborhoods. *(Hazel Hankin)*

majority of African Americans in cities such as New York, NEWARK, Chicago, Detroit, and Atlanta. These areas experienced decreasing employment throughout the 1970's and beyond; most were also stagnant or declining in their populations. The second type of neighborhood included a minority of African American residents and primarily was populated by Latinos and Asian immigrants. Employment rates in these neighborhoods were low but stable, and their populations often increased as single-family housing units were occupied by two or more families. This second type of inner-city neighborhood was often found in metropolitan areas in the West and Southwest, such as San Antonio and HOUSTON in Texas and Los Angeles and Santa Ana in California. Both types of neighborhoods shared some common characteristics: high percentages of people living in poverty, high rates of single-parent households, and high rates of crime.

Moving to the Suburbs
Beginning slowly in the 1950's and increasing significantly by the 1980's and 1990's, African Americans began to leave inner-

city neighborhoods for the suburbs. This trend was particularly noticeable during the 1970's and 1980's, when the rate of black relocation to the suburbs often exceeded the rate of white relocation. From 1970 to 1980, for example, the total U.S. suburban population grew by 17.3 percent, but black suburbanites increased in number by 49.4 percent. By 1980 about 6 percent of all suburbanites were black, and by 1988 more than one-fourth of African Americans were living in the suburbs.

The suburbs that were most likely to receive large numbers of new black residents usually had existing black populations. Although many observers pointed to this trend as an indication of improving economic conditions within the African American community, it is simplistic to view it as a cure-all.

For one thing, despite the movement of African Americans to the suburbs, African Americans continue to constitute the majority of people living in poverty in inner-city neighborhoods in the 1990's. For another, relocation has rarely produced truly integrated suburban neighborhoods. Moreover, gang activity, poverty, and other social problems encountered in the inner city continued to confront black residents in some suburban areas.

Urban Renewal

Beginning in the 1960's, a phenomenon that forced a certain amount of relocation was urban renewal. Metropolitan governments in major cities such as PHILADELPHIA, Chicago, and Miami launched large-scale urban renewal programs beginning in the late 1950's and early 1960's. These programs frequently had the effect of displacing large numbers of impoverished black residents. Some of these uprooted African Americans moved to poor suburban areas.

Urban renewal frequently includes the building of highways or complexes that divide or disrupt historic communities. It places major government buildings and other insti-

tutions in locations where low-income homes previously existed. It encourages upper-middle-class professionals to move from predominantly white suburbs back to urban centers. When such "gentrification" occurs and when older homes are removed to construct new residences that are expensive to rent or buy, impoverished black residents are forced to relocate. (In the 1960's urban renewal was sarcastically dubbed "Negro removal" by its critics.) Resulting relocation to predominantly poor black suburbs on the outskirts of these metropolitan areas does not constitute an indication of upward social mobility or substantial economic progress.

Black Suburban Residents

According to the 1990 CENSUS OF THE UNITED STATES, there were forty metropolitan districts with at least 50,000 black residents living in suburban neighborhoods or outside what the census designated as central cities in metropolitan areas. The largest concentration of black suburban residents was found in the Maryland and Virginia suburbs of Washington, D.C., with a black suburban population of more than 600,000. The District of Columbia itself has historically had a substantial black middle class, and it cannot expand its boundaries for more urban growth. Most of the movement of the city's residents has been to suburban areas such as Prince George's County, just over the border in Maryland.

The second largest group of suburban blacks was found in Atlanta, Georgia, with more than 400,000 black suburban residents. Like Washington, D.C., Atlanta has long had a stable black middle-class population that developed a substantial urban presence in the form of black-owned businesses and historically black academic institutions. Atlanta suburbs such as Brook Glen, Panola Mill, and Wyndham Park all had predominantly black populations by 1990. The third largest black suburban area was Los Angeles-Long Beach in California, followed by Miami-Hialeah, Philadelphia, Newark, and Chicago. Houston was ranked ninth, and greater New York City ranked eleventh.

For the top forty metropolitan areas, the average black suburban population stood at 135,981 residents. The distribution of such suburban concentrations was not limited to outlying neighborhoods near cities in the North and Midwest, where many African Americans had migrated in large numbers after World War II. Six of the ten largest black suburban populations were found near cities in the South and Southwest: Washington, D.C.; Baltimore; Atlanta; Houston; Miami; and Los Angeles. Only four large concentrations of black suburban residents were found in the North and Midwest: Philadelphia, Newark, Chicago, and St. Louis. The movement to the suburbs was not a regional phenomenon; it included all geographic regions of the United States.

When the percentage of black suburban residents was compared with the overall suburban population for each census tract in 1990, the ranking of these districts changed significantly. Metropolitan areas in the North and West did not have nearly the high ratio of black to white residents in the suburbs as found in the South. The city of Fayetteville in North Carolina had 29 percent of its suburban population represented by African Americans. Jackson, MISSISSIPPI, had nearly the same high percentage, and it was followed in order by Charleston, SOUTH CAROLINA; Augusta, Georgia; and Columbia, South Carolina. All these metropolitan areas are situated around medium-sized cities and are located in the South. By contrast, the ratios of black to white residents in the suburbs among large cities in the North and West were quite low even though the black populations themselves were larger than in the South. New York City had only 11 percent of its suburban population represented by African Americans. Houston

had 9 percent, followed by Los Angeles-Long Beach at 8 percent and Chicago at slightly more than 6 percent.

National figures indicate that the majority of African American suburban residents live in predominantly black neighborhoods. These suburbs often exhibit social and economic characteristics that differ from predominantly white suburbs. Such characteristics directly affect the quality of life of African American suburbanites, since it is clear that if some inner-city problems continue in suburban contexts, opportunities for residents are not as positive as they would be if such problems were eliminated. African American suburban neighborhoods have measurably higher populations of unemployed residents than white suburban neighborhoods have; they also have populations that have received less formal education than white suburbanites.

Black suburban neighborhoods tend to be larger in size than white suburbs, in part because they are usually located close to the outer boundaries of central metropolitan areas. African American residents also tend to be concentrated in relatively fewer suburbs than do white suburban residents. By 1980 there were nearly three times as many African American residents living in 72 predominantly black suburbs than there were in 643 predominantly white suburbs in the United States. Furthermore, predominantly black suburbs have generally been found to be in worse financial condition and more often operating with budget deficits than other suburbs.

Housing in black suburbs is often older and more crowded, and black suburbs have approximately three times as many residents living in poverty as do white suburbs. Per capita public expenditure in black suburbs is also higher than in other suburban neighborhoods. This situation may be the result of higher maintenance costs necessary to keep facilities running in these older suburban neighborhoods. In some areas of expenditure, however, less money is allocated in black suburbs. These areas include money spent on highways, sanitation, public health, and hospitals, even though all these expenditures are important in maintaining the residents' quality of life.

Dramatic Growth

In certain national metropolitan areas, the increase in black suburban populations has been dramatic. In California, the number of African Americans moving into the suburbs in both the Riverside-San Bernardino and San Diego metropolitan areas doubled during the 1980's. During that period, the same situation prevailed in the DALLAS and Houston metropolitan areas in Texas. Among the top ten cities that experienced this phenomenon, only two were located outside the South or Southwest: Chicago, Illinois, and Middlesex-Somerset, NEW JERSEY. Suburban growth occurred rapidly in the 1980's and 1990's even in some metropolitan areas that had slower increases in general population. In Riverside-San Bernardino, the population of the total metropolitan area increased by 66 percent, while black suburban growth was measured at 179 percent. During the same decade, Atlanta's total metropolitan population grew only 33 percent, but its black suburban population grew by 95 percent.

Affluent Black Suburbs

At the same time that lower-income black suburbs are expanding, many middle- and upper-middle-class black suburban areas have continued to grow. Such affluent black suburbs experience fewer of the social and economic problems that characterize either the inner city or the poorer black suburbs. The neighborhood of Baldwin Hills, located southwest of downtown Los Angeles, is an affluent black suburb populated by many doctors, lawyers, entertainers, and other professionals. A similar suburb is MacGregor Park, located near Houston. Developed originally in the 1930's, MacGregor Park did not begin to see an influx of black residents until the 1960's, and this trend made it a predominantly black suburb during the 1970's. Other examples of affluent black suburbs include Cascade Heights in Atlanta and Chatham in metropolitan Chicago, both of which exhibit many of the social and economic charactertistics of Baldwin Hills and MacGregor Park. In many cases, the professionals who live in the predominantly black suburbs prefer to socialize with African American neighbors and rear their children within an environment that exposes them to African American culture and tradition rather than live among suburban residents with whom they do not share ethnic ties.

A trend that began receiving scholarly attention in the 1990's is the movement of black immigrants to the suburbs. As black immigration from the Caribbean has continued to grow, especially around cities such as New York, Miami, and Washington, D.C., many of these immigrants have moved into predominantly white or Hispanic suburbs. English-speaking black immigrants from Jamaica, Trinidad, and the Bahamas often have achieved middle-class economic status and tend to identify themselves with national ties to their island homes and the British Commonwealth rather than strictly by racial heritage. Although many Spanish-speaking black immigrants from CUBA, PUERTO RICO, and the DOMINICAN REPUBLIC have arrived in the United States with few economic resources, others have middle-class origins, and some identify primarily with other Latinos. In Miami, many white suburban neighborhoods are generously populated with middle-class black immigrants from the Caribbean, while Hispanic suburbs include middle-class residents with black racial features.

—*William T. Osborne and Max Orezzoli*
See also: Immigration and ethnic origins of African Americans.

Suggested Readings:

Bullard, Robert D., et al., eds. *Residential Apartheid: The American Legacy.* Los Angeles: CAAS, 1994.

Clark, Thomas A. *Blacks in Suburbs: A National Perspective.* New Brunswick, N.J.: Center for Urban Policy Research, Rutgers University, 1979.

Darden, J. "Population Growth and Spatial Distribution." In *A Sheltered Crisis: The State of Fair Housing in the Eighties.* Washington, D.C.: U.S. Commission on Civil Rights, 1983.

Downs, Anthony. *New Visions for Metropolitan America.* Washington, D.C.: The Brookings Institution, 1993.

Gale, Dennis E. *Washington, D.C.: Inner-City Revitalization and Minority Suburbanization.* Philadelphia: Temple University Press, 1987.

Kleinberg, Benjamin. *Urban America in Transformation: Perspectives on Urban Policy and Development.* Thousand Oaks, Calif.: Sage Publications, 1995.

Lake, Robert W. *The New Suburbanites: Race and Housing in the Suburbs.* New Brunswick, N.J.: Center for Urban Policy Research, Rutgers University, 1981.

Rose, Harold M. *Black Suburbanization.* Cambridge, Mass.: Ballinger, 1976.

Sudarkasa, Niara (Gloria Marshall Clark; b. August 14, 1938, Fort Lauderdale, Florida): University PROFESSOR and administrator. In 1987 Sudarkasa became the first woman to be president of LINCOLN UNIVERSITY, the oldest HISTORICALLY BLACK COLLEGE in the United States.

In her earlier academic life, she won a Ford Foundation scholarship for early admission to college, attending FISK UNIVERSITY from 1953 to 1956 and transferring to OBERLIN COLLEGE, from which she earned her A.B. in 1957. Her M.A. (1959) and Ph.D. (1964) in anthropology are from Columbia University.

From 1960 to 1963, Sudarkasa held a Ford Foundation Foreign Area Training Fellowship, which she used to study the YORUBA language and the role of Yoruba women in the marketplace. She studied at the University of London, then lived in a Yoruba village in Nigeria. Her publications include works on African women, West African migration, African American families, and market activities of Yoruba women.

From 1963 to 1964, Sudarkasa was a fellow at the Committee for the Comparative Study of New Nations at the University of Chicago. She became an assistant professor at New York University in 1964, teaching there until 1967, when she became an assistant professor at the University of Michigan at Ann Arbor. She reached the rank of full professor in 1976, becoming the first black woman to achieve that rank in the school's division of arts and sciences. From 1981 to 1984, she was director of the university's Center for Afro-American and African studies. She then was named as associate vice president for academic affairs. In that position, she initiated, evaluated, and monitored the recruitment and retention of minority students.

In 1977 Sudarkasa married John Clark, an inventor, sculptor, and contractor. It was then that she began using her new name. The name of Sudarkasa, she says, came from her marriage. *Nia* is a Swahili word meaning "purpose," and "niara" is an adaptation meaning "woman of purpose."

Lincoln University announced its selection of Sudarkasa as president on September 29, 1986. She began serving in 1987. Among her stated goals as president were to maintain ties with the African continent. Toward that goal, she planned to add to the school's collection of African materials and to open an African museum. She also continued to stress the school's strong programs in science. Sudarkasa served as president until 1998.